Seven Virginians

Also by John B. Boles

Jefferson: Architect of American Liberty

A University So Conceived: A Brief History of Rice

Seeing Jefferson Anew: In His Time and Ours (coedited with Randal L. Hall)

University Builder: Edgar Odell Lovett and the Founding of the Rice Institute

Unto a Good Land: A History of the American People (coauthored with David E. Harrell Jr., Edwin S. Gaustad, Sally Foreman Griffith, Randall M. Miller, and Randall R. Woods)

Shapers of Southern History: Autobiographical Essays by Fifteen Historians (edited)

Origins of the New South, 1877–1913, Fifty Years Later: The Continuing Influence of a Historical Classic (coedited with Bethany L. Johnson)

A Companion to the American South (edited)

Autobiographical Reflections on Southern Religious History (edited)

The South through Time: A History of an American Region

The Irony of Southern Religion

Masters and Slaves in the House of the Lord: Race and Religion in the American South, 1740–1870 (edited)

Interpreting Southern History: Historiographical Essays in Honor of Sanford W. Higginbotham (coedited with Evelyn Thomas Nolen)

Black Southerners, 1619–1869

Dixie Dateline: A Journalistic Portrait of the Contemporary South (edited)

Religion in Antebellum Kentucky

Maryland Heritage: Five Baltimore Institutions Celebrate the Bicentennial (edited)

America: The Middle Period: Essays in Honor of Bernard Mayo (edited)

The Great Revival, 1787–1805: The Origins of the Southern Evangelical Mind

Seven Virginians

THE MEN WHO
SHAPED OUR REPUBLIC

John B. Boles

University of Virginia Press
CHARLOTTESVILLE AND LONDON

University of Virginia Press

Printed in the United States of America on acid-free paper

First published 2023

1 3 5 7 9 8 6 4 2

Library of Congress Cataloging-in-Publication Data

Names: Boles, John B., author.
Title: Seven Virginians : the men who shaped our republic /
John B. Boles. Other titles: 7 Virginians
Description: Charlottesville : University of Virginia Press, 2023. |
Includes bibliographical references and index.
Identifiers: LCCN 2022042437 (print) | LCCN 2022042438 (ebook) |
ISBN 9780813949093 (hardcover) | ISBN 9780813949109 (ebook)
Subjects: LCSH: Statesmen—Virginia—Biography. | Virginia—
Politics and government—1775–1865. | Statesmen—United States—Biography. |
Virginia—Biography. | United States—Politics and government—1775–1783. |
United States—Politics and government—1783–1865.
Classification: LCC F230 .B713 2023 (print) | LCC F230 (ebook) |
DDC 975.5/03—dc23/eng/20220920
LC record available at https://lccn.loc.gov/2022042437
LC ebook record available at https://lccn.loc.gov/2022042438

Cover art: George Washington (Library of Congress, Prints and Photographs Division [LC-DIG-pga-10095 DLC]); Thomas Jefferson (National Archives [NAID 518078]); James Madison (Library of Congress, Prints and Photographs Division [LC-DIG-pga-11881]); James Monroe (Bureau of Engraving and Printing; Wikimedia, restoration by Godot13); George Mason (Library of Congress, American Memory Collection/University of Chicago Library); Patrick Henry (From *Americana,* Beach, ed. [New York: Scientific American, 1904]; Internet Archive/Robarts Library, University of Toronto); John Marshall (Asher Brown Durand, after Henry Inman, The Metropolitan Museum of Art, New York [MET, 30.15.33]); background and numeral (Shutterstock.com/1203969238, 1734274994)

In 1972, I dedicated my first book, with love, to my wife, Nancy; now, fifty-one years later, I dedicate to her what will perhaps be my last book, again with love.

CONTENTS

ACKNOWLEDGMENTS

In the course of teaching and editing for a half century, I have read countless articles, books, dissertations, and student papers and heard scholarly presentations about much of the contents of the present book, long before I had any such book in mind. Much that I know came from this lifetime of engagement with the material as a working academic. Unfortunately, because most of these years I did not have this book in mind and hence took no specific notes, I honestly do not remember in many cases where I first learned what I now believe to be true about this particular part of the past. While I do cite specific quotations and occasionally the arguments of certain books, generally what I write simply reflects years of reading. Suffice it to say, we exist in a world of wonderful historical scholarship, and one of the pleasures of my life has been the freedom and leisure to read as much as I could if not as much as I wanted. To the hundreds of historians, academic and freelance, as well as the dedicated editors of documentary projects, who have contributed to my understanding, I owe inestimable thanks.

Various colleagues over the years have also taught me much, and librarians and archivists have assisted me generously over the decades. Rice University has long supported my endeavors, and to it—its administrators, faculty, and students—I express my heartfelt appreciation. Rice has provided a subvention for this book, whose production costs were increased by supply-chain disruptions and other COVID-related problems. I will not try to list all the individuals who have helped along the way; they know themselves and my regard for them. But I must single out Randal L. Hall, Bethany Leigh Johnson, and Suzanne Scott Gibbs at Rice. My family has always patiently supported or put up with my efforts, especially my wife, Nancy, and I here thank them all, especially Nancy. One of my oldest colleagues, from my first teaching appointment in 1969, Joseph W. Cox, again stepped up and agreed to read the manuscript to ensure its accessibility to a general audience.

I came to Rice University as a student in 1961, the age of Sputnik, assuming it my patriotic duty to study science, but calculus, physics, and chemistry in my freshman year helped redirect my interests to an even earlier enthusiasm, history, and I have never regretted that change in major. I have had several wonderful mentors, have worked with treasured colleagues, and have taught a multitude of bright, curious, and eager students, both undergraduate and graduate. What a privilege it has been! Because I became a historian as a graduate student at the University of Virginia in the mid-1960s, it is fitting that what might be my last book is published by the university's press. I would like to express my sincerest gratitude to Nadine Zimmerli of the press for her wise and patient guidance through the process of acquisition, to J. Andrew Edwards for shepherding the book through production, to freelancer Beatrice Burton for her skillful copyediting, and to another freelancer, Kate Mertes, for compiling the index. Others at the press worked to design, publicize, and otherwise promote this project. I appreciate their combined efforts. As with rearing a child, it does take a village to publish a book.

Seven Virginians

INTRODUCTION

It is one of the single most remarkable facts of American history. Within the span of slightly more than three decades, 1725–1758, seven men were born in the northeast quadrant of the colony of Virginia who would ultimately play a vastly disproportionate role in the founding of this nation. In order of birth, they were George Mason, George Washington, Patrick Henry, Thomas Jefferson, James Madison, John Marshall, and James Monroe. All household names it is true, but their closely intertwined lives and careers have never before been integrated and jointly employed to tell the story of how the colonies came to break away from their mother country, fight a revolution, and write a constitution, thereby establishing a new nation. They helped ratify that Constitution, set the infant nation in motion, develop its governing procedures, organize its first political parties, evolve the role of the president, and subsequently guide the maturation of the Supreme Court. In each of these critical events, one or more of this group of men played essential roles. That is, they were indispensable actors in the creation of the United States. Of course, there were other influential leaders from other colonies, particularly Massachusetts and Pennsylvania, but no other colony produced such a large cluster of such significant leaders as did Virginia.

I became fascinated several years ago by the extraordinarily important role these seven had in shaping the development of the political institutions and practices of the nation and the fact that they all came from a small region of one colony. That prosperous region had a stable economy based on the cultivation of tobacco by enslaved African American laborers. Out of this milieu, these seven men came of age having been provided with a basic education and a set of beliefs about local governance. From an inheritance of family name, land, and enslaved men, women, and children, they all had or soon gained the leisure and opportunity to expand that initial education and develop leadership skills. They were ambitious and were given or seized opportunities to extend their roles in local government. Their property holdings also tended to grow over time, and in various ways they quickly emerged as societal leaders. Almost automatically they, like other similarly placed individuals, accepted slaveholding as a rightful part of the natural order and presumed the wholesomeness of an agricultural/plantation way of life. Had they been born elsewhere, say Massachusetts, they likely would have thought differently, but they were from Virginia. While all eventually began to question to varying degrees the morality and financial viability of slavery, they were in the end incapable of completely divorcing themselves from the world into which they had been born. These men wove an accommodation to slavery—usually blatant but often subtle—into all aspects of society, with everything from political institutions to social etiquette bearing its influence. The presence of many who were unfree in their society may very well have led Virginia's leaders even more to value their own liberties as white men and even sense a degree of commonality among men of their race. Notably, the first rumblings of dissent against England occurred in the context of white Virginians' hypersensitivity to preserving their own precious liberty. Democracy for whites and slavery for non-whites was, to our everlasting regret, part of our founding.

I recognize that a book about seven white slaveholders will appear inappropriate or even repugnant to some readers in 2023, but I believe it is important to see these men in all their complexities—good and bad—if we are to face our history honestly and with completeness. Having often taught noncredit general education classes for decades, and in Maryland, Louisiana, and Texas, I know many otherwise well-educated Americans are unfamiliar with the background of the Founders and the political and economic issues they confronted. At a time when many of the basic principles of our nation are forgotten, unknown, or even rejected, I think it important to give a relatively full historical context for readers, more so than perhaps would have been necessary a generation or two before. I hope to offer in part at least a civics refresher.

One might ask at what point should such a book begin. Nation-building clearly did not commence in 1787 with the drafting of the Constitution or even 1776 with the Declaration of Independence. Rather, the process of creating a new nation began when colonists in mainland North America first started to see their fundamental interests as different from those of the mother country; we cannot fully understand the motives and actions of those we call the Founders unless we see them in this longer chronological context. As John Adams wrote in 1818, "the revolution was effected, before the war commenced. The revolution was in the minds and hearts of the people."[1] For that reason our story starts in the 1740s. What might be generously called the long revolutionary era ended in Virginia about 1830 when that state essentially repudiated the progressive nationalism of the Founders and began its headlong march toward an increasingly conservative state-rightism that eventually and tragically led to secession and civil war. Hence the chronological boundaries of our story.

I remember a comment a taxi driver in London had made to my son David in 2009, shortly after the first election of Barack Obama to the US presidency. "That could never happen in this country," he had said with a sense of awe. But were we truly that unique? Whether or not that comment was correct—and I doubted it—it led me to ponder the origins of this nation, its fundamental institutions, its gradual (sometimes grudging) openness over time to new people and new ideas. Could the story of these seven white men help provide some understanding of this evolution? What exactly had motivated these similar but again quite different leaders? Certainly, they all appreciated the exciting opportunity they had to break away from the control of the mother country, and most of them seized the chance to participate in the actual creation of a new nation, one larger than a single state. How had they responded to change, to crisis, to remarkable economic and geographical expansion? Did their viewpoints evolve over time? I hoped that by examining aspects of the careers of seven political leaders during a critical era of our nation's history I could develop a clearer knowledge of our past. And I wanted to relate that history in a way that was accessible to general readers throughout the nation, for this was much more than simply a Virginia story. It is an essential part of the American story.

Perhaps it goes without saying that if there were leaders, there had to be followers. Key to leadership is the ability to motivate, educate, inspire, and direct a significant fraction of the general population. These seven men had that ability in spades. Their skills were varied: Washington possessed an austere charisma that generated immense respect and support. Henry's remarkable oratory moved people to act. Jefferson's literary power and idealism persuaded people to trust in democracy. These three have famously been labeled the sword, the trumpet, and the pen of the revolution.[2] Mason's thoughtful writing gave him great influence, and everyone appreciated the penetrating intelligence of Madison's words. Marshall's plain-written logical analysis of issues built adherence to the Constitution and undergirded the growing support for the national government. Monroe was probably the least skilled of the seven, but his earnest if awkward phraseology nevertheless garnered support for his positions. Out of a mix of leadership styles—especially the power of the spoken and written word—was the nation built, and that such a democratic system of government was established in an era of powerful monarchs and nearly universal autocracy was no minor miracle. It did not begin with democracy for all people, although over time and through difficult struggles, democratic practices eventually expanded.

Admittedly our democratic prospects as a nation have been threatened over the last years. There is a huge gap between the men I focus on and most of our recent leaders, and the controversies and disputes of the last years have raised profound questions in the minds of many about the durability of our founding institutions. Looking at the dysfunctionality of our recent Congresses; the apparent lack of character, courage, and outstanding political ability in a nation of over three hundred million people; the repeated repudiation of the principle of compromise; the widespread rejection of science and distrust of experts; the persistence (even intensification) of racism and xenophobia; the shocking January 6, 2021, assault on the Capitol Building and the working of Congress; and the continuing unwillingness of millions of people to accept fair election results, how was it possible that a collection of colonies totaling only about three million people ever established a nation that is now the world's longest lasting (if imperfect) democracy?

These seven Virginians furnish a manageable sample size to investigate aspects of that story, and their ample correspondence offers insight into their beliefs and behavior. They certainly were not men without faults, even grievous ones; they had glaring blind spots about such things as race and gender; they often disagreed with one another; and their influence was clearly uneven. Still, the political ideas, institutions, and practices these imperfect men helped create contained possibilities they did not fully comprehend and that we have not always lived up to. I invite you to join me as we seek to know these men of more than two centuries ago and explore how they helped create a nation. The result was far from perfect, but it allowed—often in response to protest, civil conflict, even war—for changes to be made over time that inched the nation toward that ideal expressed in the opening line of the Constitution, achieving *a more perfect Union.*

Context is always critical to comprehending the past. If we are to make sense of the careers of our seven actors, we must situate them in their place and time in history: they were propertied, free white men who came of age in eighteenth-century Virginia. We should not forget that they most decidedly did not have the attitudes of modern Americans. How could they? In the years following 1725, the colony seemed to be approaching a golden age, at least for the white elite. But Virginia also had a larger population of enslaved persons by far than any other colony, and for them this was by no means a golden age. And the great majority of Virginia's white population were non-slaveholding small farmers and indentured servants. However, the gentry—3 percent or less of the total population—set the tone for the society and controlled politics. Although tobacco prices fell for several years after 1720, on the whole, these were prosperous times for mainland America's oldest, most populous, and most profitable colony. For a significant fraction of the non-elite whites, there was even upward mobility. Death rates had stabilized a generation before, Indian wars had become a thing of the past, and the slave agricultural economy was booming. Between 1700 and 1750, approximately 45,000 enslaved Africans were imported into the colony, and because of indigenous population growth the total number of Blacks in 1750 reached 100,000, or almost 44 percent of the colony's total population.[3] The fundamental character of the colony was evolving: whites increasingly accepted the presence of enslaved people as normative, and by midcentury, Virginia contained more such people by far than any other mainland British colony. Few whites questioned slavery's morality, and fewer still questioned its role in the economy.

Tobacco production was such—especially since by then the British had tapped the immense European market for snuff—that Virginia's trade with the mother country amounted to fully one-third of Britain's commerce with her mainland colonies. The colony largely governed itself with almost no interference or oversight by Parliament or the Crown and expected that virtual autonomy to continue. Wealthy, stable planters paid to have large, stately homes designed and constructed (usually by enslaved workers) for themselves—think Nomini Hall, Stratford Hall, and Westover and Middleton Plantations—along the lower stretch of the James and other wide, slow-moving tidal rivers, and similar homes were built in succeeding decades. Although some elite whites occasionally expressed worries (usually privately), about the morality of slavery, almost no one turned down the profits that slave-cultivated tobacco could bring. In 1730 or so, few could see on the horizon significant problems for their society. Yet perceptions could be deceptive.

The geographical setting for our beginning is, again, but a small portion of colonial Virginia as it evolved from complacency to rebellion. During this era, Virginia was a growing participant in an accumulation of protests that slowly transformed random conflicts between England and the various colonies into what would become the genesis of a self-conscious nationalizing movement. Among many political actors in Virginia, our seven men stood out for their leadership. They all knew one another, shared central viewpoints at one time or another, and contributed to the national narrative, though in time they came to disagree and oppose each other, and in doing so they represented practically the full spectrum of outlooks that defined American politics during the age. Their intertwined biographies help us to understand an eventful era in American history. Although Virginia's agriculture would over time diversify and the state eventually became a major wheat-growing and milling center, at the beginning of our story, tobacco cultivation completely dominated the colony's economy. By the middle of the previous century, tobacco planters realized that the crop quickly depleted the nutrients of the soil, so the only way to guarantee long-term prosperity was to acquire large acreages. Depleted land could be abandoned and cultivation shifted to fresh soil. Consequently, the more affluent planters soon owned most of the arable lands near waterways, essential in an age when bulk goods were most efficiently shipped by boat. Earlier, many small farmers had cultivated tiny patches of tobacco, but by the late seventeenth century wealthier men, utilizing larger work forces of enslaved Black laborers, had already begun to dominate the colonial economy.

This agricultural reality would shape the pattern of settlement for the next century and a half, and it established the procurement of additional acreage as a central concern for planters and ambitious farmers. Purchase of land and speculation in massive landholdings ever further to the west in fact came to be a defining characteristic of the wealthiest and politically dominant men of the colony, a trait the royal governors and other government officials came to share. Well-placed speculators by the late 1740s were obtaining blocks of land of up to one hundred thousand acres, and in 1749 alone the government approved land grants of more than one million acres. In 1747 the so-called Ohio Company obtained two hundred thousand acres along the Ohio River (with the prospect of more than doubling that acreage if it successfully established a fort and settled a hundred families in the region within seven years).[4] Investors in the project would soon include such men as George Washington and George Mason, who spent an enormous amount of time contemplating land acquisition. But Virginians proved not to be the only men who cast greedy eyes upon these munificent tracks of virgin land. The French in Canada were eager to occupy the region of the Ohio Valley too, and they could envision linking up with French settlements along the Gulf Coast. In 1749 they sent an expedition under the command of Pierre Joseph Céloron de Blainville south of Lake Erie and across western Pennsylvania, burying lead plates to mark the purported boundaries of French territory and establishing several small forts, meanwhile gaining the support of local American Indians who correctly saw the English settlers as permanent occupiers, not transient hunters. These French advances upset not only Virginians (and especially the powerful land speculators with investments in the Ohio Company) but authorities in England as well. Virginia lieutenant governor Robert Dinwiddie (the de facto royal governor), a fellow investor in the company, instantly saw the threat to Virginia interests and in 1753 requested approval from his superiors to erect forts in the disputed territory. From King George II came permission to send a diplomatic mission to the French occupiers to warn them that they were trespassing upon British territory and, if they did not agree to leave, "We do hereby strickly charge, & command You to drive them off by Force of Arms."[5]

Dinwiddie did not have ready at hand a militia force or military command structure, so he turned to an inexperienced young Virginian, twenty-one-year-old George Washington, to lead an eight-man expedition into the contested region to demand the French forces to withdraw. With this mission our story begins.

1

THE FIRST RUMBLINGS

What about youthful George Washington recommended him to the royal governor of Virginia as the right person to address what Britain saw as a French incursion into Virginia territory in 1753? Born northeast of Richmond in Westmoreland County, near the Potomac River, on February 22, 1732, Washington was not initially privy to great wealth, although his father came to own substantial acreage and, by his death, about fifty enslaved men, women, and children. But his father died when George was only eleven, and he was primarily raised by his mother in a farmhouse near Fredericksburg. Young George looked up to his two older half brothers, but his hypercritical, even hateful mother had a larger psychological influence. Washington coped by learning to control his every emotion and would always be extremely sensitive to criticism and eager to win approval. Early on he copied out a set of more than a hundred rules for civility and good behavior originally composed by a Jesuit scholar in the late seventeenth century, and he sought diligently to shape his life accordingly.

Washington grew to be extraordinarily ambitious both for fame and money, and he learned to obsequiously court the support of powerful men about him. Never scholarly like the famously so Thomas Jefferson or James Madison after him, or even George Mason, Washington learned surveying, studied books on military demeanor and strategy, and polished his social skills. Six feet tall, muscular, with an erect bearing and elegant on horseback, Washington cut an impressive figure. Even at an early age the worth of his character shone, and hints of his later charisma were already present. He simply sold himself and his promising leadership ability to Governor Dinwiddie.[1]

Washington signed up an experienced frontiersman, Christopher Gist, to join his squad, and the small body of men traversed rugged terrain, endured almost impossibly cold weather, escaped an Indian assassination attempt, formed a temporary alliance with Seneca chief Tanacharison, and finally reached the outpost of the French just south of Lake Erie. A naive Washington gave the French commander there the message that he should vacate the region and turn it over to the British, only to be completely rebuffed by the French officer. Washington and his small contingent returned to Williamsburg where on January 16, 1754, he handed Governor Dinwiddie a rough journal account of his efforts and a letter from the French officer dismissing the English demand. Washington's journal revealed the fruits of his reconnoitering of the territory, which included identifying the location of French positions and estimates of their troop strength. Dinwiddie asked Washington to write up and polish his report as a message to the council, and the hastily drafted report was also published in the Williamsburg and other newspapers. This report or journal gained Washington instant local fame, and although it revealed the failure of his mission, readers saw him as hardy, brave, and forthright in his stance against the French. The failed mission ironically made Washington a Virginia hero.

Governor Dinwiddie soon found additional funds and gathered a small force of Virginia men to return to the Ohio Territory. On April 2, 1754, Washington, now heading a regiment of three hundred, left Virginia to return to the disputed territory, but he quickly learned that a much larger French force had entered the region. On July 3, French forces attacked, subjecting Washington's men to withering gunfire. The Virginians, completely outgunned, took horrendous casualties. For some reason the French commander, Louis Coulon de Villiers, showed mercy. In the midst of a rainstorm, Washington surrendered. De Villiers was surprisingly generous: although the Virginia troops were required to surrender the fort, they were allowed to keep their weapons; they agreed to leave the Ohio Country for a year; and they were given a pass to return to Virginia.

Washington led the defeated troops home, where once again he was feted as a hero for resisting the French (Washington grossly exaggerated the number of casualties his men inflicted on the French forces) despite his thorough defeat. Virginia's House of Burgesses commended Washington but also deactivated the Virginia regiment that he had commanded and redistributed the forces across ten companies, each with their own leader. Ever sensitive, Washington felt slighted by the move and resigned. As if to sartorially compensate for what was in effect a demotion, he ordered from England materials to have tailored for himself a resplendent military uniform.[2]

Washington had been fighting to protect the interests of the colony of Virginia and its ambitious planters. However, in London, wiser heads with a larger perspective on international strategy understood that the issues at stake were greater than skirmishes over a fort or two claimed by Virginians—would France or England eventually control the region and the continent? This was to be a war for a North American empire. In February 1755, British officials sent General Edward Braddock with two regiments of the British army to Virginia. Braddock was an accomplished officer, but the only warfare he knew were conflicts on the open plains of Europe, where disciplined formations of men lined up and fired at one another. Confident of British military superiority and contemptuous of both Virginia soldiers and Native American fighters, Braddock assumed he would march smartly across Virginia and enter the backcountry to certain victory. Washington hoped to get a commission in the British army, but all Braddock would offer was that Washington could become a member of his staff.

A disappointed Washington in protest agreed to serve without pay. He had learned enough about warfare in the rugged terrain of the West, and the unorthodox-by-European-standards of Native American warfare, that he found the gradual British march westward infuriating. Sure enough, Braddock's progress slowed to a crawl when, on July 9, Indians and French soldiers attacked, suddenly appearing from the woods or from behind rocks to fire on the redcoats, only to disappear into the wilderness. The British took frightening losses. Braddock himself was killed, and Washington, displaying great courage and stamina, helped bring order to the rattled British forces and organized a successful retreat. The remaining British regulars went into so-called winter quarters in safe Philadelphia in the middle of the summer. Washington never received the military commission he desired, but he nevertheless had grown confident of his ability to command and had come to see that the British army was not invincible in the kind of warfare practiced on the American scene. He never forgot that lesson.

The House of Burgesses in August authorized funds to reorganize the Virginia regiment, and it named Washington in command. For the next several years he recruited men, trained them, instilled a sense of discipline in his troops, and with a still surprisingly small force attempted to bring order and a cessation of Indian warfare along the extensive western frontier. Washington was a severe disciplinarian, punishing his soldiers for infractions like drunkenness with up to a thousand lashes, and he had deserters hanged. But he succeeded in molding his men into an effective fighting force, much better than the voluntary and only slightly trained militia that he already held in contempt. By now he considered himself a far superior commander than the British officers he had met. Yet in these years the major theater of the war between the French and English had moved to the Great Lakes region and along the St. Lawrence River, where the iconic battle would ultimately turn out to be General James Wolfe's stunning victory over the Marquis de Montcalm on the Plains of Abraham near Quebec in September 1759. Before that British triumph, officials in England had in April 1758 sent General John Forbes to retake Fort Duquesne.

Forbes, with twice the number of troops that Braddock had commanded, was competent, generally willing to take advice from Washington (and others experienced in western warfare), and welcomed his aid. Forbes moved expeditiously into the Ohio Territory, and, with the military assistance of Washington and his Virginia regiment, regained Fort Duquesne. Although Washington was still young, headstrong, and perhaps too sure of his own abilities, over the past five years he had honed his martial skills to the point that he was—at the age of twenty-six—indisputably Virginia's military leader. By hard work, an iron will, study, and self-discipline, he had fashioned himself into a persona that elicited respect from his soldiers and earned the admiration of most of his fellowmen.

Meanwhile the war was coming to an end, with the French thoroughly defeated. Conflicts intensified in the final years between English colonists and Native Americans along the western and southern frontier, but hostilities with the French ceased. A comprehensive peace treaty was signed in Paris in 1763, freeing the British colonies from any threat from another European power. Most colonists were pleased with the removal of the French and proud at the moment to be British, but beneath the apparently calm surface other issues had already begun to emerge between the mainland colonies and British authorities. No one foresaw the complications that came to a head over the next few years, complications that had taken root a generation earlier. For the first four decades of the eighteenth century, English authorities had largely left Virginians to manage their own affairs, including passing laws and regulating land purchases. Virginia prospered and grew; in fact, its population doubled between 1730 and 1760—this had produced the demand for land that underwrote the worries about French ambitions in the region.

In the years following 1740, the Board of Trade in London began to take more interest in colonial affairs. What caught its attention was a complete overhaul by the Virginia Assembly in 1748 and 1749 of its whole set of laws, which had arisen, willy-nilly, over the years and had become outdated, repetitive, and sometimes insufficiently precise. The Assembly had expected no complications from the Board of Trade, but the Earl of Halifax, now head of the Board of Trade, had just begun a process of tightening administrative procedures and overseeing more carefully England's far-flung colonies. Virginia's revision of its laws became caught up in the enhanced supervisory procedures of the Board of Trade, with the result that the Board in 1751 rejected ten Virginia laws, placed seven on probationary status, sent three to the treasury for examination, and approved fifty-seven. This action stunned the Virginia legislature. Never before had the colony been subjected to such interference.

Governor Dinwiddie soon created another provocation. In part because he wanted to more closely regulate land sales and thereby collect rents due the

Crown, he decided to charge a fee on all land patents (claims). The members of the General Assembly saw this as an unprecedented attempt to gouge money from the citizens—in effect, to tax them without their consent. Protests went all the way to the Privy Council in London. Ultimately the Privy Council so limited the applicability of the fee as to render it of little effect, but the Council took care not to legally limit the power of a governor to levy such fees. The controversy raised colonial concerns about taxing authority and initiated conversations about local control of taxation.

Another unforeseen irritant between the colony of Virginia and the mother country arose in the late 1750s after several years of crop failures tripled the price of tobacco. The state religion of colonial Virginia was Anglicanism, and for years, law had set the salaries of the Anglican ministers at sixteen thousand pounds of tobacco. In 1755 (and renewed in 1758), after the sharp rise in prices had in effect given ministers very substantial raises, the General Assembly passed the Two-Penny Acts that sought to keep the ministerial real wages at their historic levels, based on two cents per pound as the average price fetched by tobacco. Five Anglican ministers protested, and one, the Reverend John Camm, traveled to London to present the ministers' cause to the Board of Trade—he was there joined by the bishop of London. The Board of Trade accordingly overruled the Two-Penny Acts without specifying whether they were retrospectively void or only void from that moment onward. This required that the five protesting ministers go to court locally in Virginia to try to recoup what they saw as their legally due wages. Four of them had their claims rather quickly rejected; the fifth, the Reverend James Maury, whose case was brought in Hanover County in December 1763, proved to be of more import. Maury, a very reputable minister who also ran a highly effective school in his home (Thomas Jefferson had been one of his students), found himself opposed by a young lawyer named Patrick Henry.

Born May 29, 1736, in Hanover County to parents who were relatively well-off, owning several thousand acres of land, a commodious house, and dozens of enslaved laborers, Henry had learned the rudiments of Latin and Greek and apparently read fairly widely, but he had not attended university and had no scholarly inclinations. In his early adult years he had flitted from career to career with little direction, and he seemed to possess no exceptional ability other than sociability. Jefferson had met him over the Christmas holidays of 1759–60 and recalled in 1815 that at that first meeting Henry's manners were coarse, he had an "idle disposition," and "his passion was fiddling, dancing & pleasantry, he excelled at the last, and it attached everyone to him."[3] (By 1815 Jefferson had broken with Henry, so this may have colored his recollection.) Henry twice tried keeping a store but both efforts failed, and then he worked as a barkeeper in a local tavern. Suddenly he found himself: he read law for several months in late 1759 and early 1760, traveled to Williamsburg to sit for his bar exam before a distinguished panel of lawyers in April 1760, and impressed them all by his natural aptitude if not by the depth of his legal knowledge. He passed the exam. At this date Henry had neither the learning, polish, nor sophistication of the other men we consider Founding Fathers, but more than any of them he had the popular touch, identified with the common people, and knew how to reach them rhetorically and persuade them of his position.

This skill became obvious when Henry argued on behalf of the vestry and against Reverend Maury. There was a grandeur to his words, a musicality to his voice, a theatricality to his body language that overwhelmed the jury and those in the courtroom. He spoke extravagantly, claiming that in overturning the just Two-Penny Acts, the Board of Trade and by extension the king had acted tyrannically. Maury and supporting ministers were taken aback by this extreme language, and though the charge was disproportionately strong, it resonated with some troubling concerns that many in the audience were beginning to feel. It also reflected a sharp disaffection with the established Anglican Church on the part of dissenting sects like the Baptists, whose numbers had exploded as the results of revivals over the past decade. Henry combined his bold charge with a moving portrait of poor parishioners starving while greedy ministers clamored for higher wages. When the jury quickly came back with a decision technically supporting the vestry but granting the clergy only one farthing (one-quarter of a penny) in recompence, it established Henry as the hero of the common people. As soon as they had a chance, in early May 1765, the people of Hanover County elected him to the House of Burgesses, where his rhetorical brilliance was to become the thing of legend. Still, the Parson's Cause case, as it became known, affected relatively few people. As of yet there was no glimmer of a break with England, no rumors of revolution. Only in retrospect did the lengthening list of irritants come to be comprehended as reflective of something of larger significance.

At the time, the late 1750s and early 1760s seemed relatively peaceful years. Teenager Thomas Jefferson, then unknown to history, traveled to Williamsburg in March 1760 to enroll at the College of William and Mary. Henry was developing his legal practice and striving to support his young wife and growing family. On January 6, 1759, Washington, having utilized every ounce of his self-control to suppress his infatuation with Sally Fairfax—the real love of his life—made the more practical decision to ask the enormously wealthy widow, Martha Custis, to become his wife. On that January date he finally ascended to the top rungs of Virginia aristocracy, becoming one of the richest men (and largest slave owners) in the colony. Having inherited the small Mount Vernon, he now began to pour money into it, buying more land, making improvements, acquiring fine furnishings and luxury goods of all kinds, purchasing a handsome carriage. He spent prolifically (the equivalent of an enormous $2–3 million in the early 1760s alone), but his expenditures would be more than matched by his business skills.[4] We tend to associate Washington with military command and the presidency, overlooking that he was a truly gifted businessman: he invested in western land, developed grist mills, bought town lots in Alexandria, made huge profits from a fishery industry focused on the Potomac adjoining his property, quickly turned from tobacco to wheat farming. (His businesses relied on enslaved laborers who worked his fields and operated his fisheries.) Washington's range of business operations hardly seem the preoccupations of a man expecting a revolution.

While no one event in the late 1750s and early 1760s rose to the point of being a cause of the break between the colonies and England, the slow accumulation of provocations established the context for sharply increasing tensions by the mid-1760s.[5] Such events as the growth of the dissenting sects (beginning with Baptists), and their active persecution by the Anglican clergy, supported by some civil officials, rankled many of the common people and began to cast the clergy and everything that smacked of English officialdom as contemptuous of the beliefs of the Baptist faithful. Soldiers like Washington who had encountered arrogance on the part of British officers in the late war against the French carried a chip on their collective shoulders and were quick to find offense at British actions. When many of the sons of the wealthier Virginia planters traveled to England to finish their educations, proud of their colonial families and sure of their merit, they were seen by British aristocrats as little more than country bumpkins and not accorded the respect the planter offspring thought their due. When tobacco prices declined and British merchants began to push their planter customers to pay their debts, the hard-pressed planters—who believed as men of honor they should be trusted to settle their accounts as soon as they could—found the merchants' importuning to be ill-tempered badgering and felt being pressured to pay was an attempt to circumscribe their personal freedom. Their liberty was under attack!

Planters' letters became filled with complaints against their British factors who facilitated their trade, with wealthy planters like Washington and his neighbor George Mason constantly expressing their annoyance even as they continued to buy luxury goods. Planters sensed that partly they were at fault for their indebtedness, but they found it difficult to change their ways; it was easier to imagine corruption, exorbitant gambling expenses, and high living among their fellow Virginians than to control their own financial affairs.[6] When in mid-1766 the longtime colony treasurer John Robinson died and it was soon discovered he had embezzled one hundred thousand pounds or more, much of it lent out to friends to help cover their indebtedness, it truly seemed that corruption was everywhere, at home as well as in Britain. A strong sense of unease began to develop, feelings of anxiety that in politics and society, things were not as they should be. Suspicion began to mount over British actions, both those of private merchants and then imperial policy itself.

Although Americans were little aware of it, conditions in England were also stressful. In consequence of having prosecuted effectively the war against France, British public debts had grown 70 percent, from £72 million in 1755 to £122 million in 1763, with no end of its increase in sight.[7] Citizens there were heavily taxed, while the total taxes raised in the colonies were negligible, perhaps less than £2,000 annually before 1763.[8] The increased empire in North America would cost more to administer and defend, and the hostilities with Native Americans that erupted in the final stages of the war intensified in 1763 as Chief Potomac of the Ottawa Indians pushed conflict eastward from the region of Detroit. One response of Crown authorities was to pass a proclamation in 1763 to limit colonial expansion west of the midpoint of the Appalachians as to such time as the animosities with the Ottawa Indians and other nations could be placated.[9] This seemed an imminently rational policy in London, but to Americans and perhaps especially to land-hungry Virginians for whom land speculation in the West was seen as a birthright, any attempt to shut off expansion westward was a huge offense. They saw it as an attempt to keep Virginians confined to the East Coast, a conspiracy to limit their future. For people like Washington and Mason, confirmed land speculators, this was an outrage. This is what Washington had fought for earlier, and Mason had been an early investor in the Ohio Company and after 1749 treasurer of that land company. Even Henry, much less well-off than Washington and Mason, was nevertheless consumed with desire for more land. Little else England could have done would have so upset so many elite Virginians. But more was to come.

England, faced with an enormous debt, high taxes at home, and growing expenses for administering her mainland colonies, needed to find new revenues. Secretary of the Exchequer George Grenville in early 1764 proposed the American Revenue Act, popularly known in the colonies as the Sugar Act. Since 1660 England had had regulations to control colonial trade, primarily intended to keep commerce within the confines of the British empire, but these so-called Navigation Acts were not revenue generators. Grenville issued new duties on a number of foreign products, increased duties on goods originally landed in England and then re-shipped to the colonies, banned French wines and foreign rum, decreased an older but seldom enforced import duty on molasses but promised to rigorously enforce the new duties, and made a long list of items that could not be sent from the colonies. The hope was these various regulations would produce revenues of about forty-five thousand pounds annually.[10] Of course, most of these duties fell on goods that the more affluent and influential colonists were apt to purchase.

It was clear that unlike previous Navigation Acts, the duties of the Sugar Act were explicitly intended to raise revenue. That is, they were taxes. Up and down the colonies protesters began to complain that the English had no right to levy taxes on colonists without their having given their consent. Massachusetts author James Otis argued powerfully in a pamphlet entitled *The Rights of the British Colonists Asserted and Proved* that "No parts of His Majesty's dominions can be taxed without their consent."[11] That viewpoint gained almost immediate assent everywhere. But not finished yet, Grenville pushed through Parliament the next year a Quartering Act that in essence required local colonies to provide quarters and rations for British troops stationed in the colony (this most affected the northern colonies), and, in a measure aimed squarely at Virginia, the Currency Act of 1764 that prohibited the colonies from issuing paper money as legal tender. This too hurt the merchants and their affluent slaveholding customers more than it did small farmers, who lived in practically a barter economy, locally exchanging products and services without the use of money. Grenville was still not finished. He had hinted in 1764 that he had in mind a more remunerative revenue measure, a Stamp Act. Members of the House of Burgesses fixated on this threat, as did outspoken colonists elsewhere. Grenville believed the Stamp Act would be noncontroversial because such a revenue mechanism had long been used in England without protest. He thought it would be easy to administer and would produce significant income. He could not have been more wrong. The Stamp Act required that revenue stamps ranging in price from a half penny to ten pounds be purchased and attached to most things printed in the colonies (newspapers, pamphlets, and almanacs), on any commercial or legal documents such as deeds and insurance policies; and on playing cards and dice. Nothing could have been formulated that would have more immediate impact on printers and lawyers, the opinion makers.[12] The act passed Parliament in March 1765, but already colonists had heard rumors of the coming measure and were developing their counterarguments and protests. Common to the opposition was the idea that control of taxation was a local matter: taxes were only to be levied when the people *at the colony level* gave their consent.

Since the organization of Virginia into county governments in the seventeenth century through the maturation of the General Assembly, the tradition of local, representative government had become a respected feature of life in the proud colony. Richard Bland, a member of the House of Burgesses and learned in the law, published a widely read pamphlet in 1764 entitled *The Colonel Dismounted: or The Rector Vindicated . . . containing A Dissertation upon the Constitution of the Colony.* This document summarized the Virginia position that local laws, so-called internal legislation, meaning taxes, could only rightfully be passed by the local assembly, for only in that forum could the people give their consent.[13] But the most influential statement of opposition to the Stamp Act came from the Capitol Building in Williamsburg on May 29, 1765. Patrick Henry, on the heels of his victory in the Parson's Cause, had been elected to the House of Burgesses in May 1765, taking the oath of office on the twentieth of that month. There had been little prior evidence of Henry's political views, though he was very much a man of the people, and in the first days or so of the session few took notice of him. He attracted attention when a farfetched and self-interested scheme to establish a loan office was debated. This proposal, recognized clearly as a bailout of sorts for the colony's treasury, was overseen by John Robinson, who would be soon discovered to have long been embezzling treasury funds and illegally using them to help out friends deeply mired in debt. Though the loan office bill passed the lower house, it was rejected by the Governor's Council, and Henry had spoken out forthrightly against the proposal. That he did this so soon after entering the House, and at such an early age—he was only twenty-eight—suggests his growing self-confidence and sense of presence.

Many of the senior members of the Assembly believed that, with the failure of the loan office proposal, most of the important work had been done and so returned home. By the end of the month only about one-third of the Assembly's members were still in place to witness Henry's next bold action. On May 29, the day he turned twenty-nine, Henry rose in the House of Burgesses and successfully moved that it resolve itself into a committee of the whole, which allowed a speaker more freedom to address his points and speak more than once. Then, having—by his own account—drafted a total of seven resolutions on a blank page torn from a lawbook (others had probably assisted in the drafting), Henry placed the first five resolutions on the floor for debate. He held back the final two resolutions, apparently to gauge the climate of the House before introducing them. The first two resolutions, though awkwardly phrased, were not controversial. The first made the point that the original colonists had brought with them the rights possessed by those living in Great Britain, and the second argued that the descendants of the original colonists currently possessed those rights and privileges just as if they still dwelled in England. The third resolution in convoluted language insisted that taxes passed only by local representatives was "the Distinguishing Characteristic of British Freedom." The next resolution made clear that the people of Virginia "have uninterruptedly enjoyed the Right of being thus governed by their own assembly in the article of their Taxes . . . and the same have never been forfeited or any other way given up." None of these ideas were new or radical; others had said as much. But the fifth resolution had more bite.

> Resolved, therefore, that the General Assembly of this Colony have the *only and sole exclusive* Right & Power to lay Taxes & Impositions upon the Inhabitants of this Colony and that every Attempt to vest such power in any Person or Persons whatsoever other than the General Assembly Aforesaid has a manifest Tendency to destroy *British* as well as *American* freedom.[14]

This was a stark denial of Parliament's right to tax the colonies without their consent and by implication to pass any legislation that dealt with exclusively colonial concerns. Previously, such ideas had been expressed abstractly; this was a flat-out repudiation of parliamentary authority.

Henry had the floor, and he spoke with uncommon power in support of his resolutions. During the reading of the fifth, the members who remained began murmuring among themselves. Henry's oratory was something no one had ever experienced before. Years later Jefferson recalled that as a student he had stood in the doorway to the House and "heard the splendid display of Mr. Henry's talents as a popular orator. They were great indeed; such as I have never heard from any other man. He appeared to me to speak as Homer wrote."[15] Amid Henry's torrent of words he legendarily stated that "Tarquin and Caesar had each his Brutus, Charles the First his Cromwell, and George the Third." Here came the interrupting shouts of "treason, treason!" A quick-witted Henry then supposedly completed his sentence with "may profit by their example! If this be treason, make the most of it!"[16] According to a French traveler who happened to hear the debate, Henry quickly apologized if he had spoken too freely and expressed his loyalty to the king, although Henry tempered his apology by stating that "what he had said must be attributed to the Interest of his Countrys Dying liberty which he had at heart."[17] This fifth resolution passed by the slimmest margin. However, the narrow margin apparently convinced Henry and his close associates not to try to advocate the final two resolutions, the seventh of which stated that anyone who defended the right of Parliament or the king to levy taxes on the people of the colonies (that is, without their consent) "shall be deemed an Enemy to this his Majesty's colony."[18]

Henry, so new to the House as to be naive about how things really worked, returned home on May 31, the day after the vote on his five resolutions. Older, more cautious members, who felt that his intemperate words would be counterproductive in their attempts to get Parliament to repeal the Stamp Act, maneuvered to have the vote on the controversial fifth resolution rescinded, and as such it does not even appear in the records of the House. But reports of all five quickly appeared in newspaper accounts elsewhere in the colonies, with no mention of the fifth having been voided. In fact, several papers printed the sixth and seventh resolutions that were not even introduced as though they had passed. These Stamp Act resolutions had an electrifying impact on the colonies, reshaping colonial debate: most other colonies soon passed resolutions that mirrored Henry's Virginia resolutions. Taken all together, Henry's resolutions were nothing less than a call to defy the Stamp Act. On June 1, Governor Francis Fauquier dissolved the House.

The major result of Fauquier's action was that the colony of Virginia, with its legislature shut down, could not choose and send delegates to a newly called Stamp Act Congress in New York City in October 1765. The Stamp Act Congress met between October 5 and 25, 1765, to discuss the controversial act and send remonstrances to England. On October 19, the Congress drafted a "Declaration of Rights and Grievances" that, in fourteen resolutions, claimed for Americans all the rights held by those dwelling in England, said that taxation without the colonists' representatives giving their consent was a violation of their traditional rights, and stated clearly that the colonists were not represented in Parliament and thus any taxes imposed on them were unconstitutional.[19] England's claim that the colonists were in fact virtually represented in Parliament was vigorously refuted in the light of the American argument that only representatives from discrete geographical districts truly were representatives of the people living within such districts, hence *constituent* representation as opposed to *virtual* representation. The two sides were talking past one another.

Just days after the conclusion of the Stamp Act Congress, George Mercer, a Virginian who had been in Ireland and therefore not privy to recent political developments at home, arrived back in Williamsburg expecting to be a stamp distributor. He was met by a swirling mob, and within a few days, sizing up the situation, he frankly acknowledged his ignorance of the issues at stake and resigned his commission. With that the Stamp Act was a dead letter in Virginia. In Virginia and in other colonies later that year and in the first months of 1766, colonial courts closed and protesters styling themselves Sons of Liberty prevented the distribution of stamps and prohibited economic transactions that required them. The pressure, economic and legal, was felt in England. Meanwhile Grenville had lost favor with the king and been replaced by the Marquis of Rockingham, who had long opposed the Stamp Act duties. Now with pressure from British merchants, on March 18, 1766, Parliament repealed the act. Parliament accompanied the repeal with the Declaratory Act, stating its supreme authority: "all resolutions, votes, orders, and proceedings in any of the said colonies . . . whereby the power and authority of the parliament of Great Britain is denied or drawn into question . . . are hereby declared to be utterly null and void to all intents and purposes whatsoever."[20] The colonists chose to ignore this face-saving gesture of Parliament.

In pamphlets and letters, colonists continued to argue the American position. Underway was a subtle transformation of American opposition to British actions. No longer engaging in narrow protests against the payment of local clergy, or opposition on the part of wealthy land speculators to British actions to control land sales and settlement, or even umbrage over the arrogance of British soldiers, Virginians and Americans generally began to see their essential constitutional rights, the markings of their liberty, as under assault. George Mason, a learned planter and near neighbor to George Washington, put the emerging American position well in a letter of June 6 to an anonymous group of British merchants.

Mason lived in a stately Fairfax County home named Gunston Hall just a few miles south of Mount Vernon, on a small peninsula jutting into the Potomac. Long a friend of Washington, Mason had a decidedly localistic orientation that limited his involvement in colonial issues, much less continental, and he suffered from bad health, especially an at-times incapacitating gout and a painful skin rash called erysipelas, which caused high fever, chills, and fatigue. More than any other of the Founders, Mason—born of well-off parents on December 11, 1725, in Fairfax County where he lived his entire life—was a homebody, but he was extremely well read and had a rigorously analytical mind. His constant illness made him seem grouchy, and he had little patience with others, but he came to be highly respected for his ideas and ability to express them. Jefferson later described Mason as "a man of the first order of wisdom of those who acted on the theater of the revolution, of expansive mind, profound judgment, cogent in argument, learned in the lore of our former constitution, . . . strengthened by a dash of biting cynicism when provocation made it seasonable."[21]

Not surprisingly, Mason reacted sharply to the publication on May 16, 1766, in the *Virginia Gazette* (printed by Alexander Purdie) of "*A letter from the Committee of merchants in* London, *trading to* North America, *directed to the merchants in New York, dated Feb. 18, 1766,*" that condescendingly referred to Americans as disobedient children who needed to be corrected by their superiors. This overused trope, Mason explained, was tiresome and "not . . . a little ridiculous, when applyed to three Millions of as loyal & and useful Subjects as any in the British Dominions, who have been only contending for their Birth-right." He explained that "We do not deny the supreme Authority of Great Britain over her Colonys, but it is a Power which a wise Legislature will exercise with extreme Tenderness & Caution." "Let our fellow-Subjects in Great Britain reflect that we are descended from the same Stock with themselves, nurtured in the same Principles of Freedom; which we have both suck'd in with our Mother's Milk: that in crossing the Atlantic Ocean, we have only changed our Climate, not our Minds, our Natures & Dispositions remain unaltered; that We are still the same People with them." "We claim Nothing but the Liberty & Privileges of Englishmen, in the same Degree, as if we had still continued among our Brethren in Great Britain: these Rights have not been forfeited by any Act of ours, we can not be deprived of them, without our Consent, but by Violence & Injustice." "These are the Sentiments of a Man," Mason took care to emphasize, "who spends most of his Time in Retirement, and has seldom med[d]led in public Affairs . . . who tho' not born within the Verge of the British Isle, is an Englishmen in his Principles." No radical he, no discontented rebel. But "I am not singular in this my Political Creed; these are the general Principles of his Majesty's Subjects in America; they are the Principles of more than nine-tenths of the People who have been so basely misrepresented to you."[22] Mason was expressing the sentiment of a large and growing majority in America. The colonial-wide response to the Stamp Act had fundamentally changed the relationship between the colonies and the mother country.

2

THE FATEFUL STEP

The small number of Tidewater elites who had controlled Virginia politics for decades emerged from the Stamp Act crisis somewhat disturbed. In May 1766 the troubling exposure of the corruption of John Robinson, who for a quarter of a century had served both as Speaker of the House of Burgesses and colony treasurer, left political fissures that younger leaders soon tried to take advantage of. But in the initial scramble to pick up the pieces, two established leaders, Peyton Randolph and Robert Carter Nicholas, won election to the speakership and treasury respectively, Randolph beating out the ambitious Richard Henry Lee who was emerging as an aggressive foe of British policies. Yet the establishment realized that in fact it had not been able to prevent the enactment of the Stamp Act and had lost a sense of local control to the oratorically gifted Patrick Henry, younger than they and particularly appealing to the growing power of middling farmers and small planters beyond the Tidewater region. It would be a mistake to describe Virginia at that time as suffering a crisis of leadership, but the sharper competition for political offices, added to the dissenter challenges to the established church and the growing sense that Parliament had no right to impose taxes on the colony, created an undercurrent of unease.

The removal of George Grenville from his position as chancellor of the exchequer in July 1765 left the British in the same financial strait that had led to the Stamp Act, so it might have been expected when Charles Townshend became chancellor of the exchequer in 1767 that he too would seek to raise revenues in the colonies. He devised a host of import duties clearly intended not to regulate trade but to collect fees, and he accompanied these new duties with a variety of enforcement measures. The American reaction was not as combative as it had been to the Stamp Act, but slowly opposition grew not just to British attempts to tax but to attempts to legislate in any other ways over the colonies. This became the background to colonial-imperial relations in the next decade. Royal governor Francis Fauquier died in 1768 and was replaced by Norborne Berkeley, baron de Botetourt, who promptly dissolved the session of the House in the fall of 1769 when he learned that it planned to send resolutions to Britain protesting recent government actions. The majority of burgesses then promptly proceeded to the Raleigh Tavern and there, in an extralegal meeting, issued a nonimportation agreement that in effect had Virginia join a nonimportation movement that had already begun in New England. A gradually worsening economy and growing colonial debt made such efforts as restricting the imports of nonessential goods and living more frugally seem both the morally and politically responsible thing to do.

George Washington played a larger role in this decision than he had ever before in colonial politics.[1] Having learned of attempts among merchants in Annapolis and Philadelphia to develop an agreement not to accept British goods, he sent copies of some documents to that effect to his learned neighbor, George Mason. They exchanged ideas, with Mason ending up drafting resolutions for the burgesses to consider. Washington introduced these resolutions at Raleigh Tavern. The tenor of the statement was revealed by its first paragraph, which stated "the Grievances and Distresses, with which his Majesty's American Subjects are oppressed . . . threaten the Ruin of ourselves and our Posterity, by reducing us from a free and happy People to a wretched and miserable State of Slavery." This was written with no sense of irony! It proceeded to outline in detail the organization of a rather complete boycott of British imports and declared that the resolves would be binding on all the signatories.[2] At this time the burgesses still had faith that strong protests could effect change in British policy; there was no desire for a full break with the Crown, no hint of revolution. But despite their modest intentions, this nonimportation agreement was supported by relatively few Virginia merchants and had little effect, perhaps because, unlike in New England, there were in Virginia no occupying British troops and Governor Botetourt was personably likable. But Botetourt died in October 1770 after a brief illness.

After some delay, a Scotsman, John Murray, the earl of Dunmore, who had been serving as the royal governor of New York, was named the royal governor of Virginia, a move he apparently regretted. He did not have the popular touch of his predecessor, and his arrogance put off his subjects, but he did share with them a hunger for western lands and promptly made war against Indigenous Americans on the western frontier, partly to defend Virginia claims to the Ohio Company. This gained him some colonial approval, though it created a need for revenue and may have been mainly a ploy to increase his control of governmental affairs. Still, there were at first no new provocations from Parliament, and relations with the mother country seemed more restrained.

The following several years of good feelings, however, were deceptive. The decline in tobacco prices increased the difficulty of paying planter debts, and hard-pressed British merchants began to pressure their colonial debtors, angering planters who tended to see debts as more like favors between equals than cold financial transactions. Planters reacted to the merchants' pressure as improper British efforts to circumscribe their liberties. George Washington, imagining future taxes that the British might impose, wrote in 1774 that unless the colonists resisted, Britain would "make us as tame, & abject Slaves, as the Blacks we rule over with such arbitrary Sway."[3] Such attitudes prepared colonists to be suspicious of British policy and ready to see impropriety even when none was intended by the British policymakers. Alas, they did not see the irony in their expressions of opposition to being treated as slaves, a moral blindness that led the acerbic English critic Samuel Johnson to question why "we hear the loudest yelps for liberty among the drivers of [N]egros."[4] Certainly Washington, who owned several hundred enslaved men, women, and children, knew precisely what the loss of freedom meant.

Lord North, who became prime minister in 1770, faced the perennial problem of needing additional revenue, and he thought he saw a way, in 1773, to find more money and simultaneously solve other problems. The vast East India Company, which both governed India and had a monopoly on imports of tea, was in dire financial trouble and near collapse. Meanwhile it had thousands of pounds of tea in British warehouses because the colonies were boycotting it and purchasing cheaper, smuggled Dutch tea. North's solution sought to save the East India Company and convince the colonists to buy its tea. His proposal, the Tea Act of 1773, would allow the East India Company to sell tea directly in the colonies and make it cheaper by removing a 12-pence-per-pound tax levied on the tea when it first landed in England and before it was transshipped to America. (The company also had to give up governance of India.) Removing the 12-pence tax meant that the tea would be much cheaper in the colonies (even cheaper than it was in England), and by removing the middleman and allowing the East India Company to sell the tea directly, it would even undercut the smuggled tea. Surely the colonists would leap at the opportunity to buy such cheap tea, and the enhanced American market would allow the company to empty its overstocked warehouses and find profit once more.

North assumed this would please everyone, but the colonists, deeply suspicious of every British move, quickly saw an ulterior motive. The real cost of the so-called cheap tea was American acquiescence to a British monopoly and the loss of a fragment of freedom. The colonists saw a threat of tyranny in every British action, an imaginary conspiracy against their liberties. Up and down the seaboard, colonists rejected the Tea Act, the most dramatic example coming in Boston on the night of December 16, 1773, when protesters dressed as

Mohawk Indians boarded three ships laden with tea and dumped all 342 boxes into the harbor. Over the next few months colonists in Charleston, South Carolina; in New York City; and in Annapolis stopped the unloading of tea. The Annapolis protesters even burned the offending ship, the *Peggy Stewart*. British officials reacted with outrage, focusing on Boston. Beginning in March 1774 and extending over several months, they produced the Boston Port Act that closed the port; the Administration of Justice Act that transferred certain trials to Britain; the Massachusetts Government Act that reshaped the government and made many positions Crown appointments rather than elective; and the Quartering Act, applicable to all colonies, which made legal the quartering of British troops in taverns and empty buildings. Tellingly, while the British called these the Coercive Acts, the colonists labeled them the Intolerable Acts. Colonists everywhere saw them as predictive of the kinds of harsh legislation an increasingly intolerant Parliament would inflict on all colonists, not just radical Massachusetts. They were all threatened.

In Virginia, Governor Dunmore had called for a session of the General Assembly because there was essential business to attend to, especially setting the fees for courts. Before the members could meet, however, word had arrived of events in Boston, and a small group of burgesses, including Thomas Jefferson, Richard Henry Lee, and Patrick Henry, met in secret to devise a resolution for public fasting and prayer on June 1, the day the Boston Port Act was to take effect. To give their resolution more power, Jefferson had even thumbed through an old book of documents, borrowing the language of the early Puritans to invest the resolution with the proper reverential tone.[5] Two days later, Governor Dunmore dissolved the Assembly.

The next day, May 27, 1774, a larger group consisting of practically every former burgess—including Washington, Peyton Randolph (who presided over the meeting), Edmund Pendleton, and Benjamin Harrison—again met at the Raleigh Tavern and drafted "An Association of Members of the Late House of Burgesses." They tasked themselves with "pointing out to our countrymen such measures as in our opinion are best fitted to secure our dearest rights and liberty from destruction, by the heavy hand of power now lifted against North America." The Association concluded with sorrow that "a determined system is formed and pressed for reducing the inhabitants of British America to slavery, by subjecting them to the payment of taxes, imposed without the consent of the people or their representatives." It ended by calling (via the various committees of correspondence) upon all the other colonies to send delegates to a "general congress" at a place and date not yet chosen to "deliberate on those general measures which the united interests of America may from time to time require."[6] The former burgesses, styling themselves the Convention, had in effect become the shadow government for the colony of Virginia. The general congress they proposed was in essence a shadow national government, though none were yet thinking quite so nationalistically.

Across Virginia, political leaders were pondering the relationship between the colony and the Crown. For example, in mid-July the voters of Fairfax County, in addition to electing George Washington and Charles Broadwater as representatives to the called August meeting in Williamsburg, adopted what were called the Fairfax County Resolves: a series of twenty-four resolutions, primarily written by George Mason, that captured the emerging political sentiment. At this moment, many of his contemporaries considered the rather austere Mason the colony's leading political theorist. The Resolves insisted on the "fundamental Principle of the People's being governed by no Laws, to which they have not given their Consent, by Representatives freely chosen by themselves."[7] Parliament was not supreme in the colonies! The Resolves also called for unity of action by the colonies and the formation of an association to enforce nonimportation of British goods. Washington would later bring the Resolves to the Williamsburg meeting, where they would be joined by similar resolutions from other counties and towns.

Consequently, on August 1, 1774, some twenty-five delegates met in Williamsburg as the Convention to consider a nonimportation proposal from Boston, the various local sets of resolutions submitted, and, most importantly, to choose delegates to the new intercolonial congress scheduled to meet in October in Philadelphia. The Williamsburg Convention chose seven delegates to Philadelphia: Peyton Randolph, George Washington, Richard Henry Lee, Patrick Henry, Richard Bland, Edmund Pendleton, and Benjamin Harrison, who together constituted a good representation of the range of political attitudes, with Henry and Lee being the most radical. Thomas Jefferson, at the age of thirty-one (having first been elected a burgess in 1768 when only twenty-five), was too junior to have been elected to the Congress; unlike Patrick Henry, Jefferson was shy, soft spoken, and known primarily for his learning, analytical skills, and writing ability. Obviously, he was what was even then called a comer, but he had not yet arrived. He had intended to submit at the August Convention a draft of instructions to the delegates to the Congress, but a sudden illness prevented his attendance. By way of his enslaved servant Jupiter he sent on two copies of his text, one for Henry, hoping that he would read and promote it, and the other copy for Peyton Randolph, who he expected would be presiding. There is no evidence that Henry read the document, but Randolph, recognizing its merit, read it aloud to a number of the burgesses gathered in his Williamsburg home. Without seeking Jefferson's permission, several decided to have the text printed, so they added a brief preface, chose a title, and had it published as *A Summary View of the Rights of British America,* a nineteen-page pamphlet.[8]

Jefferson's views, although elegantly expressed, were more radical than many members could accept at that moment, but Jefferson had succeeded in wrapping the growing list of colonial frustrations and grievances—reflected in the various sets of local resolutions that were submitted to the Convention—within a consistent ideological framework that became the intellectual and moral justification for revolution. Several of the Virginia delegates, including Washington, took copies of the pamphlet with them to Philadelphia. It was quickly reprinted in port cities such as New York, Boston, and Norfolk, and before the end of the year there had been at least two printings in London. Jefferson's statement, as he later recalled, was considered "too bold" for the moment.[9] But its impact proved to be immense.

Jefferson's words merit attention because he was the first to fully articulate what became the foundational ideas of the later revolution. Jefferson's first page revealed how radical his message was to be. Stating that he intended to lay before the king the complaints of the colonists, and to do so "in the language of truth" and not by "expressions of servility," Jefferson reminded the king that he was "no more than the chief officer of the people" and was "consequently subject to their superintendence."[10] No one previously had spoken of the king that way. Jefferson reminded His Majesty that the colonists possessed the same rights as did those who resided in the British Isles; coming to America did not obliterate their natural rights as Englishmen. Then followed a list of the actions toward the colonists that were intrusions on their natural rights: the denying them the rights of free trade, the provisions against making certain products from their own materials, various intermeddling with their internal affairs. Jefferson boldly emphasized that it was not just an issue of taxation: "the British parliament has no right to exercise authority over us," a line that no doubt went further than many colonists were yet ready to go. He made clear that one or the other such infractions at the hands of British officials could be marked up to accident or carelessness, "but a series of oppressions, begun at a distinguished period, and pursued unalterably thro' every change of ministers, too plainly prove a deliberate, systematical plan of reducing us to slavery."[11] What might Jupiter have thought of these words? Certainly the white readers failed to notice the irony, even hypocrisy, of the document, a blindness that would characterize similar readers for two centuries or more. Jefferson was warming to his subject. British authorities, he charged, had suspended legal legislatures, had imposed taxes without the consent of the colonists, had closed a major port city, had interfered with the administration of justice, had not allowed the Virginia burgesses to end the importation of enslaved people from Africa—and here Jefferson reflected much more his private belief than he did a Virginia consensus—had disallowed laws by legal legislatures, had required local people to house and feed British troops forced upon them, had arbitrarily dispersed land. He enumerated a long train of abuses no one of which lay within the proper authority of the king. Had the king "bestowed a single thought" on these kinds of actions? He should "remember that force cannot give right."[12]

Rising to a crescendo, Jefferson penned "these are our grievances which we have thus laid before his majesty with that freedom of language and sentiment which becomes a free people, claiming their rights as derived from the laws of nature, and not as the gift of their chief magistrate. . . . Kings are the servants, not the proprietors of the people. . . . Let no act be passed by any one legislature which may infringe on the rights and liberties of another."[13] He clarified that it was "neither our wish nor our interest to separate from" Great Britain, "but let them be just." "The god who gave us life, gave us liberty at the same time; the hand of force may destroy, but cannot disjoin them."[14] Jefferson concluded by stating that the colonists' sincerest prayer was reform so that the colonies could happily stay within the whole empire, but those words read more like a sop to the king than an honest statement of principle. Here was a defense of American rights, reaching all the way back to the "wilds and woods in the North of Europe," and a defense of the sole authority of the colonists themselves to legislate for their own interests.[15] Some Virginians had visceral reasons to oppose Britain. For example, Washington had felt slighted by the arrogance of British officers, and his land speculation was thwarted by Parliamentary restrictions. Mason too strongly took umbrage at restrictions against speculation and the failure of the Ohio Company to be granted additional acreage. Henry's dissenter religious identity fueled his opposition to the Church of England and other aspects of British authority. But Jefferson's opposition originated in his library. Reading in law and political philosophy lay at the heart of his intellectual and ideological protest on behalf of colonial rights.

The First Continental Congress, as it came to be known, met in Philadelphia from September 5 though October 26, 1774; its delegates—recognizing the population and economic strength of Virginia, in effect, its primacy in the eyes of the Crown—elected Virginian Peyton Randolph as the presiding officer, and it made formal the organization of committees of correspondence whereby the colonies could share information. It also put together a colony-wide Colonial Association agreement both to enforce a nonimportation decision (set to begin on December 1, 1774) and to push for additional moral reforms emphasizing frugality. It was decided that each colony would have two votes (but as many delegates as they desired), and—endorsing the Suffolk Resolves authored by a local convention in Suffolk County, Massachusetts—Congress declared the Coercive (Intolerable) Acts cruel and unconstitutional and, among other things, urged the people to call and arm their own militias. Obviously, a profound crisis in the relationship of the colonies to the Crown was in the works, but no one dared just yet to really imagine the ultimate result. The next year would bring things to a head. But as of this date, the various colonies still had not melded into a nation—they still retained their individual allegiance to the Crown, not to their emerging union. More of the delegates to the First Continental Congress had been to London than to Philadelphia.[16]

With the House of Burgesses dissolved, the extralegal Convention served as the governing mechanism of Virginia. It chose an eleven-member Committee of Safety to perform executive functions between meetings, called on counties to organize and equip militias, and dealt with the mundane issues of local governance. The Convention agreed to meet quarterly. At the March 1775 meeting in St. John's Church in Richmond, presided over by Peyton Randolph, Edmund Pendleton on March 23 spoke on behalf of a rather mild petition of protest of parliamentary actions by the Jamaican assembly. Patrick Henry, whose nerves might already have been on edge as a result of the worsening condition of his wife, who either had just died or was near death, took offense at what he considered the pusillanimity of the Jamaican petition. Asking to be recognized by Randolph, Henry introduced a resolution, clearly written out beforehand, that concluded with a call that "This colony be immediately put into a state of defence" and that a committee be formed "to prepare a plan for embodying, arming, and disciplining such a number of men, as may be sufficient for that purpose."[17] He was calling for a colony militia, not a county one. To the chorus of murmurs that this was going too far, Henry stood up and, beginning slowly and quietly, proceeded to overwhelm his fellow members with the eloquence of his oratory, giving a speech perhaps second only to Lincoln's Gettysburg Address of 1863 in the annals of American oratory.

There is no definitive text of his address; Henry was careless about keeping papers of any sort. Contemporaries and near contemporaries helped such early historians as William Wirt try to reconstruct what was said, and several witnesses in private letters left snitches of phrases. We must, with a degree of caution, take Wirt's version as the nearest we can come to Henry's actual words. Henry was no longer the rough-hewn, untutored character he had been in 1765. Realizing that his speaking ability had enormous power to shape opinion, he had since then carefully read and studied books on rhetoric and vocabulary to make even more effective his unparalleled oratorical skills.[18] Though not the profound student that either Jefferson or Mason was, Henry had, in the last decade, read widely. Possessed of more than just a mesmerizing voice, Henry now had history and ideas at his command. Mason, not one to be easily impressed, had taken the measure of Henry the previous year and described him "as by far the most powerful speaker I ever heard. Every word he says not only engages but commands the attention; and your passions are no longer your own when he addresses them. But his eloquence is the smallest part of his merit. He is in my opinion the first man upon the continent, as well in abilities as public virtues."[19] When Henry spoke, everyone was transfixed, and in his March 23, 1775, oration he forcefully rejected the idea that it was premature to talk about a resort to arms:

> We have done everything that could be done, to avert the storm which is now coming. We have petitioned—we have remonstrated—we have supplicated—we have prostrated ourselves before the throne. . . . In vain, after these things, may we indulge the fond hope of peace and reconciliation. There is no longer any room for hope. If we wish to be free . . . we must fight! I repeat it, sir, we must fight! An appeal to arms and the God of hosts is all that is left us! [Crescendoing to his conclusion, Henry thundered:] There is no retreat, but in submission and slavery! Our chains are forged; . . . The war is inevitable—and let it come! I repeat . . . let it come! . . . . Gentlemen may cry, peace, peace—but there is no peace. The war is actually begun! . . . Why stand here idle? . . . . Is life so dear, or peace so sweet, as to be purchased at the price of chains and slavery? Forbid it, Almighty God! I know not what course others may take; but as for me, . . . give me liberty or give me death![20]

The members sat stunned for a moment. Despite the undeniable power of Henry's words, the momentous resolution passed by only a 65–60 margin. Then the Convention elected seven delegates to the Second Continental Congress to meet two months later. The vote demonstrated the lingering influence of the older, most established members, though Henry had broken into that group. The top seven vote-getters were Peyton Randolph, with 107 votes; George Washington, 106; Patrick Henry, 105; Richard Henry Lee, 103; Edmund Pendleton, 100; Benjamin Harrison, 90; and Richard Bland, 90. Far behind, ranking number eight with but 18 votes was Thomas Jefferson, the youngest of the group, elected as an alternate on the supposition that Randolph would likely be called back to Virginia to preside at later meetings of the Convention, which did happen.

Before the delegates could convene in Philadelphia, events took a bloody turn. In Massachusetts, British troops had marched to Lexington on April 19, 1775, to seize a cache of arms, shots were fired, and there and the next day at nearby Concord the first battle of the American Revolution occurred. Completely unrelated to these stirring events, on the early morning of April 21, under cover of darkness, Governor Dunmore sent troops to remove the gunpowder from the magazine (armory) in Williamsburg and store it in the HMS *Magdalen* in the nearby York River, an action that outraged most Virginians.

Militia readied themselves. Patrick Henry raised a troop of militia from Hanover County and led them toward Williamsburg. He was stopped when he was met by Carter Braxton, who convinced Henry that the governor regretted his actions and had already paid for the powder. They avoided a skirmish, and Henry sent his troops home. More-cautious leaders saw this as indicative of the hotheadedness of Henry, and Dunmore condemned him, but Henry's reputation continued to grow among the small farmers beyond the Tidewater. A few days later, word of Lexington and Concord reached Williamsburg. Few could any longer deny that these were troublesome times. Shortly thereafter, Henry and the other Virginia delegates were on their way to Philadelphia, where the Second Continental Congress opened in mid-May 1775.

Almost immediately, all the delegates learned that Massachusetts was calling up an army of over thirteen thousand troops, so the reality of imminent war pressed itself on everyone. As expected, Peyton Randolph was recalled to Virginia to preside over the Convention quasi-government there, and John Hancock of Massachusetts succeeded Randolph as president of the Second Continental Congress. With Randolph's return to Virginia, Jefferson made ready to replace him in Philadelphia. There, because Virginia was the largest and most populous colony, leaders such as John Adams thought it essential that a Virginian should be placed at the head of the army. George Washington obviously thought the same, and as if he needed a recommendation, he wore his buff and blue military uniform to the sessions. He wrote his wife, Martha, that he wished to avoid such service, but his choice of martial dress suggests otherwise. On June 15 he was unanimously chosen General and Commander in Chief of the Army of the United Colonies, and in an act of magnanimity, the wealthy Washington announced that he would serve without pay (though he would expect reimbursement for his expenses). The army did not in fact yet exist; creating one was the first of Washington's tasks, and he would prove himself more than up to the challenge of military leadership.

Before Jefferson arrived in Philadelphia, the Battle of Bunker's Hill was fought in Boston. Clearly the colonies were at war. Soon the Congress felt the necessity of laying out a "Declaration of the Causes and Necessity of Taking Up Arms." Some objected to the original text, so newcomer Jefferson was named to the drafting committee, along with an older, accomplished writer named John Dickinson, famous for a series of essays published in the previous decade. The resulting revised declaration reflected Dickinson's blunt, forceful style of writing, while the strategy of the document came mainly from Jefferson. The rest of this term Jefferson had little to do, having neither experience nor skill at military matters.

By early August members began leaving the Congress to return home. Patrick Henry left, never again to participate in a continental or national congress; his orientation became increasingly, even emphatically, localistic. Jefferson also left, and by August 25 he was back in Monticello. Virginia's government now consisted of the elected members to the Convention, and no one played a more important role in that body than did George Mason, as much as he hated being away from Gunston Hall. Gout continued to plague him, he still would have preferred spending more time in his library at home, and with the death of his wife Ann in 1773 (between 1753 and 1772 she had borne twelve children, nine of whom lived into adulthood), Mason now had strong parental obligations that gave him good reasons for wanting to stay at home. Yet for the while his sense of duty to Virginia led him to stay at work, helping make many of the key decisions necessary for governing the colony.

Improving colonial defenses was a major concern, and one that brought controversy. When officials called for the creation of the First Virginia Regiment of militia, Patrick Henry had rushed home from Philadelphia to seek its leadership, and given his popular support, he was elected to the position despite his lack of real military experience or skill. Most senior state leaders were dismayed by this development, even George Washington later writing that "I think my countrymen made a capital mistake, when they took Henry out of the senate to place him in the field; and pity it is, that he does not see this and remove any difficulty by a voluntary resignation."[21] The Convention soon raised the Second Virginia Regiment and placed William Woodford in command independent of Henry's authority. Later that year the Convention ordered Woodford to counter moves made by Governor Dunmore and by doing so made clear that it preferred Woodford's military leadership. Henry resigned his commission in a huff. In Virginia, Dunmore, with news of hostility in Massachusetts, decided to take the offensive. He signed a proclamation on November 7 "declar[ing] all indented Servants, Negroes, or others (appertaining to Rebels) free that are able and willing to bear Arms, they joining his Majesty's Troops."[22] Nothing he could have done would have more inflamed most white Virginians than inciting indentured servants and especially enslaved people to take up arms against the colonists. Neither Dunmore nor British authorities at home were antislavery, and Dunmore's action was intended simply as a military strike against Virginia, but colonial leaders interpreted his move as an attack upon a key feature of their economy and social system. In their minds, the crisis had thereby escalated. A break with the mother country now seemed inevitable.

Dunmore utilized several of His Majesty's ships to make raids along the many riverbanks—burning buildings, taking supplies, receiving runaways—with the Virginia militia able only to make feeble responses. The first substantial battle, however, at Great Bridge near Norfolk on December 10, 1775, brought victory to the colonists, and a retreating Dunmore, as he withdrew from Norfolk, partially ransacked and burned the city on January 1, an event that struck Jefferson as notably barbaric in the middle of the winter. Virginians were truly shocked by the reports of what Dunmore had done, although in truth Virginia militia had done most of the destruction of Norfolk (to deprive the British of its resources) but concealed their role, casting all the blame on Dunmore. Meanwhile the runaway slaves, quartered on British ships, suffered horrendously from a smallpox epidemic. Few if any of them found freedom, as that had not been Dunmore's aim.

Several months later, Virginians and indeed all colonists were titillated by a blockbuster best-selling pamphlet by a recent English immigrant, Tom Paine. Writing with uncommon vigor and boldness, Paine proclaimed that the colonies would prosper once freed from British trade restraints. They ought by the simple logic of their size and population be independent of Britain—common sense demanded it. He ridiculed and mocked the king, whom colonists still professed to revere; he was, Paine virtually shouted out in print, nothing more than a "crowned ruffian," a "royal brute."[23] This pamphlet, aptly titled *Common Sense,* sold more than one hundred thousand copies and took America by storm. The tide was turning if it had not already: the colonies were quickly moving toward independence.

The new session of Virginia's governing Convention was scheduled to meet in May 1776, with Edmund Pendleton chosen to preside. Somewhat surprisingly, Patrick Henry was one of the more-cautious delegates, thinking that the colonies should forge alliances with one or more European nations before declaring themselves independent. Others, with Dunmore's Proclamation in mind, were far more aggressive in their thinking. Several proposals came before the body suggesting the Convention make plans to draft a declaration of rights, create a new state government with its own constitution, and send the Virginia delegates to the Second Continental Congress with directions to recommend from that body a formal statement of independence. Pendleton forged a single statement out of the variety under consideration by the Convention. His version passed unanimously on May 15, and two days later the Convention appointed a committee to prepare both a declaration of rights and a new constitution for the local government. On June 7, Richard Henry Lee in Philadelphia introduced to the Second Continental Congress the motion authored by the Virginia Convention: "That these colonies are, and of right ought to be, free and independent States, that they are absolved from all allegiance to the British Crown, and that all political connection between them and the State of Great Britain is, and ought to be, totally dissolved." John Adams seconded the motion. Not every delegate was ready to take this dramatic final step, so it was decided to delay consideration until July 1. (It would be approved on July 2.) In the meantime, Congress appointed a committee of five members—John Adams, Benjamin Franklin, Roger Sherman, Robert R. Livingston, and Thomas Jefferson—to draft a document explaining and justifying the resolution for independence. But that's getting ahead of our story.

At this time, Jefferson desperately wanted to be elsewhere, in Williamsburg, where the committee just appointed by the Convention was about to write a constitution—the fundamental body of laws—for the new state of Virginia. He thought that document was the more important work of the moment. The Convention appointed a huge committee of more than two dozen members, and George Mason quickly became its intellectual leader. Everyone recognized that his legal learning and logic were second to none. His uncle John Mercer, a talented lawyer with a scholarly bent, had lived nearby in Mason's youth, and he had an excellent library specializing in legal books and the classics; Mercer compiled several versions of an *Abridgement of the Laws of Virginia* over time. Young George Mason was given complete access to Mercer's books. Here began his lifelong hunger for reading, resulting eventually in his possessing his own substantial library. The thousands of hours Mason spent in Mercer's library and later his own (Mason's family always respected his study time) made him one of Virginia's most esteemed scholars, exceeded only by George Wythe and soon Jefferson, who was eighteen years his junior.

Now, in 1776, Mason, who had little patience for less-informed minds and the endless squabbles of committee meetings, threw himself into the task of privately drafting both a declaration of rights and a constitution for Virginia, finishing the rights draft first. Sometime between May 20 and 24, Mason drafted ten statements, and the committee added several more for discussion. A final revised draft was completed on June 12. Mason began with words that today sound familiar because Jefferson would later reflect and improve upon them in his draft of the Declaration of Independence: "That all men are born equally free and independent, and have certain inherent natural Rights, of which they can not by any Compact, deprive or divest their Posterity; among which are, the Enjoyment of Life and Liberty, with the Means of acquiring and possessing Property, and pursuing and obtaining Happiness and Safety."[24] However, in response to several who feared the first phrase might endanger slavery, Edmund Pendleton added the following parenthetical statement "(when they enter into a state of society)" immediately after the words "of which." This was intended to mean that because enslaved people were not legally citizens and hence a constituent part of society, their enslavement did not contradict the abstract idea of equality.[25] White liberty had been made complicit with slavery. Because so many of the foundational documents of the nation were written by slaveholding Virginians, the defense of slavery was a feature of the political system.

Mason continued, "That [political] Power is, by God and Nature, vested in, and consequently derived from the People." From this it followed "That Government is, or ought to be, instituted for the common Benefit and Security of the People, Nation, or Community. . . . And that whenever any Government shall be found inadequate, or contrary to these Purposes, a Majority of the Community had . . . a Right to reform, alter, or abolish it." Moreover, "no part of a Man's Property can be taken from him . . . without the Consent of himself, or his legal Representatives; nor are the People bound by any Laws, but such as they have in like Manner assented to." Mason obviously was reflecting what most progressive Virginians had come to believe. He added "That as Religion, or the Duty which we owe to our divine and omnipotent Creator, and the Manner of discharging it, can be governed only by Reason and Conviction, not by Force or Violence; and therefore that all Men should enjoy the fullest Toleration in the Exercise of Religion, according to the Dictates of Conscience."[26]

Mason included a defense of trial by jury and the separation of executive and legislative functions. The committee added more clauses that guaranteed free elections, prevented the suspension of laws without the consent of the legislature, prohibited excessive bail, and declared a militia as the best means of defense and opposed a standing army. In the final consideration, a young James Madison made a highly significant revision of the clause on religion, removing the word "toleration," and after the phrase "all men" inserting the words "are equally entitled to the free" before the rest of the sentence, "exercise of religion." This salutary change had met some opposition, and more conservative church men like Patrick Henry wanted to make sure that it would not jeopardize the concept of government-supported religion, but Mason apparently approved the change, as did Edmund Pendleton, so it was added.[27] Thus did Virginia become the first state that via its constitution disallowed any religious test for public office-holding.

This textual intervention was twenty-five-year-old Madison's first major contribution to American freedom. In fact, this was his first time to visit Williamsburg and participate in governance, and he had not yet met Jefferson. That would happen several months later, and these two, who had so much in common, including a voracious appetite for reading, would become the closest of colleagues and collaborators over the next fifty years. Though the difference in height made them an odd contrast when seen together, they quickly grew to be, in the words of a contemporary, an "intimate, confidential, and devoted friend" to each other. John Quincy Adams, who knew both well, would insightfully remark after their deaths that "the mutual influence of these mighty minds upon each other, is a phenomenon, like the invisible and mysterious movements of the magnet in the physical world, and in which the sagacity of the future historians may discover the solution of our national history."[28]

Mason's first draft was printed in a Williamsburg newspaper on June 1, and someone sent a copy to the *Philadelphia Evening Post,* which published it on June 6. Several days later, other Philadelphia papers printed the revised draft, then it appeared in an Annapolis paper, and soon it was reprinted up and down the seaboard states. Its impact as the first modern bill of rights was remarkable, for it was to have a profound effect on the drafters of other states' constitutions, most of whom decided to also attach a statement of fundamental rights to their constitutions. And Mason's words influenced Thomas Jefferson, sitting in Philadelphia and wishing he were in Williamsburg, and assigned the duty of drafting an explanation to the nation-to-be of the Congress's scheduled vote on the resolution for independence.

One more thing stood between Jefferson and that task to justify revolution, the opportunity to compose a constitution, the fundamental laws, for the state of Virginia. Jefferson felt that nothing was more important at this juncture of history than rethinking and formulating the laws that outlined the powers of and restrictions upon the new state governments. Jefferson had arrived in Philadelphia on May 14, just as the committee in Williamsburg was beginning to meet, and he took residence in a spacious house on Seventh and Market Streets, where he hoped to find quiet and that had room for many of his books. As he wrote to Thomas Nelson Jr., he wished he could be recalled from his duties in the Congress and retire to Williamsburg, for the work about to begin there was "of the most interesting nature and such as every individual would wish to have his voice in. In truth it is the whole object of the present controversy": establishing a proper and good government.[29] Although he was reassured to learn that George Mason, as Edmund Pendleton wrote him, "seems to have the Ascendency in the great work," Jefferson wanted to try his hand at the project.[30] So, sitting at his work desk, Jefferson proceeded to write out a proposed constitution for Virginia. Actually, between mid-May and before June 12, he wrote three versions of a constitution as his ideas evolved.[31]

Jefferson's first draft began with a long listing of the transgressions against the colonies made by the Crown and Parliament, a list he would come back to in the Declaration of Independence, and all of which were meant to justify the conclusion that the colonies "are out of allegiance to the" king. Then he proceeded to outline the shape of the proposed government: there would be two separate houses, members of the lower one annually elected and the other appointed for life by the lower house; the executive powers would be in the hands of a weak administrator (and that's what he was called) who could not veto bills or dissolve the legislature; neither could he declare war, pardon crimes, or affect other tasks. In fact, Jefferson called for a notably powerless executive.[32]

He laid out a judicial structure for the state, arranged for the state to give from its public lands sufficient acreage to allow every white man to meet the property qualifications for voting, did away with entail and primogeniture (techniques of inheritance that were bulwarks of aristocratic landholding), called for the election of sheriffs, disallowed private purchase of Indigenous lands, gave to citizens in the western territories the same rights possessed by those in the original states, guaranteed "full & free liberty of religious opinion," and protected the rights of gun ownership and freedom of the press.[33] Perhaps it hardly needs saying, but Virginia, like the other former colonies, was not a modern democracy: those enslaved could not vote, women could not vote, and even for free white male citizens, there were property requirements that precluded about half of them from voting. A vast chasm existed between the lifestyles of the planter elites (i.e., all the Founders considered here), and the enslaved men, women, and children they held in bondage and also propertyless whites below. Jefferson's second draft of the state constitution expanded on several issues, stated that "No person hereafter coming into this country shall be held in slavery under any pretext whatsoever" (i.e., stopping the importation of new slaves from Africa), and disallowed the existence of a standing army. It specified that the new constitution would take effect only after voters gathered for this sole purpose were assembled in every county and two-thirds of the counties voted to accept it.[34] The third draft made no major changes.

Jefferson's three drafts arrived too late in Williamsburg to have much influence, other than his listing of the infractions against colonial liberties by the Crown and his sketch of a judicial system. By way of Richard Henry Lee, John Adams's ideas about the ideal form of a state constitution did arrive and joined the mix—along with the writings of Mason and Jefferson—under consideration by the Assembly. The resulting Virginia constitution, adopted on June 29 and primarily the work of Mason, was far more conservative than Jefferson's would have been.[35] Mason's initial notion of a bicameral legislature was retained, as was a weakened executive branch (with the governor's decisions requiring the approval of an executive council chosen by the General Assembly), along with a separate judicial branch.

Mason had wanted to negate the impact of rotten boroughs by giving each county two votes in the lower house, but the General Assembly resisted this reform and maintained votes for Jamestown, Williamsburg, Norfolk, and the College of William and Mary. The members of the lower house were popularly elected, but those of the upper house were chosen by a complicated procedure involving a double filtering of potential candidates by a process resembling the later electoral college. All laws would originate in the lower house. Missing was Jefferson's suggestion to broaden the franchise, guarantee full self-rule to future states carved out of current Virginia land claims, and prohibit the importation of additional enslaved people. Sheriffs and justices of the peace were appointed, not elected, and the governor and council would choose them following the recommendations of the county courts, hence perpetuating existing political cliques.

Jefferson was particularly concerned that the new constitution, drafted by a legislative committee, was not submitted to the voters. (Actually, none of the constitutions first adopted by the several states were drafted in specially called conventions, and only that of Massachusetts, two years later in 1778, was submitted to the voters for ratification.) Nevertheless, Jefferson would always see it as a regular act of legislation, not the fundamental law of the commonwealth. Still, when the Virginia constitution was completed, it was the first one drawn up in America to "endorse expressly the separation of powers and the first to recognize the courts as a distinct branch of government."[36] It was less progressive than Jefferson's would have been, but he had no time to dwell on disappointments: there was a Declaration of Independence to write.

The five-person committee established by Congress to compose a justification for a resolution of independence had two of the most senior American statesmen on it. Benjamin Franklin was the most famous American in the world, and John Adams was the preeminent constitutional scholar and a leader of the movement in Massachusetts. Jefferson tried to demur to their rank, but Franklin insisted he was too ill, and Adams, recognizing his gruff nature had made him unpopular, and aware, as he put it later, of Jefferson's "happy talent of composition" and "peculiar felicity of expression," likewise insisted that Jefferson, from the nation's most populous and wealthy state, should be the primary draftsman. So, sequestering himself in his quiet library (although he could not escape the news that a large English flotilla was heading toward New York City, nor, on July 1, a report that a squadron had arrived off the coast of Charleston), and using a small, slant-top writing desk, Jefferson produced a manuscript. He wrote from no notes—after all, he had been thinking about these issues for years, he knew the writings of Locke and Montesquieu intimately, was familiar with the pamphlet literature of Richard Bland and others, he had just gone over Mason's Virginia Declaration of Rights, and certainly the language of his own *Summary View of the Rights of British America* was fixed in his mind. John Adams later wrote that Jefferson had not really said anything new. To this charge Jefferson readily admitted. He had not sought to invent a political philosophy but rather to capture the sentiment of the moment and write it in memorable language. Almost fifty years later Jefferson explained what he had attempted to achieve: "Not to find out new principles, or new arguments . . . but to place before mankind the common sense of the subject, in terms so plain and firm as to command their assent, and to justify ourselves in the independent stand we are compelled to take. Neither aiming at originality of principle or sentiment, nor yet copied from any particular and previous writing, it was intended to be an expression of the American mind, and to give to that expression the proper tone and spirit called for by the occasion."[37]

Once Jefferson had completed his draft, he submitted it to Franklin, who was too sick to attend meetings. Whether Franklin offered any suggestions is unknown. Adams and the other committee members made minor changes, then apparently a printer rushed out a hurried version of the document as submitted by the committee and gave this printed copy to the full Congress on July 1 for their discussion and suggestions. Jefferson took great effort and pride in his writing, and he found it excruciating to sit in session as members of Congress haggled, fussed with his prose, and edited his draft. They cut his text by about a quarter, changed some of his wording (sometimes for the better), and omitted sections, notably a long section in which Jefferson attacked the king for supporting the Atlantic slave trade. Jefferson, philosophically opposed to slavery (he had several times in the past tried to make manumission easier, had defended the natural rights of indentured servants, and had attacked the slave trade in his *Summary View*), stated in his text that the king had "waged war against human nature itself, violating it's [*sic*] most sacred rights of life and liberty in the persons of a distant people who never offended him, captivating & carrying them into slavery in another hemisphere . . . . Determined to keep open a market where MEN should be bought & sold."[38] This passage was cut because the southernmost states would not accept such language. The Congress also added two additional references to God. As a result, the final version, the one we see in textbooks, though it does consist mostly of Jefferson's words, is notably different from his original manuscript.

The brief document as known to posterity contains riches we are prone to overlook. In its very first sentence—"When in the course of human events it becomes necessary for one people"—the phrase "one people" stands out. Using it, Jefferson was in essence creating the concept of the nation. This was no longer a collection of individual colonies, banding together, but *one people!* The sentence goes on to lay down the gauntlet to England and other nations: this new nation, the United States of America, was prepared to "assume among the powers of the earth that separate & equal station to which the laws of nature and of nature's God entitle them."[39] Key here was the insistence on the *equal status* of this infant nation among the older, longer established nations. The second paragraph contains the most famous words in American history, wherein Jefferson took previous ideas, for example Mason's first

Virginia Declaration of Rights, and rewrote them in memorable, elegantly concise prose. "We hold these truths to be self-evident: that all men are created equal; that they are endowed by their creator with inherent and inalienable rights; that among these are life, liberty, & the pursuit of happiness." (He meant, by the word *men,* not the male gender only but humankind.)

Following this stage-setting proposition, Jefferson borrowed from the commonplace Lockean compact theory of the origin of government to craft a statement rendered in syllogistic form, that is, as an argument that if you accept certain initial ideas, then a logical conclusion follows. So Jefferson posited, first, that "to secure these rights, governments are instituted among men." Second, "whenever any form of government becomes destructive of those ends, it is the right of the people to alter or abolish it." Setting forth those propositions, Jefferson then proceeded, in the great bulk of the Declaration, to list, in ascending order of importance, all the things the Crown had done or permitted to be done to attack the rights of the colonists. He made clear that a people are prone to overlook such actions when minor or rare, "But when a long train of abuses & usurpations begun at a distinguished period and pursuing invariably the same object, evinces a design to reduce them under absolute despotism, it is their right, it is their duty to throw off such government."[40] Given the original purpose of government, simple logic demanded this conclusion.

Jefferson's listing of Crown offenses is today tedious reading, and it is actually rather an unfair presentation of events, but Jefferson was not attempting to write objective history. He was writing as a lawyer, marshaling the evidence to prove his point, arguing the Americans' cause to the jury of the world as persuasively as he could. He was making history rather than writing history. Following this long recitation of abuses, Jefferson returned to his philosophical mode. He adopted the language of the resolution Richard Henry Lee had introduced to Congress on June 7 and stated, the representatives, "appealing to the supreme judge of the world for the rectitude of our intentions, do . . . solemnly publish and declare that these united colonies are & of right ought to be free & independent states; that they are absolved from all allegiance to the British crown, and that all political connection between them & the state of Great Britain is, & ought to be, totally dissolved." His final sentence, including a reference to religion added by Congress, concluded passionately: "And for the support of this declaration, with a firm reliance on the protection of divine providence we mutually pledge to each other our lives, our fortunes, & and sacred honor."[41] After all, they were committing treason against Great Britain.

After three days of spirited discussion, on July 4 Congress approved the Declaration as revised without dissent, although New York abstained. Publicly proclaimed in Philadelphia on July 8, read before General Washington and his troops in New York City on July 10, proclaimed at the Capitol, Governor's Palace, and courthouse in Williamsburg on July 25, and subsequently universally printed in newspapers, the colonists at last had a formal justification for the conflict with the mother country. With an army and a cause, the American Revolution was truly begun. Jefferson's primary authorship of the Declaration of Independence was not instantly known and recognized, but it was to become his greatest legacy to the nation. The Declaration was subtly infused with the spirit of the Enlightenment, and had delegates from the more southern colonies not eliminated Jefferson's powerful words about slavery, those who were beginning to question the institution might have encountered fewer obstacles in the future. But on this issue Jefferson was ahead of his time, so the revolutionary moment reflected less of a Jeffersonian than a Virginia spirit.

3

WINNING INDEPENDENCE

The same day the Virginia Convention approved a constitution for the new state of Virginia, June 29, 1776, it also voted to elect the state's first governor. George Mason had put forward Patrick Henry's name, and on the first ballot Henry beat out Thomas Nelson Jr. for the position. But by the time Henry was sworn in, on July 6, he had fallen extremely ill, so much so that some feared for his life. Luckily the constitution had provided for an eight-member Privy Council, whose approval was required for gubernatorial decisions to take effect. John Page, who had served on the Committee of Safety of the Convention and hence had executive experience (at this time Henry had none), was chosen president of the Council and stepped in during Henry's weeks of recuperation. Throughout his three terms Henry was frequently absent from the capital, and Page had to repeatedly provide essential executive duties.

The new state government was faced with an onslaught of problems. Luckily for Virginians, the main theater of war was in the northeastern states for the first three years of statehood. In its initial week, the state had to deal with former royal governor Dunmore, who with several hundred troops was hunkering down on Gwynn's Island, just off the coast of the peninsula of land (called by Virginians the neck) between the York and Rappahannock Rivers. But a quick and accurate bombardment of his position and shelling of his main ship forced the hated Dunmore to evacuate and soon flee toward New York City. Virginia would be safe from a major invasion until 1779.

However, no bureaucratic structure had yet been created, so Page and Henry had to respond even during relatively peaceful conditions to literally hundreds of requests that a fully formed administrative system would normally handle before they ever got to the governor. Although Henry had limited administrative experience beforehand, he proved adequate to the demands of his office. The drafters of the new Virginia constitution, reacting to the opposition to the king and overbearing royal governors, had created an almost powerless governor who on most matters could not act without Privy Council approval. The drafters had expected the governor's duties to be primarily routine—in fact, in his proposed constitution Jefferson had called the chief executive of the state simply the administrator. Still, requests from soldiers to buy supplies, questions about regulating ferries, demands for more defensive assistance at certain locations, the need to increase the supplies of food, gunpowder, guns, cannons, salt (for food preservation), and on and on poured in to the governor's office and required action. The mundane administrative demands threatened to overwhelm Henry and his successors.

Much of the business, however, was not simple routine; important decisions had to be rendered on a wide variety of matters. A constant problem proved to be the calling up and arming of militia, and related to this was recruiting soldiers to send to George Washington's Continental Army. These dual demands severely stretched the ability of the state, and Virginia could never fully supply the number of troops Washington requested, although neither could any other state. Many of the militia recruited were undisciplined and otherwise untrained, there were devastating shortages of ammunition and weapons, and logistic difficulties hampered the ability of the troops to get to where they needed to be in time to counter threats from British marauders. These problems were extremely frustrating to state leaders, and at times the needs—for money, for food, for weapons, for clothing, for manpower—were almost overwhelming.

In the absence of a fully operational bureaucracy, the state came to rely on one especially able assemblyman, George Mason, who became busier as a delegate than he had ever been before when serving his state. He and Jefferson proved to be the workhorses of the House of Delegates. Jefferson's efforts were soon focused on reforming the laws of the state. Mason was more involved with the immediate issues facing the commonwealth. He helped write and pass legislation to try to control inflation, to stop the hoarding of food, to gather additional supplies of salt, to develop lead mines and foundries, and to prevent the export of food supplies badly needed at home. Henry and the other legislators came to turn to Mason whenever legislation was needed for a discrete purpose. Mason authored dozens of legislative acts aimed at meeting the necessities of war, such as providing boats for the protections of rivers, clothing the troops, speedily recruiting troops for the Continental Army, investigating unrest in the southwestern portion of the state, and purchasing iron to manufacture cannons.[1]

Henry, Mason, and other leaders tried to inspire, shame, or force communities to provide militia, and they ended up, in near desperation, passing several varieties of draft legislation in an effort to provide for the defense of the state and to send men to the Continental Army. James Madison, incidentally, was missing from the House after the final months of 1776. He was not reelected in early 1777 because he refused to treat the voters with cakes and ale, and they apparently took that failure as either stinginess or arrogance. The leaders of the government, already having recognized Madison's enormous ability, chose him to be a member of the Privy Council instead. In that capacity he handled "a great deal of routine paperwork and administrative detail" for Henry, who, although the most popular man in the state, was never known for the hard work of drafting legislation or dealing with details.[2] On December 16, 1779, however, Madison was elected as a delegate to the Second Continental Congress sitting in Philadelphia, the first of a series of national offices he would hold, and did not return to the Virginia House until 1784. Jefferson had gone back to Williamsburg in 1776 as soon as he could after the Second Continental Congress approved the Declaration of Independence. He recognized how important the work of the House of Delegates would be, and he had large plans for continued reform of the state. In late September 1776 he had received a letter from John Hancock, president of the Congress, notifying him that the Congress had appointed him, along with Benjamin Franklin and Silas Deane, as commissioners to France. After days of agonizing, Jefferson, as much as he would have liked to go to Paris, declined the appointment. The delicate situation of his family (namely his wife's frailty), as he later explained his decision, "was such as I could not leave it, nor could I expose it to the dangers of the sea." But he also believed that the more important work for him lay in Virginia. As he said in his autobiography decades later, "I saw too that the laboring oar was really at home."[3]

But truth be told, the welter of decisions pressing on the infant state government threatened to exceed the capability of the executive, currently Henry, given the circumscribed powers of the position as defined by the state constitution. The issue came to a head at the end of 1776 when news from the battle scenes in the North were especially distressing. If the theater of war moved south, could the creaking machinery of Virginia's government cope with the situation? Seeking a remedy, George Mason took the extraordinary step in December of bringing a resolution to the House of Delegates to confer "emergency powers on the Governor and Council." Mason was no hothead; rather, he was exceedingly cautious and prudent. That he authored this resolution indicates how at risk the state seemed to its legislators. It authorized the governor, "with the advice & consent of the Privy Council," to raise troops, send them into battle, and draw funds from the treasury, but the resolution made clear that this was not intended to set a precedent for future actions.[4]

The bill passed, and though it gave practically dictatorial powers to the governor, these additional powers had a precise time limitation and in fact the precedent for this procedure went back to Roman law. But Jefferson took great umbrage at the decision, blamed Henry for being power hungry, and saw it as evidence of why the present constitution, passed as regular legislation, did not have the steadying role of a proper constitution, one approved by the people in specially charged assemblies called to vote on the state's fundamental law. Despite Jefferson's fear (and his growing dislike of Henry), Virginia never evolved into anything remotely resembling a modern dictatorship.

The British did not move on Virginia in a serious way until 1779. In the interval, there were occasional quick raids along the riverbanks of the major tidal rivers, and several scares that a major invasion was about to occur, which necessitated the calling up of militia and sending them toward expected invasion routes. But no invasions came, and as the war dragged on, with repeated calls for additional manpower and additional taxes, the people began to tire of the demands. Trying to maintain a constant state of military readiness was exhausting, and militia, called up time and again to no effect, became reluctant to serve. Supplies were so limited and transportation so execrable that it took days for the troops to get into position, and by then it was too late: after a teasing invasion maneuver, the British always withdrew. Understandably, militia grew ever more resistant to calls for service, and the governor, whether it was Henry at first or later Jefferson, came to hesitate before calling on them in hopes of first finding out how imminent the threat was. Everyone was exhausted.

Land issues forced themselves on the House of Delegates at the very beginning. By its colonial charter Virginia owned the territory all the way west, at least to the Mississippi River. Jefferson had distinctly reformist ideas about western lands, and he succeeded in getting legislation passed that sought to protect the rights of squatters, small farmers who aspired to settle on the land. He also pushed to guarantee the rights of settlers who lived in the West, and he would later try to control how land was purchased from Native Americans. He worked with George Mason to regularize land purchases and both hoped to sustain a reformist vision, yet they would be defeated by other, stronger interests. Jefferson's original bill in 1777 was intended to regularize and reform land sales in the western territory of Virginia. It had a secondary purpose of raising revenue to pay toward the state's debt and other financial needs. But more interesting is what the bill aspired to do. For example, a stated purpose was "the Encouragement of Foreigners to settle here, and an Inducement to Import Inhabitants from Foreign Countries."[5] To further this goal, it provided that anyone who paid the way for a person from a foreign country to come here and settle (enslaved Africans were excluded from this proviso), would be able to purchase fifty acres of land. Moreover, it sought "to encourage Marriage and Population, by making provision for the natives of the Country." Each free child born in Virginia, once an adult and married for a minimum of one year, would be granted seventy-five acres of land from the current unappropriated lands in the West.

The goal was the spread of small, free farmers across the state.[6] But the visionary aspects of this bill were defeated by the strenuous opposition of its foes, land speculators. It would not be the last time Jefferson's reformist ideals were thwarted. At this juncture, Patrick Henry was the most popular man in the state, but he had little skill or interest in writing legislation, and he had no overarching reform goals he wanted to achieve as governor other than winning the war and doing what was necessary to meet that important objective. Jefferson, on the other hand, approached his position as a member of the new House of Delegates fired up to effect change, to remake the state. No sooner had he entered the House in October 1776 than he introduced a bill calling for the appointment of a five-man committee to be tasked with considering all the existing laws with the "authority to revise, alter, amend, repeal" them. The aim was a significant reformation of the state's entire legal system. This bill passed the House two days later and the Senate on October 24.[7] Now Jefferson had permission to revise the laws of the state, and he intended to make the most of the opportunity.

On November 4, 1776, the legislature appointed Jefferson, George Wythe, Edmund Pendleton, George Mason, and Thomas Ludwell Lee to the committee of revision, but Lee soon became ill and died, and Mason, rather incredulously claiming he was no lawyer, resigned. Jefferson, the visionary, was thinking about the future of the state; Mason, the practical realist, planned to focus on the immediate issues at stake in the midst of an ongoing war. Most of the reform work, then, fell to the remaining three, with Jefferson taking in effect the superintending role in the whole process. Mason apparently consulted with the committee and probably played a role in their drafting of laws treating land matters, one of Mason's special concerns. And Mason would work to help get as many as possible of the revised laws enacted. Many of them, though, would have to wait until Madison rejoined the House of Delegates in 1784. Jefferson proved himself a legislative phenom. Years later John Adams recalled of Jefferson's service in the Continental Congress that he was "prompt, frank, explicit, and decisive upon committees and in conversation."[8] Service on the committee of revision was one of the greatest pleasures of Jefferson's career. Here was really the chance of a lifetime to reform his beloved commonwealth, to make up for the failures of its 1776 constitution (which he felt was mere statutory law, not genuinely fundamental law).

The committee discarded many older laws because they were no longer necessary, and of course many laws, now written in clearer, less cluttered prose, dealt with mundane affairs of governance, such as "A Bill for Preventing Infection of Horned Cattle" or "A Bill for Establishing Public Ferries." But Jefferson had powerful reformist ideals that undergirded his attempt to remake the state. The whole corpus of the revised laws, some 126 bills, was delivered to the House of Delegates on June 18, 1779, but certain ones had been pulled out of the report and submitted earlier. Two of the first were Jefferson's proposals to end primogeniture and entail, which were more a statement of principle than a real reform because the practices had mostly gone out of fashion. Jefferson wanted to strike a symbolic blow against aristocracy anyway.

Other bills reflected long-held attitudes of Jefferson. Number 55, "A Bill Declaring Who Shall Be Deemed Citizens of This Commonwealth," stated that all white persons born in Virginia, or those who had resided in the state two years prior to the bill's passage, and who proved by oath or affirmation that they intended to continue their residence, and "give assurance of fidelity to the commonwealth . . . shall be deemed citizens of this commonwealth." Jefferson hoped to populate the state with small farmers who were white, not enslaved Africans, and acceding to the dominant viewpoint of the time, he only considered whites as potential citizens. Number 64, "A Bill for Proportioning Crimes and Punishments in Cases Heretofore Capital," significantly changed how criminals were to be treated. Rather than prescribing capital punishment for dozens of crimes large and small, Jefferson—who had read the recent European literature on criminology—sought to develop a system by which the punishment inflicted was proportionate to the crime, with reformed behavior being the desired result. Only those convicted of treason and murder would be liable to death.[9] Jefferson explained in his autobiography that a proposed "Bill Concerning Slaves," which would have limited the importation of additional enslaved Africans, was a kind of decoy bill; the intention was, whenever it came up for debate, to insert a substitute bill that would have called for a program of gradual emancipation, but Jefferson determined not to introduce the bill because "it was found that the public mind would not yet bear the proposition." This substitute bill has not been found, but there is little doubt what Jefferson and supporters like George Wythe had in mind.[10]

One of the bills that Jefferson took most pride in, Number 79, "A Bill for the More General Diffusion of Knowledge," was one of the most progressive. It did not pass the much more conservative General Assembly, and in fact, Virginia would not enact a statewide system of free public education for more than a century, but that was what Jefferson was forecasting in this innovative bill. He called for a free three-year education for all white boys and girls; thereafter, by means of a carefully laid out winnowing system, a decreasing number of the most talented boys would be chosen for additional education, through what would today be high school, twenty of them throughout the state, and then the top-ten male students throughout the state each year would be chosen for a free education at the College of William and Mary. Jefferson believed a republic depended on a literate, informed public, and the free universal three years of learning reading, writing, and arithmetic would provide that. Jefferson admired the public schools of New England, and he believed that talent was not confined just to the children of wealthy families. Regrettably, he did not provide for equality of education for young women and African American students. Nevertheless, his proposals were far in advance of what the legislature would accept even if it did hint at what education eventually became in the state.[11]

Jefferson's final legislative landmark, one of the three things (along with the Declaration of Independence and the creation of the University of Virginia) that he wanted mentioned on his tombstone, was "A Bill for Establishing Religious Freedom," famous not only in Virginia and US history but in the history of Western Christendom. In part because his own religious views were so far outside Anglican orthodoxy—he rejected the concept of the Trinity, did not believe in miracles and the resurrection, and did not accept Jesus as divine—Jefferson was personally susceptible to prosecution, at least technically. He thought that no person or human institution should stand between an individual and that person's understanding of God. He knew the renamed Episcopal Church had the legal right to censor a person's religious beliefs and practices; he was aware that religious dissenters were currently persecuted in the state, and he wanted to establish the principle of religious (and intellectual) freedom. People should not have to pay taxes to support a church they disagreed with, and they should not be prevented from attending any church they liked, or none if that was their choice. But there was currently a state-established, tax-supported church in Virginia, a church with buildings, lands, and a public role beyond religion. Jefferson took all this on, and he had on his side such powerful thinkers as George Mason and the young Madison. Jefferson's bill opened with the assertion that "Almighty God hath created the mind free," and all attempts to control it or rein it in "are a departure from the plan of the holy author of our religion." God chose to promote religion "by its influence on reason alone." Efforts to control personal religion by legislation, mandatory contributions, and restricted civil capacities were "sinful and tyrannical." Jefferson (and Madison) believed in the moral autonomy of the individual—religion was an entirely private matter and should be beyond the reach of the state. After a long preamble that laid out the basis for religious liberty, the bill concluded that "no man shall be compelled to frequent or support any religious worship, place, or ministry whatsoever, nor shall be enforced, restrained, molested, or burthened in his body or goods, nor shall otherwise suffer, on account of his religious opinions or belief; but that all men shall be free to profess, and by argument to maintain, their opinions in matters of religion, and that the same shall in no wise diminish, enlarge, or affect their civic capacities."[12]

These were radical ideas for the time, denying that the state had any right to interfere in any way with religious behavior.[13] Passage of this bill was hard fought, and many otherwise progressive legislators hesitated to disestablish the Episcopal Church. Another ploy was to defend the principle of a state religious tax that would be distributed proportionally among all churches; Patrick Henry fought for this.[14] One of the difficulties facing the bill's approval was that Madison was no longer in the House, and neither was Jefferson, who now served as governor. The House approved it in 1786, after Madison had retired from the Continental Congress and was back to shepherd it through the Virginia House (and Jefferson was in France). To promote the bill, Madison anonymously published a petition in 1785 titled *Memorial and Remonstrance against Religious Assessments* that complemented the ideas in Jefferson's bill and itself became an important text in the history of religious freedom. Jefferson's bill and Madison's petition would later have influence on the First Amendment in the nation's Bill of Rights and the full development of the principle of separation of church and state.

But that very consequential development lay in the future. At the moment there was a revolution to win. Just weeks before the complete package of bills was submitted to the General Assembly, that body elected Jefferson governor of the state on June 1, 1779. Patrick Henry's three-year reign had ended by the term-limitation provision of the state constitution. Until this moment, the closest the war had come to Jefferson was when several thousand captured British and Hessian soldiers had been relocated from New England to a plot of land just outside Charlottesville in January 1779, and Jefferson had in fact befriended the British and German commanding officers and invited musically inclined captives to Sunday afternoon musicales at Monticello. That gentle intrusion of war barely reflected the harsh realities of the conflict: death, hardship, the almost desperate plight of the soldiers and officers of the Continental Army, led with extraordinary devotion by George Washington. Everything that had happened in Virginia since independence occurred with the horrors of war at a distance. That was about to change as Jefferson took office, but Washington's role in the mostly northern war to this point deserves close attention.

When the Continental Congress had named Washington as General and Commander in Chief of the Army of the United Colonies on June 15, 1775, there really was not yet an army to command. The American forces who engaged the British troops two days later in the first pitched battle of the revolution, the so-called Battle of Bunker Hill that really occurred on Breed's Hill in Boston, was fought by local militiamen. The British suffered horrendous casualties. Not until July 3, 1775, did Washington arrive to take over. Washington's instinct in warfare was to be aggressive, sometimes unwisely so. His first initiative was to mount an expedition supposed to seize Canada, so in the fall he sent two forces, one led by General Richard Montgomery and the other by Colonel Benedict Arnold. The terrain was terrible, supplies were almost nonexistent, and the weather horrendous. The American forces attacked Quebec on the last night of December in the middle of a blinding snowstorm. The battle turned into a disaster for the American troops. Montgomery was killed, Arnold seriously wounded, and the campaign a complete failure. Luckily Washington next directed his attention to Boston, which the British still controlled. Here Washington studied the topography and managed to inspire the American troops, under the command of General Henry Knox, somehow under cover of night on March 4, 1776, to drag forty-three cannon and sixteen mortars to the top of Dorchester Heights. From there they could bombard practically the whole city of Boston. British general William Howe marveled at this exploit and instantly recognized that his troops occupied an untenable position. Three days later the British forces pulled out of Boston and departed for Halifax, Nova Scotia. Washington expected them to soon attempt to take New York City, so he began moving his troops southward. For many months afterward he was fixated on that city, which the British, with thirty-two thousand troops, soon invaded and occupied.

Washington's original task was to create an army, and he knew immediately that he wanted a standing army, with men signed up for several years' service, not a collection of militia who came and went after several months so that the army was constantly in flux, impossible to train effectively. Most Americans had long been opposed to standing armies, which were seen as productive of military despotism, but Washington knew waves of amateur soldiers would be no match for the well-disciplined British forces. Washington was doggedly persistent in his entreaties to the Congress, which grudgingly gave in to his logic. Had he been required to adhere to an army made up of militia, his ultimate success would have been unlikely if not impossible. Washington also had the self-confidence necessary to surround himself with talented assistants and associates. He maintained a stable of highly literate, strongly motivated aides-de-camp, young men such as Joseph Reed, John Laurens, and most notably Alexander Hamilton. They could write for him, even think for him. From their pens came hundreds of orders, letters, and requisitions.

Washington also had an eye for effective leaders, especially Nathanael Greene (a brilliant strategist) and Henry Knox; and he quickly accepted almost as a son the Marquis de Lafayette, a teenage volunteer from France who brought enthusiasm, money, and soldiers. During the terrible winter at Valley

Forge in 1777 and 1778, Washington welcomed the assistance of Prussian lieutenant general Friedrich Wilhelm Augustus von Steuben (the title of baron was fake), who, despite broken English liberally sprinkled with salty profanity, methodically drilled and trained Washington's unprofessional troops. Steuben wrote a detailed drill manual (it even explained how to lay out a camp), taught marching and discipline, and helped create an effective fighting force. Washington learned from his own mistakes, was open to advice, and understood that despite his complete authority over the army, he himself was subject to the authority of the civilian leadership of the nation. His demeanor, his bravery, his steely resolve no matter the problems or hardships, led his men to almost worship him. In strictly military terms, Washington was no tactician of special skill, but as the personification of the cause for which they were fighting, he was extraordinarily successful. American victory depended on him.

Ironically, during the days while the Continental Congress was discussing Jefferson's draft of the Declaration of Independence, July 2–3, 1776, British troops began pouring into New York City. Washington would later attempt to dislodge them only to suffer a humiliating defeat. Still Washington continued to linger in the vicinity, hoping eventually to see a chance for victory, which never came. After another devastating loss at Fort Washington on Manhattan Island, the American troops reluctantly began to retreat toward Trenton, New Jersey. Howe (who actually was somewhat sympathetic to the American cause and had hoped a reconciliation could be achieved) inexplicably left New York and deployed near Trenton for the duration of the winter. Desperate to find some way to recoup from the losses in New York, Washington daringly ferried his troops across the Delaware River on Christmas night, 1776, and successfully attacked a small British encampment, inflicting substantial casualties on the foe at the cost of but two American deaths (both from freezing) and just a handful of wounded, including a young lieutenant from Virginia, James Monroe, who almost bled to death.[15] Washington followed up this victory with an equally daring attack on British troops at Princeton. The British quite easily brushed off these losses, but they gave Washington and his troops a powerful psychological boost. Americans could fight, and the British could be defeated. Throughout 1777 Washington stayed near Philadelphia, which Howe's forces were beginning to bear down on. Washington engaged the enemy twice that year, once in September at Brandywine, which was an embarrassing defeat, Howe badly out-generaling Washington, and the next month near Germantown (where incidentally, John Marshall was wounded in the hand), which could be considered a draw except that the Americans had many more casualties than the British. Afterward, Howe occupied Philadelphia.

But the key battle of 1777 occurred far away, in New York State. The British planned to send an army commanded by General John Burgoyne southward from Canada via Lake Champlain and the Hudson River, ultimately hoping to rendezvous with General Howe. Burgoyne had not expected to meet the resistance he did, yet American general Horatio Gates was more than his match. Gates, managing to pull together more men than Burgoyne had, engaged the invaders near Saratoga. On October 17, 1777, to avoid utter disaster, Burgoyne surrendered his entire army, almost six thousand men. The surrender terms were labeled the Convention of 1777, and these so-called surrendered Convention troops, consisting of both British regulars and Hessian mercenaries from Germany, were eventually marched south and by January 1779 arrived in Albemarle County, Virginia, where they were barracked in a prisoner-of-war camp just northwest of Charlottesville.

Burgoyne's defeat at Saratoga had far more importance than merely producing captives; it also provided a powerful psychological boost: Americans could fight, and the British could be defeated. Even more importantly, this American victory so impressed the French that American victory was possible that it led to the French-American alliance—thanks to the canny negotiating skills of Benjamin Franklin in Paris—and recognition of the independence of the United States. Saratoga proved to be the turning point of the war, even though Washington was not there.

Readers today are sometimes surprised to learn that actual hostilities between the American colonies and England preceded the Declaration of Independence by more than a year. And it is also surprising to learn that the colonies fought most of the revolution without a real national government, instead limping along under the vague authority of the impromptu Second Continental Congress. On the day that Congress had appointed a five-man committee to draft the Declaration of Independence, it also appointed a committee to draft a confederation agreement to more formally bind the colonies together into a nation. That committee labored for months, trying to create an effective central government for thirteen new states that were in rebellion against central authority, especially one that claimed to be able to raise taxes. Finally, on November 13, 1776, the draft was completed and submitted to the states for ratification, which finally came on March 1, 1781, when Congress learned that Maryland had ratified on February 2. That government, the Articles of Confederation, did not even have an executive but rather a rotating executive committee. It had no effective mechanism for raising taxes (it could merely request taxes) or troops. It was barely a central government and more a treaty loosely linking thirteen independent states, but that truly reflected the political sentiment of the time and place. The locus of power was seen to be in the individual states. But it did not make for a government that could mount an efficacious war against England.

Herein lay George Washington's largest handicap. He had to wage war not just against the redcoats but against the lethargy of his home government, the miserliness of its provision of the matériel of warfare, and the shortage of troops. Often his troops were without ammunition, adequate clothing, and sufficient rations. No wonder he became an advocate for a stronger central government! Washington's greatest accomplishment was simply holding his army together, maintaining morale in almost hopeless conditions, demonstrating courage that inspired confidence, and persisting in promoting the American cause in the face of endless disappointment and frustration. In a bold show of leadership, recognizing that a virulent smallpox epidemic was wreaking havoc among his forces, he made inoculation mandatory in the fall of 1777, a farsighted move that ultimately had significant consequences for his army. The low point of the war was the terrible winter quarters, 1777–78, at Valley Forge, where his cold, hungry, often barefooted soldiers left bloody footprints in the snow. Having at best crude wooden huts without floors as shelter, with shortages of food as well as adequate clothing, the troops suffered dreadfully. Somehow, against all odds, Washington had the charisma to forge a winning army in the midst of these conditions. This accomplishment, not strategic genius, was the essence of his greatness.[16]

British general Howe with his superior forces spent that winter comfortably ensconced in Philadelphia, but he did not try to disperse Washington's troops. In May 1778 Howe was replaced with General Henry Clinton, who the next month began preparations to move his forces to New York. Although Washington made a courageous but futile effort to stop him at the Battle of Monmouth in New Jersey, thereafter Clinton maintained his forces in New York. French forces under the command of Admiral Jean Baptiste Charles Henri Hector, comte d'Estaing, arrived in July 1778 to assist the Americans, but because d'Estaing's ships were too large to allow an easy unloading of troops for a land-sea attack on New York City, he decided to move toward Newport. He soon withdrew to the West Indies. Up to this point, the British had only made temporary raids along the coast of Virginia, but British strategy was soon to turn to the South, where they believed there were many Tories who had just been waiting for His Majesty's forces to direct their attention to them. Virginia of course lay between the major theater of war in the North for the first three years and the emerging theater in Georgia and South Carolina.

While Washington remained focused on Clinton in New York City, the British broadened the conflict, invading and capturing Savannah in December 1778. Through the early months of 1779, there were skirmishes across Georgia, although in May the British made a quick raid on Portsmouth and Norfolk,

Virginia, setting them afire. Governor Patrick Henry rather belatedly called out troops, but when they arrived, three-quarters of them did not have arms. Virginia was having recurrent problems trying to maintain its militia and simultaneously send troops to Washington's Continental Army. Meanwhile, Washington was biding his time in vicinity of New York City, doggedly preoccupied with that city.

One of his young aides, John Laurens, son of the wealthy South Carolina slave trader and plantation owner Henry Laurens, proposed to Washington that a force of three thousand enslaved people be raised in South Carolina and Georgia to fight for the American cause, after which they would be freed. Washington did not summarily reject the proposal—he knew hundreds of Blacks from the New England states were already serving in the Continental Army—but he did not think recruiting enslaved soldiers from the southern states would be advisable because it might destabilize the plantation work force. Henry Laurens reported to Washington that he found absolutely no support for the idea among southern delegates to the Continental Congress. So Washington did not attempt to advance the proposal despite the dire need for additional troops.[17]

Nevertheless, desperate to motivate leaders throughout the colonies to push their local governments to support the Continental cause more generously, Washington wrote letter after letter describing the needs of the Continental Army and promoting the cause of independence. To his longtime friend George Mason he admitted in March 1779 that "I have beheld no day since the commencement of hostilities that I have thought her liberties in such eminent danger as at present.... We seem to be verging so fast to destruction.... Nothing therefore in my judgment can save us but a total reformation in our own conduct, or some decisive turn to [our] affairs in Europe."[18] He even lamented that so many able men like Mason himself and Jefferson were serving in state capacities rather than in the Continental Congress that was managing the national effort. But the European assistance he hoped for did eventually come from France, boosting the American resolve and contributing significantly to their ultimate victory.

It was at this moment, on June 1, 1779, that Virginia's General Assembly elected Jefferson governor of the state. With British intentions now having shifted to the southern colonies, it was an inauspicious time to enter the gubernatorial office. Jefferson himself wondered if the occupant should have at least some military experience—he had none. Jefferson faced the same problems that had bedeviled Henry: the constant need to raise funds, matériel, and soldiers. Jefferson worked tirelessly, trying to promote arms manufacture, obtain wagons and the horses to pull them, and increase the production of clothing, saddlery, and foodstuffs. He wanted to build fortifications along the major rivers, send troops northward to Washington, and especially now, send troops southward, reasoning that it was better to fight the British in South Carolina or Georgia than in Virginia. The inefficiency of the governor's office made effective actions doubly difficult. Jefferson as governor needed to have the signed consent of the Privy Council to authorize any action, and slow communication, combined with the frequent absence of members of the Council from Williamsburg, often made rapid response impossible. At times decisions could simply not be executed. This would have been merely inconvenient in peacetime, but in wartime it was devastating.

In early September 1779 the French admiral d'Estaing bore down upon Savannah, sank four British ships, and began to move against the city, hoping to regain it from the British. Supporting American troops under the command of General Benjamin Lincoln moved too slowly to be of assistance. In the ensuing battle, d'Estaing was injured, and he withdrew. The British remained in control of Savannah. The following spring, 1780, with General Sir Henry Clinton having left Rhode Island and New York and transported almost eight thousand troops to Charleston, the British took that city as well after a siege of several months. Charleston surrendered on May 12, 1780, General Lincoln was captured and gave up his army of 5,400 men. Before the end of the month Colonel Banastre Tarleton smashed a crack Virginia regiment at Waxhaw Creek, devastating news for Jefferson and all Virginians. The loss of Charleston was the largest single American defeat of the war. After this signal success, Clinton sailed back to New York.

The month before, the state capital of Virginia moved inland from Williamsburg to Richmond, intended to prevent the government from falling easy prey to an invading force. Two months after the move came word of the disheartening defeat in South Carolina. Morale continued to fall. Jefferson, like Henry before him, found it excruciatingly difficult to raise sufficient revenue and militia to mount a defense of the state. As Henry wrote him in February 1780, "Do you remember any Instance, where Tyranny was destroyed and Freedom established on its Ruins among a people possessing so small a Share of Virtue and public Spirit? I recollect none; and this more than the British Arms, makes me fearful of our final success."[19] Madison wrote much the same the next month from Philadelphia, where he was serving as a member of the Continental Congress: "Our army threatened with an immediate alternative of disbanding or living on free quarter; the public Treasury empty; public credit exhausted."[20] The situation was bleak. On June 2, 1780, the General Assembly reelected Jefferson as governor. Despite the continuing bad news from the South, when he learned that General Horatio Gates had replaced the captured Lincoln, Jefferson reluctantly worked to recruit men to augment his forces. Then word came in September that General Charles Cornwallis had defeated Gates at Camden, pressing him to move into North Carolina. Jefferson began to worry about how to defend Virginia if the conflict continued to move northward. He contemplated resigning so that a military man could replace him as governor, but his closest friends talked him out of this drastic move.

On December 9, 1780, George Washington sent Jefferson a vague warning that it looked like there was an embarkation of British troops from the northern states headed somewhere southward, but Jefferson could hardly call up the exhausted and under-equipped militia and try to position them somewhere based on such imprecise information. But sure enough, on January 2, 1781, it became clear that there was an invasion. British troops, led by the traitorous turncoat Benedict Arnold, led a force up the James River, came ashore at Westover Plantation, and then made a quick, destructive raid on Richmond, even storming the governor's house (Jefferson had earlier sent his wife and children to safety). Jefferson had worked endlessly to move valuable supplies and papers beyond the reach of the invaders. But then the British departed almost as quickly as they had arrived, settling in Portsmouth. Meanwhile, enslaved people continued to escape their bondage and flee to British troops. Thousands so joined the British, with dozens of enslaved people even leaving Monticello and Mount Vernon, increasing both Jefferson's and Washington's antipathy toward the redcoats. Neither believed the British were committed to Black liberty and recognized the welcoming of runaways as a military measure to weaken the southern economy. The policy certainly hardened whites' animosity toward the British. The situation looked grim for the Commonwealth of Virginia. Luckily, Washington, recognizing the strategic importance of his home state, sent the young French general, the Marquis de Lafayette, to the state with 1,200 regular troops of the Continental Army, and Lafayette, who became a lifelong friend of Jefferson, was soon joined by another foreign volunteer, the profane Prussian general Steuben, who quickly began transforming the Virginia militia into a more formidable fighting force. Both Lafayette and Steuben found it difficult to understand why Jefferson could not just commandeer supplies and men, and he had to patiently instruct them both on the limited powers of his office and the American attitudes toward maximum freedom from government.

Another ominous turn came in March 1781, when British general William Phillips joined up with Benedict Arnold in Portsmouth. Cornwallis subsequently moved into Virginia and took control of all British troops there. The following month they began moving toward Richmond. Shortly thereafter, Cornwallis sent one force northwestward seeking to capture or destroy the state's limited supplies, and another force, led by Banastre Tarleton, headed straight for Charlottesville, hoping to capture members of the state government who had fled there and perhaps even take Jefferson himself at Monticello. The state's government was falling apart. Legislators had abandoned the Capitol, and even the executive council could not be gathered.

In early June, as Tarleton was rushing toward Charlottesville, an alert militiaman saw members of the British forces taking refreshment at a tavern en route and raced ahead to Monticello to warn Jefferson. The British would have liked nothing better than capturing the governor of the state; a small group of state militia that was stationed east of Monticello precisely to hinder such raids panicked and fled when the British approached. Jefferson hustled the few legislators who had been staying at Monticello away to safety, continued to gather up and conceal papers, sent his family to a friend's plantation some miles distant, and just minutes before the would-be captors arrived on June 4, he rode westward on his horse Caractacus (named after a mythical first-century British chieftain who had fought against the invading Romans). Jefferson escaped, but the British did catch several of the dilatory legislators in Charlottesville.

Actually, Jefferson's term of office had expired two days before, but the legislature was in such a state of panic and disruption that it could not elect a successor until June 12, when it chose the person Jefferson himself would have picked, Thomas Nelson Jr., commanding general of the militia of lower Virginia and a fellow signer of the Declaration of Independence. Jefferson was later charged by political enemies—and even by some modern historians—with cowardice and abandonment of his office, a charge that wounded him to his innermost core. He still later was exonerated by the state legislature, and the Senate passed a resolution unanimously praising his gubernatorial conduct. But incorrectly believing that Patrick Henry was behind the accusation, Jefferson was thereafter a bitter enemy of the great orator. The so-called pen and voice of the revolution would never be reconciled.

This nadir of Jefferson's political career occurred in early June 1781. Ironically, had he stayed in office for another term, he likely would have been hailed for managing the affairs of the state as the last major battle of the war took place just a few miles from Jamestown and Williamsburg. Cornwallis's army was on the neck of land between the James and York Rivers, well positioned, he reasoned, for future excursions up the peninsula and easy to be provisioned via the port at Yorktown. But suddenly Lafayette with his troops were in the state, then he was joined by troops under the command of General "Mad" Anthony Wayne, blocking Cornwallis's path up the peninsula. Far away in New York, Washington's forces had been mightily fortified by the arrival in July 1780 of French general Jean-Baptiste-Donatien de Vimeur, comte de Rochambeau, with six thousand troops. Rochambeau was positioned in Rhode Island, while Washington kept watch on New York City, contemplating a joint attack with his newly arrived French colleague.

Rochambeau learned in the summer that French admiral François-Joseph-Paul, comte de Grasse, with his fleet and several thousand troops were headed for the mouth of the Chesapeake, where he could prevent British ships from provisioning or rescuing Cornwallis. Rochambeau succeeded in persuading Washington that the two of them should march, posthaste, to Virginia, with de Grasse ferrying them part of the way. It all came together at the end of September. Cornwallis could not escape; Virginia's militia, assisted by the troops commanded by Lafayette and Wayne, were marching toward him, soon to be joined by the combined forces of de Grasse, Washington, and Rochambeau; and Washington, recognizing the superiority of the military engineers in the French army, let Rochambeau direct the battle, complete with trenches and artillery bombardment.

The siege began on October 6. Cornwallis realized only too late his dilemma. He asked Washington for twenty-four hours to consider a surrender agreement; Washington gave him two hours. There, on a site so near to where English colonial America had begun at Jamestown, Cornwallis on October 19, 1781, surrendered his eight thousand men. Cornwallis wanted to be able to surrender his troops with full military honors, but Washington, knowing that Cornwallis had not shown such respect to the Americans in their defeat at Charleston, denied the request. The petulant Cornwallis then refused to attend the final signing of the surrender agreement, sending another general in his place. Washington, alert to the intentional insult, had the British replacement general hand over the ceremonial sword to his assistant, General Lincoln. The British officers were haughty and condescending to the end, behavior Washington had first experienced from them in the 1750s.[21]

The last major battle of the American Revolution had just been fought, and the Americans had won, in Virginia no less. Of course no one was immediately aware of the significance of the victory, but an indication occurred less than a week later when General Clinton, having sailed south from New York, arrived in the vicinity expecting to reinforce Cornwallis. Discovering what had happened five days before, Clinton turned around and sailed back. When the news reached London, Lord North resigned ("Oh God," he had blurted out, "It is all over."), to be replaced by Lord Rockingham, who quickly decided to begin negotiations to end the war.

There were minor skirmishes in the months after Yorktown, but the British realized they had lost their former colonies. In September 1782, meeting in Paris, Benjamin Franklin, John Jay, and John Adams negotiated with the British peace commissioner. By the terms of the US-French treaty of 1778, neither side was supposed to negotiate independently with England, but the English, wanting to give the Americans lenient terms in the hope of weaning them away from their connection with the French, had reached out. The terms were generous: recognition of American independence, transfer to the United States of all former British territory east of the Mississippi River from the Great Lakes to the boundary with Spanish Florida, rights to fish off the coast of Newfoundland and Nova Scotia, validation of debts mutually held between the two nations, an American promise to respect the property rights of former Loyalists, and the promise on the part of the British to remove all forces from territory now granted to the new nation. This preliminary treaty was signed on November 30, 1782, and the final treaty took effect on January 20, 1783, after the French and British agreed to the terms, France reluctantly so. The United States now was to play its role upon the world stage as an acknowledged nation state, though it would in fact take decades for established European countries to grant it its due respect. Washington had witnessed the entire struggle, from his commissioning in June 1775 to the victory at Yorktown, and in the process he had become the most famous American in the world.

4

UNRESOLVED PROBLEMS

In Annapolis, on December 23, 1783, General Washington stood before the members of the Congress in a ceremony orchestrated by Thomas Jefferson. Impressive in his uniform, Washington addressed them. He declared that he had the "honor of . . . presenting before them to surrender into their hands the trust committed to me. . . . Having now finished the work assigned me, I retire from the great theatre of Action; and bidding an Affectionate farewell . . . take my leave of all the employments of public life."[1] With that he surrendered his military commission. Unlike other victorious generals in other places and times, Washington did not seek to transmute his fame into a military dictatorship but rather completely accepted the supremacy of civilian government. Nothing he did in warfare so became him as this abdication of martial authority. As Jefferson said, "The moderation and virtue of a single character has probably prevented this revolution from being closed as most others have been by a subversion of that liberty it was intended to establish."[2] Finally, after eight years of warfare and absence from Mount Vernon, the general had laid aside the sword for the plow. The one-time planter and dedicated agricultural reformer was ready to return to his beloved homesite.[3]

Washington had long abandoned the traditional Virginia plantation focus on tobacco, both because the soils around Mount Vernon were exhausted and because the price of tobacco had fallen. Instead, Washington had shifted to the cultivation of wheat. He experimented with several varieties of crop rotation, he had invested heavily in fishing in the Potomac and the commercial selling of fish, and he had built grist mills. Still he came to realize that the land surrounding Mount Vernon itself could not be made prosperous. In fact, it was a losing proposition. What kept him afloat were profits from land leases from the tens of thousands of acres he owned in the West. He had been a dedicated and successful land speculator, with a hunger for land that was off-putting, but now the rent revenue from small leaseholders allowed him to continue his "baronial lifestyle."[4] He was well aware that his slave-based agricultural operations did not and would not support his way of life. Privately he said he would like to sell (not free) all his bondspeople. At this stage of his life he was more a hard-headed businessman than an emancipationist. Paradoxically, while he abhorred the British government and its previous control of the colonies, he wanted to live as the British upper class did on their great estates. Before the war, he had grown accustomed to prolific spending, and now in peacetime he expected to live at a standard associated with British aristocrats. (Washington did not have democratic sensibilities in terms of lifestyle, though he understood that political power inhered in the citizenry.)

Washington, despite an outer demeanor of humility, lived every bit the ideal of the country squire, conscious always of his public image and determined to preserve the version of himself that he wished to project to posterity. The enslaved people who worked in the house and drove his carriage were dressed in livery. He had employed well-educated clerks during the war to ensure that his notices, orders, and requests were grammatically correct and that his letters were gracefully written. In peacetime he even employed skilled wordsmiths to make sure that he expressed himself properly. Confident of his ability in most aspects, he was conscious that he did not possess the education of many of the other leaders and took care to present a written record that reflected his high expectations. More than any of the other Founders, Washington worked to improve, promote, and protect his image, both for himself and he believed for the reputation of the nation. He was extraordinarily sensitive to criticism. His personal character, his home, his public presentation befitted his role as leading citizen of his country. He always dressed exquisitely. His fame had grown to such an extent that Mount Vernon was overrun by visitors, many of whom expected to be fed and their horses boarded. Not only did this drain his financial accounts but it also absorbed much of his time. Washington's behavior toward his guests, invited or not, was always proper, but he was seldom outgoing. His wife, Martha, on the other hand, was genial and welcoming. His correspondence grew to such an extent that he had to employ assistants to reply to his extensive mail. And of course there were no government retirement benefits to reimburse him for these expenses, although he was allowed franking privileges for his correspondence.

As a result of his experiences during the war, Washington had become disenchanted with the weaknesses of the Articles of Confederation government that had been only an incremental improvement over the practically powerless Second Continental Congress it replaced in 1781. On March 31, 1783, Washington had written Alexander Hamilton, originally one of his most trusted staff members and later a junior officer, that

> No man in the United States is, or can be more deeply impressed with the necessity of reform in our present Confederation than myself. No man perhaps has felt the bad effects of it more sensibly; for the defects thereof, & want of Powers in Congress may justly be ascribed the prolongation of the War. . . . More than half the perplexities I have experienced in the course of my command, and almost the whole of the difficulties & distresses of the Army, have their origin here.[5]

He understood that a government that could not raise tax revenues would not be able to secure loans, would not be able to support an army, and in the last resort would not be able to defend and maintain the nation.

Washington also sent a long and heartfelt circular letter to the various state governments on June 8, 1783, imploring them to strengthen the central government, honor its requests for funds, and pay the debts incurred as a result of the war. Otherwise, he feared ultimate chaos and dissolution, making all the sacrifices and deaths of the revolution in vain.[6] But Washington assumed that his public career was over, and he did not believe that the nation would summon the political will to address the weaknesses of its present form of government until some severe crisis of undetermined nature simply forced it to. He did not expect to play a role in this response; it might be years away, he was conscious of his age (he was of a short-lived family), and he wanted to focus on improving Mount Vernon, take his ease, and read more deeply than he had ever before had time to. As he put it in his circular letter, now, "remote from the noise and trouble of the world, I meditate to pass the remainder of my life in a state of undisturbed repose."[7]

Washington's neighbor and friend George Mason responded to the end of the war very differently. As a relatively young man Mason had hired two wonderfully skilled British craftsmen, William Buckland and William Bernard Sears, to design and build his plantation home, Gunston Hall, a jewel of a house, between 1755 and 1759, and—unlike Washington or later Jefferson—Mason never felt the need to enlarge or improve on the original structure. Smaller than Mount Vernon, Gunston Hall, in the Georgian style, had elegant, richly decorated interiors with exquisite carvings. No wonder Mason resented ever having to leave this stately home for the sake of politics. Sickly, often grumpy, and quick to find fault with his fellow legislators, Mason had retired from the General Assembly in 1781. Since his first wife, Ann Eilbeck Mason, had died in 1773, Mason had often used the need to attend to his children to excuse his refusal to more actively engage in politics, but in 1780 he married Sarah Brent, who was about fifty years of age.[8]

This marriage did not release him from parenting duties and allow for enhanced participation in the governance of Virginia. Rather, he resigned from the legislature in 1781, professing disgust with many of his fellow legislators—Mason was not a patient man. Still, he was active serving as an informal, local commissary general for the Continental Army, buying supplies and forwarding them on. Mason was extremely concerned about the state's shortage of tax revenue and constant need for funding, and he just as constantly pushed for government frugality. Therefore, he resisted efforts of the Articles of Confederation Congress to raise the taxes required by its revenue quotas suggested for the states. Mason was opposed to any government beyond his state—really, his county—having taxing powers. He simply distrusted government beyond the county level. He was a decided localist, never becoming a nationalist: his identity would remain totally Virginian. Mason also did not have Jefferson's faith in the people or in democracy. The squire of Gunston Hall would later be opposed to having the president elected by the people, saying it would be "as unnatural to refer the choice of a proper character for chief Magistrate to the people, as it would, to refer a trial of colours to a blind man."[9]

When Mason learned in 1781 that some land promoters were scheming to create a new state in the West out of Virginia's traditional territory, he sent off a remonstrance to Jefferson, now back in the General Assembly. Several years later, when he heard that a committee of the Articles of Confederation Congress had drawn up a proposal for regularizing the creation of new states, he objected. This proposal, of course, was authored by Jefferson, and it advocated an orderly process based on population growth for the creation of new states, it called for the support of education and freedom of religion, and Jefferson even proposed that in the new states slavery would be ended in 1800. Mason did support the validity of debts owed by Virginians to British creditors because he did not want it believed that narrow self-interest drove the revolution. He was a cautious conservative, fearful that the people did not have sufficient virtue to maintain liberty. As he wrote to Patrick Henry in 1783, "We are now to rank among the Nations of the World; but whether our Independence shall prove a Blessing or a Curse, must depend upon our own Wisdom or Folly, Virtue or Wickedness; judging of the future from the Past, the Prospect is not promising."[10]

Mason's negativity led to his opposition to the idea of revising the existing Virginia constitution of 1776, which of course Mason had substantially drafted and Jefferson believed substantially flawed. When Mason heard a rumor in 1783 that plans were afoot to write a new constitution, he opposed the idea. Jefferson, hearing the same rumor, was so excited he wrote out an entire new constitution for the state.[11] Alas for Jefferson, no new constitutional convention was called, so the 1776 constitution stayed in force until it was revised in 1830.

As might be expected from such a dyed-in-the-wool localist as Mason, he was no friend of cities, but he had such faith in the western lands (as long as they were deemed an expansion of Virginia, not organized as new states) to which thousands of settlers were migrating annually, that he supported transportation improvements of the Potomac River with the hope of facilitating trade with the West. This would bind that section more securely to the original states, and by the by, send profitable trade by way of Alexandria and down the Potomac past Mason's plantation. Mason always had a keen eye on his economic interests and his plantation profits. Washington had exactly the same enthusiasm for commerce via the Potomac, and this shared idea would later bring them together in 1785 and 1786 to discuss methods of addressing the needs of river transportation. With a forward-looking sense, these two plantation owners also recognized how internal transportation improvements to the West benefited large-scale commercial agriculture and the entire state. These discussions ultimately led in a direction neither of them originally foresaw.

Patrick Henry, forty-seven-years old when the American Revolution formally ended, was living at his plantation called Leatherwood a little under two hundred miles southwest of Richmond. Interestingly, although Washington, Mason, Jefferson, and Madison would always be associated with their iconic homes, Henry and his family lived in half a dozen or more homes, only settling at the relatively plain Red Hill, with which today he is often associated, in the final years of his life. Not surprisingly, he was unstintingly busy at his legal practice in the years after 1779 when he ended his first three terms as governor of Virginia, and he too was enthralled with the idea of acquiring land in the West.[12] By this time, Henry's financial situation had markedly improved. In addition to several plantations in Virginia and perhaps fifty enslaved laborers, he owned more than thirty thousand acres in Kentucky. He would end his life a wealthy man.

Having broken with Jefferson in 1781, Henry was becoming, year by year, more conservative and more localistic in orientation. He was elected to the Continental Congress but refused to serve, though he did accept election to the Virginia House of Delegates in 1782, where he devoted himself to looking after the economic interests of his constituents. Breaking also with his friend Mason, Henry was opposed to Americans having to repay their (legitimate) debts to British merchants, and he was vigilant against taxation. Although he understood that the central government's inability to raise revenue damaged the wartime effort, he feared that any attempt to strengthen its taxing authority over the states would lead to oppression. He already felt that the Articles of Confederation gave too much power to the central government at the expense of the states.[13] Governor again (1784–86) of Virginia, Henry paradoxically felt that the Confederation was too weak and indecisive to militarily protect settlers in the West from Indian attacks. He along with other westerners came to believe that the central government was almost worthless to them, a belief that strengthened Henry's suspicion of the Confederation. Despite all that he had done to promote Virginia's revolt against England, he—like Mason—never evolved a nationalist identity and persisted in his resolutely Virginian identity.

Henry maintained his political popularity; no one could match his oratory, and he had a populist, anti-tax, localistic following, especially among small, isolated farmers, not the elites. He also opposed the strong desire of Jefferson and to an extent Madison to replace what they considered the flawed 1776 state constitution with a new one. And, devout Christian that he was, Henry opposed Jefferson and Madison's efforts to promote complete religious freedom and supported instead what was called a general assessment plan, whereby the revenues from a state tax to support religion would be distributed to a range of Protestant churches while the state merely tolerated other faiths. These stands contributed to the friction that arose constantly between this once radical firebrand and his revolutionary colleagues Jefferson and Madison. Their differences festered in the years following the revolution.

James Madison had been elected to the Second Continental Congress on December 16, 1779, and took office the following year. Only twenty-eight years old, very slight of build, and so youthful-looking that people mistook him for a student, Madison soon became recognized and respected in the Congress because of his ability, knowledge, and strong work habits. He had quietly emerged as a national leader. He entered the College of New Jersey (which would become Princeton) in 1769 as a sophomore, completed the junior and senior curriculum in only one year, and stayed for an additional year of graduate study. Like Jefferson who was sometimes rendered incapable of work because of severe migraine headaches, on rare occasions Madison was temporarily incapacitated for several days by mild epileptic seizures that left him in a dazed state for several minutes.[14]

In 1784, Madison's term-limited membership in the Congress ended, and he returned to Virginia, where he would become an extraordinarily hardworking member of the House of Delegates. A bachelor, Madison lived in his parents' home, just then beginning to be called Montpelier, in Orange County, about eighty miles southwest of the later city of Washington, DC, and twenty-two miles northeast of Monticello. The home plantation contained over four thousand acres, and his father, James Madison Sr., enslaved more than one hundred people. Madison grew up in a society based upon slavery. He even brought his enslaved servant Sawney to college to serve him there. Small in stature, reserved in personality, conservative in dress (usually all black), not a powerful or lively speaker but a persuasive writer, Madison was to have a huge impact on American history.

Before he had completed his term in the Articles of Confederation Congress, Madison had come to believe that as a structure of government it was too weak, inefficient, and cumbersome in practice to suffice over the long run. Although his nationalism was not, like that of Washington's, a result of serving in the army, Madison was an acute student of political theory and recognized that the Confederation government needed to be given significantly more executive authority and the ability to raise revenue and regulate commerce. In the years after 1784, he began a methodical course of study, investigating all known attempts to create self-governments, independent of rule by a monarch. He collected a substantial library on the subject, asking Jefferson, then US minister to France, to secure books for him in the bookstalls and bookshops of Paris. After Jefferson sent him a "literary cargo," Madison labeled it "perfectly to my mind."[15]

Jefferson and Madison had discussed what Jefferson considered the flawed 1776 Virginia constitution, both bemoaning that the influential Patrick Henry opposed any efforts to revise it. Jefferson only half-jokingly quipped to Madison that "What we have to do I think is devoutly to pray for his death."[16] During these years, when Madison served in the House, he effectively advocated for the reform legislation that Jefferson had drafted in the late 1770s, countering Henry's efforts to defend the principle of a general assessment religious tax and pushing through ratification in 1786 of the Virginia Statute of Religious Liberty, one of Jefferson's highest priorities. By the middle of the 1780s Madison had become the preeminent scholar of constitutionalism in the nation. Jefferson may not have been fully aware of what drove Madison's interest in constitutions at this time—what the precise purpose of his research project was—though it would soon become obvious.

Jefferson himself had reached a low point in his public life in 1781, following his narrow escape from being captured or killed by the British marauding party in June, followed by the hurtful allegations of cowardice or dereliction of duty hurled at him later in the year. Even the full vindication offered him in November by the House of Delegates, and the defeat of Cornwallis just a month earlier, did not salve Jefferson's wounded feelings. His wife's illness associated with a recent pregnancy put him further on edge, especially after her continued decline following the birth of a daughter in May 1782. A distraught Jefferson seemed on the verge of abandoning politics altogether, or so he wrote a young friend, James Monroe, who had just a year or two before studied law with Jefferson and was a newly elected member of the House of Delegates. Jefferson stated to Monroe that the recent charges against him had "inflicted a wound on my spirit which will only be cured by the all-healing grave." He reported that the last thirteen years of public service had left his "private affairs" in "great disorder and ruin," and that he had closely examined his heart to see if any "particle" of "political ambition" remained only to discover that none did. He now "ventured to declare to my countrymen my determination to retire from public employment."[17]

When that coming September his dear wife, Martha, died, Jefferson was devastated. He fainted, and for days was utterly disconsolate. Family and friends worried about his state of mind: would he recover from his grief? Thankfully his eldest daughter, also named Martha (at the time he called her Patsy), helped pull him from the realm of darkness, creating a bond between the two that would last the remainder of Jefferson's life. His closest friend Madison sought to throw him a lifeline, maneuvering to have the Congress send him an offer to go to Paris and help negotiate a treaty ending the Revolutionary War. Jefferson seized the opportunity to get away from Monticello and its sad memories, but in the midst of preparations to depart, word arrived that the final peace treaty was so near achievement that there was no need for his going. This was a great disappointment, but the weeks spent in Philadelphia preparing for the diplomatic assignment had reacquainted Jefferson with close personal associates and the excitement of ideas, thus providing him a new sense of duty. Jefferson found renewed purpose in living. Returning to Virginia, Jefferson was gratified when the General Assembly elected him, in July 1783, as a delegate to the Congress of the Articles of Confederation.

Shortly thereafter, hearing rumors that Virginia was about to call a convention to consider writing a new constitution—Jefferson had long disparaged the 1776 state constitution—Jefferson quickly drafted a new one, determined not to be too late to get his suggestions in as he had been in 1776. He changed several aspects of the existing constitution: making the Privy Council truly advisory only, strengthening the role of the executive, outlawing the importation of new enslaved people to the state, and declaring that children born to enslaved mothers after December 31, 1800, would be free, following the guidelines for emancipation pioneered by the state of Pennsylvania. But alas, the state did not call for a new constitutional convention, so this effort to end slavery in Virginia came to naught.[18]

In the middle of October 1783, Jefferson arrived in Philadelphia, the seat of the Confederation government, but shortly thereafter the Congress temporarily relocated to Princeton, then to Annapolis. Unlike the Continental Congress of 1775–76 that was filled with eminent men, this Congress was much less distinguished, Jefferson in fact being the leading member. He was to play a dominant role in its proceedings, beginning with arranging the ceremony on December 23, 1783, at which George Washington resigned his military commission, even drafting the remarks made by the president of the Congress, Thomas Mifflin. Jefferson was primarily worried that because often not enough states had sufficient delegates present to constitute a quorum, the Congress might not be able to formally accept the 1783 peace treaty with Britain before the time limitation for approval expired. Finally at the last moment a sufficient number of states were represented, so on January 14, 1784, the treaty was unanimously ratified. Jefferson drafted the ratification agreement to end the war whose purpose he had eloquently declared in 1776.

A few weeks later he drew up the agreement whereby the Congress accepted the grant of Virginia's western lands, an agreement that had been necessary to achieve ratification of the Articles of Confederation three years previously by mollifying several of the smaller states that had no western land claims. In April he was the primary writer of an ordinance that dealt with how the lands east of the Mississippi granted to the new nation by Britain would be eventually divided into states coequal with the original thirteen states. In other words, the United States would not have colonies the way Britain had. Jefferson included a provision that after the year 1800 slavery would not exist in any of these future states. That fateful proposal was defeated by one vote in the Congress, perhaps the most consequential single-vote refusal in the nation's history. (Jefferson did not elaborate on how and when he would have freed his own enslaved people had this proposal been successful, but state laws passed later did make individual emancipation far more difficult.) Had Jefferson's provision been accepted, there would have been no slavery in Alabama, Mississippi, Louisiana, and Arkansas, among others, and probably no deadly Civil War decades later. This Ordinance of 1784 was later revised, reduced in scope, and emerged as the Northwest Ordinance of 1787 that disallowed slavery only from the states to be carved out of the territory north of the Ohio River.

Jefferson also chaired a committee that produced instructions for American ministers to European nations to attempt to work out treaties of "amity and commerce with the commercial powers of Europe."[19] Within weeks, word arrived from the American minister to France, Benjamin Franklin, that trade commissioner John Jay was returning to the United States. Almost immediately Congress elected Jefferson a minister plenipotentiary to replace Jay in Paris. At last Jefferson would be on his way to France, a destination he must have long desired but little expected would come his way again.

Jefferson made preparations to go to Paris, accompanied by his daughter Martha and an enslaved man named James Hemings. They set sail on July 5, 1784, and upon arriving in the city, Jefferson leased a house, got more fashionable clothes for his daughter and himself, put her in an exclusive boarding school, and arranged lessons in the French language and in French cooking for Hemings. Jefferson set forth to explore the city—especially the book stalls, where the books he purchased later became the nucleus of the Library of Congress—and promptly presented his credentials at the Court of Versailles. Soon he began working with his colleagues John Adams and Benjamin Franklin to advance the nation's commercial interests. This proved to be an essentially hopeless task, for the European nations did not know if the new nation would endure, they already had their own established trade networks, and they wanted—as England had—to keep their maritime commerce confined within their own imperial systems.

The trio of American negotiators—Adams, Franklin, and Jefferson—were very different individually, yet even with the fabled conviviality of Franklin and the philosopher-statesman credentials of Jefferson, they could make no headway against European nations set in their ways.[20] In less than a year, Adams was reassigned to American minister to Britain, Franklin at long last retired and returned to Philadelphia, and Jefferson became the minister to France. He worked tirelessly to open the French markets to whale oil and salted fish from New England fishermen, tobacco and wheat from Maryland and Virginia, and rice and deer skins from South Carolina and Georgia. He had limited success, though he did succeed in working out a consular agreement with France, which became the first treaty signed by the United States under the Constitution.

In truth Jefferson proved to be more a cultural ambassador than a commercial negotiator. To French intellectuals curious about the new nation, he was an endless source of information. Jefferson made several extensive travels, one trip to England, another to the south of France, and another to the Netherlands and parts of Germany. Constantly he sought to collect information about canals and locks, vineyards, tools, gardening, livestock, and everything imaginable that he thought might be useful to the American people. When Virginia state officials asked him to suggest a design for a new state Capitol in Richmond, he quickly thought of the Maison carrée, an eighteen-century-old Roman temple in Nimes. Jefferson had a plaster-cast model of the Maison carrée made, and he added architectural plans for almost doubling the size of the structure. Thus Jefferson introduced the Roman temple style of architecture to America, where it would over the next two and a half centuries be the prototype of countless government and financial buildings.

Although Jefferson appreciated many displays of art, he believed architecture was particularly important for Americans to learn because the growing nation would be the site of extensive construction in the course of the coming decades. He especially admired the east facade of the Louvre, and recommended it, to good effect, years later to Pierre Charles L'Enfant when he was designing Washington, DC, at the end of the eighteenth century. More personally, Jefferson fell in love with a stylish new urban palace, the Hôtel de Salm, being built for a German prince. It was a low, white, horizontal house with a flattened dome, and from this infatuation would come Jefferson's later determination to fundamentally reshape his mountaintop home Monticello into the iconic house we recognize today. Jefferson would become the pioneer American architect. Jefferson also loved the witty and intellectual conversation he encountered in Paris; he became a committed oenophile, and he acquired a lifelong love of French cooking, later even introducing macaroni and cheese, for example, to the United States. And he was a one-man book buyer for readers back home like Madison. Perhaps most of all he enjoyed the Paris music scene, though he found it harder to replicate this experience once he returned to his homeland.

In 1787 he was shocked to learn that his smallest child, Lucy, who had stayed back in Virginia under the care of an aunt, along with her sister Maria, had died of whooping cough. He instantly determined to bring Maria to Paris. She was accompanied by a fourteen-year-old enslaved girl named Sally Hemings—the sister of the James Hemings already with Jefferson and the half sister of Jefferson's deceased wife—to be her nursemaid and playmate. Within several years, Thomas Jefferson and Sally Hemings would develop an intimate relationship, a relationship that would thereafter remain a part of Jefferson's life and later become a political scandal.[21]

During his first years in Paris, Jefferson completed and expanded a written response to a set of questions put to him several years earlier by the secretary of the French embassy in Philadelphia, François Barbé-Marbois, a series of inquiries about all aspects of Virginia. Jefferson, who loved compiling data, threw himself into this task. The final result, published in English in 1787 as *Notes on the State of Virginia,* was filled with the kind of aphoristic writing that makes Jefferson so quotable. There are famous passages throughout and an outrageous, now infamous passage on so-called African American characteristics that has come to haunt Jefferson's reputation today, although at the time it raised few hackles because it largely reflected commonplace French philosophical thinking about races. From today's perspective, however, it was starkly racist.[22]

Jefferson clearly loved his time in France: the food, the wine, the philosophical conversations, the art, the architecture, the cosmopolitanism. But he was constantly aghast at the poverty he saw everywhere he traveled, with beggars surrounding his carriage when it paused and looks of hunger and desperation on the faces of the people. This poverty existed side-by-side with the over-the-top extravagance of the Court of Versailles, aristocrats' homes of up to several hundred rooms, and a church establishment of enormous wealth. Jefferson explained the paradox of the people living in passive desperation amid such ostentatious wealth as the result of France being a monarchy. He saw this all over Europe. Powerful monarchs believed their authority came from God, not the people. They had no sense that legitimate political power inhered in the people, and they thought the purpose of government was to increase royal wealth and prestige, not to benefit the people of the nation. As Jefferson wrote Washington, "I was much an enemy to monarchy before I came to Europe. I am now ten thousand times more so since I have seen what they are."[23] Jefferson never lost this powerful antipathy to monarchy, and it would later be the root of his opposition to Alexander Hamilton and the Federalists, who he saw as unabashed monarchists. His deepest political belief was that the basis of government authority rested in the people. He was the profoundest democrat of the leading Founding Fathers. For that reason he was an admirer of the Articles of Confederation government in part for its absence of a strong executive and its limited powers, both of which truly represented the American political consensus in the midst of the American Revolution when the Confederation government was being drafted. Jefferson's political antennae were usually sensitive, but at a distance of four thousand miles they completely failed in the mid-1780s to pick up signals of distress and crisis from the United States.

Already by early 1784 there were intimations of economic problems in the US. Individual states and the central government itself had accrued debts, both to individuals and to British merchants, and none of the governmental bodies had adequate funds to pay them off; some people even wanted to repudiate the debts to British creditors, which struck more principled leaders like George Mason and James Madison as outrageous. A fever of irrepressible land speculation arose, and the disruption of traditional trade relations with England led to economic distress, foreclosures, and a collapse of agricultural markets. Exports of rice and tobacco fell by at least a quarter, damaging the southern agricultural economy and rendering both states and individuals incapable of paying their debts. One estimate suggests the five southern states owed 84 percent of the total debt to England.[24] Britain prevented American shippers from trading with her West Indies colonies and disallowed imports into Britain of goods from the United States that could be imported directly from British colonies, both serious blows to the US economy.[25] Desperate debtors pressured state legislatures for relief, with demands for stay laws to delay payment dates and even develop installment plans for debt repayment. Such actions angered creditors, but many farmers were truly destitute.

In fact, the American economy as a whole plummeted into a deep depression in the years following the revolution. Land prices and rental rates fell, credit dried up, tax revenues collapsed, and there were shortages of currency. The Confederation's requests to states went unheeded. In such hard times, many could not afford to pay their taxes, and rising tax rates only exacerbated the problems debtors faced. National leaders like Washington and Madison understood that maintaining full faith with European creditors was absolutely essential for the nation's survival. A bankrupt Confederation could not field an army, could not enforce its laws, or put down riots and insurrections. For such men, the fiscal failures of the Confederation threatened the survival of the nation.[26]

Those who had experienced the difficulties of the late revolution, people like Washington and Alexander Hamilton, were fully aware that the Articles of Confederation government required some changes to meet this spectrum of difficulties, especially giving the government the power to compel the payment of taxes to settle legitimate debts; enforcement of levies, not just polite requests, were necessary. Merchants increasingly realized that the states needed to act as one in order to work out commercial agreements with nations like Britain and France. Although the Articles had created a quasi-nation that was essentially a league of friendship among independent states, more unity of action was needed. The central government simply had to have the authority to work out trade agreements. Even trade disputes between two or more states, like Maryland and Virginia over commerce on the Potomac, or New York, Connecticut, and New Jersey over the harbor afforded by the Hudson River, suggested that bilateral or multilateral agreements were essential. The shortage of hard currency led several state legislatures to issue paper money that soon became worthless because of rampant inflation, and conservatives like Mason and Madison were inveterate foes of such currency not backed up by the full authority of a national government that could guarantee its value across state boundaries.

Issuances of paper currency were but one of the many problems caused by state legislatures. These bodies had been significantly democratized in the aftermath of the revolution and their members become more responsive to local pressures. Turnover was extremely high, so legislative experience was minimal. Many of the new legislators had only local and parochial interests in mind, so acts often were passed that pardoned debts, regulated prices, gave special privileges to certain constituents, and funded what later would be called pork-barrel projects.[27] Such legislative abuses worried many, especially Madison. As he wrote Jefferson, irresponsible actions by state legislatures were "so frequent and so flagrant as to alarm the most stedfast friends of Republicanism." In fact, he believed that "the evils issuing from these sources contributed more to that uneasiness" that eventually led to the call for governmental reform than did "the inadequacy of the Confederation [government]."[28]

Inflation and attempts to raise some funds by local taxation led to popular unrest, most notably in Massachusetts, where in 1786 and early 1787 several thousand farmers in five counties, led by Daniel Shays, protested, shut down courthouses, and resisted the efforts of local officers. Eventually the state militia, led by retired general Benjamin Lincoln, was called out to quell the so-called Shays' Rebellion, but not before the event had raised horrors of a more general protest. The Bay State was thought to have crafted the ideal state constitution, now this was happening? Because neither the Confederation nor the state government had funds sufficient to pay the state troops, wealthy merchants stepped forward to loan money to support the military expedition. Had the nation won its independence only to fall into internecine conflict, lawless mob rule, economic collapse, and a helpless government? Concerned nationalists in other states reacted in horror. As Washington wrote General Lincoln in Massachusetts, "Are your people getting mad? Are we to have the goodly fabric that eight years were spent in raising pulled over our heads? What is the cause of all these commotions? When & how will they end?"[29] Two months later he wrote that if the government "shrinks, or is unable to enforce its laws . . . anarchy & confusion must prevail."[30] Washington's fears were shared by many of his fellow citizens, and Shays' Rebellion contributed to a widening sense of crisis. Would the new nation survive, or were drastic measures called for?

John Marshall, an up-and-coming political leader in Virginia who had just recently married and was beginning his law practice in Richmond, reacted with similar fear to news from Massachusetts. In a letter, he reflected what appears to have been a common view:

> These violent, I fear bloody, dissentions in a state I had thought inferior in wisdom and virtue to no one in the union, added to the strong tendency which the politics of many eminent characters among ourselves have to promote private and public dishonesty cast a deep shade over that bright prospect which the revolution in America and the establishment of our free governments had opened to the votaries of liberty throughout the globe. . . . I fear we may live to see another revolution.[31]

A distraught John Jay in New York City wrote Washington that events caused him "to look forward to Evils and Calamities."[32] In a thoughtful reply Washington responded:

> Your sentiments, that our affairs are drawing rapidly to a crisis, accord with my own. What the event will be is also beyond the reach of my foresight. We have errors to correct. We have probably had too good an opinion of human nature in forming our confederation. Experience has taught us, that men will not adopt & carry into execution, measures the best calculated for their own good without the intervention of a coercive power. I do not conceive we can long exist as a nation, without having lodged somewhere a power which will pervade the whole Union in as energetic a

> manner, as the authority of the different state governments extends over the several States. . . . What astonishing changes a few years are capable of producing! I am told that even respectable characters speak of a monarchial form of government without horror.[33]

Having no strong executive officer, the Articles of Confederation government could not energetically enforce its legislation or respond to crises, and corrective changes to the system of government were prevented by the necessity of obtaining unanimous consent by all the states for any amendments. The three-year term limitations on government service meant that no body of legislators could emerge with expertise at governance on the national level. Structural flaws in the political system, therefore, hampered effective responses to the problems encountered. Slowly, concerned leaders came to realize that some kind of action was required to save the new nation from economic collapse and political turmoil.

Ironically, in faraway France, Jefferson, upon hearing of the farmer protests in Massachusetts (and other problems), saw little to worry about. He even wrote Madison in January 1787 that "the late troubles in the Eastern states. . . . do not appear to threaten serious consequences."[34] Jefferson seemed blissfully unaware of the severe economic problems besetting his homeland. In fact, the ever-idealistic Jefferson, surrounded by a passive population in France that submitted supinely to the tyranny of a monarch and a domineering church, found absolutely refreshing the image of hearty American farmers standing up for their rights. In this frame of mind he wrote Abigail Adams one of his most famous if misunderstood letters: "The spirit of resistance to government is so valuable on certain occasions, that I wish it to be always kept alive. . . . I like a little rebellion now and then. It is like a storm in the Atmosphere."[35] He specifically had in mind the absence of popular democratic protest to political tyranny in a monarchial polity. Jefferson's sentiment was much different from Madison's evaluation of events. Three days after Jefferson's quotable letter to Abigail Adams, Madison wrote Edmund Pendleton, "Our situation is becoming every day more & more critical. . . . [T]he existing Confederacy is tottering to its foundation."[36]

For Jefferson and Patrick Henry—oddly linked on this occasion—another worry loomed far more perilously than the farmers' revolt in Massachusetts. Practically the entire export trade from the growing western territories flowed down the Mississippi River and through the Spanish-held port of New Orleans to the world. Trans-Appalachian farmers had to have this access for their agricultural products if they were to prosper. Spain, opposed to the American growth in the West, in July 1784 closed the river to US navigation, a devastating blow to the western population. Governor Henry of Virginia was passionately opposed to the closure. Congress appointed Secretary of Foreign Affairs John Jay to attempt a settlement with Spanish diplomat Don Diego de Gardoqui, an extraordinarily skilled negotiator who, certainly from a southern and western perspective, decidedly bested Jay. Gardoqui offered to open trade to Spain of New England fish and naval timbers (but not southern tobacco), which could be transported in US ships, all in exchange for Jay accepting the closure of the Mississippi. Jay agreed to Gardoqui's proposal—lucrative for New England and catastrophic for the West. Henry was apoplectic, and Jefferson—a lifelong defender of US trade via the Mississippi—categorically opposed the Jay-Gardoqui agreement.

Jefferson always believed that American farmers' prosperity depended upon their ability to export their bumper crops. Keeping the Mississippi River open, not Shays' Rebellion, was the critical issue to Jefferson. As he wrote Madison, "The act which abandons the navigation of the Missisipi [*sic*] is an act of separation between the Eastern and Western country."[37] Madison and Washington agreed. This was the most explosive and intractable political controversy during the Confederation era. The treaty could not pass because the Articles of Confederation had specified that approval required the support of nine states, and the proposed treaty with Spain could only garner seven. From this controversy dated Henry's implacable opposition to strengthening the central government, and it almost fractured the fragile nation.[38]

Amid this backdrop of financial and diplomatic stress, a series of seemingly unrelated meetings to discuss commerce along the Potomac had consequences no one could have imagined. Washington and Mason, whose plantation estates were on the Potomac, had long envisioned expanding the river's role in trade. Both men, who had been devoted speculators in the lands in the West, believed that if the Potomac could be cleared of obstacles, and locks and canals were constructed to get around rapids, it could be an artery of trade and commerce to the West that would promote population and growth, unite the eastern and western states thereby strengthening the union, and bring additional prosperity to Alexandria, which lay just a few miles from both Mount Vernon and Gunston Hall. Yet there were controversies with the state of Maryland over which state had sovereignty of the river, and clearly both would need to share expenses if the river were to be improved and would need to agree on commercial regulations. For this purpose, the Virginia General Assembly on June 28, 1784, resolved that a commission consisting of Mason, Madison, Edmund Randolph, and Alexander Henderson would arrange to meet the following year with representatives from Maryland to discuss commerce on the Potomac.

Governor Patrick Henry was supposed to notify these four men of their appointment, but whether from laziness or opposition to the plan, Henry did not contact any of them. Mason accidentally learned about the plan when two delegates from Maryland, making preparations to attend, wrote to ask him if they could stay at Gunston Hall while the meeting was held in Alexandria. Washington, learning of the proposed meeting, graciously offered to host the conference at Mount Vernon on March 28, 1785. Mason, arriving there and discovering that the other three Virginians failed to show up, realized that none of them had been notified. Without a Virginia quorum, Mason met only informally with the Marylanders. The delegates did agree to some minor improvements to navigation on the Potomac, for example sharing the costs of lighthouses.

Perhaps most important, the delegates at the Mount Vernon convention proposed that they should meet annually, with the Marylanders deciding to invite Pennsylvania and Delaware delegates to attend the next meeting scheduled for Annapolis in September 1786. The state of Virginia expanded the invitation list still further to include all the states (rather ironically, Governor Henry signed the circular letter inviting them to attend). Only five states actually sent delegates. New York did not send a full delegation, but Alexander Hamilton came unofficially. Initially James Madison feared little would result from this proposed meeting, but he soon wrote to James Monroe that "it is better than nothing, and it may possibly lead to better consequences than at first occur."[39]

Madison grew more optimistic about the prospects for change. Virginia leaders who had been frustrated by their membership in the existing Congress began to hope that out of an Annapolis meeting would come proposals to strengthen the national government. Probably next to Madison, Hamilton—who had been Washington's aide-de-camp during much of the Revolutionary War—was the strongest advocate for a drastically strengthened national government, and he was Madison's equal in learning and brilliance. The two of them spent hours discussing the political situation and the nature of a political solution, conversations rich with importance for the next significant moment in American history. The under-attended 1786 Annapolis convention could not really do much of substance, but it did send a petition to the Articles of Confederation Congress, written by Hamilton (Madison persuaded him to tone down his language), requesting "with the utmost deference" that Congress direct the individual states to send commissioners to a proposed convention to meet in Philadelphia in May 1787 "to devise such further provisions as should appear to them necessary to render the constitution of the federal government adequate to the exigencies of the union."[40] In other words, they would merely consider revisions and amendments to the existing frame of government, nothing too controversial.

With characteristically little sense of urgency, the Congress approved the recommendation on February 21, 1787, that such a convention meet in May to consider revising the government, with no hint of anything more. The states would choose their own delegates by whatever method they thought best. The Virginia General Assembly quickly chose Madison, Mason, and Washington. Madison had to spend days convincing Washington to attend, for although Washington emphatically agreed that the national government needed changing, he was hesitant to become once more heavily involved in the affairs of state until he had a better idea of the chances of success. The Assembly also appointed John Blair, George Wythe (Jefferson's revered law professor), and James McClurg, who was only asked after Richard Henry Lee and Patrick Henry refused to accept appointment. Henry famously (and perhaps apocryphally) saying he "smelt a rat" because he incorrigibly opposed doing anything to strengthen the central government after his displeasure over the Jay-Gardoqui imbroglio. Word that Washington would be attending persuaded several hesitant states to choose and send delegates to the convention.

Jefferson, fully absorbed in his diplomatic duties in France, nevertheless was eager for news from America, but the long delays in getting letters meant that he was always months behind events. Although he believed the Articles needed some slight changes (despite calling it a "wonderfully perfect instrument, considering the circumstances under which it was formed"[41]), he did not grasp the sense of crisis that gripped many who believed the Confederation near collapse. Madison, his closest advisor, did not reveal to Jefferson (as he did to other correspondents) just how concerned he was by the state of affairs. He sent Jefferson a partial list of those expected to meet in Philadelphia and stated that he believed it would be "expedient . . . to lay the foundation of the new system in such a ratification by the people themselves of the several States as will render it clearly paramount to their Legislative authorities," but Jefferson, at the moment traveling in the south of France, did not get the letter until June and may not have, in the rush of catching up on his correspondence, understood immediately what Madison meant by the phrase *new system*.[42] Jefferson had already received a letter, actually written after Madison's, from Benjamin Franklin, reporting that "Our Federal Constitution is generally thought defective and a Convention . . . is to assemble here next Month, to revise it and propose Amendments. The Delegates . . . are Men of Character for Prudence and Ability."[43]

Jefferson must have been beside himself with curiosity about what would be the result of their labors, and he must have sorely wished he could be present in Philadelphia. (Ironically, neither Jefferson nor John Adams, minister to England, would attend the Constitutional Convention.) More letters arrived, one from Madison saying Washington would probably attend, then one from Edward Carrington characterizing the Philadelphia meeting as having the purpose of "revising and thoroughly amending the Confederation." John Jay reported that he was not very sanguine about prospects for reform, saying that he thought "Calamity" was required to make "their Dictates effectual."[44] Madison wrote on May 15 that the convention had finally begun, with Washington present, and on June 6, Madison sent Jefferson a complete list of the participants but then said that with that listing, "I have exhausted all the means which I can make for gratifying your curiosity. It is thought expedient . . . to restrain even a confidential communication of our proceedings." He went on to relay that in Virginia Patrick Henry was still advocating for paper money and that there was "good reason to believe too that he is hostile to the object of the convention and that he wishes either for a partition or total dissolution of the confederacy," the latter words written in code.[45]

These were extremely busy months for Jefferson, for in addition to traveling to the south of France he was engaged in the delicate matter of bringing his younger daughter Maria to Paris to join him and her sister. But Jefferson was aware that important consideration was being given to the matter of governance in Philadelphia, so he found time to write Edward Carrington that he believed the ideal was to "make the states one as to every thing connected with foreign nations, and several as to every thing purely domestic." What would result from the deliberations in the convention? Jefferson complained to John Adams about the secrecy of their discussions ("tying up the tongues of their members," as he put it), but, ever optimistic, confessed that "I have no doubt that all their other measures will be good and wise. It is really an assembly of demigods."[46] Little did he suspect the extent of the changes to the Articles of Confederation being proposed, changes that would at first take him aback when, in a few months, he received copies of the fruit of their efforts, the US Constitution. The young nation had just completed another turning point in its history.

5

CREATING A NEW GOVERNMENT

Three years having passed since James Madison's last service in the Articles of Confederation Congress, and hence eligible once again, his constituents promptly reelected him. In late January 1787 he began his journey northward, traveling the last few days through a snowstorm and finally reaching New York City in early February. Madison's mind must have been racing ahead as he anticipated what might transpire in Philadelphia in three months. Having spent much of the last few years preparing for just such an occasion, he was busy now organizing his thoughts, producing in April a long document that he titled "The Vices of the Political System of the United States," a tour de force of political analysis that laid bare the flaws of the Articles of Confederation government.[1] Although during the previous couple of months he had written a series of letters to George Washington, Thomas Jefferson, and Edmund Randolph laying out his views in bits and pieces, in the document "Vices," Madison brought all his ideas together.

The document listed and elaborated eleven categories of weaknesses (labeled "vices") of the existing political system, the first being the failure of the government to force the states to comply with requisitions of taxes and manpower during the late war. Equally frustrating to Madison were the ways that the various state legislatures "encroach[ed]" on the national authority, the ways states violated treaties and trade agreements with other nations, and how states trespassed on and otherwise violated the rights of other states. He highlighted the unrestricted ability of legislative majorities within states to trample on the rights of minorities. With Shays' Rebellion in mind, he noted that the states could not protect their people against internal violence, the confusion in states over the efficacy of national laws within their bounds and the multiplicity of laws, and the "injustice of the laws of the States" caused by factions within states where sometimes well-organized minorities could harm the interests of the majority.

In a brilliantly innovative analysis, Madison argued that the key to the problem was that the geographical sphere of local governments was too narrow, making it possible for various small factions to organize and dominate. If the geographical extent of sovereignty were enlarged, then the multiplicity of potential factions within them would be so great that no one could dominate and instead they would check each other. In other words, he turned upside down the prevailing thinking that republics could work only in small territories, arguing that in such limited regions factions could communicate and concert to bad effect. Instead, he reasoned, the larger the territory, the safer the rights of all and the less occasion for such tumults as had arisen in Massachusetts. The conclusion was obvious: expanding and strengthening the focus of government at the national level would bring tranquility, prosperity, and, most important, better protect the rights of free men and women.[2]

Madison would elaborate this central idea over the next months, eventually resulting in the definitive essay known as Federalist No. 10, published in 1788 in the landmark volume known as *The Federalist,* consisting of eighty-five essays by Madison, John Jay, and especially Alexander Hamilton, who wrote the bulk of them. But that was later. "Vices" was only a private document in which Madison worked out his thoughts. In the letters sent to several friends during this period, he pushed the ideas that helped form what became known as the Virginia Plan, which shaped the early discussion within the Constitutional Convention. Even before he authored "Vices," Madison had written to Jefferson, who was still serving as minister to France, about the need to devise a "new system" to deal with the mounting problems in the various states. Jefferson probably did not realize just how dramatic a governmental change Madison was contemplating. Madison advocated a radical increase in the powers of the national government: "To arm the federal head with a negative [that is, a veto power] *in all cases whatsoever* on the local legislatures."[3] There could have been no clearer indication of how serious a problem Madison felt the irresponsible (to his mind) state legislatures were, and how dramatically he wished to increase the power of the national government. Jefferson, however, did not like the idea of the negative. He replied to Madison from Paris three months later that the concept "fails in an essential character, that the hole and the patch should be commensurate. But this proposes to mend a small hole by covering the whole garment. . . . Would not an appeal from the state judiciaries to a federal court . . . be as effectual a remedy?"[4] But Madison was fixated on the idea of the negative.

A letter to Washington, whom Madison knew would be attending the convention, on April 16 more fully reflected Madison's emerging views and expressed clearly what changes he thought necessary to the national system of government. To begin, he wrote that he conceived "an individual independence of the States [to be] utterly irreconcileable with their aggregate sovereignty; and that a consolidation of the whole into one simple republic would be as inexpedient as it is unattainable; I have sought for some middle ground, which may at once support a due supremacy of the national authority, and not exclude the local authorities wherever they can be subordinately useful."[5] Madison next proposed a change away from equal representation by the states in favor of representation based on population—to equate tiny Delaware or Rhode Island with Massachusetts or Virginia made no sense to him. He strongly believed the national government should be given "a negative *in all cases whatsoever* on the legislative acts of the States." He then proposed that the national government be given complete authority in matters requiring national uniformity, as in regulating trade, determining the requirements for naturalization, and so on.

National supremacy should also pertain to the judicial branch—most laws should be uniform. Madison called for two branches of the legislature, and he believed what he called a "national Executive" should be provided for, in contradistinction to the current system that had none. There needed to be provision for maintaining peace and putting down rebellions; the government should have the coercive power to enforce its laws, raise taxes, and protect the nation. And precisely because this new government would unavoidably encroach on the "existing Constitutions of the States," it was "essential" that "a ratification . . . be obtained from the people, and not merely from the ordinary authority of the Legislatures."[6] Madison understood how important it would be for George Washington to understand and buy into his conception of a new system of government. An eager Madison came down from New York to Philadelphia on May 3, a full eleven days before the convention was scheduled to begin, and took a room in a boardinghouse where he had stayed during his prior service in the Continental Congress, but no other delegates were yet present. When Washington with his three enslaved servants arrived on May 13, greeted by cheering throngs of people, he chose to stay in financier Robert Morris's luxurious townhouse rather than with Madison at the boardinghouse. The next day, when Madison and Washington walked over to the Pennsylvania State House, today known as Independence Hall, they found almost no other delegates had yet arrived except those from Pennsylvania. Perhaps the unusually rainy weather had slowed travel on the muddy roads.

However, Edmund Randolph arrived on May 15, and George Mason on the seventeenth, so at Madison's suggestion the Virginians, joined by James Wilson, Gouverneur Morris, and Benjamin Franklin of Pennsylvania, decided to meet for several hours each day to discuss their ideas and rehearse their arguments. Wilson, who had a degree from the University of St. Andrews in Scotland, was brilliant, learned, articulate, and strongly committed to devising a stronger government. The debonair Morris, equally brilliant, was witty, a skilled speaker, and dedicated to constructing a stronger government as well. Franklin, both internationally famous and locally beloved, would prove to be the oldest delegate, and although he made few substantial contributions, occasionally with his trademark humor and pithy stories he helped the delegates get through rough patches of controversy. This small group—dominated by Madison, Wilson, Morris, and Mason—met in an almost seminar format for a week, preparing for the moment when enough delegates (twenty-nine representing seven states) arrived to constitute a working quorum.

Finally, eleven days later than scheduled, the convention began on Friday, May 25. The convention was held in what had been known as the State House, a red brick, Georgian-style building constructed in 1753. The ground floor of the State House consisted of two large rooms with a broad vestibule running between them, the room on the west accommodating the state supreme court. The room on the eastern side, known as the assembly room—where the Declaration of Independence had been debated, voted on, and signed in 1776—was forty feet by forty feet, with a twenty-foot high ceiling. Its walls were a bluish gray, and on the easternmost side there was a small dais, with a table upon it behind which was a high-backed mahogany chair. Here George Washington, almost immediately and unanimously elected president and presiding officer of the convention, sat every day the convention met, never speaking except to recognize speakers and otherwise supervise the proceedings. Yet his presence bestowed a sense of essential gravitas. Eventually a total of fifty-five delegates participated, representing every state but Rhode Island. The delegations ranged in size from Pennsylvania with eight and Virginia with seven down to New Hampshire with two. Most delegations numbered between three and four. When Washington looked up, he faced a total of thirteen tables, covered in a green, felt-like cloth, arranged in roughly concave rows, with the six northern states sitting to his right (the table for Rhode Island remained empty), and to his left were tables for the seven states south of New York. Madison sat apart, sharply to Washington's right and against the rear wall, with a table for himself and a convention secretary, Major William Jackson, hired to keep the official journal and record the votes, not take verbatim notes on what was said. Even so, it turned out that Jackson did a poor job of his narrower task.[7] Madison attended every day and took copious notes. Using his own form of shorthand, and expanding and correcting his notes at night, Madison prepared almost a verbatim account of all the proceedings. From his journal comes most of what we know of the convention.

Probably never were all fifty-five delegates in attendance at any one time; usually about thirty were present. The delegates as a whole were an impressive group. Jefferson had been correct to call them an "assembly of demigods."[8] What strikes one today is how young they were, the average age being forty-four, ranging from twenty-six-year-old Jonathan Dayton of New Jersey to octogenarian Benjamin Franklin. Nearly all of them were men of wealth, twenty-nine of them had college degrees (interestingly, the two most famous, Franklin and Washington, did not), and the same number had studied law. A striking forty-two of them had served in the Continental Congress, eight had even signed the Declaration of Independence, and twenty-one had served militarily in the American Revolution, a significant nationalizing experience. Forebodingly, twenty-five slaveholders were among the delegates, including all the Virginians.[9] (Four especially notable men were absent: Jefferson was serving as the American minister to France, John Adams was the American minister to England, and 1776 firebrands Patrick Henry and Samuel Adams refused to participate—the absence of the latter two contributed to the dominance of the nationalist viewpoint.)

The fifty-five delegates who met in the stately room of the State House over the course of an uncommonly hot and humid summer were to create the basic framework for the nation we know today. The only thing of substance done that opening day, Friday, May 25, was the reading of the credentials of the delegates, a formality that included each states' rationale and hopes for sending delegates. Then those present elected Alexander Hamilton of New York, George Wythe of Virginia, and Charles Pinckney of South Carolina to a Rules Committee to draw up the procedures by which the convention would operate.[10] Wythe, a signer of the Declaration, was of course well known and universally respected (though within days he had to return home to care for a sick wife), and Pinckney would turn out to play a significant role in the convention. Hamilton's uncommon ability was recognized, although many found him insufferably vain. He was to play a relatively minor role in the actual convention, though his Federalist essays after the Constitution was signed proved to be somewhat influential in shaping the ratification process and extraordinarily useful to later thinking about the Constitution's meaning. With the appointment of the committee, the full convention adjourned, but the committee worked over the weekend.

On Monday, May 28, Wythe presented their deliberations to the assembled delegates. These rules helped ensure the kind of free debate and decorum that would eventually lead to a successful outcome. Also on Monday, nine more delegates arrived, and George Wythe, speaking on behalf of the rules committee, outlined its detailed recommendations. One of the rules said any member at any time could request that the votes on an issue be formally entered into the journal; George Mason quickly objected, arguing that members should feel free to change their minds after discussion and such recordings of votes would inhibit free debate. Mason's suggestion carried, a decision that proved to be very important, for in the course of lively and honest debate, men changed their minds many times. The other rules, as adopted, guaranteed formal proceedings with free discussion and civil debate. It specified that seven states had to be present to constitute a quorum (no matter the number of delegates a state had, each state had only one vote). If a delegate wanted to speak, he stood, faced the president of the convention, and while he was speaking others could not walk between him and the president or read or talk privately. The president would recognize the speakers and decide their order if several rose simultaneously. No one could speak twice on the same issue without permission from the president, and only after everyone else had had an opportunity to speak. All committees would be appointed by ballot, and when an adjournment was called, all delegates would stand at their desk until the president had exited.

The next day several important additions were made to the rules: no one could make copies of any entries in the official journal without permission of the body of delegates, members alone could read the journal, and, most important, "nothing spoken in the House [could] be printed, or otherwise published or communicated without leave."[11] This decision to keep the proceedings secret was essential, for it allowed absolutely free discussion of all issues, issues presumed to have been decided could be returned to, and delegates could change their minds without threat of later being attacked for inconsistency. And it allowed frank debate of issues that clearly went beyond the narrow commissions attached to the appointment of many of the delegates. Guards were posted at the doorway to prevent members of the public from wandering in and to ensure that no documents were irresponsibly or inadvertently removed from the room.

After the passing of these amendments to the initial set of rules, Washington, in a move clearly planned in advance, recognized delegate Edmund Randolph from Virginia to speak. Randolph, tall and considered handsome, with what one delegate called a "most harmonious voice," was the current governor of Virginia, and he had evidently been primed for his presentation by the discussions with Madison, Mason, Wythe, and Washington.[12] Effecting a stance of humility, Randolph would speak for the rest of the morning and most of the afternoon, briefly laying out the nature of the present crisis and responding with a series of resolves (what became known as the Virginia Plan) to correct the deficiencies of the present governmental system. Although he fulsomely praised the authors of the Articles of Confederation, Randolph's depiction of the current crisis was devastating, so much so that it upset many of the delegates who came directed by their states merely to consider revisions to the Articles. But the next day attention quickly shifted away from the failures of the system and toward the remedies Randolph had proposed.[13]

In his initial address, Randolph had resolved "that the Articles of Confederation ought to be so corrected & enlarged as to accomplish the objects proposed by their institution; namely 'common defense, security of liberty and general welfare.'" Then he began with his more substantive resolutions: representation in the national assembly should be based on free inhabitants' monetary contribution or population or some combination of the two; and the national legislature should consist of two branches, the lower branch popularly elected (with no set term yet), the upper branch chosen by the lower branch (again with no term yet established).[14]

Among other things, he called for a national executive chosen by the legislature but did not specify whether this should be a single individual, nor was a set term recommended. Another resolution called for a council of revision composed of the national executive and some number of the national judiciary that would examine the acts of the national legislature and certain legislation of the several states (Madison pushed for this for weeks, but in vain). He called for a national judiciary composed of judges appointed for good behavior who would have a broad jurisdiction, including impeachment of national officers. Each legislative branch would be able to initiate acts, and the national legislature should have the power to "negative [veto] all laws passed by the several states." (Madison strongly advocated this national negative over state legislation almost to the end.) Provision should be made for the admission of additional states and for amendment of the articles of union. Moreover, state officials should be bound by oath to support the new articles of governance. These new articles should be submitted to the people, gathered in specially called conventions for just this purpose, to be ratified. He concluded, as Madison recorded it, "with an exhortation, not to suffer the present opportunity of establishing general peace, harmony, happiness and liberty in the U.S to pass away unimproved."[15] After Randolph was finished, Charles Pinckney of South Carolina was recognized and laid before the convention his own draft of a new form of government, but we know relatively little about this because Madison gave it such short shrift in his notes. The convention then adjourned.

The following day, May 30, the convention went into a committee of the whole to facilitate free discussion of Randolph's resolutions, with Nathaniel Gorham of Massachusetts chosen chair of the proceedings while the convention acted as a committee of the whole. Gorham, perhaps because of a prior arrangement, made sure that the Virginia and Pennsylvania advocates of a strong national government dominated the early discussion, with Gouverneur

Morris—who as it turns out spoke more often than any other delegate at the convention—leading the way. Morris quickly offered three resolutions: one that a federal system (such as the existing Articles) would not suffice, no form of treaty linking the colonies would do either, then his third resolution revealed his real desire—"A *national* government ought to be established consisting of a *supreme* Legislative, Executive and Judiciary."[16] Quickly Charles Pinckney rose to ask if Morris wanted to completely abolish the state governments; Elbridge Gerry of Massachusetts asked essentially the same question. Clearly some from the smaller states in particular thought they were moving too fast, with Roger Sherman from Connecticut fearing to do so would risk the whole effort. Mason spoke up to say the present system wasn't working and a government should be able to compel individuals, not just requisition state governments. Without doubt, the new government needed the power of compulsory taxation. In the end a majority of the states voted for Morris's resolution. Thus, the basic federation principle of the Articles was rejected in favor of a truly national form of government.

But this fragile consensus soon broke down. Madison was dedicated to changing the Articles' principle of the states having equal representation in the national legislature. He wanted some system of proportional representation based on population. Knowing that if population was explicitly based on free inhabitants he might lose the support of Deep South states, he proposed just stating proportional suffrage. Then several spokespersons of smaller states objected, foreseeing that they would be dominated by the three most populous states. (Virginia alone had more inhabitants than New Hampshire, Vermont, Connecticut, New Jersey, and Delaware combined.) As the discussions continued, it became obvious that proportional rather than equal representation in a national legislature was extremely controversial. It proved to be the most contentious issue of the convention, with the smaller states digging in their heels to defend their position. With no compromise in sight, the convention adjourned.

The next day they decided to leave the issue of representation unresolved for the moment and began to discuss the nature of the legislature. Most delegates desired two branches, but even popular election of the lower branch proved surprisingly controversial, with Sherman arguing that "the people . . . should have as little to do as may be about the Government. They want information and are constantly liable to be misled."[17] Sherman, described by William Pierce of Georgia as "the oddest shaped character I ever . . . met . . . . Awkward, un-meaning, and unaccountably strange in his manner," nevertheless had a sharp intellect and played a large role in the convention.[18] Mason, a born-and-bred aristocrat, rebutted Sherman, describing the legislature as "the grand depository of the democratic principle of the Government." Madison added that popular election of at least one branch of the national legislature was "essential to every plan of free Government."[19] It soon became clear that the idea of popular election would carry the day for the lower house. For the upper branch of the legislature—although it was still undetermined whether states would be equally represented—the Virginia Plan called for its members to be elected by the lower house. Quickly those who feared that an attack on state governments was underway called for the state legislatures to choose the members of the upper branch of the national legislature. Madison defended his original proposal, but on this point he lost.

Next, the convention decided on the powers of the national legislature in its broadest contours. It could legislate in those cases where the individual states were "incompetent," though that phrase was left undefined, could "negative all laws passed by the several states," and could utilize the "force of the Union" against states that refused to fulfill their duties as proscribed by the national government. These general principles were approved, but of course the devil was in the details, and those were yet to come. Still the momentum was on the side of those advocating a much stronger, more decisive national government. There was a growing consensus that the Congress's powers should be enhanced.

The delegates then turned to consider the nature of the so-called national executive, with the discussion somewhat muted because everyone assumed that Washington, sitting there before them, would be the first such leader. In fact, it had been Charles Pinckney, in his plan for the government, who first explicitly called for a president, but for many in the convention, the memory of King George cautioned against a single chief executive. Sherman wanted an executive with minimal powers, while Randolph feared an executive consisting of but one man could be "the foetus of monarchy." Wilson forthrightly called for a single magistrate, saying such would give the most "energy . . . and responsibility to the office."[20] Randolph persisted in his worries, and his fellow Virginian George Mason feared they were proposing an elective monarchy. On June 4 a majority of seven states agreed to a single executive.

Many delegates joined in the subsequent discussion regarding the chief executive. Should his term be for three years, or seven? Should he be eligible for reelection? What should his salary be? (Franklin suggested no salary.) How should he be elected? By the national legislature? By only the upper branch? By some as yet unspecified process determined by the various state legislatures? By a popular vote? Wilson, who more than any other delegate shaped the discussion and the ultimate nature of the office of president, strongly advocated direct popular election, though filtered through a process that resembled the eventual electoral college. Many delegates thought this impractical if not foolish, and the idea of popular election was not even voted on. For the time being, the process hung, as it were, in limbo, with the original proposal of election by the national legislature remaining the most popular choice.

The issue was complex: how could the executive be independent of the legislative branch yet not prone to accumulate excessive power? Almost as controversial was whether or not the executive should possess a veto over legislation. Wilson believed he should have sole power to veto, independent of some council of revision as the Virginia Plan had proposed. Sherman, who wanted the weakest possible executive, wanted no veto power. Others accepted the veto but suggested the legislature should have the right to overturn a veto if two-thirds of each branch agreed. Madison sought some halfway point (although he hoped the judiciary could be involved in some fashion along with the legislature), and finally the convention agreed to delay the final decision until the members had discussed the role of the judiciary. In the midst of these discussions, the question arose as to whether and how a president could be removed from office. Sherman believed the legislative branch could remove him "at pleasure"; John Dickinson of Delaware suggested that on the request of the majority of the state legislatures; Mason opposed both because he believed they threatened the principle of separation of powers.[21] The delegates turned down both suggestions and the issue remained open.

As the discussions continued, it became increasingly clear that the issues were whether the individual states would still exist under a strong national government, and whether the interests of the smaller states would be crushed by the more populous states. Dickinson insisted that the "preservation of the States in a certain degree of agency is indispensable," and Mason agreed that the "State Legislatures . . . ought to have some means of defending themselves ag[ainst] encroachments of the Natl. Govt." Wilson and Madison countered by insisting on the primacy of the national government, with Madison continuing to push the idea of a negative power: "He could not but regard an indefinite power to negative legislative acts of the States as absolutely necessary to a perfect system."[22] On June 9, William Patterson of New Jersey sought to bring everyone back to the wording of their original commissions, to revise the Articles but keep them as the basis of their proceedings. In other words, all this discussion of a strong national government was inappropriate, and as for New Jersey, she "will never confederate on the plan before the Committee. She would be swallowed up. Patterson had rather submit to a monarch, to a despot, than to such a fate."[23] Before things got out of hand, the convention adjourned for the day.

When the delegates reconvened, Roger Sherman offered a compromise of sorts, suggesting that in the lower branch of the legislature, representation should be proportionate to the number of free citizens, and in the upper branch each state should have only one vote. But without a decision on that point, discussion moved on to the precise matter of representation, specifically to what degree property would be considered, or would it be solely a matter of population. Deliberations moved along smoothly until South Carolinians John Rutledge and Pierce Butler moved a resolution to add a phrase following wording about "the whole number of white & other free Citizens . . . including those bound to servitude." Specifically, they proposed inserting "and three fifths of all other persons not comprehended in the foregoing description."[24] This wording, borrowed from a 1783 decision regarding the requisitions placed on states, was not meant to count enslaved people as only partially human but was intended as an estimate of their per capital contribution to the wealth of a state. It was seen as a compromise: southern states would be expected to push for their enslaved populations counting 100 percent to gain more representation, and so the three-fifths compromise was hoped to gain the support of non-slave states.

Madison and others took care to phrase the clause in euphemistic language so as not to have the word *slave* explicitly mentioned in the emerging document. They understood pragmatically that if their work was to be approved by all the states, it had to tread carefully on this issue, but idealistically believing that slavery would eventually die out, they did not want the nation's foundational document besmirched with the offensive word. Nor did they want slavery permanently established in national law.[25] But despite these nuanced concerns, the final Constitution would guarantee the continued existence of slavery—seen as essential for the southern economy—far into the future.[26]

By June 14, most of the essentials of the Virginia Plan were still in place, with a few details added. The committee as a whole believed a national government should be formed consisting of a "supreme" legislature, executive, and judiciary. The legislature should have two branches, the lower branch elected by the people for three years terms, the upper branch chosen by individual state legislatures for seven year terms; among the powers of the national legislature was a negative, or veto, over acts of state legislatures; and the rights of suffrage for electing the lower branch was proportional to the white citizens and inhabitants and "three fifths of all other persons." There should be a national executive, a single person, elected by the national legislature for a single term of seven years; his powers were not limited by an executive council, but he could be impeached upon "conviction of malpractices or neglect of duty." This executive had the right to veto legislation, though his veto could be overturned by a vote of two-thirds of each branch of the legislature. A national judiciary should be founded, a provision would be developed for the admission of new states and for the adoption of amendments, and the legislatures of the various states should be under oath to support the new articles of union.[27] There was no council of revision, but Madison could take pride in what had been achieved and in the apparent progress toward the full-blown national government he had envisioned.

The following day, June 15, William Patterson of New Jersey instantly asked to be recognized and stated that the members of several states wished to offer another plan. Patterson, one of the ablest men at the convention, put before the convention a completely new proposal in opposition to the Virginia Plan that had so shaped prior discussion. Patterson's resolves rejected the clearly national orientation of the Virginia Plan and replaced it with a federal system that restored the power of the states. Accordingly, he emphasized that the Articles should be "revised, corrected & enlarged"—not summarily rejected—to enable the government to meet the "exigencies" of the moment and promote "the preservation of the Union." The Congress should be authorized to pass acts to raise revenue, regulate trade and commerce, and have other needed powers. Taxes and other requisitions should be based on the number of free citizens and three-fifths of other persons. The government should be authorized to elect a federal executive(s) (number and length of term unspecified), establish a federal judiciary, provide for the admission of additional states, and other powers not dissimilar from the Virginia Plan, the stark difference being there would be one legislature and the states would retain most of their powers.[28]

Sovereignty would lie in the individual states, not in the aggregate nation. The intent was clear. The government remained a federated one—that is, a confederation of powerful states—not a truly national one with supreme power. It acted by request upon the states, not having the power to pass laws binding citizens. As such, it repudiated the underlying principle of the Virginia Plan and harkened back to the Articles of Confederation, and its basic flaw. Quickly known as the New Jersey Plan, it meant that now the convention had two starkly different fundamental schemes of government to consider. Weeks of debate, controversy, and careful consideration lay in the future.

Monday, June 18, opened with Alexander Hamilton asking to be recognized, and he proceeded to speak for five or six hours, during which he said frankly that he was opposed to both plans heretofore announced (the Virginia and New Jersey Plans) but agreed that something had to be done given the emergency situation of the nation. He admitted that he considered the monarchial British government "the best in the world" and "doubted whether any thing short of it would do in America." But he recognized the current national revulsion against things British. Hamilton thought, given "the amazing violence & turbulence of the democratic spirit," that monarchial tendencies had to be gradually introduced into any American form of government. The members of the upper branch of the legislature should serve for life (assuming good behavior), and the executive should "also be for life," and he proscribed extensive powers for the executive.[29] When Hamilton finished his discourse, there apparently was astonished silence. No one replied, agreed, or refuted him, and the delegates simply rose and adjourned.

The next day, with no reference to Hamilton's comments, Madison gave a long critique of the Patterson proposal, continuing to defend the strengthening of the national government and minimizing that of the states, including his infatuation with the right of the national government to negative or void state legislation. Madison then had Edmund Randolph's original resolutions, as revised by the several weeks of discussion, reentered on the record, and James Wilson spoke again in defense of the so-called Virginia Plan. By June 19, it was clear that in its broad outlines, the Virginia Plan would win out, but for almost two weeks the debate went on, with various delegates advocating their ideas. Mason, though from Virginia, insisted that despite his desire to form an effective national government "he never would agree to abolish the State Govts. or render them absolutely insignificant."[30]

On June 30, Franklin offered one of his trademark homilies about how in order to make a handsome table out of uneven pieces of wood, the skilled carpenter had to plane the edges off each just a bit to make them fit together, but this folksy call for compromise had little effect.[31] On July 2, just before the break for the Fourth of July, Charles Cotesworth Pinckney of South Carolina (first cousin once removed of fellow South Carolina delegate Charles Pinckney) suggested that a Grand Committee consisting of one person from each delegation be formed to settle the question of the nature of the two branches. The suggestion was adopted, with Mason serving for the Virginia delegation. On July 5, the Grand Committee's decision was as follows: the various states in the lower house would have one delegate for every forty thousand inhabitants of their state; in the upper branch, each state would have an equal vote.[32] The next day, by the slimmest of margins, this recommendation, which later became known as the Great Compromise, passed. (On July 23 it was further decided that each state should have two senators.) It was later decided that a census of the total number of persons in each state would be taken every ten years, and each state's representation adjusted accordingly.[33]

Madison opposed the conclusion of the Grand Committee because he still insisted on proportionate representation in both branches, but the larger issue quickly became how to count inhabitants. Rufus King of Massachusetts stated what others must have realized but did not want to admit, that the real matter at stake was not large states versus small states but between the southern and northern (then called eastern) states. That is, slavery. Gouverneur Morris thought if enslaved people were counted as inhabitants, the southern states would have disproportionate representation in the legislature. Again the bugaboo of three-fifths arose. Butler and Charles C. Pinckney of South Carolina believed enslaved persons should be counted equally with whites, not as three-fifths. Mason objected, even though their proposal would favor Virginia, because he believed it unjust. Rufus King, whom William Pierce opined "ranked among the Luminaries of the present Age," thought counting them at all would outrage those from the non-slaveholding states.[34] Gouverneur Morris argued that to count them would give southern states added incentive to support the Atlantic slave trade. Still, giving in to the reality of the southern intransigence on slavery, Morris on July 12 accepted that for both the calculation of taxes required of the southern states (a concession to non-slave states) and their representation in the national legislature, enslaved people should be counted at the ratio of three to five. Again, this was not a comment on the degree of humanity of enslaved persons but rather an effort to accommodate the interests of both slave and non-slave states; morality was never part of the discussion.

On the next day, Friday, July 13, Butler stated forthrightly that "the security the Southn. states want is that their negroes may not be taken from them." He basically wanted a constitutional guarantee of slavery. Madison made clear that "the institution of slavery & its consequences formed the line of discrimination" between the states.[35] (Ironically, that very day in New York City the Articles of Confederation government, in one of its last significant acts, passed the Northwest Ordinance, prohibiting slavery from any future states that would be organized north of the Ohio River. This was a truncated version of the land ordinance that Jefferson had written in 1784 that disallowed slavery after 1800 in all the future western states, a proposal that had failed by one vote.[36]) For all the delegates present, the most pressing issue was to create a compromise that would allow the formation of a strengthened national government. It was assumed now was the moment to make the nation and the opportunity must not be missed. Ending slavery was considered a cause for another time. After additional discussion, the Grand Committee Report, as revised in relation to counting Blacks at the three-fifths ratio, was narrowly accepted on July 16. One of the most divisive issues of the convention had been resolved through a compromise, although Randolph and Madison in particular were upset that their desired principle of proportional representation in both branches was not accepted.[37]

On July 17, the day began with Delaware delegate Gunning Bedford introducing a resolution supporting one of Edmund Randolph's initial resolutions, calling for the national government to "legislate in all cases for the general interests of the Union, and also in those to which the States are separately incompetent." This of course was music to Madison's ears, but Randolph himself opposed it now, fearing it essentially obliterated the powers of the states. Randolph would eventually refuse to sign the Constitution, something no one would have expected from his opening day introduction of the so-called Virginia Plan. Bedford's proposal passed, but Madison's subsequent recommendation of a national negative failed after only three of ten states accepted it. This proved to be one of his biggest disappointments.

Discussion moved on that afternoon to the nature of the executive, now seen as a single individual. The term of this person was completely unsettled, as was the process by which he would be elected. And could this person be removed from office? Suggestions for term length began with seven years, then six. Some proposed only one term, others called for multiple terms, still others suggested serving for life or good behavior. Mason strongly opposed the latter, considering it only "a softer name for an Executive for life. . . . The next would be an easy step to hereditary Monarchy." (There was an undercurrent of fear of monarchy in the convention.[38] At least seven delegates spoke against it at various times during the deliberations.) The good behavior proposal failed, though the length of the term and whether service was limited to one term were left undecided. The original Virginia proposal had called for the executive being chosen by the national legislature, but now that seemed, to Madison and others, to violate the principle of separation of powers.

Wilson of Pennsylvania pushed for popular election, but the majority of states believed the nation so large that it would be impossible for the public to make an informed choice. In the absence of national newspapers, most doubted that any person, Washington excepted, could have national appeal or even be known outside his state. As we have seen before, Mason thought it "would be as unnatural to refer the choice of a proper character for chief Magistrate to the people, as it would, to refer a trial of colours to a blind man."[39] In this environment, the idea of popular election failed overwhelmingly. Elbridge Gerry suggested the executive should be chosen by electors appointed by the several state executives, a proposal approved on July 19.

The issue of impeachment was equally divisive. Some, like Charles Pinckney and Gouverneur Morris, thought the executive should not be impeachable; Wilson and Mason strongly believed he should be. Indeed, Mason thought nothing was more important: "Shall any man be above Justice? Above all shall that man be above it, who can commit the most extensive injustice?" Madison agreed, thinking it "indispensable that some provision should be made for defending the Community ag[ainst] the incapacity, negligence or perfidy of the Chief Magistrate." With what in retrospect seems astonishing sagacity, Madison worried that the chief executive "might pervert his administration into a scheme of peculation. . . . He might betray his trust to foreign powers."[40] Impeachment was approved by eight of the ten states voting, although for what crimes was not yet decided. All other issues were pushed ahead for another time. William Davie of North Carolina strongly supported impeachment: "If he be not impeachable whilst in office, he will spare no effort or means whatsoever to get himself re-elected."[41]

The delegates continued to wrangle over a number of points, sometimes points that had been much discussed earlier in the summer. Fairly little time was given to the precise functions of the national judiciary and far more on how its members should be appointed, whether by the national legislature or by the national executive. More discussion ensued on the nature of executive impeachment. Then there was debate over how the new system of government being proposed should be approved, by the state legislatures or directly by the people through specially called conventions? Wilson and especially Madison advocated ratification by the people. But now most delegates realized that out of the plethora of ideas and conclusions some order needed to be drawn. On July 23 the convention decided to appoint a five-man Committee of Detail to gather all the proposals and pull them together into a workable set of tentative conclusions, with the exception of the nature of the executive.

Then for the next few days there was intense debate over how the national executive should be chosen. While the majority still wanted the national legislature to make the choice, Wilson and Madison among others pushed for a popular election. But everyone worried about how the voters, spread across the nation, could be sufficiently informed to make a wise choice. Madison in a long address advocated either popular election or election by electors chosen by the people in the various states. But no decision could be arrived at. The perceived practical problem of the lack of a really informed public trumped the philosophical desire to have the people make the choice of the executive. The issue still stewed as the convention prepared to give all the relevant documents and passed resolutions to the Committee of Detail prior to adjournment and a two-week break on July 26, during which time the committee would do its work.

Little is known about exactly how the committee members of John Rutledge, Edmund Randolph, Nathaniel Gorham, Oliver Ellsworth, and James Wilson proceeded, but Randolph created the first draft, a fitting choice since he had outlined the original Virginia Plan at the beginning of the convention. And he made several wise decisions, including having the draft address broad principles only and be written in clear, precise language instead of legalese. And he chose to begin the document with a brief philosophical preamble. It suggested the name of the government be the United States of America; stated the government would have "supreme" legislative, executive, and judicial powers; and specified a lower branch of the legislature serving terms of two years, the upper branch six years, with the first elected by the people, the second by the various state legislatures. It laid out in great detail the powers of the legislative branch, including the power to set and collect taxes, regulate commerce both within the nation and internationally, declare war, raise armies, make all laws "necessary and proper," make treaties with foreign nations, and appoint national judges. It specified that the executive—now for the first time called the president—would be a single individual, serve a term of seven years, and not be eligible to serve a second term. The president's powers were summarized (including command of the military apparatus) but not the mode of his election.[42]

The Committee of Detail's work was impressive, and its members made decisions that might have been implied in the open meetings yet had not been explicitly approved, and overall it clearly took a powerful step toward a national government. But on several issues it contained language that just as clearly showed a deference to the demands of the southernmost states. Surely this was the influence of South Carolinian Rutledge on the committee, but just as surely the other four members, whatever their personal feelings, understood that without this language the southern states would refuse to sign the final document. The creation of the national union overrode all other concerns for the committee members, as it would later prove to do for the convention members as a whole. The language was unambiguous: "No tax or duty shall be laid by the Legislature on articles exported from any State; nor on the migration or importation of such persons as the several States shall think proper to admit; nor shall such migration or importation be prohibited. . . . No navigation act shall be passed without the assent of two thirds of the members present in each House."[43] The southern states whose economies were based on the export of certain crops insisted that their commerce not be threatened by any export tax, and their commitment to keeping the Atlantic slave trade open was unbending even though they used euphemism to hide that ugly truth. Likewise, the exporting states wanted to protect themselves from potentially restrictive laws regarding all aspects of international commerce. These words were a capitulation to the practical necessity of keeping the states united as they formed a new nation.

On August 3 the committee arranged for a Philadelphia printer to secretly print enough copies of their document to provide each delegate with a copy to work over. When the convention assembled again, all those present worked for over three weeks in August with remarkable diligence to pore over the document line by line, often word by word. Much was quickly accepted, but the meticulous examination led to intense discussion. Some of the more aristocratic members like Gouverneur Morris and Charles Pinckney wanted property qualifications for voters for the lower branch of the legislature, but the convention insisted that none in excess of what various states already imposed should be added. A compromise was reached on the length of time new citizens had to have been residents before they could serve as members of the legislature (seven years for the House, nine years for the Senate).

On several occasions over the duration of the proceedings, delegates expressed concerns about potential corruption on the part of government leaders. As early as June 17, Edmund Randolph had suggested that the document prohibit "any emoluments [compensation or perquisites] from foreign states" "to exclude corruption and foreign influence." George Mason, ever vigilant against improper influence, commented on June 23 that "if we do not provide against corruption, our government will soon be at an end." Similarly, Elbridge Gerry had worried on August 13 that "[f]oreign powers will intermeddle in our affairs, and spare no expense to influence them. Persons having foreign attachments will be sent among us & insinuated into our councils, in order to be made instruments for their purposes."[44] (At the time, the foreign powers feared were England, France, and Spain.)

In an attempt to foreclose such interference, delegates added a clause to the Constitution on August 23 and accepted it unanimously. This so-called Foreign Emoluments Clause, in Article 1, Section 9 of the Constitution, states that "no person holding any office of Profit or Trust . . . shall, without the consent of the Congress, accept of any present, Emolument, Office, or Title, of any kind whatsoever, from any King, Prince, or foreign State." Precisely because corruption was understood to have been a consistent problem in English politics, the convention members put safeguards in their proposed new system of government.

On another critical issue, Gouverneur Morris and George Mason on moral grounds strenuously attacked the defense of the slave trade. Many slaveholders, like Mason, disapproved of the Atlantic slave trade, but Charles Pinckney insisted that "South Carolina can never receive the plan if it prohibits the slave trade," a stark reality that could not be effectively rebutted. The day before, Rutledge had insisted that "religion & humanity had nothing to do with their questions. Interest alone," he stated, "is the governing principle with nations."[45] A time limitation was inserted—the year 1808—before which the importation of enslaved Africans could not be banned. Madison amid the debate over the importation of enslaved people essentially defended the euphemistic references to the institution, declaring that he "thought it wrong to admit in the Constitution the idea that there could be property in man."[46] After all, this was to be a document for all time, and he and others believed that slavery would eventually die out. (We today find this belief wildly foolish, but by the summer of 1787—before the invention of the cotton gin—five states, beginning in 1780, had already ended slavery or begun the process, the first time in history this had happened. Hence total abolition was not inconceivable in this context. The majority did not want to lose this critical opportunity to create a stronger nation in a controversial fight over a system of labor they believed was already on the path to extinction. We now of course see this as a tragic miscalculation.)

Chillingly, on August 29, Pierce Butler of South Carolina asked to add a new article to the draft stating that "If any person bound to service or labor in any part of the U. States shall escape into another State, he or she shall not be discharged from such service or labor, in consequence of any regulations subsisting in the State to which they escape, but shall be delivered up to the person justly claiming their service or labor."[47] This escaped-slave clause was accepted unanimously and without discussion. It was simply assumed to be necessary to gain the approval of the Deep South delegates: the delegates' highest concern was the formation of a new government, not taking action against slavery that was widely believed to be a dying institution.

It was decided that navigation acts could be passed by a simple majority. Even most of the delegates from the Deep South states came to accept this, but not Mason, a ferocious proponent of requiring a two-thirds vote to protect southern commerce from what he considered rapacious northern shippers.[48] This would turn out to be a major reason Mason ultimately did not sign the Constitution. Debate ensued over the location of the permanent capital, and over the decision to create a special capital district ten-by-ten miles square. (Mason particularly opposed such a federal district.) And despite Madison's desire, no national negative over state legislative acts was accepted, nor was another pet idea of Madison's, a national council of revision. It was decided that the final document would eventually be sent to specially elected conventions in the states, and the approval of nine states was deemed necessary before the new government would go into effect. Obviously, the delegates recognized the Constitution to be far more than simple revisions to the Articles of Confederation but rather a completely new form of government.

By the end of August the convention sensed that it was coming near to the completion of its work, though the precise nature of the executive still needed to be resolved. On Friday, August 31, Sherman proposed that a Committee on Postponed Parts, consisting of a delegate from each state, be established to provide the final details. Among those on the committee were Sherman, Rufus King, Gouverneur Morris, and Madison. Clearly, the convention chose men who had been heavily involved in the deliberations so far.[49] By Monday the committee had recommendations for the convention to begin considering. On Tuesday the committee took up the contentious matter of the election of the executive. The committee, and this was apparently the work of Madison, now proposed that the executive, whose term was set at four years, should be chosen by a set of electors: each state would elect a group of electors equal to the number of their members in the House, plus their two senators, and this group would meet in their state and vote for two persons, one of whom could not be from their state. They would then send a list of all those voted for to the presiding officer of the Senate, who would then subsequently open and count the ballots. The person with the highest number would be named president; if there were a tie, the top five vote-getters would have their names submitted to the Senate, where, each state having one vote, a president would be chosen, the runner-up being named vice president.

The committee also decided that only natural born citizens (or a citizen at the time the Constitution was approved) would be eligible for the presidency, and the vice president's sole role was to preside over the Senate and vote only in the case of ties. The power of the president was enhanced; now he, not the Senate, would appoint judges, ambassadors, and other officials. At the same time, the president could now be impeached by the House, with conviction voted on in the Senate, but only for treason and bribery. Much earlier, "mal-practice or neglect of duty" was listed; later, "corruption" was inserted; still later, "maladministration" was substituted for mal-practice.

After further discussion, the convention revised the document to have tied electoral votes decided in the House, not the Senate, with each state having one vote to choose from among the top five in electoral votes. (In 1804 the Twelfth Amendment specified that only the top three would be considered.) Further discussion led to the reasons for impeachment being expanded to, in Mason's words, "high crimes & misdemeanors ag[ainst] the State."[50] The precise definition of misdemeanors was left unclear, but the whole phrase was a term of art drawn from ancient British legal usage, with the "high" referring to the office of the malefactor, not the severity of the crime. These most important matters were resolved by the committee with apparently little discussion or dissension. The delegates were exhausted and wanted to finish. A year later Hamilton, in an essay titled Federalist No. 65, commented that the trials of impeachment dealt with "offenses which proceed from the misconduct of public men, or in other words from the abuse or violation of some public trust [i.e., not necessarily from the breaking of any statutory law]. They are of a nature which may with peculiar propriety be denominated POLITICAL." And he accurately foresaw that as such, being decided in the Senate, "there will always be the greatest danger, that the decision will be regulated more by the comparable strength of parties than by the real demonstrations of innocence or guilt."[51]

By the end of the first week of September, the Constitution was nearing completion, so on September 8 a Committee on Style & Arrangement was elected, with Hamilton, Gouverneur Morris, Madison, Rufus King, and William Samuel Johnson of Connecticut chosen to draft the final document. It was Morris who did most of the writing and put the final "finish," as Madison called it, to the document, including the eloquent preamble that most people in the United States memorize at some point in their education.[52] In retrospect it seems odd, and it proved to be a mistake, that no explicit bill of rights was included, an omission that Mason (author in 1776 of the Virginia Declaration of Rights) quite expectedly noted with dismay. Over the weekend, the assistant clerk of the Pennsylvania legislature, Jacob Shallus, was asked to prepare a handwritten final copy of the Constitution, ready to be signed. Working apparently almost without stop, and with a succession of quill pens, he wrote out in handsome calligraphy on four parchment pages, each approximately 23 by 28 inches in size, the full Constitution (in his hurry making several errors that he had to cross over and rewrite). The delegates assembled for one final time on September 17. Franklin, perhaps anticipating some dissenters, asked his colleague Wilson to read out a speech Franklin had written. "Mr. President," read Wilson,

> I confess that there are several parts of this constitution which I do not at present approve, but I am not sure I shall never approve them: For having lived long, I have experienced many instances of being obliged by better information, or fuller consideration, to change opinions even on important subjects. . . . I agree to this Constitution with all its faults, if there are such; because I think a general Government necessary for us. . . . I doubt too whether any other Convention we can obtain, may be able to make a better Constitution. . . . It therefore astonishes me, Sir, to find this system approaching so near to perfection as it does. . . . I consent . . . to this Constitution because I expect no better, and because I am not sure, that it is not the best. . . . I can not help expressing a wish that every member of the Convention who may still have objections to it, would with me, on this occasion doubt a little of his own infallibility, and to make manifest our unanimity, put his name to this instrument.[53]

In the closing moments, Nathaniel Gorham of Massachusetts spoke up to say if it was not too late, he would like to change the ratio of representation in the House from one in forty thousand to one in thirty thousand. Suddenly, no doubt to the surprise of all, George Washington spoke for the first time in the entire convention to support this change. It was accepted unanimously. Then, despite Franklin's entreaty, several delegates announced that they would not be able to sign the document, Edmund Randolph apologetically so, although he did not preclude supporting it in the ratification process. George Mason objected too because of the absence of a bill of rights, because he thought the new government smacked of monarchy, and because he feared it threatened the economic security of Virginia. Crotchety Elbridge Gerry feared the rights of the citizenry were not sufficiently protected. After a few more desultory comments, George Washington stepped forward to sign the parchment document first. In total, thirty-nine delegates signed. As the last delegates were signing, Franklin spoke again, this time to those near him. He confessed that throughout the convention he had looked at the half sun carved into the high back of the president's chair, wondering throughout if the artist had meant a rising or setting sun. Now at last he had, he said, the pleasure of realizing it was a rising sun.[54]

Within minutes the convention adjourned for the last time, and the delegates went together to the City Tavern to have a farewell dinner. They had produced a new system of government, in effect, produced a revolution. The so-called Virginia Plan had essentially carried the day. The result was, to paraphrase the Founders, a marvelous piece of political machinery, one that greatly enhanced the powers of the national government but carefully limited its possible excesses through an elaborate system of checks and balances. It was the result of profound discussion and ample compromise, even on such profound moral issues as slavery. All in all, as Washington later wrote to Lafayette, it was "little short of a miracle, that the Delegates from so many different States . . . should unite in forming a system of national Government."[55] But at the moment the Articles of Confederation Congress was still the operative government. Yet to be seen was whether the nation's people, assembled in conventions in every state over the next few months, would approve this radically changed form of government. And if approved, would it suffice as a viable system? If their present endeavors failed, Madison wrote Jefferson less than two weeks before the Constitution was signed, "it is hard to say what may be our fate."[56]

6

THE VIRGINIA RATIFICATION DEBATE

The Articles of Confederation Congress had been in session in New York City while the Constitutional Convention was meeting in Philadelphia, so as soon as the convention finished its work on September 17, 1787, some ten of its members prepared to journey to New York to take up their positions as regularly elected delegates to the Congress. The Congress had received a copy of the final convention document on September 20, and within days it began to consider how to proceed. Already, opponents of the new Constitution were making their views known, especially George Mason, whose antagonism toward the document he had refused to sign seemed to grow daily. As James Madison reported to Thomas Jefferson, "Col. Mason left Phila. in an exceedingly ill humour indeed.... He returned to Virginia with a fixed disposition to prevent the adoption of the plan if possible."[1]

Opposition to the Constitution quickly emerged in the Congress, although with almost a third of the delegates present having also been at the Constitutional Convention, the advocates for the Constitution seized the upper hand. Madison again demonstrated his mastery of the document and managed to keep opposition from dominating. Several delegates wanted the Congress to positively recommend the Constitution to the states, while others wanted to include possible amendments as well, but the advocates—who already had styled themselves the Federalists—carried the day. On September 28 Congress, having decided that the Constitution should be considered whole, without debate over its parts, "Resolved unanimously" that it would transmit the Constitution to the various state legislatures so that they in turn could submit them "to a convention of delegations chosen in each state by the people thereof" for each state's approval or rejection.[2] (The word "unanimously" referred to the vote to simply *send* the proposed Constitution to the various state legislatures and did not actually mean unanimous support *for* the document, but the astute Federalists knew many would not be aware of this subtle distinction.) This set in motion a remarkable series of state conventions wherein the proposed new form of government underwent rigorous examination. The debates were learned, passionate, impressively thoughtful, lucid, and a testament to the political acumen and seriousness of the American people. No one knew in late September 1787 what the final outcome would be.

Perhaps no person was more supportive of the new Constitution than George Washington, who since his days as Commander in Chief of the Continental Army had advocated a stronger, more effective central government. The day after the convention had closed, he sent copies of the Constitution to Thomas Jefferson and the Marquis de Lafayette in France.[3] Anticipating controversy in Virginia over the proposed change in government, Washington a week later sent copies of the Constitution to three Virginians whom he suspected might be opponents: Patrick Henry, Benjamin Harrison, and Thomas Nelson Jr., all three former governors of the state who in fact did become opponents. Attempting to forestall their feared opposition, Washington stated that he wished that the Constitution "had been made more perfect, but I sincerely believe it is the best that could be obtained at this time—and as a constitutional door is opned [*sic*] for amendment hereafter—the adoption of it under present circumstances of the Union is in my opinion desirable."[4] Alexander Donald, who visited Washington at Mount Vernon in late September or the first of October, said of the general in a letter to Jefferson six weeks later, "I never saw him so keen for any thing in my life, as he is for the adoption of the new Form of Government."[5] Indeed, Washington throughout the period conducted an extensive correspondence with men from across Virginia and the nation itself to keep track of the progress of the Constitution and privately make known his firm support.

Washington and Madison knew Mason would be active in opposition, and, sure enough, Mason on October 7 sent Washington a paper that summarized the reasons he could not accept the Constitution. His initial objection was the absence of a declaration of rights, but Mason's list had grown longer the more he stewed over the new scheme of government. He did not believe the lower house was large enough to be truly representative; he feared that the upper house had too much influence over money bills and would have undue influence over other aspects of governance; he thought the federal judiciary would in effect destroy the state judiciaries; he thought the presidency (and indeed the entire government) would eventually evolve into "a Monarchy, or a corrupt oppressive Aristocracy"; and he was convinced the government's control of "Commercial & Navigation Laws" would be destructive of the interests of the South (and of course Virginia particularly, which was really Mason's major concern).[6]

Whereas Mason was outspoken, neither Washington nor Madison knew for sure where Henry—the most popular and powerful politician in the state—would come down on the Constitution.[7] He was apparently delaying his decision until he could be certain which way the political winds were blowing. But Washington and Madison's uncertainty was removed when on October 19 Henry wrote Washington to say, "I have to lament that I cannot bring my Mind to accord with the proposed Constitution. The Concern I feel in this accord, is really greater than I am able to express." He did say that "perhaps mature Reflection may furnish me Reasons to change my present Sentiments," but if anything his opposition hardened and deepened over the coming months.[8]

It suddenly became clear that the ratification debate in Virginia, whenever it was scheduled, would feature Washington and Madison against Mason and Henry. Most citizens of the state assumed that they would be asked to elect delegates to a specially called statewide convention to make a decision on the new Constitution, and the House of Delegates, meeting in Richmond on October 25, began to debate precisely what the procedure should be to arrange for such a convention. Delegate Francis Corbin introduced a resolution stating "that a Convention should be called, according to the recommendation of Congress." Patrick Henry instantly objected on the grounds that such wording suggested the document as it existed could only be voted up or down. He wanted to add wording that provided that the convention might add amendments. George Nicholas objected to that proposal, saying that such a phrase suggested that the House believed the Constitution was lacking in some form and needed amendments. Mason reminded everyone that he had participated in the convention that drafted the Constitution, and said—holding up his hand—that he would sooner have it cut off than sign the document as it emerged from the convention. Tensions rose until John Marshall, in the most important political action so far of his young life, offered a satisfactory compromise that all could accept: "That a Convention should be called, and that the new Constitution should be laid before them for their free and ample discussion."[9] More debate followed over the next several days regarding exactly how delegates should be elected, with the conclusion that each county would have two delegates and the towns of Norfolk and Williamsburg each have one, and that requirements for voting on the delegates should be the same as existed for voting for delegates to the House. Finally, the date for the opening of the convention was set for the first Monday of the following June.

Even before the House concluded this discussion, however, Madison understood that Henry and Mason were going to be powerful opponents. As he wrote Washington on October 28, "I am not without fears that their combined influence and management may yet create difficulties."[10] As he suspected, over the next seven months Mason, Henry, and other objectors did everything they could to generate opposition to the Constitution, hoping to get as many delegates elected as possible who could be counted on to vote against it. Meanwhile, the Constitution was being considered in other states and as far away as Paris, where minister plenipotentiary Jefferson contemplated the political changes underway in America. We tend to forget how significant an event the series of ratification conventions in the various states were, but more than seventeen hundred delegates, chosen in a variety of ways, eventually served in state conventions, with the cumulative amount of discussion and debate far more than that produced during the four months the Constitutional Convention had sat in Philadelphia, and never before or since has there been such a national concentration on the central issues of governance. For months it was a leading topic of conversation in pubs and taverns, town meetings, and around courthouses. Most of the nation's newspapers wrote in support of it, and pamphlets on both sides proliferated. As Madison wrote Jefferson in Paris, "The Constitution proposed by the late Convention engrosses almost the whole political attention of America."[11] For several reasons the debate in Virginia was the most consequential, but the totality of the ratification debates bears testimony to how significant everyone realized the issue at stake was.

No sooner was the Constitutional Convention over than Pennsylvania politicians began planning to vote on it, but they had to wait until word came from the Articles of Confederation Congress that it was appropriate to do so. Then there had to be elections for delegates to the ratification convention.[12] The Pennsylvania convention opened on November 21. Supporters of the Constitution had the advantage of having James Wilson in their convention, who next to Madison, was the most knowledgeable and articulate defender of the Constitution. In clear, elegant language that delegates at later conventions echoed, Wilson made the case for the Constitution. There were in reality but three options, he said. Abolish the state governments and make one supreme government; form thirteen independent nation states; or create a federal republic that, recognizing the sovereignty of the people, created a limited national government that protected the rights of the individual states. Moreover, all Pennsylvanians knew that the venerable Ben Franklin approved of the new Constitution too. Although the outcome was preordained, the Federalists (as the supporters of the Constitution called themselves, thereby implicitly suggesting that those on the other side, the Antifederalists, were mainly naysayers) gave the opponents sufficient opportunity to express their concerns.

The whole debate was lifted by the quality of the viewpoints printed in newspapers. Practically every point pro and con eventually voiced in subsequent state conventions were first stated in Pennsylvania. Finally though, everyone seemed to realize that there had been enough discussion, so on December 12 the vote was taken. The tally was 46 for, 23 against. A large, powerful state was now on board. But Pennsylvania was not the first state to ratify. The small state of Delaware, wanting protection from its neighbors, had rushed to form a convention and on December 7 voted unanimously in support of the Constitution, and six days after the Pennsylvania decision, New Jersey, similarly feeling threatened by its larger neighbors, also voted unanimously for the Constitution. Momentum was certainly behind the new system of government. In various ways, Pennsylvania forecast the ensuing debates. The majority of well-to-do, educated citizens supported the Constitution as did the majority of newspapers. Urban areas that prospered via commerce were strongly Federalist (and most conventions turned out to be held in cities, making it convenient for pro-Constitution delegates to participate). And in Pennsylvania and elsewhere, with Virginia a strong exception, Federalist delegates possessed the most oratorical skills.[13]

State ratification continued in quick succession in early 1788. Georgia's ratification convention on January 2 unanimously approved the Constitution in large part because of fear of Indian attacks on its western frontier and the danger represented by Spanish Florida to its south. Two days later Connecticut, a small state that was concerned about import duties placed by Massachusetts and New York on goods intended for Connecticut, approved by a vote of 128 to 40, largely because the new Constitution prohibited such duties.[14] Now five states had accepted the new government. Next to consider it would be the influential and populous state of Massachusetts, where a much closer contest was expected.

Virginia Federalists were already heartened by the ratification by three states before the end of the year, and they were gratified to read the pamphlet published in Richmond on December 27 by former governor Edmund Randolph, who had famously introduced the so-called Virginia Plan to the Constitutional Convention in May but ended up not signing the document. In his December 27 pamphlet he laid out in detail his recognition that the present Articles of Confederation government was utterly ineffective but also his various objections to the proposed Constitution and the amendments he would like to see adopted. But in the penultimate paragraph he confessed that "if after our best efforts for amendments they cannot be obtained, I scruple not to declare, . . . that I will, as an individual citizen, accept the constitution; because I would regulate myself by the spirit of America."[15] These words gave great umbrage to Antifederalists, who accused Randolph of hypocrisy and dishonesty, but his words reassured both Washington and Madison. Still, they knew that nothing was certain until delegates voted in the Bay State, in Virginia itself, and in New York—all large, powerful, economically important states whose support was essential if the new nation was to prosper under a new government.

The weather was unusually cold on January 9, 1788, when the Massachusetts ratification convention opened in Boston, and eventually an astounding 355 delegates attended. This was the first convention held in a state in which there was strong opposition to the Constitution, especially in the western part of the state where there persisted sympathy for those who had participated in Shays' Rebellion, and in the faraway Maine section that was already planning for individual statehood and feared the new government might complicate that process.[16] Virginia Federalists like Washington and Madison were deeply worried about the outcome in Massachusetts. In the previous conventions, the Federalists had been insistent that the Constitution either be voted up or down; they resisted any attempts to revise it or call for another convention. Likewise, they opposed attempts to suggest amendments that had to be passed before approval, arguing that even discussion of amendments suggested that somehow the Constitution was faulty. But in Massachusetts, whose citizens were notable for their feisty independence, Federalist leaders both permitted discussion of the Constitution paragraph by paragraph—spending a day and a half on one paragraph alone—and agreed to allow amendments that, if passed, would be presented as "recommended" to be part of the Constitution but not required for passage.

Two old revered revolutionaries, John Hancock and Sam Adams, were given respectful roles in the convention, and finally both—thought to be skeptics—importantly ended up supporting the document. There were some disgruntled remarks about the three-fifths clause in the Constitution, but others pointed to the fact that slavery was explicitly protected only for twenty years—that was seen as an opening for abolition. In part because of popular support by artisans and mechanics in the coastal port cities, where maritime commerce was so important, the convention voted its approval of the Constitution on February 6 by the close margin of nineteen votes, 187 to 168. Because they had been treated well in the convention by the Federalists, the Antifederalists graciously accepted defeat and the decision of the majority, a good omen for the future. Madison and Washington were gratified by the Massachusetts vote, though Madison was concerned over the recommended amendments. Edward Carrington of Virginia, on the contrary, was unrestrained in his pleasure over what the Bay State had done, calling "[t]he decision of Massachusetts . . . perhaps the most important event that ever took place in America, as upon her in all probability depended the fate of the Constitution."[17]

The following week the New Hampshire convention met but could not reach a decision for the moment and adjourned. Rhode Island, which had not even bothered to send delegates to the Constitutional Convention, did not call a ratification convention but rather submitted the Constitution to the voters at large, who overwhelmingly rejected it, and did so in four additional elections over the next two years. (This unruly state did not accept the Constitution until January 1790, after George Washington had been elected president and the new government was well underway.) Massachusetts was the sixth state to ratify, but the matter was far from settled in the nation. In Virginia both Washington and Madison had their ears to the ground, eager for news about not only progress outside the state but the status of the controversy in Virginia itself. They knew that an embittered Mason was pushing his views as effectively as he could, although he was considered less rigid in his position than Henry and, with a series of amendments, Mason could perhaps be expected to accept a revised Constitution, aware as he was of the inadequacies of the Articles of Confederation government.

Patrick Henry was another matter. His opposition was now incorrigible. Federalists feared he opposed the whole idea of a strong central government over all the states and that he believed that Virginia was so powerful the other states would bend to its position. As Carrington, a former officer during the Revolutionary War and a strong nationalist, wrote Madison in January, "Mr. Henry, it is said, is determined to amend & leave the fate of the measure to depend on all the other States conforming to the Will of Virginia. His language, is, that the other States cannot do without us, and therefore we can dictate to them what terms we please."[18] With his immense popularity in the state and unparalleled oratorical skill, Henry was feverishly working to generate opposition to the Constitution. Even with the momentum created by the approval of Pennsylvania and Massachusetts, the final issue was by no means settled. As Madison had written Jefferson in December, "Mr. Henry is the great adversary who will render the event precarious."[19]

In early March, elections were held throughout Virginia for delegates to the ratifying convention scheduled to meet in June, with 170 eventually being chosen. Five of Virginia's seven delegates to the Constitutional Convention were elected to the ratifying convention also, but Dr. James McClurg and George Washington chose not to run. That did not mean that Washington would be inactive on behalf of the cause. He wrote numerous letters and in other ways let his opinion be known, and of course his unrivaled prestige meant that he was an important, indispensable force in the campaign even from Mount Vernon. Jefferson was in France and played no role, and opponent Richard Henry Lee opted not to put himself up for election. Madison, who wished he could watch from the sidelines as did Washington, got intense pressure to run, and finally he gave in reluctantly to the urgings of his friends in Orange County, confessing to Washington, "I can say in great truth however that in this overture I sacrifice every private inclination to considerations not of a selfish nature. I foresee that the undertaking will involve me in very laborious and irksome discussions; that public opposition to several very respectable characters whose esteem and friendship I greatly prize may unintentionally endanger the subsisting connection; and that disagreeable misconstructions . . . may be the fruit of those exertions."[20] In spite of his reservations, Madison would go on to play a dominant role in the ratifying convention.

At this moment no one could predict the outcome, or even how particular men might vote. For example, Washington was yet unsure of James Monroe's position. Of one person, however, there was no doubt. Henry was busy sowing dissention, first calling for a second Constitutional Convention, then saying numerous amendments were needed, and many felt he really wanted not one central government but three confederations representing the different sections of the county. Still as late as May, Mason could write, "I think the Convention of Virginia will be so equally divided, that no man can at present form a judgment of what may be the determination."[21]

Maryland was the next state to consider the Constitution. Here the Federalists were in full command, and the state voted its approval on April 28. South Carolina's delegation assembled in May, and once more those with strong maritime and commercial involvements dominated. Moreover, with the state's slavery interests having been well protected through the labors of its delegates to the Constitutional Convention, as well as the ban on export taxes, no significant opposition arose in this proud and touchy state. Its convention voted 149 to 73 in approval of the Constitution on May 23. So by the end of the month eight states had approved the document, one short of the nine necessary to set the new government in motion. But the oldest, richest, and most populous state had not yet decided, and everyone doubted that the government could be a success without the support of Virginia.

Federalist leaders across the nation felt by the first of June that the fate of the nation hung precariously in the balance: what would be the outcome in Virginia? On the one hand, if Virginia rejected the Constitution, would North Carolina then follow suit, and would that persuade New York to vote negatively too? How could the Constitution survive if both Virginia and New York rejected it? On the other hand, if Virginia accepted it, surely North Carolina would also, and that would likely pressure New York to accept it too. The contest in Virginia, whatever the decision, would be immensely important.

Meanwhile, in distant France, Thomas Jefferson was struggling to come to terms with the new Constitution, with his opinion shifting as he learned—and thought—more about it. Eventually he would describe it as "unquestionably the wisest ever yet presented to men," but it took him many months to come to that conclusion.[22] His absence from the scene in the United States meant that Jefferson was not as aware as were local statesmen of the economic problems that beset the nation, but Washington had written him at the end of May 1787, just before the Constitutional Convention was to open in Philadelphia, that the "situation of the General Government . . . is shaken to its foundation. . . . Unless a remedy is soon applied, anarchy and confusion will inevitably ensue."[23] Madison followed up with a letter giving Jefferson the names of many of the delegates assembling, and although he was unsure what the result of the convention would be, he reported auspiciously that "there can be no doubt but that the result will in some way or other have a powerful effect on our destiny."[24] Jefferson had previously remarked that the "Confederation is a wonderfully perfect instrument, considering the circumstances under which it was formed," but by mid-1787 he recognized that changes were needed. As he put it, he would like to "make the states one as to every thing connected with foreign nations, and several as to every thing purely domestic." And he understood the executive office needed to be strengthened and made more effective.[25]

Before he learned the results of the convention, Jefferson had triumphantly praised his nation's resiliency, writing that "Happy for us, that when we find our constitutions defective and insufficient to secure the happiness of our people, we can assemble with all the coolness of philosophers and set it to rights, while every other nation on earth must have recourse to arms to amend or to restore their constitutions."[26] But then Jefferson began to get word that the result of the convention was far more than just some revisions to the Articles and was instead a strikingly different new system of government. When by mid-November he began receiving copies of the new Constitution, he was taken aback. He quickly wrote John Adams, "There are things in it which stagger all my disposition to subscribe to what such an assembly has proposed." He especially disliked the fact that there were no term limitations for the president; like a Polish king, Jefferson quipped, a president could be repeatedly reelected for life.[27]

And after Jefferson received on November 26 a letter from Adams commenting on the absence of a bill of rights, that too instantly became another chief Jefferson criticism of the Constitution. Perhaps after popular opinion was heard, Jefferson pondered, it would be advisable to hold a second constitutional convention, clearly not appreciating what a can of worms that would be. Then he received several letters from Madison first outlining the parameters of the newly proposed government and then justifying it in great detail.[28] Slowly Jefferson began to come around, though his concerns did not vanish immediately. He engaged in a flurry of correspondence, both about the Constitution itself and the political scene in Virginia as its ratifying convention approached. Soon Jefferson came to believe that the good outweighed the problematical in the Constitution, leading him to write Madison that he was glad to hear that the document was being "received with favor. I sincerely wish that the 9 first conventions may receive, and the 4. last reject it. The former will secure it finally, and the latter will oblige them to offer a declaration of rights in order to complete the union."[29] Madison did not reply to this letter. Every politically sentient person in Virginia was alert to the political issues at stake as the ratifying convention drew near. Edward Carrington wrote Jefferson on May 14, remarking that soon eight states would have approved the Constitution—and South Carolina did approve on May 23—so the ultimate issue was dependent on the outcome in Virginia. The Virginia delegates would gather, believed Carrington, "under very critical circumstances, because upon her decision will, in my opinion, depend not the fate of the Measure, but whether some degree of convulsion shall, or shall not, attend its Maturation. . . . Should Virginia adopt, [and thereby effect a revolution without violence] . . . we may exhibit to the world this instance of our superior wisdom and benevolence."[30]

By this point Jefferson's opinion had significantly evolved on the basis of additional information—especially from Madison but from others as well—and much consideration. (Madison here and elsewhere over the duration of their long friendship had the ability to calm Jefferson's fears or hopes and moderate his often expansive and even at times naive idealism.[31]) No longer did he believe a second convention was needed. Writing to Carrington even before receiving his most recent letter, Jefferson said that he learned "with great pleasure the progress of the new Constitution. Indeed I have presumed it would gain on the public mind, as I confess it has on my own. At first, tho I saw the great mass and groundwork was good, I disliked many appendages. Reflection and discussion have cleared off most of these."[32] By late July, having learned—to get ahead of our story—that Virginia had ratified, he wrote that although he still desired a bill of rights, he assumed that would come through the amendment process. "We can surely boast of having set the world a beautiful example of a government reformed by reason alone without bloodshed."[33] He was pleased to write Madison that "I sincerely rejoice at the acceptance of our new constitution by nine states [it was actually then eleven]. It is a good canvass, on which some strokes only [a bill of rights] want retouching." And by August 12 he was writing that this defect "will pretty certainly be remedied."[34] In the coming months he became a strong advocate of the Constitution. Jefferson—and the nation—had made a remarkable intellectual journey over the last two years, and no state better illustrated the debate and discussion that produced that political transformation than Virginia, whose ratification convention opened June 2, 1788.

The city of Richmond, with a population of hardly two thousand, had been the capital of the state for less than a decade, and the Jefferson-designed Capitol Building was not yet completed. The city was filling up in late May and early June as the 170 delegates, plus hundreds of citizens who wanted to hear the debates, crowded in. The stagecoach line accommodated the crush of visitors by adding Sunday coaches. Ironically, Madison, who in 1787 had arrived at the Constitutional Convention days early, incorrectly assumed nothing would happen on Monday, June 2, the day scheduled for the opening of the ratification convention, so he arrived in the evening, but the convention had begun on time.

That first day the delegates elected the elderly Edmund Pendleton, a highly respected judge renowned for his legal discernment, president of the convention. Though he was on crutches and seemingly physically infirm, he was mentally sharp and summoned forth the energy to play an important role in the convention. The delegates on the first day organized several committees; arranged to have key documents printed and distributed to the delegates; named a chaplain who would daily open the meetings with prayer; chose clerk of the House of Delegates John Beckley to be secretary of the convention; and permitted a non-delegate, David Robertson, to attend each day and from his seat in the gallery take notes of the proceedings. For that reason, we have for Virginia by far the most complete notes—almost verbatim—of the debates of any ratifying convention.

On June 3, the delegates decided that the convention would sit as a committee of the whole for the debates, a process that allowed much freer discussion. By appointing others—George Wythe for most days, Benjamin Harrison for one day, and Thomas Mathews for two—to preside, President Pendleton was free to enter into the discussion, and he was extraordinarily skilled at debate. The overall quality of the debates was astonishingly high: the speakers were generally eloquent, respectful to each other, and informed. Unlike in all the previous states that had held ratifying conventions and in which the great majority of the most talented, educated, and influential delegates were firm supporters of the Constitution, in Virginia those in opposition were a good match for the supporters in both ability and prestige. While no Antifederalist could compare with Madison's knowledge of the Constitution, no Federalist could equal the persuasive oratory of Patrick Henry. Both sides had advocates of real distinction, and what was to follow over the next three and a half weeks was an exchange of ideas, political theories, and serious intellectual consideration of the Constitution that was equaled in no other state.

Shortly after being elected presiding officer of the convention, the venerable Pendleton offered remarks that to a substantial degree set the tone for the next three weeks of deliberations:

> We are met together on this Solemn Occasion as Trustees for a Great people, the Citizens of Virginia, to deliberate & decide upon a Plan proposed for the Government of the United States.... The Trust is *Sacred & important,* and requires our most Serious *Attention.* Let us calmly reason With each other, as Friends, having all the same end in view, the real happiness of our *Constituents,* avoiding all *heats, Intemperance & Personal Altercations,* which always *impede,* but never *Assist Fair* Investigation. Let us Probe the Plan to the Bottom, but let us do it with *Candor, temper* & mutual *Forbearance:* & finally decide as our Judgment shall direct.[35]

On the next day, Mason spoke, recommending that the body discuss the proposed Constitution "clause by clause" before any portion of it be voted upon. Madison instantly agreed, and the convention delegates approved unanimously.[36] This decision has often been declared a victory for the Federalists, but in fact the convention quickly moved away from such a methodical consideration and, led by Patrick Henry, began discussing the document in its entirety in general terms. Henry effectively hijacked the proceedings to the advantage of his forte, spoken argument.

Unable to contain himself, Henry spoke up after George Nicholas of Albemarle County gave a lengthy speech on the proposed lower house (that is, the first article of the Constitution) and how its members were to be elected. He ignored Nicholas's comments completely and questioned the purpose of the new government. Henry said the commonwealth of Virginia had been in "perfect repose," prosperous and in no sense of danger. Now this new government "goes to the utter annihilation" of the good order of the various states, threatened treaties with other nations, endangered the people's liberties, and brought on consolidated government that will lead to tyranny. The phrase "We, the people" forecast such a change, he thundered, voiding the traditional "We, the States." The convention delegates should have simply amended the Articles, Henry argued passionately, not proposed such a dangerous threat to the tranquility of the state and the liberties of its citizens. "You ought to be extremely cautious, watchful, jealous of your liberty; for instead of securing your rights you may lose them forever."[37] Henry knew that fear was a mighty force, and he intended to wield it to squash the Constitution.

Governor Edmund Randolph replied, refuting Henry's claim that there were no problems under the Articles. After all, the previous year Randolph had begun the Constitutional Convention by outlining the crisis the nation faced. He admitted that he had later objected to the Constitution as written, and still hoped changes could be made by the amendment process, but with now eight states having already approved it, the time was past for demanding changes before voting. To insist on them now would bring "ruin to the Union, and the Union is the anchor of our political salvation." For that reason, he would now vote for the Constitution.[38] That admission was a serious blow to the Antifederalists, who had expected Randolph to side with them. After Randolph's shocking news, George Mason tried to pull the discussion back to an orderly examination of the Constitution, clause by clause, beginning with the new government's power to levy direct taxes and the overall authority of what he insisted on calling a consolidated government. Mason believed the central government should first ask the states to pay their share of taxes and only if they failed to meet their requisition should then intervene to collect the monies. Of course, this had not worked well under the existing government and there was suspicion it would not work under the proposed one, but at least Mason seemed not totally opposed to the new government. *Henry was.* It was clear that Henry and Mason were taking different approaches in their opposition. As Madison wrote to Washington that evening, "Henry & Mason made a lame figure & appeared to take different and awkward ground."[39]

On June 5 Pendleton likewise rebutted Henry's claim that everything was fine under the Articles, and taking particular aim at Henry's attack on the Constitution's phrase "We, the people," replied "Who but the people have a right to form Government."[40] Henry "Light Horse Harry" Lee of Westmoreland County followed Pendleton and also defended the use of "We, the people." Then Henry rose to speak, and he would hold the floor for the rest of the day, addressing first one topic and then another, as though he found so much to despise in the Constitution that he could not control himself. He described the document as an attempted revolution, and he couldn't care less that eight states had already accepted it. He found absolutely no part of it he could approve and by turn labeled it tyrannical, despotic, abhorrent, frightful, detrimental to our liberties, and "among other deformities, . . . it squints toward monarchy." He concluded, after hours of impassioned rhetoric, by saying, "yet I have not said the one hundred thousandth part of what I have on my mind."[41] Already it was clear that Henry was going to dominate the convention, and the Federalists realized that closely reasoned analysis stood little chance against the powerful fulminations of the impassioned Henry. In what one scholar has called Henry's "desperation to defeat ratification," he "was not above resorting to personal invective, disingenuousness, and outright demagoguery."[42]

Friday, June 6 began with Governor Randolph, speaking as "a child of the revolution," emphasizing how important was the union. Virginia could not stand by while already eight states had ratified, for not only would that risk the union, but Virginia could not thrive going alone. "I believe, that as sure as there is a God in Heaven, our safety, our political happiness and existence, depend on the Union of the States; and that without this Union, the people of this and the other States, will undergo the unspeakable calamities, which discord, faction, turbulence, war, and bloodshed, have produced in other countries."[43] Madison spoke up, drawing upon reason and historical evidence to make his points with impressive erudition, but he spoke so softly that note-taker Robertson said he could not hear everything Madison said. Madison emphasized how innovative the newly proposed government would be: "In some respects, it is a Government of a federal nature; in others it is of a consolidated nature."[44] While the central government would have clear strengths and prescribed authority, the state governments would continue to play an important role.

Throughout the convention Madison emphasized this balance between the national and the state governments, as he did the balance, within the constitutional framework itself, between the executive, legislative, and judicial branches of government. (This was, after all, a key point he had made with great clarity and vigor in his essay known as Federalist No. 51.) Alluding obviously to Henry, Madison said the delegates should not aim their "arguments to the feelings and passions" of the people but rather should "enquire whether [the Constitution] will promote the public happiness."[45] George Nicholas closed the long day with further attacks on Henry's complaints about the size of the legislature—how could such a relatively small number of delegates truly represent the nation?

In the convention's Saturday deliberations, Francis Corbin, Governor Randolph, and Madison continued to defend the method of representation proposed by the Constitution, discussed its powers to levy taxes, and in general elaborated on issues already addressed. That afternoon Henry replied to all, arguing that he sought to defend the nation's liberties, which were under threat by the new government. He specifically addressed the three earlier speakers, concluding by arguing that a bill of rights was "indispensably necessary."[46] With that, the convention adjourned until Monday morning. That first week, Henry had spoken extensively on three days, and every advocate for the Constitution who addressed the convention had focused their remarks on what Henry had said. He was dominating the convention even when silent.

Monday opened with Henry again holding forth, and he would continue for most of the day. As was Henry's wont, he did not analyze particular portions of the Constitution but railed against it in general. That Monday he suggested that 80 percent of the citizens of Virginia opposed the new plan and said that "No Government can flourish unless it be founded on the affection of the people." Taking scattershot jabs at the Constitution, he said he agreed with George Mason that the presidency of such a large nation would become an "absolute despotism." Commenting on foreign policy, the nature of representation, and whatever else came to mind, he insisted that "Congress by the power of taxation—by that of raising an army, and by their control over the militia, have the sword in one hand, and the purse in the other." The implication of course was that the people's liberty was at grave risk.[47]

Here and elsewhere Henry was employing both explicit and coded language to suggest that a powerful central government would threaten the South's institution of slavery. Congress could use its implied powers "to liberate every one of your slaves."[48] Henry of course was a slaveholder, but he spoke not primarily out of self-interest but because he understood how prevalent such proslavery sentiment was in the state. With what was left of that afternoon, Henry Lee and Edmund Randolph responded to Henry, Lee quite sharply, but the actual details of the Constitution were not being considered in an orderly fashion, a procedure—with Madison's mastery of the document—that would have clearly favored the Federalists. Randolph continued his remarks the next day; however, gradually, in random fashion, the Federalists as they replied to Henry's wide-ranging attacks were elaborating and defending the Constitution, but their elucidation was less effective than it might have been had the discussion proceeded more systematically.

On June 10 a new speaker was heard. James Monroe, a delegate from Spotsylvania County, had just recently turned thirty, and Madison had expected him to be a "cool" supporter of the Constitution. Monroe's background suggested that. Born April 28, 1758, in Westmoreland County (also the birthplace of Washington and Madison—and later, Robert E. Lee), he had dropped out of the College of William and Mary to join the Patriot cause. Monroe served in the military for more than two years, impressed General Washington, and was badly injured at the Battle of Trenton but after recovery rejoined the fighting. As an aide to Lord Stirling, one of Washington's brigade commanders, Monroe came to know Alexander Hamilton, John Marshall, and others who would play a major role in American history. In 1780 he made acquaintance with then-governor Jefferson, read law under his tutelage, and broadened his viewpoints, although he never finished his college degree. Monroe's military experience had a nationalizing influence on him, as it did on so many others, and convinced him of the inadequacies of the Articles government and the need for broader taxing powers, a stronger executive, and national authority over militias and international trade. He also developed great interest in the West.

In the spring of 1782, he was elected to the House of Delegates from King George County (where he owned both land and enslaved laborers), became a member of the Governor's Council, and in late 1783 was elected to the Confederation Congress. While it met in Annapolis, Monroe shared a house with Jefferson and befriended Madison. He married in February 1786, returned to Virginia, began establishing his law practice, and eventually won election to the ratification convention from the Spotsylvania County, where he lived at Fredericksburg. At first, he apparently was quite positive toward the Constitution, but during the spring of 1788, surrounded as he was in his neighborhood by Antifederalists, he began to back away from that support. By the time he took his seat in the convention, he had evolved into a mild opponent. Fully aware of the failures of the Articles, he nevertheless saw imperfections in the Constitution.[49]

To those imperfections, Monroe now, on June 10, gave voice. While he admitted the flaws in the existing government, he objected to the Constitution's giving the central government the right to levy direct taxes. He feared that without a term limitation, the president could become a monarch. He was concerned that foreign nations could corrupt the president and his counselors. He feared the unrepresentative nature of the Senate and, with the Jay-Gardoqui debacle over navigation of the Mississippi River in mind, he thought treaty-making should require more than a two-thirds vote by the Senate. He concluded by lamenting the absence of a bill of rights, although he made clear that he supported the general aim of the Constitution and believed, unlike Patrick Henry, that several amendments could correct its flaws. Why such a hurry, Monroe asked, to approve the Constitution? Why "this wild precipitation"?[50]

Perhaps emboldened by the youthful Monroe's speaking up, another new speaker, John Marshall, now addressed the convention, and he wished to answer that question of urgency. Marshall, elected from Henrico County, in which Richmond was located, had been born in 1755, so he was youthful too. Marshall's maternal grandmother, Mary Isham Randolph, was the sister of Jefferson's maternal grandfather, Isham Randolph. Hence, Marshall and Jefferson were cousins. Marshall's parents were of the lower gentry class, and his father, who owned a sizable library, strongly valued education and pushed his son to excel. As disagreements arose between England and the colonies, Marshall soon joined the local militia and then the Continental Army, serving under Washington at battles near Trenton, at Princeton, and enduring the terrible winter at Valley Forge. For him too, the army had been a nationalizing experience, and he also came to see the necessity of a strong, effective central government, one that could raise taxes, enforce its laws, and support an army. In early 1780 Marshall began studying law with George Wythe, passing the bar that August. By 1783, now married, Marshall was living in Richmond and had opened his practice, greatly aided by his friendship with Edmund Randolph, then the city's leading lawyer, and the political influence of his father-in-law, Jaquelin Ambler, who was the state treasurer.

As Marshall's practice prospered, his prestige grew. He had been elected to the House of Delegates in 1782 (along with Monroe), and then named to the

Privy Council. Later elected to the Confederation Congress, Marshall was almost instantly a member of the conservative establishment: men who wanted a stronger central government, one that could provide for national defense and promote international trade, and one that had the stability to protect property rights. In Richmond he was surrounded by this sentiment, so when, in the spring of 1788, he was quite expectedly elected to the ratifying convention, his position as a strong Federalist was foreordained. To that position he also brought a rigorous legal mind, crisp logic, and the lawyerly ability to craft an argument.[51]

In his opening remarks to the convention, he point-by-point refuted Henry's scare tactics and strongly supported accepting the Constitution. If it turned out to be lacking in some particulars, he argued, corrections could be made via the amendment process.[52] On June 20 he discredited the idea that the national Congress could, willy-nilly, go beyond their designated powers and pass laws on any topic. "If they were to make a law not warranted by any of the powers enumerated," Marshall stated, "it would be considered by the Judges as an infringement of the Constitution which they are to guard:—They would not consider such a law as coming under their jurisdiction.—They would declare it void."[53] Here, unnoticed, was a preview of the doctrine of judicial review by the Supreme Court.

By now the pattern of the debates was established. Mason and especially Henry would expound on the dangers to the liberty and safety of the nation that the Constitution represented, and Pendleton, Randolph, and Madison would reply, repudiating what they called the exaggerations of their opponents. Henry described the dangers of the taxing powers of the new government, its potential to misuse the militias, its threat to the survival of slavery, its probable inability to protect the navigation of the Mississippi and thereby jeopardize the economy of the western states. George Nicholas, who planned to soon move to Kentucky, eloquently rebutted Henry's fears for the prosperity of the West. "That country contains all my wishes and prospects," he stated. "There is my property, and there I intend to reside. I should be adverse to the establishment of any system which would be injurious to it. I flatter myself that this Government will secure their happiness and liberty."[54] Randolph discounted the concern about the "danger . . . of the President receiving emoluments from foreign powers. If discussed, he may be impeached."[55] On and on such give-and-take ensued for days, with Henry speaking often, once for seven hours at one stretch. Mason seemed to dig in the more the debates continued, perhaps even moving from "healthy skepticism" to "virtual paranoia," while Madison, suffering through a bout of illness, responded calmly, reasonably, and with careful attention to the Constitution itself as amplified by reference to the actual debates attendant to its composition.[56]

The high quality of the remarks by speakers on both sides—Madison, Henry Lee, Pendleton, Randolph, and Marshall for the Federalists; Henry, Mason, Monroe, and William Grayson for the Antifederalists—made it impossible to predict in advance how the final vote would turn out. (Fewer than 20 of the 170 delegates spoke during the proceedings, and only about a dozen made substantive remarks.) A frustrated Madison wrote Alexander Hamilton on June 16 that the proceedings were "wearisome beyond expression," and four days later he added that there is "a very disagreeable uncertainty in the case."[57] Federalists began to worry that the Antifederalists were dragging the issue out, delaying, hoping that New York, whose convention was underway, would vote in the negative and thereby swing the Virginia delegates to vote similarly.

During the days of debate, each aspect of the Constitution was considered, with the Antifederalists critical of practically every phrase. As Henry said on June 20, "I despise and abhor it."[58] Daily, Henry and his colleagues attacked the taxing policy, the role of the courts, every part of it, repeating their general charges. They were primarily spokesmen for Virginia, not the nation; they foresaw Virginia and the South being marginalized by the new government, putting slavery at risk. Again and again Madison, speaking as a nationalist, effectively defended the Constitution against their specific criticisms, and when he spoke on behalf of the proposed federal judiciary, he could draw on the expert legal knowledge of Pendleton and Marshall. On one issue alone the Antifederalists found traction, the popular demand for amendments, but after even Madison came to realize that accepting amendments would be necessary to win ratification in Virginia, the Federalists succeeded in their argument that any such amendments offered should be addressed *after* ratification in the way prescribed in the Constitution itself, not as a precondition for ratification.

In the waning days, Henry and Mason began to sense they were losing the larger battle. (On June 23 Madison wrote Washington that "the opposition . . . to day seemed to betray despair."[59]) They could attack the Constitution, but, critically, they had no alternatives to promote, and practically everyone except Henry recognized the failures of the Articles of Confederation. The Antifederalists' projections of fear, no matter how dramatically expressed, ultimately could not counter the spirit of hope offered by the Federalists.

The General Assembly of Virginia was scheduled to open its new session on June 23, and sixty-three members of the ratifying convention were also members of the General Assembly, so an accommodation was made by having the General Session meet only for an hour or so in the morning. The ratifying convention could begin shortly thereafter. Accordingly, June 24 began with George Wythe making one of his rare speeches. Speaking so lowly he could barely be heard, he proposed that the convention should ratify the Constitution, with whatever amendments delegates thought necessary being "recommended to the consideration of the Congress which should first assemble under the Constitution, to be acted upon according to the mode prescribed therein."[60] Subsequently a number of speakers then addressed the body, some, like John Dawson and William Ronald, for the first time, and Madison sought to sum up his positive advocacy.

Instantly Henry rose to counter Madison's positive portrayal. "He tells you of important blessings which he imagines will result to us and mankind in general, from the adoption of this system," Henry stated. "I see the awful immensity of the dangers with which it is pregnant.—I see it—I feel it."[61] At that moment a violent thunderstorm struck the area, "putting the House in such disorder," recorded the record keeper, "that Mr. Henry was obliged to conclude."[62] While Henry speaking was like a force of nature, he was no match for the real thing. His dramatic conclusion, however, did not sway any additional delegates. In fact, it is not apparent that any minds were changed over the duration of the debates. Every delegate knew that George Washington supported the Constitution and that if Virginia voted for ratification—but only if—Washington would certainly be the nation's first president. That was the Federalist's ace in the hole that the Antifederalists could not beat.

The next day, June 25, they were to vote on the Constitution. George Nicholas promptly moved that the convention clerk should read Wythe's resolution from the previous day, and then the delegates should vote. John Tyler moved to have the proposed amendments read out also. As was to be expected, there followed discussion by Benjamin Harrison, James Innes, John Tyler, all widely known, then comments by the lesser known Adam Stephen and, notably, Zachariah Johnston, who spoke, as he put it, "without erudition or eloquence, but with firmness and candour." He had, he said, listened "attentively" to the speeches of "Gentlemen of great abilities" and had been convinced, in contrast to the "strained construction" outlined by the Constitution's opponents, "of the safety and propriety of this system." He ended by saying that he was "contented to rest my happiness on that footing."[63] Johnston in his rough-hewn manner may have upstaged James Innes, who even Henry remarked spoke with "great eloquence." Innes, the state's attorney general, was brief and effective. He argued against both the idea of suggesting amendments—let the Congress do that—and holding a second ratifying convention. Delegates should not expect a perfect Constitution, he said with sober reasonableness. "Let us no longer pursue chimerical and ridiculous systems," he said. "Let us try [the proposed Constitution]—Experience is the best test."[64]

Mason had nothing else to add at this late state, but Henry, who had spoken so often, so passionately, and at such length, now clearly understood that he was on the losing side of the great debate. He gracefully begged the pardon of his listeners for having taken up so much of their time and announced that if he "should be in the minority, . . . I will be a peaceable citizen!" But he had not given up the fight, stating, "My head, my hand, and my heart shall be at liberty to retrieve the loss of liberty, and remove the defects of that system—in a constitutional way."[65] And he would be heard from in the future.

After Randolph had a final word, Pendleton, the presiding officer of the convention, announced that Thomas Mathews, chair of the committee of the whole, reported that the committee had resolved to ratify the Constitution. At that moment an unspecified Antifederalist offered a substitute amendment stating that a series of amendments should be submitted to the other states for their consideration before the Constitution was ratified. When put to a vote, the substitute amendment was defeated 88 to 80. Following that, the original resolution was approved by a vote of 89 to 79. A committee consisting of Madison, Randolph, Nicholas, Marshall, and Corbin—all Federalists—was appointed to prepare the formal document for sending the ratification notice to the Congress, and a committee of twenty was appointed to prepare a list of all the recommended amendments. On this committee were several (nine in total) of the most vociferous proponents of amendments, including Henry and Mason, but eleven Federalists were represented also, with Wythe serving as chair. The engrossed copy of the ratification form was approved on June 26, 1788, and the next day Wythe reported the list of some forty amendments, twenty of which were a bill of rights, with the others being structural amendments to the Constitution itself. Pendleton closed the convention the next day by congratulating the delegates on their behavior during the course of the debates and called on them all now to take pride in serving the nation with zeal.[66]

On June 28 President Pendleton sent all the documents to the Congress. In recognition of how close the vote had been, Federalists did not gloat or celebrate in victory, nor did most Antifederalists publicly respond in anger. A truculent Mason seemed the most aggrieved by the outcome, and at the conclusion he called together many of the delegates and attacked the Constitution in such an intemperate manner that several delegates left or simply sat in dismay. Finally Benjamin Harrison suggested they accept their defeat, leave peacefully, and hope for the best. Mason never really got over the acceptance of the Constitution and never reconciled with former friends such as Washington, though he did continue to respect Madison. Just before the conclusion of the ratification convention, Mason had sent a letter to Washington that obviously was intended to patch up their frayed friendship: "I can truly say there is not a Man in the World, who more sincerely wishes you every Felicity, than—dear Sir, Your most obedient Servt."[67] Washington never replied, and after a brief, businesslike request four months later, Mason never wrote to him again.

Mason did have some subsequent correspondence with Monroe and Jefferson, and he even asked Jefferson in early 1791 to effect for him a rapprochement with Madison: "I beg the Favour of you to present my best Respect to our Friend Mr. Madison. He is one of the few Men, whom from a pretty thorough Acquaintance, I really esteem; tho' I have been apprehensive some late Difference . . . on political Questions has caused a Coolness between us. I am sure it has not on my Part; for if I know my own Heart, I have more Liberality than to think the worse of a Friend for a Disagreement on any theoretical Questions."[68] But in the immediate aftermath of the ratification vote, even firebrand Patrick Henry seemed more at peace with events than Mason was, although a skeptical Madison suspected that in time Henry would try to "undo . . . the work."[69] No doubt Henry was already thinking about his political future and preparing to recalibrate the tenor of his opposition.

Virginia had ratified the Constitution—but as it turned out, in so doing it was not the ninth state to ratify. While the convention was underway, the delegates from tiny New Hampshire had reassembled and, unbeknownst to the Virginians, on June 21 reconsidered the matter, this time approving the Constitution by a vote of 57 to 47. Yet it was the Virginia decision that made all the difference. Still to be determined was what the powerful state of New York was going to decide. The New York ratification convention had opened on June 17, while Virginia's was still in session, and for several weeks the debate raged, with Alexander Hamilton, fortified by the *Federalist* essays, working tirelessly on behalf of the new government. Governor George Clinton was one of the leaders of the state's Antifederalists. Then on July 2 word arrived of Virginia's approval, and the news deflated the arguments of the Antifederalists in New York. For a time they proposed a list of fifty-five amendments, then they proposed a second convention. Hamilton and John Jay began to talk of a possible New York City secessionist movement if the state rejected the Constitution. That threat, along with the knowledge of Virginia's approval, led to a narrow 30 to 27 vote for ratification on July 25.

Obviously, the new nation would soon be underway, but this knowledge did not sway the powerful Antifederalist sentiment in North Carolina, where intense localism and a distrust of any form of centralized authority created, contrary to earlier expectations, almost invincible opposition. The state rejected the Constitution in July 1788 but scheduled another convention for November 1789. Madison bemoaned that just before the new government was to commence there was "such a display of locality, [which] portends the continuance of an evil which has dishonored the [previous Congress]."[70] But by the meeting of the second convention, Washington was already elected president, and a sense of reality had conquered ideology. After more than a year, a recalcitrant North Carolina approved the Constitution on November 21, 1789. That left only incorrigible Rhode Island, which finally ratified on May 29, 1790. By that date the United States of America was well underway. But by no means were all political differences settled in the nation or in Virginia. As we will see, newly elected Virginia governor Henry effectively prevented James Madison from being elected to the federal Senate and even tried, unsuccessfully, to stymie his election to the federal House of Representatives by recruiting Monroe to run against him in the redrawn boundary lines of Madison's expanded congressional district. The new nation still had many political challenges to meet, and seven notable Virginians would remain at the center of them all.

7

LAUNCHING THE NEW NATION

Patrick Henry was not about to let the ratification vote in Richmond stop his efforts to fundamentally change the Constitution. James Madison had written George Washington on the final day of the ratification convention that he expected Henry "to seize the first moment" to begin undermining the result of the convention, and that insight proved accurate.[1] On October 29, 1788, Henry declared in the Virginia House of Delegates that he would "oppose every measure" for putting into effect the Constitution unless the House called upon Congress to summon a second convention to change the document because, he charged, "the most precious rights of the people if not cancelled are rendered insecure" by the Constitution as written.[2] Washington was equally worried about Henry's plans to sabotage the new government, and by November, Madison was stating that the "secret wish of [Henry's] heart" was "the destruction of the whole System."[3] They all understood that Henry exercised almost complete control over the General Assembly, and that body would play a large role in how Virginia responded to the new government.

The House of Delegates would select Virginia's two senators, and the new Constitution gave to each state the responsibility for designating the new congressional districts that would in turn elect that state's representatives to the new Congress. The House of Delegates would draw the district lines. As of midyear, however, the existing Continental Congress had not decided when the new elections would take place or when the presidential electors of the electoral college should be chosen, cast their votes, and have them counted. Nor had it decided when the new government would be inaugurated or where it would sit: New York, Philadelphia, or elsewhere. The Continental Congress had appointed a committee to decide these matters, but even though it presented its report on July 8, the Congress did not act on its recommendations until September 13. On that date it decided that the site of the new government would, at least for the time being, be New York City. It set January 7,

1789, as the date for the appointment of the presidential electors, February 4 for their balloting, and it proclaimed that the First Congress of the new government would open on March 4, 1789.[4]

Those deadlines meant that Virginia, along with the other eleven states that had by then ratified the Constitution, had to conduct a variety of elections. Everyone understood that what would happen in the next few months, and certainly in the next couple of years, would have an enormous impact on the nascent nation. No one had thought harder about all these issues than had Madison—it would be fair to say that he had been consumed with them since 1785—and in August he had commented to Washington, who everyone expected would be the first president, that "the first year or two will produce all the great arrangements under the new system, and which may fix its tone for a long time to come."[5] Madison obviously desired and expected to play a role in shaping the government.

Patrick Henry also realized that the first months of the new government would be extremely important, and he was determined to minimize Madison's role in every way he could. Certainly, he would use his control of the Virginia House of Delegates to prevent Madison from being chosen a senator. Henry Lee wrote Madison that Patrick Henry had "exclaimed against your political character & pronounced you unworthy the confidence of the people in the station of Senator. That your election would terminate in producing rivulets of blood throughout the land."[6] Such was Henry's control of the legislature that, on November 8, it chose Richard Henry Lee and William Grayson, two firm Antifederalists, as senators, with Madison coming in third. Madison was in New York City, serving in the Continental Congress, but he soon got word.

Madison's only other chance to play a legislative role in the new government was through popular election to the federal House of Representatives, but that would prove far more difficult than he could have imagined a year or two previously. Pursuant to the need to create congressional districts, the General Assembly on November 13, 1788, had designated the ten districts Virginia was granted (more than any other state), and Orange County, where Madison lived, was placed in the middle of the new Fifth Congressional District that consisted of eight contiguous counties. Unfortunately for Madison, this was a region where Antifederalist sentiment was strong, and he was not personally known very well outside his home county, but the district was fairly drawn.[7] It did not have the geographical extremes we are accustomed to today under the hyper-gerrymandering common in many states. Henry had not caused the district to be drawn in such a way as to discriminate against Madison, but he did work to persuade the popular James Monroe to run against him. Monroe, from neighboring Spotsylvania County, was a moderate Antifederalist and posed a real threat to Madison. Madison soon realized, after receiving letters from friends, that he would have to come to Virginia to actively campaign, which, as he wrote Jefferson, "was very disagreeable . . . on account of its electioneering appearance."[8]

Madison found such politicking distasteful. He was a creature of the eighteenth century, not the coming nineteenth century where running for office meant eagerly seeking it. He wanted to be chosen for his merits without having to do something as crass as ask for votes. Madison was not a natural campaigner—short and diminutive, with a soft voice and timid demeanor—he was a thinker. But he could write convincing letters. He had learned that his opponents had spread charges that he believed the Constitution was perfect as written and needed no amendments of any kind, that he favored direct taxation, that he was not "a friend to the rights of Conscience."[9] Madison appealed through letters to Baptist leaders like John Leland to counter the final charge. He used letters to address the Constitution. True, he had in the ratifying convention opposed amendments, but he had learned since then there was a popular desire for a bill of rights; even Jefferson had harangued him about that, insisting that "a bill of rights is what the people are entitled to against every government on earth . . . and what no just government should refuse."[10] In a congressional district where the sentiment for amendments was strong, Madison was politician enough to realize he had to make an accommodation to the popular will. He answered the issue by writing letters to individuals such as the prominent Baptist minister George Eve, then by a letter published in a Fredericksburg newspaper, the *Virginia Herald.* He explained that before the Constitution was ratified and was still under consideration in several states, he found it necessary not to complicate the process by having Virginia (and other states) add a variety of amendments. To have done so would have simply stimulated endless debate. But now that the Constitution was ratified, he was willing to discuss "such amendments as will, in the most satisfactory manner, guard essential rights, and will render certain vexatious abuses of power impossible." Moreover, he made clear his belief that such amendments "ought to be recommended by the first Congress."[11] In the final days of the campaign, such as it was, Madison and Monroe spoke together at several venues in Louisa County.

The weather was uncommonly cold on February 2, 1789, when the votes were cast. In Orange County, where the voters knew him, Madison won 96 percent of the vote, 216 to 9, but in the other counties the vote was much closer. Still, he ended up with slightly more than 57 percent of the total votes cast and hence won election to the House of Representatives. The contest between Monroe and Madison was not personal, and they continued to be friends. A little over two weeks later Madison returned to New York City, stopping at Mount Vernon for a week to visit with Washington. This visit sealed their friendship. The two Virginians would work together for the next two years to get the federal government underway, and theirs would prove to be an essential partnership in nation-building.[12]

In the final months of 1788, the critical issue nationwide was the election of the first president. Everyone assumed it would be George Washington. No one else came close to his reputation, his name recognition, his image as the father of the nation. But Washington himself felt conflicted. He realized that he was practically destined for the position, but he did not want to be seen as grasping for it. Furthermore, he worried about the difficulties ahead and feared his abilities did not measure up to the task. Despite his worldwide fame, Washington knew he did not have the sheer brilliance of a Jefferson, a Madison, or a Hamilton. He also truly treasured his retirement. Finally, with pressure from all quarters—and with Madison pushing subtly and unrelentingly, insisting that he was the indispensable man at this time—Washington gave in and accepted what he expected to be a burden. As predicted, when the electoral ballots were cast and counted for the first time on February 4, 1789, he was unanimously elected president. The vice presidency had been harder to predict, with Washington being scrupulously neutral in the matter, but in the end John Adams was chosen: he had 34 votes, John Hancock 9, John Rutledge and Robert H. Harrison 6 each, and seven others shared a total of 14 votes.

Washington and Adams were never particularly close, neither during the era of the revolution nor now in peacetime. Back in September the Continental Congress had set March 4 as the date for the opening of the new federal Congress, but on that day, unpropitiously, only eight senators and thirteen congressmen were present, so no quorum existed. Unusually bad weather slowed travel. Even Madison did not arrive in New York until March 19. Finally, on April 1 the House of Representatives organized and the Senate followed five days later. The first task of the Senate was to choose a temporary presiding officer (John Langdon of New Hampshire) and proceed to an official counting of the electoral ballots. After declaring Washington president, the Congress sent Charles Thomson, the secretary of Congress, to carry the official news to Washington, who was still at Mount Vernon.

Washington had very carefully given no indication of his election (although he obviously knew the electoral result) until he was officially notified, wanting to show no unbecoming eagerness to hold the position. But he had prepared for the journey northward, so on April 16 he, his aide David Humphreys, and Thomson set forth in Washington's elegant carriage. Along the way, at every city of any size, the party was met by exultant crowds cheering Washington. A stiffly formal man without the common touch, Washington nevertheless responded respectfully to the outpouring of public affection and addressed admirers in Alexandria, Baltimore, Wilmington, Philadelphia, Trenton, Princeton, and New Brunswick. Everywhere, church bells rang, cannons fired, and crowds stood in the streets to hear his words and celebrate his victory. As he approached New York City on April 23, he was ferried across the Hudson River on a large, handsomely decorated barge. He walked through streets thronged with well-wishers to his official home on Cherry Street, where he prepared for his inauguration on April 30, 1789. Most people, it seemed, even those who had not been actively Federalists, were at least willing to give the new government a chance.

The location for taking the oath of office was what had been City Hall, but in preparation for this occasion the city had hired a French engineer, Pierre Charles L'Enfant, to transform the building into the much more elegant Federal Hall, complete with a cupola and an eagle-adorned pediment. Washington spurned the idea of wearing his military uniform and instead wore a brown suit made of American-manufactured cloth. He rode partway in an elaborate carriage, then dismounted and walked the final two hundred yards, symbolically rejecting excessive pretensions of monarchial splendor. (He knew there were remnants of monarchial sentiment, especially in New York City and the New England states, that he wanted to scotch.)[13] Shortly after 12:30 in the afternoon, the state's highest judicial officer, Chancellor Robert R. Livingston, standing on the small balcony overlooking Wall Street, administered the oath, after which Washington, clearly moved by the occasion and awed by his new responsibilities, replied in a hushed voice, "I solemnly swear to faithfully uphold the duties of the President of the United States and to do all that is in my power to preserve, protect and defend the Constitution of the United States." With that, Washington stepped into the Senate chamber and read, haltingly, nervously, his inaugural address, prepared for him weeks earlier by Madison.[14]

Washington's aide Humphreys had written a much too long address for him months before, but Madison sensibly recommended Washington reject it because of its length and its litany of suggestions for legislation. Madison replaced it with a short speech that stuck to big themes. Washington again seemed nervous as he read it, beginning with humble expressions of his fear that his abilities did not measure up to his present responsibilities, and he made an uncharacteristic number of allusions to Divine Providence. He obliquely warned against "local prejudices" and "party animosities." Deigning to recommend any "particular measures" to the Congress, not wanting to overstep the boundary between the executive and legislative branches, he stated that he would leave it to Congress's "judgment to decide, how far an exercise of the occasional power delegated by the Fifth article of the Constitution [the amending power] is rendered." Here Madison's hand was most obvious. "For while I assure myself," Washington read, "that whilst you carefully avoid every alteration which might endanger the benefits of an United and effective Government, . . . a reverence for the characteristic rights of freemen . . . will . . . influence your deliberations."[15] That evening, as part of the inaugural celebrations, fireworks lit the dark sky for two hours, heralding the initiation of a new era.

Madison was subtly beginning the process of having Congress add amendments to the Constitution to both defuse the Antifederalist anger and undercut their ambition to so modify the Constitution through amendments as to fundamentally change its nature. He had obviously persuaded Washington that it was necessary to add amendments but to control the ones considered. Madison had learned during the Virginia ratification debates just how powerful was the desire for amendments in the state, and he had had to agree to support at least some in order to win his seat in Congress. But Madison was determined to monitor which amendments would be voted on.

In addition to the amendment issue, Washington was fully aware that as the first president, every action he took would be carefully observed. He wrote Madison on May 5, "As the first of every thing, in our situation will serve to establish a Precedent, it is devoutly wished on my part that these precedents may be fixed on true principles."[16] That very day, Washington prepared to receive from the House its response to his inaugural address. Fittingly, Madison, already seen as unofficial leader of the House, wrote the response, and after praising the first president, the House, in Madison's words, assured Washington that "The question arising out of the fifth article of the Constitution, will receive all the attention demanded by its importance; and will, we trust be decided, under the influence of all the considerations to which you allude."[17] Three days later Washington thanked the House for its good wishes, Madison having drafted his reply. Soon Madison would begin to go through the two hundred or so proposed amendments that had been sent to Congress, preparing to choose those he thought reasonable and proper to be ratified. But this was only one of a myriad of tasks facing the Congress, and there was no clear roadway ahead. As Madison wrote Jefferson at this time, "We are in a wilderness without a single footstep to guide us."[18]

By midyear, there were some eighty-one congressmen present in New York, with twenty of the twenty-two senators and forty-six of the fifty-nine representatives being Federalists, but the government itself barely existed. There were no executive departments, almost no employees, no Supreme Court. Political parties did not yet exist, there were no rules for the managing of Congress, no procedures yet determined. Washington wanted to establish the role of the presidency as one of dignified leadership, but the Senate was embroiled in a seemingly endless squabble over his title and how he should be addressed, with all kinds of monarchial nonsense bandied about (especially by John Adams) until finally, on May 14, the Senate accepted the good sense of the House and determined that he should simply be called the President of the United States and addressed as "Mr. President."

The leading men at the time were steeped in the classics. Most of them admired the tradition of Roman simplicity, and ultimately those preferences shaped political culture. Even the basic vocabulary of government—the words president, congress, senate, and so on—were adopted from Roman history. Washington shared these ideas, wishing to avoid extravagance and pretension, though he did ride about the city in an elegant carriage pulled by four horses, with an enslaved driver in livery sitting in the coachman's box. A stern man with a regal bearing, Washington understood that as president he had to be seen as a person of dignity and importance, aloof from the public yet not contemptuous of the people in the abstract. Never by temperament a glad-hander, Washington sought to establish an austere manner. He decided to hold punctiliously formal levees for thirty minutes on Tuesday afternoons. At 3:30 a small number of citizens were slowly allowed to enter his dining room, where a formally dressed Washington, wearing a sword, stood erect by the fireplace. The line of guests would walk by, Washington would bow ever so slightly (but never shake hands), utter a few words of innocuous small talk, and the whole charade would end promptly at four o'clock. No one found the occasions gratifying.

More significant than how the president should be addressed or present himself to the public was the matter of creating the offices of government that would do the nation's business. Slowly, after painstaking debate, the various executive departments were created. The Constitution had mentioned the existence of such departments but had not named them. Now, month by month, with the titles evolving as the discussion unfolded, departments were established: the office of the treasury, the secretary of war, the secretary of state. The most controversial aspect of the various departments was the matter of removal from office. The Senate had to approve the appointments of the various secretaries, but could the president on his own dismiss them, or would that too be the prerogative of the Senate? This of course had much to do with the principle of separation of powers and the authority of the president. Madison pushed hard for dismissal being something solely within the authority of the president, and that position eventually won out. He understood how important it was to have not only a strong but an independent president. The Department of Foreign Affairs was established on July 27 (renamed the Department of State on September 15), and Jefferson would be named secretary of state on September 26 (but did not take office until March 22, 1790); the War Department was created on August 7,[19] and Henry Knox named secretary of war on September 12; the Treasury Department was established on September 2, and Alexander Hamilton named secretary of the treasury on September 11; and the Office of Postmaster General on September 22, with Samuel Osgood appointed postmaster general on September 26. A government was quickly taking shape. No one played a larger role in the opening months of the federal government than James Madison. He simply knew the issues better than anyone else, worked harder, was more persistent, and had thought more deeply.[20] And at least in the beginning, Madison had the closest relationship with Washington, who depended upon him for advice as to policy, candidates for positions, and for assistance in writing letters and addresses.[21]

The moment Madison had arrived in New York City, he knew there was much that needed to be done and decided, and quickly. He and Washington realized that the federal government had to demonstrate that it could actually govern. The problems of the nation that had led to the desire to reform and then replace the Continental Congress still existed. The Constitution was only a blueprint for government. The government, to be effective, had to act, and in many places the Constitution had only vaguely suggested what now needed to be created. Step one for Madison and others was raising the revenue necessary to operate the government, a stark failure of the Confederation. Accordingly, Madison addressed the House on April 8 on the subject, which, he stated, "requires our first attention, and our united exertions." He went on to say that the "deficiency in our treasury has been too notorious" to require explanation, so the new federal government should endeavor "to remedy the evil." To do this, he said, "a national revenue must be obtained; but this system must be such an one, that, while it secures the objects of revenue, it shall not be oppressive to our constituents."[22]

This could be achieved by a two-part plan, which Madison then laid out. First there should be a specified impost or duty levied on certain imported goods—spirits, wines, teas, pepper, sugar, cocoa, and coffee—and then an ad valorum tax on all other goods. Then there should be tonnage duties assessed on all vessels arriving in American ports, and these duties should discriminate between US ships and foreign ships and between ships from nations that had agreements with the nation and those that did not.[23] Madison here hoped to pressure England to adjust its trade relations with the United States, with special attention to American trade with the British colonies in the West Indies. He had then, and throughout his career, a belief that such economic pressure via commerce could force other nations to accommodate American interests. Expectedly, Madison's proposal produced instant responses from the various states, most of which wanted changes that benefited them. New England complained about import duties on molasses, Pennsylvania delegates wanted in essence protective tariffs on infant industries, and southern states feared a rise in freight rates. Madison listened, cajoled, reasoned, and implored the states to put the common good above parochial interests. After months of struggle he got the impost duties approved in July (after the first committee conference between the two houses). Because of impassioned opposition from New England merchants whose trade was dominated by England, the effort to discriminate against nations who had no trade agreements failed. Two less controversial bills passed in July, one setting up tariff collection offices at the various ports of entry, with port collectors and other necessary staff, and the other bill providing for the national government (not individual states) to control and maintain lighthouses, beacons, and navigation buoys.

In mid-June Washington was afflicted by a tumor that developed on his left thigh, a tumor that grew rapidly and made it exceedingly painful for the president to sit. Washington and his doctors worried that it could become fatal, and Dr. Samuel Bard elected to excise it. Operating without anesthesia, Bard cut and scraped out the growth. Washington underwent the painful procedure with great courage. Luckily, Washington in general had a strong constitution and fully recovered. By the end of the summer, the Congress had established a system to regulate commerce and raise revenues sufficient to support the government. Quite an achievement!

Madison had addressed the most pressing problem. Now he moved on to attack the most momentous one that threatened the government: would the call for amendments, or, worse still, a second constitutional convention, destroy all that had been achieved? These were not false worries. As part of the deal to get ratification in New York, that state's Federalists had allowed the Antifederalist governor George Clinton to send a circular letter to the other states urging the First Congress to issue a call for a second constitutional convention. And just as concerning, North Carolina still had not ratified the Constitution (nor had relatively inconsequential Rhode Island), in large part because its delegates demanded amendments. The permanence of the new federal government was yet to be proven. The politically savvy Madison had himself grudgingly come to accept the practical necessity of adopting at least some amendments in large part as an act of conciliation to the nation's moderate Antifederalists. He suspected opposers like Patrick Henry were permanently irreconcilable, but many like James Monroe were not.

Madison received permission from Washington to address the House on the subject of amendments, and so he told the Congress on June 8, 1789, that it was time to address the issue of amendments because there was popular support for them and further delay might arouse suspicions that Congress intended to ignore the subject. He also pointedly said that he believed it was appropriate to amend the Constitution and the Congress had, "if we proceed with caution, nothing to lose." He stated emphatically that he would "be unwilling to see a door opened for a re-consideration of the whole structure of government" because that would place the government itself at risk.[24] Madison acted now because he wanted to foreclose the possibility that Antifederalists would begin to propose amendments, and he left unsaid the fact that he had laboriously gone through the more than two hundred amendments (many were duplicates) that had been proposed by the various state ratifying conventions to eliminate the ones he thought ill-advised, unnecessary, or injurious to the vitality of the Constitution. His intent was to protect personal rights, not states' rights. Madison proceeded to list the nineteen amendments he recommended, beginning with a philosophical proposition that all political power came from the people and they possessed the right to "reform or change" their government. Next, he proposed making more flexible the Constitution's limitation on the size of congressional districts to accommodate future population growth. His third proposal called for the delay of implementation of any congressional pay raise until the subsequent Congress. Not until his fourth proposal did he begin to address the issues of religious freedom, freedom of speech, the right to assemble peaceably, the right to bear arms (though clearly in the context of a closely regulated militia), and the other rights we associate today with the Bill of Rights. Madison proposed that these amendments should be folded into the Constitution, not listed separately at the end. He included an amendment that explicitly prevented *state* governments (not just the federal government) from interfering with freedom of religion, freedom of the press, and trial by jury, and another amendment expressly stating that "powers not delegated by this constitution, nor prohibited by it to the states, are reserved to the States respectively," which was in a way a sop to the Antifederalists.[25]

In the congressional committee there was substantial objection, some from Federalists who felt that no amendments were needed and many from Antifederalists who wanted amendments primarily to change the structure of the Constitution, such as limiting its taxing power and setting a term limitation for the presidency. But Madison was better prepared on the issues than anyone else, worked tirelessly, and—importantly—he had the support of Washington, who normally did not get involved in matters before Congress but on this occasion wrote a private letter he expected to be shared. In this letter Washington stated that he supported Madison's proposals because he believed a constitutional protection of "essential rights" was a good thing. Because amendments had been strongly recommended by the Virginia ratifying convention, he felt himself "bound" to support them now; if these were not accepted, Antifederalists were sure to offer amendments of their own; and if Congress approved the proposals, they would "kill the opposition every where, and by putting an end to the disaffection to the Govt. itself, enable the administration to venture on measures not otherwise safe."[26]

Once Washington's viewpoint became known, support for the measures grew. As the result of discussion and committee consideration, out of Madison's original list of nineteen amendments, seventeen were approved by the House on August 24 but placed at the end of the Constitution. On September 9, after debate, the Senate approved twelve of these seventeen, and with slight word changes, both chambers, having reconciled the minor textual differences between the two versions, voted to approve all twelve on September 25, 1789. This was the key vote. On September 28, the twelve proposed amendments were submitted to the individual states (as the Constitution had prescribed for the amending process) for approval. Ultimately, on December 15, 1791, ten of those proposed officially became what we have come to know as the Bill of Rights. The two proposed amendments regarding legislative districts and congressional pay had been eliminated from consideration. President Washington notified the Congress on January 18, 1792, of this important achievement.[27]

The Congress decided one other significant matter in its opening months: the development of a federal judiciary system.[28] On this topic the Constitution was surprisingly brief. Article 3 had simply said that "the Judicial Power of the United States shall be vested in one Supreme Court, and in such inferior courts as the Congress may from time to time ordain and establish." Accordingly, Congress on April 7 appointed a ten-man special judicial committee chaired by Oliver Ellsworth of Connecticut. Ellsworth was a highly respected jurist who had served in the Constitutional Convention, and he was exceptionally hardworking. He understood the need for a federal court system but also realized that many congressmen feared that federal courts would destroy their state judicial systems. States had particular interests, as well, that they wanted to protect. So Ellsworth had to be careful to produce a blended system that respected the roles of the states but simultaneously prioritized the authority of federal law. There would not be, however, a unitary system of national courts and no one system of national law.

The political and legal compromise was worked out through the Senate expeditiously, with the result announced in late April. The bill Ellsworth had shepherded called for a Supreme Court with a chief justice and five associate justices who would meet twice annually in the capital city for sessions of two weeks; thirteen district courts drawn up for the nation, each of which would have a US attorney and federal marshal; and the creation of three overarching regional courts, consisting of one permanently appointed district judge and two rotating members of the Supreme Court who would travel about the nation. The bill also called for the creation of the office of the attorney general.

There was, as could have been expected, spirited debate in the Senate. Some claimed there were too many or too few judges on the Supreme Court. There was controversy over the jurisdiction of the federal courts, over the expense, over the complicated overlay of federal and state law. Some, like Madison, thought the entire system "peculiarly complicated"—Madison played almost no role in the development of the judicial system, which was largely a creature of the Senate.[29] Ellsworth's version, practically intact, was approved by the Senate on July 17 and sailed through the House on September 24.

Washington did not attempt to meddle in the legislation, but he believed the federal courts would be essential to the success of the new nation and thought the character of the judges to be appointed as important, if not more so, than their legal or judicial background. He promptly appointed as chief justice the distinguished New York statesman John Jay, who had been a member of the Constitutional Convention. Washington diligently chose the other federal judges, attentive to their reputation and their support of the Constitution, and paying due consideration to a fair regional representation on the courts. For example, the six members of the Supreme Court came from six different states.[30] Washington also appointed Virginian Edmund Randolph to be the first attorney general, which was then a part-time position. (Washington very intentionally appointed no known Antifederalist to any position.) The court system, the respective jurisdiction of state and federal courts, and the full legal authority of the Supreme Court and its role in the life of the nation were yet to be determined. That would turn out to be the life work of a subsequent chief justice, John Marshall, who would be appointed in January 1801.

But by the end of the First Session of the First Federal Congress, on September 29, 1789, its achievements were notable. Certainly, the most consequential single session of any Congress, it had gone a long way toward creating a working, self-funding, administratively proficient government based on the principles of the Constitution. Washington himself summed up its progress: "So far as we have gone with the new Government (and it is completely organized and in operation) we have had greater reason than the most sanguine could expect to be satisfied with its success."[31]

On September 2, 1789, Congress had created the Treasury Department and on the eleventh confirmed Alexander Hamilton as secretary of the treasury. Washington of course had known Hamilton since the revolution and had also received Madison's positive recommendation of him. Hamilton lived right at hand in New York City, and with his characteristic super abundance of energy, began work immediately, the afternoon of his Friday appointment and throughout the weekend. Hamilton did not have Thomas Jefferson's encyclopedic breadth of interests, but within his expertise, he was unequaled in America. Brilliant, energetic, bold, he wanted to transform the United States into an economic, manufacturing, and military powerhouse, equal to the greatest nations of Europe, and he was absolutely certain he knew how to wield financial and banking resources in such fashion—concentrating and mobilizing wealth—as to achieve his goal. Congress gave the Treasury Department more freedom of action than other executive departments, and Hamilton made the most of it.[32]

Meanwhile, Washington prepared in mid-October to begin an extended tour of New England. As a southerner, he deemed it important to be seen as a president of every section of the nation. Traveling in a coach attended by three staff members and six enslaved men in livery, he would step out of the carriage before entering a town or city and ride in mounted on a white horse. Never one for small talk or impromptu speeches, and bothered by his painful false teeth, Washington persevered nevertheless, determined to meet local officials with respect and represent personally the face of national authority. The tour was a resounding success, and most observers were inspired by Washington's politeness and dignity. His attendance by enslaved persons attracted no protests. Clearly, the nation was at the time a democracy for whites only, with little notice of the contradiction that meant.[33]

The Second Session of the First Congress convened on January 4, 1790. On January 14, Hamilton laid before Congress a forty-thousand-word Report on Public Credit. Here he proposed paying off the $12 million in foreign debt owed by the government and assuming the $67 million in domestic debt owed by the national government and the various state governments. No one objected to paying the foreign debts, but Hamilton's proposals for paying the domestic debt were more controversial. During the revolution, many patriotic citizens had bought bonds to finance the war, but these bonds had never been paid off and had lost most of their original value. In subsequent years speculators had traveled across the hinterlands swooping the bonds up at a fraction of their original cost. Hamilton proposed to pay off these debts by reissuing new bonds to the present holders of the old ones, and the new bonds would have the initial full value, not the current depreciated value. He also proposed assuming the various state debts and reissuing new bonds for them too, using federal funds to pay the total costs. All the bonds would be folded together into a common debt, full interest on which would be annually paid to all the bondholders.

Everyone supported the idea of paying government debts, but Hamilton's plan upset many. First, people like Madison thought some attempt should be made to identify the many original holders of bonds (who had purchased them for patriotic reasons, not speculative) and splitting the proposed interest payments between them and the far fewer present-day owners, whom Madison disparaged as "Stockjobbers."[34] Hamilton thought this would be an accounting nightmare and, in fact, he did not want the funds spread about the nation to numerous small investors but wanted the monies concentrated regionally in the hands of a few well-connected merchants who would then use the windfall to invest in new enterprises.[35] The several states (mostly southern: Maryland, Virginia, North Carolina, and Georgia) that had already paid their domestic debts felt it unfair that now they would in effect be charged with paying off the debts of those states (mostly northern) that had been lax in repayment. Hence the assumption plan raised obvious sectional issues. Again, Hamilton was less interested in fairness and wanted to attract all bondholders to support the federal government. Current bondholders would realize that payment of their interest would occur only if the new nation were successful. Hence, because the nation's success would greatly redound to the benefit of the wealthy and powerful, they would throw their wholehearted support behind the federal government. For Madison (and later Jefferson), Hamilton's policies conjured up fears of the kind of government corruption that had afflicted the Walpolean era of British politics in the 1720s and 1730s.[36]

Thus Hamilton was proposing a financial glue to bind together potential investors whose actions would contribute to national prosperity and strength. For him, financial interests, not political ideals, would unite the nation. And the new bonds, their full value now guaranteed, could also serve as money by being negotiable. Later, in December 1790, Hamilton would propose a schedule of taxes on spirits (alcohol) that would finance the interest payments his fully funded debts would require. His taxation scheme passed both the House and the Senate by February 26, 1791. Madison led the fight in Congress against Hamilton's funding proposals, considering them simply unfair.

This break between the two men was probably as unexpected by Madison as by Hamilton because they had previously worked so effectively in tandem to promote the Constitution. But Madison had more respect for the state governments than did Hamilton, who wanted, in effect, to obliterate them. Madison saw Hamilton's funding of the state debts as a way to reduce states' role at the same time as it maximized the support for the federal government. Even though the terms cause confusion today because of the way they were used at the time, Madison truly believed in a *federal* form of government (that is, a sharing of state and national authority) while Hamilton wanted an all-powerful *national* government. In terms of having the Constitution ratified, Madison was a self-labeled Federalist, but he always did believe in a blending of governmental sovereignty in a way that Hamilton did not.

While we have come to remember this beginning of political discord as a fight between Jefferson and Hamilton, it really began with Madison leading the opposition.[37] Jefferson only entered the picture later and bit by bit allied with Madison against Hamilton. Meanwhile, Madison's influence on Washington was slowly receding, in part because with various executive departments having been created and staffed, Washington now had more able officials than Madison alone with whom to consult. No doubt remembering how valuable his informal council of officers and aides-de-camp had been to him during the Revolutionary War, Washington as president eventually began to gather his various department heads together for consultation. They first all met on November 26, 1791, then came together two more times that year, assembled six times in 1792, and met fifty-three times in 1793. This "cabinet"—the Constitution had mentioned no such institution—grew in influence, and of all its members, Washington, who had personally been involved in a variety of commercial and semi-industrial enterprises at Mount Vernon, was increasingly attracted to Hamilton's merchant-capitalist position.[38]

Initially, on April 12, Congress turned down Hamilton's proposal to repay bondholders without discriminating between original and present owners, greatly distressing Hamilton, and it likewise on the first vote rejected the assumption of all domestic debt. But Hamilton was extraordinarily persistent. And a new participant joined the scene. On September 26, 1789, Washington, aware of Jefferson's five years of diplomatic experience in France, nominated him to be secretary of state, with the Senate confirming the recommendation the very next day. However, Jefferson was in France and knew nothing of the appointment, although on the very day Washington appointed him, Jefferson and his two daughters (along with James and Sally Hemings) had begun their trip from Paris to return to Virginia, the girls supposedly forever and Jefferson for several months to wind up unfinished family financial matters before returning to France for the final two years of his diplomatic appointment. The Hemingses knew they could have stayed as free persons in France, but Jefferson persuaded James to return to Virginia so he could teach the techniques of French cooking to his enslaved brother Peter at Monticello, after which Jefferson promised to free James, which he did. And Sally, being importuned by Jefferson also, decided to return and live in her special relationship to Jefferson, doing only light housework, and with the promise that any children she might bear would eventually be freed, which they were.[39] Upon their ship's arrival in Norfolk on November 23, Jefferson learned from a newspaper that he had been named secretary of state.

He subsequently received a letter from Washington (dated October 13, 1789) tendering him the offer but giving him the right to refuse. Jefferson's initial reaction was to turn the offer down—the position included domestic as well as diplomatic responsibilities, and Jefferson thought the duties too extensive to be manageable—and he felt he could be more effective in Paris. Madison pressured him, minimizing the domestic duties. Washington wrote a second letter (dated January 21, 1790) imploring him to accept the position:

> I consider the successful Administration of the general Government as an object of almost infinite consequence to the present and future happiness of the Citizens of the United States.—I consider the Office of Secretary for the Department of State as *very* important on many accounts: and I know no person, who, in my judgement, could better execute the Duties of it than yourself.[40]

Jefferson, understanding how much Washington desired him to accept the position, reluctantly did so, although he requested time to settle several personal financial matters in Virginia, visit some relatives (he had been in France for five years), and attend his older daughter's marriage. So it was not until Sunday, March 21, 1790, that Jefferson reached New York prepared to take over the State Department.[41]

Jefferson was soon immersed in his duties but slowed by another of his occasional debilitating migraine attacks, and he was not at once fully caught up in the intricacies of the legislative battle over Hamilton's proposals. But then, in Jefferson's words, he was accosted one June evening just outside Washington's door by a "haggard, and dejected" Hamilton, who proceeded to tell Jefferson that the proposal to assume the state debts was about to be rejected with finality, that this would fatally complicate his proposal to arrange the general financial affairs of the nation, would especially upset the New England states, and would thereby threaten the survival of the nation. Jefferson told Hamilton that he had not yet had time to completely comprehend the issues but that if the controversy might destroy the union, then Jefferson would do what he could do to affect a compromise. He proposed hosting a dinner for Madison and Hamilton (along with Virginia congressmen Richard Bland Lee and Alexander White, whose House votes were needed), with Jefferson serving as simple mediator, on the grounds that sensible men, listening to one another, could come to an agreement.

Subsequently at the dinner, Madison agreed not to fight with his normal energy the proposal to assume the state debts. Critically, one of the men, either Hamilton or Madison, realizing assumption would be a difficult pill for the southern states to swallow, proposed that in return Hamilton use his influence to have the national capital permanently located somewhere along the Potomac, and that to help Pennsylvania support this deal, the capital would almost immediately be moved to Philadelphia for ten years, after which its permanent location—far more central than New York City—would be in Maryland.[42] This had been a contentious issue for almost a decade, and more than thirty sites had been suggested for the capital. Jefferson's account simplifies a complex process, aspects of which had been previously discussed by Madison himself, by Washington, and by other interested parties (for example, Jefferson had mentioned the idea of moving the capital to Philadelphia temporarily, and then to the Potomac, to Senator Maclay on June 15, 1790[43]), but it accurately captures in a general sense what happened at the dinner. The evening cemented whatever prior understandings had been worked out. Madison tempered his opposition, Jefferson put in a good word for the compromise, Hamilton kept his promise, and everyone involved knew that President Washington passionately but discretely preferred the southern location of the capital.[44]

Consequently, Congress passed on July 10, 1790, a Residence Act that determined the site of the future national capital would be in a district ten miles square along the Potomac (the precise location to be chosen by the president), and be ready for occupancy by December 1800. The Assumption Bill itself passed on July 26, 1791, before the Second Session ended on August 12.[45] The day before the Assumption Bill finally passed, Madison, attempting to forestall anticipated political objections, had written Monroe in Virginia (who was campaigning for a Senate seat in that fall's election) that although he had opposed the measure, he could not "deny that the crisis demands a spirit of accommodation to a certain extent. If the measure should be adopted, I shall wish it to be considered as an unavoidable evil."[46] (Clearly, Madison and Monroe had reconciled after their recent election contest.) Washington, Madison, and Jefferson would be primarily responsible, in the coming years, for the siting and development of what became the city of Washington in the District of Columbia, almost exactly equidistant between the northernmost tip of Maine and the southernmost tip of Georgia. The actual city planning would be primarily the work of the French engineer L'Enfant, who had readied New York City's city hall into Federal Hall for Washington's inauguration.

In the midst of the tense congressional debates over the assumption issue, with their clear regional dimension, another issue exploded on the congressional scene that exacerbated sectional conflict and in fact even produced fears of the fragile union coming apart. This episode brought the slavery problem to the nation in a way that had only been foreshadowed by the debates in the Constitutional Convention and the Virginia Ratification Convention. Many might have been lulled into thinking that slavery had receded as a political issue because it had not been raised during the First Session, but in February 1790 three antislavery petitions were delivered to Congress, two of them from Quaker societies and one from the Pennsylvania Society for the Abolition of Slavery. All three petitions explicitly focused on stopping the Atlantic slave trade, but all three also had implications for the future of slavery itself.

According to Senator Maclay of Pennsylvania, Senator Pierce Butler (a rice planter from South Carolina) charged that the whole issue was "designed to overturn the Constitution."[47] Butler and the other senators and congressmen from South Carolina and Georgia instantly and harshly responded to the petitions, and moved to throw them out. The Congress should not even discuss them![48]

This raised the question whether citizens had the right to petition Congress. Most congressmen from the Upper South initially supported the right to petition. Yet in the Lower South, slavery was still an expanding institution, and whites there, especially in the fertile coastal regions where they were vastly outnumbered by enslaved people, believed their economies were fully dependent upon slavery. Their congressmen vehemently attacked this immediate and any related threat to slavery and praised the institution as absolutely essential for their way of life. They made clear that efforts to end slavery would end the union. In fact, they frequently claimed that any attempts to interfere with what they called southern rights violated the principles of the Constitution.

Other members of Congress were shocked by the vitriolic tenor of the proslavery comments of their southernmost colleagues and genuinely feared for the future of the nation. According to Senator Maclay, the House debate was marked by "base invective indecorous language . . . manifest signs of passion. . . . Many of them do not Hesitate to declare, that the Union Must fall to pieces, at the rate we go on. Indeed, Many seem to wish it."[49] Ominously, this discussion of slavery could lead to a fracturing of the nation. Previously the right to petition Congress had been deemed an almost sacred right. Madison tried to separate the Congress's support for the right of petition from necessarily supporting the stands advocated by particular petitions. In this he was not alone. But the result of the acrimonious commotion and intransigence from the southernmost states was that congressmen from the Upper South backed away from their support of even the right to petition and in effect agreed that discussion of abolition should be forbidden. After several votes on the issue, Congress ended up prohibiting any talk in Congress of abolishing the slave trade or otherwise interfering with slavery—in effect, a gag rule. Madison, while never rejecting the right of petitioning, counseled his fellow members to avoid actions that might push the Deep South over the edge. He emphasized that the national government had no authority over either the emancipation or treatment of enslaved people, so potentially explosive language should be avoided.

Formerly moderate congressmen simply proved more concerned to protect the survival of the union than to end slavery, which most largely believed was already a dying institution. Slavery had not yet been invigorated by the invention of the cotton gin (1793) and the rapid spread of cotton cultivation across the Deep South. In truth, southern agriculture had not completely recovered from the devastating effects of the Revolutionary War. Congressmen had also witnessed, beginning with Pennsylvania in 1780, a steady procession of northern states passing acts to end slavery within their bounds. Perhaps the movement would spread southward. Jefferson, for instance, had written to a French correspondent in 1786 that "the disposition to emancipate" was growing in Virginia, and "I flatter myself it will take place there at some period of time not very distant."[50] As some states like Virginia and Maryland had begun to shift away from the cultivation of tobacco to growing wheat, which was less labor intensive, the perceived need for additional enslaved laborers declined and more planters were willing to prohibit further slave imports from Africa. Manumissions also grew slowly but noticeably, increasing the number of free Blacks.

Still, not a single major Founder acted in a significant way to end slavery at this time. Even normally outspoken Hamilton was unwilling to risk losing votes for his economic system, currently under debate at the time of this first congressional proslavery blowup, by speaking out against slavery or defending the antislavery petitions.[51] The congressional response in the spring of 1790 shaped the national response for decades. As George Washington commented to fellow Virginian David Stuart in late March 1790, the "Memorial of the Quakers" had just "at length been put to sleep."[52] When the slavery issue eventually awoke, the nation's political institutions would fail and civil war ensue.

During the late autumn of 1790, the federal government began to move its papers and staff (tiny by today's terms) from its first home in New York City to its second home in Philadelphia. The city of Philadelphia rented the home of wealthy financier Robert Morris and restyled it the President's House for Washington's use—he had first stayed there during the Constitutional Convention. Washington had to make additions to house his large household staff, including nine enslaved persons from Mount Vernon—among them his favorite cook, Hercules, and his wife Martha's personal slave, Ona Judge.[53] Washington knew that the state had passed a gradual abolition act in 1780 that allowed slaveholders from other states to bring their enslaved laborers into Pennsylvania, but they could remain only six months, after which they were freed. Washington got around the law by shuffling his various enslaved people back to Virginia just before they had been in Philadelphia for six months, and after staying a week or so at Mount Vernon, they were brought back to the city, where the six-months clock began again.[54] Washington seemed morally unconcerned about these maneuvers to evade the intention of the local laws, and that there was no public protest over this obvious subterfuge cautions against imagining there was at that time a staunchly antislavery North arrayed against a solid slave South.

In the midst of this larger cultural context, the unexpected slave-petition controversy of earlier in the year intensified the sectional aspects of the debates over Hamilton's economic plans, which clearly advantaged the elite merchant class of the northeastern states. The Third and final session of the First Congress convened in December 1790 in the new but temporary capital. Visionary Alexander Hamilton was ready to submit the third portion of his expansive economic plan, a proposition to establish a national bank to be situated in Philadelphia. First though, on December 13, he presented to Congress his proposal for new taxes to be levied on whiskey to provide the necessary funds to pay the interest due on the newly created federal bonds. Despite some debate, everyone realized that these funds were essential. Not even Madison opposed them. The excise tax act passed both House and Senate by late February.

Far more controversial was the proposal Hamilton laid before Congress on December 14, an innovative plan to create a national bank, to be called the Bank of the United States and chartered for twenty years. It would be capitalized at $10 million (more than all the nation's other banks combined), but the government would put up only $2 million; the rest of the funds would come from wealthy private investors, mostly in the Northeast, and they would be able to use their newly guaranteed federal bonds to make up the funds. The bank would serve a number of useful functions: it would hold tax revenues, disburse federal funds, and provide short-term loans to large merchants (but would not extend loans to farmers, small entrepreneurs, and artisans). Its bank notes could serve as negotiable tender, thereby expanding the money supply.[55] Clearly the Bank of the United States would be financially beneficial to the government and to merchant capitalists, but like the refunding of the domestic debt, would be of little use to small businessmen and infant manufacturers, who ultimately became the backbone of the American industrial economy. In a sense, for all his innovative economic ideas, Hamilton here was looking backward to the kind of merchant class that had propelled British growth in the eighteenth century.[56]

Hamilton knew more about banking than anyone else in the nation, and despite its flaws, his report was lucidly written and persuasive. Because it was closely modeled on the Bank of England, Hamilton had the success of that institution to bolster his case. Moreover, Hamilton was more than willing to answer any questions, respond to any criticisms. As a result, the proposal easily passed the Senate on January 20, 1791, was sent on to the House for concurrence, proceeded through three readings, and became the subject of serious debate on February 2. The leading opponent, Madison, was clearly in the midst of a complete break with Hamilton. Madison feared the concentration of funds in the hands of a few men, all of whom lived in one section of the nation. He believed the benefits and burdens of governmental policies should be balanced across the United States. He also revealed the typical farmer's fear of banks as institutions, and he worried that as the bank grew in power, located as it was in Philadelphia, it would likely lend its influence to an effort the keep the national capital in that city. But, almost as if he were looking for reasons to oppose—as he may have been—Madison seized upon a constitutional objection. Nowhere in that document was a national bank explicitly mentioned, so Madison argued that it was improper to try to stretch the necessary and proper clause of Article 1, Section 8, of the Constitution to validate such an institution.[57] The bank would no doubt be useful but certainly not necessary for the economy to function.

Despite Madison's so-called strict constructionist arguments, the House passed the Bank Act in February 14 in a starkly sectional vote. Congressmen from the northern states supported the bank 33 to 1, while the southern representatives opposed it 19 to 6, a bad omen for the union.[58] The only option left for Madison was a possible Washington veto, something the president had not done before. Washington turned to Attorney General Edmund Randolph and to Jefferson—whom he had known longer and more closely than any of his other advisors—for their informal opinions. Randolph replied quickly, giving his opinion that the bank was not justified by the Constitution. Jefferson replied in more detail, and he was apparently conflicted by his decision. He may have opposed the bill in good part to stand in solidarity with Madison, adopting and indeed expanding Madison's strict constructionist logic. "To take a single step beyond the boundaries thus specially drawn around the powers of Congress," Jefferson wrote, "is to take possession of a boundless field of power, no longer susceptible of any definition."[59] He came down on the side of rejection, but he wrote to Washington that if he were having trouble in making up his mind, Jefferson thought the president should err on the side of accepting the legislative opinion.[60]

Washington gave the written opinions of Randolph and Jefferson to Hamilton, and with them in hand, Hamilton composed an effective reply on February 23, arguing that "necessary" did not mean absolutely essential, and that because the bank promoted the financial functioning of the government and was not explicitly forbidden by any clause of the Constitution, it was appropriate. Hamilton concluded his rebuttal with forceful language: "Every power vested in a government is in its nature *sovereign* and includes by *force* of the *term* a right to employ all the *means* requisite and fairly *applicable* to the attainment of the ends of such power."[61] These two contending ways of interpreting the Constitution would reverberate down through the more than two centuries of American history. Hamilton's reply had benefited from his having their objections before him, and he actually quoted a convincing passage that Madison had written in Federalist No. 44 to clench his case.[62] (The authorship of the various Federalist essays was not then publicly known.) Two days after receiving Hamilton's masterful reply, Washington signed the bill on February 25, 1791, though apparently without a lot of enthusiasm. Hamilton would go on, in December, to issue a report on manufacturing, which called upon the government to actively intervene in the economy by supporting certain industries, providing them subsidies (Hamilton called them bounties) and tax relief, and promoting the employment of women and children, but Congress was uninterested in this proposal, and it went nowhere.

With the passage of the bank bill in February, the First Federal Congress had completed its great work, and what an achievement it represented. The roles of two Virginians in particular stand out. Washington's gravitas and sound judgment, along with Madison's mastery of detail, had been essential in transforming the abstract language of the Constitution into a functioning national government. But national harmony was still elusive; sectional and regional differences were very much alive. It was precisely to assess these differences and hopefully to tamp them down that Washington set forth, on March 20, 1791, after Congress had recessed, to tour the southern states. Riding in a carriage accompanied now by a retinue of enslaved men, a baggage wagon, and a white parade horse—apparently the president's preferences—Washington over the next three and a half months went on an 1,800-mile tour, visiting Virginia, North Carolina, South Carolina, and Georgia.[63] Everywhere he was lionized, and the crowds exulted as President Washington rode into town on the white steed. It was an absolutely triumphant tour, and the reverence for Washington transcended sectional tensions and generated support for the nation. Yet sectional tensions did not long remain abated. Nor did Washington's leg tumor, which recurred shortly after his return in early July. It had to be lanced, and within a month the president recovered. Alas, there was to be no lancing of sectional woes.

8

POLITICAL FISSURES

None of the Founders expected or approved of the emergence of what we now call political parties; the highest political value of those elected to the national government was the survival of the union, which implied at the time a seeking of consensus. That was the sentiment that underlay the agreement, finalized at the dinner Thomas Jefferson hosted for Alexander Hamilton and James Madison in June 1790: both Hamilton and Madison were willing to make a difficult compromise for the benefit of the nation. But month after month, as Madison and Jefferson came to understand more about Hamilton's policies and Washington's general acceptance of them, their opposition mounted. At stake were two fundamentally different conceptions of what the government and economy should be. Hamilton wanted to create a much stronger central government, modeled after the economic system of England, that promoted commerce, extensive manufacturing for export, had a powerful central bank, supported a strong army, and had imperial ambitions. Madison and Jefferson, on the other hand, preferred a less intrusive central government, maintaining more of the traditional powers in the hands of the various states, with an economy based on trade, domestic manufacturing, and commercial agriculture—but not, as is sometimes thought, subsistence farming. The Revolutionary War had been a formative influence for Hamilton, teaching him the necessity of a strong and effective central government. Jefferson's experience in France and other European nations with powerful monarchs had completely soured him against anything that hinted of monarchy, which Hamilton's plans did.

As the Treasury Department under Hamilton multiplied in size and reach throughout the states, Madison and Jefferson took alarm. During a May 1791 vacation trip to upstate New York, where they admired the scenery and fished, they shared political concerns and considered a response. Among other issues, they saw that the only newspaper with national pretentions, the *United States Gazette* published by John Fenno, flush with government publishing contracts, had become essentially an uncritical mouthpiece for Hamiltonian policies. Madison and Jefferson, eager to have their perspective communicated, determined to create another newspaper that would present, in their view, a more accurate portrayal of the news, which of course meant from their perspective. Madison cajoled a former Princeton classmate, poet Philip Freneau, to edit a paper, and with Jefferson's importunings, too, along with the provision of a minimal job as translator in the Department of State, Freneau finally accepted. The first issue of the *National Gazette* was published in late October, and it grew increasing partisan. These two newspapers, offering divergent news of the administration, in effect made it official that there were two very different perspectives on what should be the nature of the national government.

Nothing like parties yet existed, and both sides found it difficult if not impossible to accept the legitimacy of the other side. Each perceived their rival to be a real threat to the nation. Hamilton and Washington saw Madison and Jefferson's political perspective as an illegitimate attack on the government and the Constitution itself, while Madison and Jefferson believed they represented the true national consensus for republican government rather than the slide into monarchism that was occurring because the myth-like status of Washington warped public opinion. For the remainder of the decade, these two opposing viewpoints, with rare exceptions, shaped the words and actions of the major governing leaders. Without anyone planning or even expecting it, a set of attitudes and practices having some of the features of what we now consider political parties gradually emerged among the two contending groups. Jefferson, who never liked interpersonal contention, was finding government service distasteful. In February 1792, he had a long, private meeting with Washington. There he suggested to the president that the newly created post office system[1] should be moved to the Department of State from the Treasury because that department was already so huge it threatened to overwhelm the other aspects of government. He told Washington this was not a power move on his part because he planned to shortly retire. Washington urged Jefferson to stay in office because he himself planned to retire; he did not want the public to come to believe that he craved the "sweets of office." Jefferson instantly replied how essential it was that Washington stay in office, though he reminded the president that he himself had only reluctantly accepted the State Department position and now wished to retire. He found the whole direction of government—and as he outlined it, it was clear he meant Hamiltonian economic policies—counter to the true principles of the Constitution.[2]

Jefferson's views hardened as the months passed. On May 23, 1792, he laid out his apprehensions in a long letter to Washington. He detailed aspects of the economic plans, concluding with the stark statement that "the ultimate object of all this is to prepare the way for a change, from the present republican form of government, to that of a monarchy, of which the English constitution is to be the model." These policies also threatened to divide the nation into opposing sections, and he could "scarcely contemplate a more incalculable evil than the breaking of the union into two or more parts." He referred to the Hamiltonian faction as "Monarchial federalists" and used the fear of sectional disruption as the primary reason he considered Washington's "continuance at the head of affairs as of the last importance. The confidence of the whole union is centered in you. . . . North and South will hang together, if they have you to hang on."[3] Jefferson feared a growing concentration of economic and political power in the hands of the central government.

For his part, Washington believed that most of the animosity Jefferson complained of came not from Hamilton but from the newspapers. The dueling newspapers were exacerbating the tensions, and after the summer of 1792, Hamilton began pseudonymously authoring blistering attacks on Jefferson in the *United States Gazette.* Washington had shown Jefferson's letter to Hamilton without revealing the author, to which Hamilton responded with a brief letter attached to a long rebuttal on August 18. In great detail Hamilton refuted all charges of impropriety, stockjobbing, and corruption, and he strongly responded to the charge that he and others had monarchical ambitions for the nation. "The idea of introducing a monarchy or aristocracy into this Country," he wrote, "is one of those visionary things, that none but madmen could meditate and that no wise men will believe." He said, not a little disingenuously, that "No man, that I know of, contemplated the introducing into this country of a monarchy." Continuing, Hamilton wrote that "it is certainly much to be regretted that party discriminations are so far Geographical as they have been; and that ideas of a severance of the Union are creeping in both North and South."[4]

Washington strongly wished harmony could reign in his cabinet, and he apparently found Hamilton's point-by-point rebuttal largely convincing. Several days after receipt of Hamilton's reply, Washington wrote to Jefferson about how "unfortunate, and how much it is to be regretted then, . . . that internal dissentions should be harrowing and tearing our vitals." He found these problems more upsetting than international dangers, and feared that

> without more charity for the opinions and acts of one another in Governmental matters . . . , [the government would be] torn asunder—And, in my opinion the fairest prospect of happiness and prosperity that ever was presented to man, will be lost—perhaps for ever!
>
> My earnest wish, and my fondest hope therefore is, that instead of wounding suspicions, and irritable charges, there may be liberal allowances—mutual

> forebearances—and temporizing yieldings on *all sides.* Under the exercise of these, matters will go on smoothly, and, if possible, more prosperously. [Otherwise,] the Ruin of the goodly fabric we have been erecting.[5]

Washington added that he had communicated the same sentiments to others in his administration. He later wrote to Jefferson, "I regret—deeply regret—the difference of opinions which have arisen, and divided you and another principal Officer of the Government; and wish, devoutly, there could be an accommodation of them by mutual yieldings."[6] But neither Jefferson nor Hamilton was dissuaded from their worries about the implications of the ideas and actions of the other. Practically every issue that arose was perceived through the prisms of these differing outlooks. Each side believed it alone was advancing the best interests of the nation. After one meeting with the president, Jefferson recorded that Washington had said he "thought it important to preserve the check of my opinion in the administration in order to keep things in their proper channel," an indication that Washington had at the time some concerns about Hamilton.[7] At first Washington *was* apparently in the middle of the differences between the two men, attempting to mediate and make judicious decisions, but soon he was clearly in what might be called the Hamilton camp. In the absence of a party system, Washington considered any criticism of governmental actions an attack on him, the Constitution, and the very government itself, and Hamilton pushed that personalistic interpretation.

One of the chief causes of the fundamental differences between the political factions was international. At the beginning of the French Revolution in 1789, US sentiment was extremely hopeful for a favorable outcome, and most Americans still had great affection for France as their essential revolutionary-era ally that had so materially contributed to their winning of independence. But as the French Revolution became more radical and deadly, American attitudes began to change, especially among the Federalists. The turning points were January 21, 1793, when King Louis XVI was beheaded, and February 1, when the French Republic declared war against Britain. The two great European powers at war instantly created a diplomatic problem for the United States, given the treaty of alliance with France dating from 1778. All the government actors realized that the US could not afford to become embroiled in a major European war. Despite his strong affection for France, Jefferson fully understood the reality of the situation and made clear that despite treaties, any nation had the right to jettison treaty obligations if failure to do so could be self-destructive. Washington, always cautious, called his advisors together to craft a response. He, like Jefferson, did not want to harshly break from France but did not want the nation to be dragged into war. Hence something like a declaration of neutrality was needed.

Hamilton, ever the enemy of France, wanted to do so in such a way as to diminish all sentiment favorable to France and enhance all sentiment favorable toward Britain. Jefferson for legalistic reasons based on the terminology of international law did not want to use the word *neutral.* He won that argument. The proclamation that resulted on April 22, 1793—although it has come down through history known as the Neutrality Proclamation—really only called for impartial behavior. Discussion of these issues further inflamed Hamiltonian fury against everything French and further convinced the Jeffersonians of Hamilton's relentless support of everything British. Hamilton wanted to reject any new French minister and refuse payments of debts to France on the grounds that the government now in charge was not the government with whom the United States had negotiated the treaty. On both issues Jefferson won: a minister would be accepted but with minimal attention, and Washington agreed with Jefferson that treaties were made with nations, not the government in charge at the time.

In the midst of these discussions in Philadelphia, the French had indeed sent a new diplomat, the young Edmond Charles Genet—handsome, vivacious, confident, naive, headstrong, extravagantly pro-French—to the United States. Arriving in Charleston in early April 1793 to great acclaim, Genet proceeded to act in a completely unrestrained manner, signing up American ships as privateers aimed against Britain, rousing support for the French cause, expecting to raise funds and troops for the benefit of his home country. He assumed that the popular support he found, as he wound his way slowly toward the nation's capital in Philadelphia, in effect repudiated the Neutrality Proclamation. Jefferson, although initially impressed by the charming diplomat, quickly realized how out of touch with the American scene and polity he was. Jefferson patiently tried to explain things to Genet, but the French minister resisted instruction, somehow still believing that popular pro-French sentiment trumped official government policy and even the prestige of Washington. The climax came when a captured British ship, the *Little Sarah,* docked in Philadelphia and renamed the *Petite Democrate,* was armed, outfitted as a privateer, and readied to sail. Jefferson met with Genet and explained that the ship could not depart until permission was obtained from the president. When Washington returned from Mount Vernon, he learned that Genet had proclaimed the *Petite Democrate* could depart at any time. Washington was furious, and after authorities detained the ship, Genet was equally furious, claiming public opinion overruled proclamations and threatening to go over the head of Washington and appeal to the people. This broke the camel.[8]

Jefferson had already come to realize that Genet had to be recalled, as had Washington. They wanted to do so with as little offense as possible to France. Hamilton, on the other hand, along with others like John Jay and Rufus King, wanted to play up the issue as much as possible to torpedo all remaining pro-French sentiment and disparage the popularity of all political leaders who still had sympathy for the French nation. On August 1, 1793, at Washington's direction, Jefferson prepared a careful letter to the French government, spelling out in detail Genet's inappropriate behavior. As expected, France relieved Genet of his duties. Jefferson explained in a letter to Madison, who was more supportive of the intemperate young French minister than was Jefferson, why he had to go: "Finding at length that the man was absolutely incorrigible, I saw the necessity of quitting a wreck which could not but sink all who cling to it."[9] Jefferson, though anti-British, was more politically savvy here than was Madison. Genet's actions had become very harmful to the Jeffersonian cause. Notably, throughout this episode, Washington was the most thoroughly neutral of those in government, seeking a middle path between the pro-British and pro-French views of Hamilton and Jefferson, respectively. But his two main cabinet members had grown even further apart. Jefferson's antipathy toward remaining in government service increased throughout this politically grueling year, and despite several more entreaties from Washington that he stay, Jefferson announced definitively that he would be leaving on the final day of the year.

Meanwhile another controversial issue arose that further divided Hamilton from Jefferson and Madison. Many years later, in a letter to Dr. Benjamin Rush, Jefferson recalled a dinner he attended with John Adams and Hamilton (probably in June 1791) at which Hamilton had commented that "the greatest man . . . that ever lived was Julius Caesar."[10] This remark stuck with Jefferson, in part because Hamilton clearly had an infatuation with military leadership that emerged on several occasions in the 1790s, most notably with the so-called Whiskey Rebellion. This was a revolt among farmers in the West, particularly in western Pennsylvania, that arose as a protest against the excise tax placed on distilled spirits as part of Hamilton's plan to raise the revenue sufficient to pay the interest on the newly reissued government bonds. Because of the transportation costs of shipping bulky wagonloads of corn over the mountains to markets in the eastern states, farmers typically distilled the corn into far more valuable corn whiskey. These farmers believed the excise tax unfairly singled them out. As a response, the excise tax was met first by anger and then protest, which grew as time passed. Tax collectors were harassed, even tarred and feathered, and other forms of extralegal violence and protests were carried out.[11]

There had long been opposition to excise taxes in the nation, predating the revolution, and distressed farmers had occasionally protested, as in the Shays' Rebellion of Massachusetts in the 1780s. But as the protests continued and escalated, the administration began to see this so-called Whiskey Rebellion as a real threat to the authority of the government. Washington, egged on by Hamilton who wanted to use force, issued an initial proclamation in 1792 condemning the protests and urging obedience of the law and payment of taxes. For two years, Washington's policy was moderation, and Attorney General Randolph and Jefferson helped restrain the president. But the protesters continued to resist, even after Washington threatened more serious action in early August 1794. In his "Proclamation Calling Forth the Militia," Washington used over-the-top language when describing the protesters, words like "dangerous and criminal," "vindictive menaces," "cruel and humiliating," and "armed banditi."[12] By this time Jefferson had resigned, and Hamilton had become Washington's most influential advisor.

What increased the administration's concern over the protests was the emergence of so-called Democratic-Republican societies, beginning in April 1793.[13] Soon there were thirty-five or more of these societies, organized in practically every state. Their membership was mostly drawn from the middling class: mechanics (manual workers), artisans, small businessmen, farmers. They believed people such as themselves should have a larger voice in the governance of society, and they were not shy about expressing their viewpoints, most of which were critical of the policies of the administration. These societies arose spontaneously and were not the result of the actions of leaders such as Jefferson and Madison, who purposefully steered clear of the radicalism the Democratic-Republican societies represented. But in the eyes of the administration, the Democratic-Republican societies were associated with the widespread farmers' protests, the specter of the French Revolution, and the more polite opposition of Jefferson and Madison. As such, the societies were seen as a significant threat to the government, especially since there had been no abatement of organized complaints despite Washington's warnings. The mere existence of the societies outraged Washington, who took their protests personally.

Washington fully identified himself with the office he held. In several overwrought private letters Washington called the farmers' protests "the first *ripe* fruit of the Democratic Societies"; he said the societies were "pernicious to the peace of Society"; he said these societies were "destroying all confidence in the Administration"; he charged them with wanting to "destroy the best fabric of human government . . . that has ever been presented for the acceptance of mankind."[14] To John Adams he wrote that "meetings in opposition to the constituted authorities" were "at all times, improper and dangerous."[15] Washington believed that after an election, all citizens should passively accept the policies of constituted authorities without protest.

At issue here was acceptable public dissent: how should it be expressed, and what differentiated healthy democratic protest from treason? Madison was more than disappointed by Washington's attacks on the Democratic societies, which merely represented citizens organized to express political opinions, calling his vituperative remarks an "attack on the most sacred principle of our Constitution and of Republicanism." Madison concluding that "the Citadel of their liberties" were "menaced."[16] Jefferson was more than shocked that Washington had, in his words, "permitted himself to be the organ of such an attack on the freedom of discussion, the freedom of writing, printing and publishing."[17]

By the summer of 1794, Washington, along with Hamilton and other New England Federalists, thought not only the authority but the actual continuance of the government was threatened. Following the insistent Hamilton's urging, Washington raised a militia force of fifteen thousand men, larger than any army he had commanded during the revolution, but though he ceremonially led the force westward into Pennsylvania, he put Hamilton effectively in charge of it.[18] Hamilton exulted at the prospect of leading an army to crush this opposition, but as soon as the military forces appeared, the protests collapsed.[19] (Washington nevertheless proved to be the only president ever to lead an army in the field.) Eventually some twenty men were arrested and two convicted, but Washington pardoned them all. The full authority of the central government had been tested and proved. As Hamilton wrote in October, "The insurrection will do us a great deal of good and add to the solidity of every thing in this country."[20] In Washington's summation of the events of the year in his annual message to Congress in November, he, in addition to attacking the protests themselves, blasted the role of the Democratic-Republican societies for inflaming public opinion, suggesting even their existence was improper.[21]

Jefferson had resigned from the State Department at the end of 1793 still in the good graces of the president. Washington had written Jefferson, upon the receipt of his resignation letter, that "the opinion, which I had formed, of your integrity and talents, and which dictated your original nomination, has been confirmed by the fullest experience; and that both have been eminently displayed in the discharge of your duties."[22] But the events of 1794 had produced a sea change in mutual opinions of matters of politics. The Hamilton-led campaign against Genet and all things French, and what Jefferson saw as a massive overreaction to the threat posed by the so-called Whiskey Rebels, caused Jefferson's feelings to harden. He found particularly outrageous Washington's attack on the Democratic societies in his message to Congress, seeing it as a desire to repress the rights of citizens to organize and express opinions critical of the administration. By the end of the year, political opinion in the nation had clearly bifurcated, with the ruling party described by Jefferson as monarchists or monocrats, and the Jeffersonians (self-described as Republicans) seen by their opponents as radical Jacobinists and enemies of the government and Constitution. Nothing like modern-day political party apparatuses yet existed, but clearly strong, self-identified coalitions had emerged, with advocates pushing their rival agendas and writing letters (both private and to newspapers) to rally voters. Much had happened since that May 1791 vacation trip through upstate New York that Madison and Jefferson had taken during which they must have discussed the direction that politics seemed to be heading. Although they did not appear to have been seeking supporters then, their private conversations with other leaders must have helped them see the emerging shape of the political scene.

The result was a situation by 1794 in which members of both proto-parties tended to overreact to the actions of the other. Politics had become poisonous. No doubt the government had needed to intervene in some fashion to put down the western protests against taxes, but the specter of a huge armed force called to crush popular protest—while it certainly strengthened the position of the central government—also highlighted the fears of what a standing army, under the control of a government not responsive to majority opinion, could do. Jefferson's always strong fear of monarchy was on hyper-alert, and Washington came to almost totally distrust Madison and have real doubts about Jefferson.[23]

Perhaps in his retirement at Monticello, Jefferson reminisced about happier days of cooperation with the president, especially regarding the siting and design of the new capital city, one of their signal accomplishments. Nothing would be more symbolic—then as well as today—of the newly established national government than a new city purpose-built to house the offices of government. Congress had narrowly passed the Residency Act in early July 1790, which called for "a district of territory, not exceeding ten miles square, to be located as hereafter directed on the river Potomack, at some place between the mouths of the Eastern-Branch and Conococheague . . . , and [the] same is hereby accepted for the permanent seat of the government of the United States." Jefferson and Washington had long wanted a Potomac location for the Federal City, Jefferson for its centrality in the nation and for the opportunity to design from scratch what he called a capital town, and Washington for those reasons as well as for the economic boost such a location would provide for Virginia. He was also not unaware that such a city would enhance the value of his town lots in Alexandria (and Mount Vernon was only seven miles distant) and his property holdings upstream on the Potomac. Washington in fact wrote in late 1793 that he had "no doubt" but that the "Federal City" would become the "emporium of the United States."[24] When the government moved there in late 1800, the center of the nation's population was nearby, in Howard County, Maryland, eighteen miles west of Baltimore.

It is fair to say that both these Virginians were ecstatic about the opportunity to create a new city for the government's offices offered, and despite the political vicissitudes of the next years, Washington and Jefferson worked in unison to shape a suitable capital for the new nation. Nowhere else had their partnership been so evident. Washington was politically astute enough to realize that he needed to act quickly in response to the Residency Act because persons in both Philadelphia and New York still hoped to somehow recapture the permanent capital for their own cities. Jefferson quickly met with the president to clear up a vagueness in the act. Conceivably it could be interpreted to mean that just enough acreage should be chosen as to accommodate a Capitol Building, a residence for the president, and several more public buildings, nothing more. Jefferson wanted Washington to seize the opportunity to claim the entire one-hundred-square-mile territory and plan on it what Jefferson called a capital town. Washington instantly agreed with Jefferson's plan and in fact probably was already thinking similarly. Jefferson had in mind government buildings, market places, gardens, and homes. He proposed a grid of streets set at right angles, with most streets 100 feet wide, with 15-foot walkways on the sides. Major streets should be 120 feet wide. He later suggested that streets running north–south should be designated by numbers and those running east–west should be listed alphabetically. He thought at first an area of approximately 1,500 acres might be laid out, which seems small today but was about the same size as the built-up portion of the nation's largest city at the time, Philadelphia. Jefferson suggested that as in Paris, a height limitation should be placed on houses.[25]

In the spring of 1791 Washington made a fateful decision, hiring Pierre Charles L'Enfant to design the capital. Washington of course knew L'Enfant from his having renovated Federal Hall in New York City. L'Enfant proved to be a real visionary, though he had been trained as an artist, not an engineer, and he had never before had such an immense project. But he had ambition, energy, and arrogance in abundance, and he was not about to be constrained by the three commissioners that Washington appointed, as the Residency Act directed, to oversee the project. Earlier, Washington had appointed Andrew Ellicott, assisted by the Black surveyor Benjamin Banneker and others, to survey and set the stone markers designating the bounds of the federal district. It is clear that despite pretensions of considering a range of locations along the Potomac, Washington already had the site in mind, a ten-by-ten-mile square positioned like a diamond with one corner pointed north, more or less centered at the spot where the Eastern Branch fed into the main branch of the Potomac. This site encompassed the preexisting cities of Alexandria and Georgetown, and to ensure it included Alexandria, the territory went below the Eastern Branch and included more than thirty square miles in Virginia. In March 1791 Congress amended the Residency Act to authorize these boundaries, although it specified that all government buildings should be on the eastern (Maryland) side of the Potomac. (Years later, in 1846, the Virginia portion of the original federal territory was ceded back to Virginia.)

Washington and Jefferson knew for political reasons they should not turn to Congress for funds sufficient to construct an entire city, so they intended to survey the town, lay out lots (with grounds reserved for the key public buildings), and auction off alternating city lots to raise the monies necessary to build the capital. L'Enfant did not understand such parsimonious caution. He seems to have imagined the new government simply authorizing ample funds, Versailles-like, to bring into existence quickly a grandiose capital city. He incorrectly expected it to rapidly become a large city in terms of population.

L'Enfant enlarged several-fold Jefferson's proposed capital town into a large capital city. He superimposed upon Jefferson's suggested grid pattern of streets a series of broad diagonal boulevards, punctuated by a number of squares and parks. He suggested the Capitol Building be placed atop Jenkins's Hill (Washington had chosen this site also), the highest point in the landscape, and what he called the president's palace more than a mile to the west. (Jefferson erased *palace* from L'Enfant's map and inserted *house,* thereby removing the taint of monarchy.) A broad mall ran westward from the location of the Capitol Building toward the Potomac.

Jefferson gracefully accepted L'Enfant's much grander vision of a city, as did Washington, though they would not budge from their cautious method of funding it. In part, a larger design would offer more lots to be auctioned, and that may have been the deciding factor. L'Enfant refused to provide preliminary maps intended to promote the selling of lots. He also prematurely demolished the house of prominent landowner Daniel Carroll because it turned out to be located in the middle of one of L'Enfant's proposed streets. When questioned about this, L'Enfant had said he "had as much right to pull down a house, as to cut down a tree."[26] Such highhandedness, and repeated refusals to cooperate with the commissioners despite Washington's patience and Jefferson's repeated efforts to explain what was both legally and practically necessary, ultimately led to Washington's firing the headstrong French visionary in February 1792. But not before his impractical plans had shaped the general design and layout of the Federal City, which the commissioners had in September 1791 named *Washington* and the federal territory the *District of Columbia.*[27]

Throughout these months of trying to move the project along, Jefferson had written many letters to L'Enfant, had mediated conflicts between him and the commissioners, and had worked with Washington to try to arrange auctions of lots (which proved exceedingly disappointing in terms of sales). On numerous occasions Washington had summoned Jefferson to come have dinner with him so they could strategize how to handle L'Enfant and deal with a multiplicity of issues, often inviting Madison to join them. But with L'Enfant now gone, and with his having completed designs for neither the Capitol Building itself nor the President's House, Jefferson proposed alternatives. He devised a plan to have competitions and offer prizes or premiums for winning designs for these two major construction projects. The commissioners subsequently received numerous proposals for the President's House and ultimately chose the one submitted by James Hoban, an Irish-trained practicing architect from Charleston. It was a fairly traditional, boxy design with features common to English and manor houses, but it pleased Washington and was acceptable to the others.[28] The President's House ended up just barely being sufficiently finished for John and Abigail Adams to move in at the very end of 1800.

The actual Capitol Building proved more complicated. Sixteen designs were submitted and none pleased the commissioners nor Washington and Jefferson, but they saw sufficient promise in the drawings of Stephen Hallett, who was really just a draftsman, to ask him to refine his proposal. Meanwhile, a Scottish-born physician, William Thornton, then living in Philadelphia, decided to try his hand, quickly skimming such architectural design books as he could find in the city. Although the completion deadline was passed, in late 1792 Dr. Thornton showed his design to both Washington and Jefferson, both of whom were so impressed they recommended it to the commissioners, Jefferson calling it "simple, noble, beautiful, excellently distributed, and moderate in size."[29] Closer inspection found some problems in the design, so the commissioners hired Hallett to correct Thornton's plans and prepare drawings for the builders. Thornton's design featured a tall dome, with wings on either side for the two branches of Congress.

Washington and Jefferson were instrumental in shaping the character of the new nation's new capital city. Washington was present at the laying of the Capitol Building's cornerstone on September 18, 1793, although this magnificent building would not be completed until after the Civil War. While the first president and his secretary of state would be largely responsible for the siting, planning, and physical construction of the capital, most of the actual physical labor employed in its building was provided by enslaved workers. Because of L'Enfant's absence, Jefferson directed Ellicott to finish the drafting of a complete map of the city, necessary for the selling of lots to finance the public buildings. Jefferson, who had long been interested in Indian languages, also asked Ellicott to try to determine the original name of the Eastern Branch of the Potomac, and based on ancient surveys, Ellicott reported it variously as Annakostia and Anna Kastia.[30] Jefferson anglicized the name and had it inserted on the revised map as Anacostia, as it is known today.

Sales of lots went far slower than Washington could have imagined, and financial problems plagued the construction of the capital city. But neither Washington nor Jefferson ever gave up on their hopes for a capital worthy of the nation. These two Founders should be recognized as city-builders as well as nation-makers. Washington did not live to see the government move to its new location. Jefferson did not expect to ever live there. After 1793, he was in retirement at Monticello, and in 1794 he began a massive renovation of Monticello based on an urban palace, the Hôtel de Salm, he had watched being constructed in Paris years before. Over the next few years, Jefferson was uninvolved with the making of national policy, and he never imagined returning to the halls of power. Little did he foresee his political future.

In a sense, the national political rosters were in fact changing. George Mason, never reconciled to the Constitution and even more upset by Hamilton's economic policies, had died on October 7, 1792, at the age of sixty-seven, a "great loss," as Jefferson recorded it to Madison.[31] Meanwhile, the Virginia General Assembly in 1790 had appointed James Monroe to the Senate, where he quickly became a leader of the Jeffersonian or republican faction against the policies of Hamilton. Despite Monroe's authoring a series of newspaper articles critical of administration policies, Washington would appoint him the US minister to France in 1794 to balance his appointment of John Jay as minister to England.

Madison's life took a highly significant turn in 1794. That spring the forty-three-year-old bachelor noticed in Philadelphia the attractive young widow Dolley Payne Todd, whose husband and infant son had died in late 1793 in the yellow fever epidemic that struck Philadelphia. (She had a one-year-old surviving son, John Payne Todd.) Madison, realizing that Aaron Burr stayed in the same boardinghouse where Mrs. Todd resided, asked Burr to introduce him to the vivacious Dolley, who was three or four inches taller than him and seventeen years younger. She had various suitors, but "the great little Madison," as she called him at first, won her hand.[32] They were subsequently married on September 15, 1794. Dolley Madison's winning personality proved a wonderful adjunct to her husband's seriousness, and she possessed astute political instincts. She would go on to serve as an occasional hostess for Jefferson in the presidential house, and later, during her husband's two terms as president, she essentially created the modern role of First Lady.[33]

Amid these changes, Patrick Henry, the once vociferous foe of the Constitution, vigorously opposed Hamilton's economic proposals, but he still revered Washington and detested Jefferson. Henry worked with John Marshall on several important legal cases in the early 1790s, becoming closer to Marshall both personally and politically in the process. By 1793 Henry had retired from politics and was concerned primarily with enhancing his own economic prospects, but his ties with Marshall and his continuing (his most recent biographer says "instinctive"[34]) admiration of Washington recommended him to the president, who in the mid-1790s offered to Henry successively the ambassadorship to Spain, the office of secretary of state, and a seat on the Supreme Court, all of which Henry declined. His oratorical fame persisted, but he was mostly politically inactive after 1793. (In 1799, at Washington's urging, Henry successfully ran for a seat in the state legislature but, seemingly old before his time, died later that year, before he could take office, at the age of sixty-three.)

Like Henry, Marshall in the early 1790s was focused primarily on his own affairs, his legal career blossoming as he became one of the state's leading attorneys. In 1788 he built a nine-room, two-and-a-half-story house in Richmond and pursued his own interests. In 1793, while Genet's antics were agitating the nation's politics, Marshall had emphatically (though temporarily) ended his friendship with Monroe primarily because of disagreement over France, and slowly he was identifying more with the political faction associated with Washington and Hamilton. Of all the Founders from Virginia, Marshall was the only one not personally involved in agriculture (though he did own many enslaved persons who lived and labored on several of the plantations he owned, and he leased out the plantations and their enslaved workforces), but kept about a dozen enslaved men and women who worked as domestics in and around his home. It was obvious that as the careers of Mason and Henry slowed and ended, those of Monroe and Marshall were accelerating.

Political careers waxed and waned, but some political issues seemed perennial. International issues again significantly impinged on what otherwise might have remained local controversies. For example, from the earliest days of US settlement beyond the Appalachians, farmers in the western regions had wanted access via the Mississippi River to the markets of the East Coast and beyond. Flatboats would float down the Ohio and Mississippi Rivers to New Orleans, and there goods were transferred to ocean-going vessels. The expectation was that such goods could be unloaded and temporarily stored until loaded unto sea-worthy vessels. This so-called right of deposit, without the paying of cargo fees, was essential to the economic well-being of western settlers. In 1784 when John Jay had worked out a treaty with Spanish minister Diego de Gardoqui that gave up navigation rights on the Mississippi in exchange for trade agreements that favored the northeastern states, there had been huge outrage in the West. Jefferson and Madison then had feared that any treaty that abandoned the right of deposit in New Orleans would be an invitation to western secession. The Jay-Gardoqui treaty had failed because of congressional opposition, but the issue had never been satisfactorily resolved.

In the early 1790s, western farmers again became concerned about their ability to ship their goods via the Mississippi, and during the first years of the decade when the so-called whiskey tax threatened the western economies, some westerners began to openly talk of secession and alignment with Spain, or, worse yet, contemplate a rebellion against Spain and seizure of the territory and erection of an independent nation. At just this time, Spain became disenchanted with her failing alliance with England against France and indicated a willingness to renegotiate the matter of the Mississippi as well as a long-simmering dispute with the United States over the boundary between Spanish Florida and the US territory: Spain had begun claiming the 32nd parallel while the US pushed for the more southern 31st parallel. When Spain hinted at an opening, Washington sent Thomas Pinckney, who had been minister to England, to Spain. There on October 27, 1795, Pinckney and Don Manuel de Godoy of Spain signed what became known as the Treaty of San Lorenzo, which was extremely favorable to the United States.[35]

The treaty recognized the 31st parallel as the boundary, it designated the US-Spanish boundary on the west as the middle of the Mississippi River all the way to its northern end (which neither Spain nor the United States knew at the time) and guaranteed to both nations free commerce the whole length of the river to its mouth. The free right of deposit in New Orleans was guaranteed for three years, with the proviso that at the end of that period the agreement could either be renewed or another appropriate location found. This treaty, ratified by Congress on March 7, 1796, met with great acclaim in the West, from Kentucky and Tennessee (which became a state on June 1, 1796) into the territories north of the Ohio River. It greatly stimulated trade, settlement, and land speculation in the entire region and was a resounding success for the Washington administration. Yet it was soon swallowed up by a far more controversial treaty that inflamed public opinion like nothing else had in the 1790s.

In June and November 1793, England issued Orders in Council (in effect, a form of legislation issued by the king upon the direction of his highest advisors) that changed its behavior regarding neutral trade, and by the terms of these new orders, British vessels seized over two hundred US ships involved with commerce with British West Indian colonies. It also seized ("impressed") dozens of sailors on US ships and arrested them. This caused great outrage in the United States, even irritating committed anglophile Hamilton, and there were demands for war. Republican leaders called for trade restrictions against the British. Washington understood the danger of war against powerful Britain and moved to defuse the issue. In April 1794 he nominated Chief Justice John Jay as a special envoy to England to try to negotiate the differences between the two nations. The Republicans were furious because this act limited their ability to push for economic retaliation while diplomacy was underway, and they feared that Federalist Jay, advised by Hamilton, would likely be prone to favoritism toward England. Southern and western legislators, remembering Jay's earlier failed negotiations with Diego de Gardoqui that had sacrificed western interests to favor northeastern merchants, had reason to worry. While Jay was in London, Washington sent James Monroe, a confirmed Republican, as minister to France, hoping his appointment would appear to balance the administration's diplomacy.

Months went by, and on November 19, 1794, Jay signed a treaty with England. Following delays, the treaty arrived in the United States, but only after Congress had adjourned. The treaty was kept secret, but rumors arose that once again Jay had caved in to British diplomats and signed a treaty that gained little for his own nation. Washington himself was so disappointed by the treaty that he delayed submitting it to Congress. Finally in June 1795 the Senate began to discuss the treaty. The administration tried to keep the terms of the treaty secret, but several senators leaked portions of it. Eventually the entire text was published, but meanwhile the Senate narrowly approved the treaty. Public outrage erupted, with the Republicans charging the treaty was far too favorable to the British. They said it essentially created an alliance between the United States and England and in effect repudiated long-standing treaty obligations to France. Would Washington sign the treaty as accepted by the Senate?

Public protests broke out across the nation. Both Republicans and Federalists resorted to appealing to the public, letters were published in newspapers, charges were made that Washington was abandoning our revolutionary-era ally, the actual treaty was attacked point by point. England had not liberalized its stand on trade and did not agree to stop impressment, although smaller US ships of under seventy tons were permitted to trade with the British West Indian colonies. A commission was authorized to settle old claims about debts owed British merchants and certain boundary disputes with Canada. Nothing was settled about British dealings with Indigenous nations, or with southern claims regarding enslaved people taken away by British vessels during the revolution. Perhaps Jay had gotten as much as any diplomat could have, and the treaty did prevent a war between the two nations, but many Americans with some legitimacy could feel that the administration had been too willing to come to an agreement with England, who dominated American trade, and thus through the resulting import taxes supported Hamilton's economic plan. To the Republicans, the treaty seemed part-and-parcel of the pro-British tendencies of the administration. There were even calls for Washington's impeachment, and the tenor of debate reached heights of acrimony not seen before in the young nation.[36]

Federalists read the opposition as the result of uncritical support of French interests, while the Republicans interpreted the treaty as a servile acceptance of little short of British rule. The result was political turmoil of unprecedented scale in the nation, and both factions again feared the fate of the nation was perilously at risk. Washington, who could only believe that criticisms of the treaty were veiled attacks upon him, the Constitution, and the nation, was aghast at the opposition. He wrote Hamilton that the treaty had "received the most tortured interpretation, & that the writings agt. it (which are very industriously circulated) are pregnant of the most abominable misrepresentations."[37] Jefferson, on the other hand, claimed that "this infamous Act . . . is really nothing more than a treaty of alliance between England and the Anglomen of this country against the legislature and people of the United States."[38] Even Dr. Benjamin Rush, who had friends on both sides of most issues, wrote in 1796 that many in Philadelphia "complain of British influence in all our cities, which extends through the medium of commerce to our country and is reflected back again from thence to the councils of the United States."[39]

Both Washington and Jefferson honestly believed that the future of the nation was at stake. Because fundamentally neither accepted the legitimacy of parties, both viewed their support of their own stance as patriotic attempts to save the union and the Constitution from the mistaken policies of the other. Therefore, the opposing position was detrimental to the nation. Both sides believed that in time the opposing positions would be recognized to be false and their own position accepted as in the best interest of the nation. Hence public protest served to stiffen Washington's resolve, and Jefferson only became more convinced that in due time the people would see through the Federalists' policies and come to accept the Republican position. What was becoming solidified were in fact two dominant sets of party positions that shaped the opinions and actions of most political actors. These differing viewpoints and their adherents were in the process of becoming what we now label political parties, but they were not quite parties yet. Neither side believed the other was really legitimate or ultimately supportive of the constitutional government as it existed. Meanwhile, both sides were engaged in the continuing bitter fight for and against the treaty Jay had negotiated and the Senate had approved. Republicans argued against portions of the treaty because they alleged its decisions regarding commerce trespassed on the responsibilities of the House of Representatives. The treaty had certain provisions that required federal funding, and of course only the House could authorize such funds. Madison and others in the Republican camp (having met in what was in effect the first party caucus) called for more information on precisely how the treaty had been negotiated and these provisions had been decided upon. If the treaty required congressionally appropriated funds, they reasoned, they should have more information on how the treaty had been arrived at.

There were calls for Washington to release his instructions to Jay and all the papers regarding the negotiations, which outraged Washington as intrusions on the president's sole authority to conduct foreign policy. Breaking harshly with Madison, Washington said the Constitution gave foreign policy design and treaty-making exclusively to the executive branch, claiming that he knew this because he had been present at the Constitutional Convention. Madison respectfully argued against this totalizing view of executive power, even drawing on debates in the ratification conventions to broaden the responsibility of Congress. Washington, visibly angry, completely refused. The result was a total break with the Virginia contingent, except for moderate Federalist John Marshall, who was destined to rise in the Federalist hierarchy. Washington never again invited Madison to visit Mount Vernon, stopping all communication with him.[40] Washington had always found it difficult to accept criticism and could not differentiate between policy disputes and personal disputes, a blindness that both puzzled and hurt Madison. Meanwhile, word kept arriving that Ambassador Monroe in Paris, a confirmed Republican who was unashamedly pro-French, was making comments critical of Jay, his treaty, and administration policies in general. Monroe insisted to French officials that US citizens were overwhelmingly Francophiles. Monroe's political clumsiness in this instance and his disloyalty to the administration so irritated Washington that in July he instructed Secretary of State Timothy Pickering to recall him.

Washington had already seriously considered not running for reelection in 1792. Now in 1796 he was absolutely determined to retire. There of course was no requirement that he do so; many Federalists wanted him to run again. But Washington was simply exhausted by the political criticism and the acrimony of politics in general. Hamilton, who had resigned from Treasury at the end of January 1795 and returned to the practice of law in New York City to bolster his financial standing, remained Washington's most trusted advisor and the de facto head of the Federalist faction. Previously, in 1792, Washington had asked Madison to prepare a farewell address announcing his retirement, but because Washington had since broken with Madison, he now turned to Hamilton, sending him both a copy of Madison's earlier work and some ideas of his own. He asked Hamilton either to refashion these writings or prepare something entirely new. Hamilton not unexpectedly did the latter, though he borrowed some from Madison for his beginning and incorporated most of Washington's ideas. But the finely crafted document known to posterity as Washington's Farewell Address was mainly the work of Hamilton. Washington went over it carefully, editing it, and making sure that it represented his own ideas, so the result was an artful blending of the two capable men's ideas. But it was not meant to be simply a form of avuncular advice from the Father of the Country to his political offspring. It had a sharp political bite, and it has to be interpreted within its historical context. Washington still believed himself a man above party (even writing to Jefferson in July 1796, "I was no party man myself"), but by this time in his administration he had in fact become a committed partisan.[41]

Hamilton was thinking of who would follow Washington as he contemplated preparing the address. He knew Vice President John Adams would be the logical successor, but Hamilton disliked Adams and favored Thomas Pinckney. However, Hamilton would greatly prefer either of them to Thomas Jefferson, and he knew that the public respect for Washington was so profound that no one would dare put their name forward as long as there was a prospect that he would choose to remain in office. Hamilton reasoned that the longer Washington delayed making his decision clear, the less time the supporters of Jefferson would have to build up political support for him (unbeknownst to Hamilton, Jefferson had no intention of seeking the presidency, although Madison, behind Jefferson's back, was strongly promoting him[42]). So Hamilton urged delay on Washington's part, until about two months before states would choose the members of the electoral college. As a result, the address did not appear until September 19, 1796, when it was published in the *Philadelphia Daily American Advertiser* and soon thereafter in many other papers. Washington never delivered it orally.

The address opened with an expression of humility and affection for the nation, after which Washington wrote, "Here, perhaps, I ought to stop. But a solicitude for your welfare"—he was speaking to the public at large—"urge me . . . to recommend some sentiments which are the result of much reflection . . . and which appear to me all important to the permanency of your felicity as a people. These will be offered," he said disingenuously, as "the disinterested warnings of a parting friend, who can possibly have no personal motive to bias his counsel."[43] What followed was in fact much good advice, useful across time, but intended in 1796 to warn the public against the ideas, practices, and leaders Washington then saw as his, and hence the nation's, political enemies. First there were heartfelt paeans to the value of the union, which, he wrote, provided many undeniable advantages to the people of the nation. Hence any "attempt to alienate any portion of our country from the rest" should be frowned upon, as should all "local discriminations."[44] Each of the nation's sections offered benefit to the others, and in turn benefited from the others. The union provided the "greater security from external danger" and is the "main prop" of the people's liberty.[45] The public should "distrust the patriotism" of those who might weaken the union, and that danger extended to "characterizing parties by geographical discriminations." Sectionalism endangered the union. Those who suspected "the Atlantic states unfriendly to their interests" in the West were doing harm to the union.[46] Here Washington meant those southerners and westerners who opposed first the Jay-Gardoqui negotiations and then the Jay Treaty.

Washington next argued that the Constitution was "sacredly obligatory upon all," which sounds impartial until one reads the next paragraph, where he attacked "all obstructions to the execution of the laws"—meaning the Whiskey Rebels—and "all combinations and associations under whatever plausible character"—meaning the Democratic societies (but not the Society of the Cincinnati, of which he was a member). Likewise, any attempt to "direct, control, counteract, or awe the regular deliberation and action of the constituted authorities, are destructive" of constitutional government, meaning political opposition to the ruling power was wrong. Such organization and protest against the administration constituted "faction . . . often a small but artful and enterprising minority of the community." He warned against any "irregular oppositions" without specifying what kind of opposition to the party in power was acceptable.[47] This all led to a strong warning "against the baneful effects of the spirit of party," from which arose all kinds of evils, including "the ruins of public liberty." For that reason, "the common and continual mischiefs of the spirit of party are sufficient to make it in the interest and the duty of a wise people to discourage and restrain it," for it "foments occasionally riot and insurrection." In short, Washington believed practically all opposition to the policies of duly elected authorities was ill-advised.[48]

Still, much that he advocated was uncontroversial, such as support for the role of religion and morality in government, the importance of supporting "institutions for the general diffusion of knowledge" and the public credit, and the avoidance of debt. Likewise, he urged leaders to "observe good faith and justice towards all nations; cultivate peace and harmony with all."[49] Who could object to such admonitions? Then came the partisan thrust: "In the execution of such a plan nothing is more essential than that permanent, inveterate antipathies against particular nations and passionate attachments for others should be excluded and that in place of them just and amicable feelings towards all should be cultivated."[50] But here he was castigating the Republican favoritism of France and antagonism toward Britain, not at all the opposite tendencies of the Federalists. One set of actions was wrong, the other set wise, in the eyes of Washington, yet he recognized no bias toward his own position. Partiality for one nation, he warned, "gives to ambitious, corrupted, or deluded citizens (who devote themselves to the favorite nation) facility to betray or sacrifice the interests of their own country."[51] Washington here obviously meant

Jefferson and like-minded politicians. The president continued in this vein, attacking "excessive partiality for one foreign nation and excessive dislike of another." Of course he was warning here against partiality toward France and dislike of England, the tendency he accused the Republicans of. They would have warned him similarly but with a switch of affections, but the point is, Washington was employing his farewell address for partisan purposes. Some of the most famous words of the farewell address came next:

> The great rule of conduct for us in regard to foreign nations is, in extending our commercial relations, to have with them as little *political* connection as possible. . . . Europe has a set of primary interests, which to us have none, or a very remote relation. Hence she must be engaged in frequent controversies, the cause of which are essentially foreign to our concerns. Hence therefore it must be unwise in us to implicate ourselves, by artificial ties, in the ordinary vicissitudes of her politics or the ordinary combinations and collisions of her friendships or enemies.
>
> . . . . It is our true policy to steer clear of permanent alliances with any portion of the foreign world—so far, I mean, as we are now at liberty to do it—for let me not be understood as capable of patronizing infidelity to existing engagements. . . . We may safely trust to temporary alliances for extraordinary emergencies.[52]

Throughout this section Washington was attacking the Republicans for their presumed inappropriate attachment to the French, unaware that they could just as legitimately accuse his administration of rank partiality toward all things British. In fact, leaders on both sides were alert to the inadvisability of complicated and permanent arrangements with either Britain or France regardless of which nation they were more favorably disposed toward. After all, it was Jefferson, in his first inaugural address, who would famously advocate "peace, commerce, and honest friendship with all nations, entangling alliances with none."[53] With his final admonition, Washington concluded by stating that he "anticipate[d] with pleasing expectation that retreat in which I promise myself to realize without alloy the sweet enjoyment of partaking, in the midst of my fellow citizens, the benign influence of good laws under a free government—the ever favorite object of my heart, and the happy reward, as I trust, of our mutual cares, labours and dangers."[54]

While Washington's many supporters praised the address as well-meaning advice to the nation, his political adversaries saw it as the highly partisan and polemical document it was. As Madison wrote Monroe, "the valedictory address of the president . . . shews that he [is] completely in the snares of the British faction" and reveals that in his mind there is "a rancor against [France] . . . and suspicions of all who are thought to sympathize with its revolution."[55] With the passage of time and the dimming of memories, most Americans now, if they know it at all, remember the farewell address as a salutary warning against foreign entanglements that can lead to war. It is today rarely connected to the political controversies of the 1790s that contributed to its issuance.

Though many of the Virginia leaders were at odds with one another by the end of Washington's administration, they had jointly made major contributions to the new nation over the period of his tenure. Washington and Madison's close partnership had been key to the successes of the First Congress, the beginnings of a stately national capital had been laid out by Washington and Jefferson working in tandem, skillful diplomacy had eased several international problems, and the outlines had been established for what became the first political parties, with Jefferson and Madison leading the way. As members of the older generation like Washington and Henry left the scene, newer Virginia leaders like Monroe and Marshall were emerging. The government was still but a fledgling, but in future years Jefferson and Marshall would, for example, further develop the office of the presidency and magnify the importance of the Supreme Court. For another generation, Virginians would continue to play the role of nation-makers.

9

POLITICAL CRISIS

While all the Founders who were in office in the early 1790s hoped for a general consensus in government, it had become clear during the First Session that that was not to be, despite the reverence for George Washington. Though in retirement at Monticello in 1794, Jefferson was greatly dismayed by the president's condemnation of the principle of political opposition as indicated by his attacks on the Democratic-Republican societies. Jefferson wrote Madison, upon hearing rumors his fellow Virginian was contemplating retirement from Congress, that he hoped instead someday to see Madison "in a more splendid and a more efficacious post." Jefferson stated that he was somewhat embarrassed to be wishing higher office for Madison when he himself had withdrawn from the political world, but "I would not give up my own retirement for the empire of the Universe," he wrote, and said he would explain his views in more detail at a later time.[1] No doubt looking forward to the time in several years when Washington would retire, Madison replied that Jefferson "ought to be preparing yourself . . . to hear truths, which no inflexibility will be able to withstand."[2] Madison, at this point more politically astute than his mentor, knew that Jefferson would be the most likely person to succeed Washington and rebalance the government away from what he saw as proto-monarchial tendencies. Jefferson was unmoved by Madison's warning. He replied that his mind was totally made up; his health was bad, he said, his financial affairs were in a distressed situation, and whatever "little spice of ambition" he had once had "has long since evaporated. . . . The question is for ever closed with me."[3] Maybe so in Jefferson's mind, but not in Madison's.

In the midst of the political turmoil the Jay Treaty had engendered, thoughtful Federalists in 1796 worried about the decision of Washington not to seek another term. In many ways Vice President John Adams seemed his obvious successor, but support for him was lukewarm. Even in his own party some considered him vain, irritable, and too independent, a trait that particularly bothered Alexander Hamilton, who expected to still be able to have the same influence over the next president that he had had over Washington. Hamilton decided to secretly support Ambassador Thomas Pinckney, whose successful negotiation of a treaty with Spain was thought to have gained him significant support in the South and West. Hamilton wanted to appear to support Adams and Pinckney equally so as to gain both the presidency and vice presidency, but he intended to engineer a process by which one or more electors would throw away their supposed vote for Adams so as to deliver the presidency to the more pliant Pinckney. Whichever way it went, Hamilton favored either prospect over Jefferson, but he was aware that if word got out about his scheme, either Adams or Pinckney electors might drop their votes, inadvertently causing Jefferson to win.[4] In Hamilton's view, "there can be no doubt that the exclusion of Mr. Jefferson is far more important than any difference between Mr. Adams and Mr. Pinckney."[5]

Madison, if not Jefferson, had some whiff of these plans, and the Madison faction feared the centralizing tendencies of the Federalists would increasingly place the nation in the power of the British. Federalist politicians wrote letters and through pamphlets, sermons, and other methods worked to maintain their control of the presidency. Adams, as was the fashion, did nothing publicly to advance his campaign, seeing such open politicking as crass. Madison and his cohorts had an even more complicated plan; they were working feverishly on behalf of Jefferson who did not even know his name was being pushed for the office. Madison never consulted with him and abstained from visiting Jefferson at Monticello over the summer lest the issue come up. Jefferson's proponents were more comfortable with campaigning than were Adams's supporters, and the Jeffersonians had command of a much broader range of newspapers across the nation. Newspapers with partisan editors were becoming an essential arm of the emerging party system. Full-fledged campaign operations had not yet arisen, but Madison did have colleagues who wrote and otherwise advocated for Jefferson. It is almost inconceivable that Jefferson did not have an inkling of what was happening, but he certainly did not in any way engage in electioneering and did not lift a finger to help his cause.[6]

This was the first real or competitive election in the new nation's history. In December, Madison wrote Jefferson several letters, the first suggesting that the members of the electoral college might interrupt Jefferson's "repose" at Monticello, then a letter warning that should he be elected as vice president rather than president, he should accept the position. Jefferson replied that although he wished Madison, not him, could be elected, he surely would accept the call of the voters for either office but in fact thought it appropriate that Adams have the superior position: "He has always been my senior from the commencement of our public life, . . . and this circumstance ought to give him the preference."[7]

When the electoral votes were counted, Adams received 71, Jefferson 68, Pinckney 59, and Burr (expected to be Jefferson's vice president) only 30. (Nine other candidates got a smattering of votes.) Adams would be the next president. Jefferson prepared a generous letter to send to Adams, both congratulating him and expressing his long affection for him. Jefferson also made an oblique reference to Hamilton's plotting, calling him "your archfriend of New York." Jefferson had the good judgment to show the letter first to Madison, who counseled him not to send it both because he said the prickly Adams already knew of Jefferson's warm feelings toward him and, should the letter become public, it would anger those who had worked hard for Jefferson's election. So Adams never saw the letter. Still, if Jefferson were aware of Hamilton's activities, certainly Adams was ("his intrigues in the election I despise," Adams wrote in January of the new year[8]). And this internal conflict among the Federalists would grow and eventually erupt into bitter attacks by Hamilton upon the head of his own party, contributing not a little to Adams's eventual defeat by Jefferson four years hence. Meanwhile, Jefferson was content with the outcome in 1796; he even thought it would perhaps be good for the nation, especially if Adams "administer[ed] the government on it's true principles, and . . . relinquish[ed] his bias to an English constitution." More important, though, in Jefferson's mind, "He is perhaps the only sure barrier against Hamilton's getting in."[9] That, for both Adams and Jefferson, was the primary concern.

In 1796 the electoral college included electors from sixteen states—Vermont, Kentucky, and Tennessee having been added to the original thirteen—but still the proto-parties did not offer voters what is now called a ticket. Instead, whoever won the most number of electoral votes became president, and the winner of the second most votes became vice president. Hence in what now seems an oddity, the two central opponents, Adams and Jefferson, became, respectively, president and vice president. At first, because both men at that time still thought well of the other, there seemed a fleeting possibility of a diminishment of domestic political tensions. When, almost as soon as he took office, Adams was faced with the French rejection of American diplomat Charles Cotesworth Pinckney and then a decision by the French government to designate all trade with Britain or its colonies subject to seizure, he wanted to cool the animosity with France. He proposed to Jefferson sending him to Paris, although Adams stated he imagined that might interfere with Jefferson's vice presidential duties, which it obviously would. He then asked Jefferson to sound out Madison about his going, but Jefferson stated he was sure that Madison would refuse.

After Jefferson later reported Madison's negative decision to the president, Adams remarked that when he had brought Madison's name up with his cabinet—all committed Hamiltonians—they angrily rejected it. Adams did not really control his own administration. And, Jefferson said, Adams never again consulted him on any policy issue. (Years later Adams admitted to the same, writing that "party violence" was the reason, and "this party violence was excited by Hamilton more than any other man."[10]) In truth, Jefferson did not want to be involved in presidential decisions. Because the vice president's only constitutionally mandated job was to preside over the Senate, Jefferson saw himself as a member of the legislative branch, not the executive.

Later that year an embarrassing personal letter Jefferson had written in 1796 to an old friend, Philip Mazzei, in Italy, came to light in a badly translated version. Amid his letter about local Virginia news and friends, Jefferson had made a sharp comment about Washington, commenting that "It would give you a fever were I to name to you the apostates who have gone over to these heresies, men who were Samsons in the field and Solomons in the council, but who have had their heads shorn by the harlot England."[11] Of course he would never had said something like this in the United States, or for public consumption, but Mazzei, in an act of astonishingly bad judgment, had the letter translated into French and published in a Paris newspaper. There it was seen by a US merchant, who brought the paper back to New York City and gave it to Noah Webster, who translated the letter back into English and published it in May 1797 in his own paper. The comments obviously about George Washington proved to be a political bombshell, casting Jefferson as a critic of the revered Father of the Country and hence a rank partisan. This huge blunder by Jefferson caused the Federalists to see him as the personification of the opposition.

With public furor high over France's recent actions, and at Adams's behest, Congress built up the nation's defenses, including, along with naval vessels and harbor defenses, authorizing the president to call up a militia force of some eighty thousand men. War seemed imminent. The Jeffersonian faction did not believe that France was a military threat to the United States and instead expected it to soon invade England; the Hamiltonians fanned the anti-France fervor. Yet Adams knew that the nation could not sustain a war against a strong European nation, so he insisted on sending a delegation of negotiators to Paris, choosing Charles Cotesworth Pinckney, whom the French had rejected before; an old friend, the quirky and independent-minded Elbridge Gerry of Massachusetts; and John Marshall, the moderate Federalist from Virginia.

The wily French foreign minister, Charles Maurice de Talleyrand-Périgord, spoke English and knew the United States well, having lived there for several years, and he expected through his government position both to serve his nation and enrich himself. He assigned a set of envoys (known as X, Y, and Z) to meet with the American negotiators and make several demands: First, that Adams apologize for remarks France considered insulting. Second, pay some French debts owed by Americans. Third, make a loan to France. And finally and most outrageous in the Americans' eyes, provide Talleyrand and the members of the Directory (five men who controlled the French government following 1795) a healthy bribe. To the latter demand Pinckney exclaimed "No! No! Not a sixpence!" No substantial easing of tensions between the two nations was achieved.[12] France continued to harass US ships at sea. Adams informed Congress in March 1798 that the diplomatic mission had failed, although he did not release details of the negotiators' reports from Paris. Jefferson and other leading Republicans thought Adams was covering up the diplomatic failure and believed he in fact favored war with France. Adams asked Congress to ramp up defensive measures, a move that Jefferson thought bordered on insanity, but in the context of the moment, Adams was the moderate. The Jeffersonians demanded that Adams reveal the content of the diplomatic dispatches, and when Adams did so, a national outrage erupted. The Republicans were sobered and disappointed, but the Federalists were exultant at this demonstration of French perfidy. Petitions poured in praising Adams, who became almost giddy over his newfound popularity. When Marshall arrived back in Philadelphia, the first of the delegates to return, he was feted as a hero.

War fever erupted. Rumors circulated that French agents were planning to burn Philadelphia. During the first portion of the 1790s, thousands of immigrants from Ireland, France, and Haiti had come to the nation, and anglophile Federalists feared these groups constituted a severe internal danger. To make things seem more sinister, former French ministers Edmond Genet and Pierre Adet had openly indicated their opposition to Federalist policies.[13] With a series of military victories in Europe, Napoleonic France was now the leading military power. Would Napoleon soon invade England? Or America?

War fever became war hysteria, with anti-French resolutions pouring into Congress. A riot ensued in Philadelphia between pro-English and pro-French advocates. Federalists genuinely feared that American Jacobins were plotting with the French Directory. Rumors abounded that Virginia, seen as the hotbed of pro-Jefferson sentiment, was stockpiling arms. Was civil war about to break out? International issues seemed to be ripping apart the fabric of American unity. Even President Adams, basking in his popularity, took to wearing a ceremonial sword as military action was increasingly called for. Any form of public protest against administration policies was now deemed unpatriotic and threatening.

At this point in its young life, the nation and its leaders did not know how to handle such political unrest. In May 1797 a federal grand jury in Richmond had recommended that Congressman Samuel Cabell, who represented Albemarle County, be charged with libel because of criticisms of the administration he had expressed in letters to his constituents. Jefferson was offended by this flagrant affront to the freedom of a congressman to communicate with his constituents. Believing it was fruitless to protest this judicial interference with the right of free correspondence to either the courts or the Congress, both controlled by Federalists, Jefferson instead turned to state officials. He drafted an anonymous petition to the Virginia House of Delegates, calling upon it to institute impeachment proceedings against the members of the offending grand jury. In fact, Cabell was never indicted, and the impeachment effort petered out, but Jefferson had indicated that in pursuit of a fundamental right of speech, when the federal courts and legislature offered no relief, citizens should turn as a last resort to the states.[14] This federal infringement upon freedom of expression was mild compared to what came in subsequent years, but it hinted at what would be Jefferson's response later to far more serious matters.

Most Federalists were truly worried about the state of the nation and, being in power, attempted to make the nation safe, from their perspective, from both external and internal enemies. Congressional Federalists more than President Adams pushed these issues: Adams throughout his term advanced few policy issues. First came enhanced measures to build up military defenses, including war ships (the Navy Department was created) and an enlarged standing army of some twelve thousand troops, but because of the opprobrium of the term *standing,* it was called the *New* Army. An additional ten thousand–force Provisional Army could be called up in case of actual invasion. Federalists pressured Adams to call Washington out of retirement to take command, but Washington only accepted on the condition that he could have Hamilton as his second-in-command.

Hamilton was exhilarated by his new military command and by the potential opportunity it offered him to crush the political opposition. By 1799 Hamilton privately was talking of suppressing Virginia (his correspondence is quite shocking), breaking up the larger states, and even contemplating joining arms with England to take Florida and Louisiana from Spain and maybe invade Latin America to liberate it from European (except English) control, with he himself commanding the joint military forces. Hamilton had Napoleonic dreams of a military empire with himself at the helm.[15] None of Hamilton's dictatorial or imperial ambitions came to fruition.

The Federalist Congress was able, however, to enact legislation intended to squelch any possibility of homegrown political opposition, which they saw as treason. In March 1798 Adams officially announced that the previous diplomatic initiative to France was a failure because of French arrogance and obstinacy. Federalist congressmen, far more anti-French (and generally anti-foreign) than was Adams, began to draft legislation to protect the home front. Concerned about the recent immigrants already in the nation and fearful of others who might come, they passed a new Naturalization Act on June 18, 1798, that lengthened the residency requirement for citizenship from five years to fourteen. The act required that all aliens register with a federal official within forty-eight hours of entering the nation, created a national registry of aliens, and made naturalization solely a federal, not a state, matter. The hope was to stop immigration.

This was followed up a week later by the Alien Act, which dealt with aliens already resident. The original Senate version was shockingly draconian, clearly intended to make aliens leave the nation, but the final version was moderated by the House, where there was vehement Republican opposition to the measure. The bill as enacted allowed the president to decide which if any aliens were dangerous and should be deported. Foreigners were denied access to the courts and had none of the protections bestowed upon citizens by the Constitution. They were completely subject to the whim of the president, who could expel them without giving a reason. As Jefferson said even before it was passed, it was an "act worthy of the 8th. or 9th. century."[16] Even the most casual or thoughtless word of criticism could theoretically result in deportation.

Thankfully, the act was slated to retire after two years. Edward Livingston of New York and Albert Gallatin of Pennsylvania ferociously opposed the bill. Livingston said it so obviously violated the Constitution that people and states should not obey it. This alien bill was far stronger than Adams wanted, and he ended up not expelling anyone. But in part that is because many nonnative intellectuals and public figures, fearing the worst, left in advance, a dozen or so shiploads fleeing the nation.[17] However, in July 1798 when the US minister to England, Rufus King, notified President Adams that the French writer and economic thinker Pierre Samuel Du Pont de Nemours and a delegation of scientific thinkers planned to visit the United States to promote the advancement of science, Adams refused to grant the French scholars permission to visit. He commented that "We have had too many French philosophers already."[18]

A second alien act passed on July 6, the so-called Alien Enemies Act, which was far less controversial. It allowed the president, in case of an actual declared war against another nation, to be able to arrest or deport resident aliens subject to the enemy nation. This bill remains in effect still today. Congressional Federalists thought even citizens constituted a threat to the nation: those who criticized, ridiculed, or in other ways harmed the government and thereby assisted enemy nations. Anyone who opposed the administration was deemed a "traitor."[19] The Federalist response was a Sedition Act that underwent substantial revision, with Republicans fighting it line by line. Even several staunch

Federalists, Hamilton included, feared it went too far. John Marshall both argued and voted against it. The final version, passed on July 14, 1798, made it a crime, punishable by fine and imprisonment, for anyone, citizen or alien:

> To write, print, utter or publish, or cause it to be done, or assist in it, any false, scandalous, and malicious writing against the government of the United States, or either House of Congress, or the President, with intent to defame, or bring either into contempt or disrepute, or to excite against either the hatred of the people of the United States, or to stir up sedition, or to excite unlawful combinations against the government, or to resist it, or to aid or encourage hostile designs of foreign nations.[20]

Other sections of the bill (which was set to expire on March 3, 1801, the final day of Adams's administration) outlined these provisions in even more detail, clearly with the intention of shutting down every form of criticism of the existing government, though proponents of critical viewpoints could offer truth as a defense in courts. This Sedition Act absolutely outraged Jefferson, and it, along with the other alien acts, were, he wrote, "so palpably in the teeth of the constitution as to shew they mean to pay no respect to it."[21] (Notably the vice president, Jefferson, was not protected against verbal attack.)

Behind the Federalists' attacks on freedom of expression were the concerns, first raised in opposition to the Democratic-Republican societies for their organizing and comments against administration policy, about the proliferation of newspapers increasingly seen as perpetrators of opinions rather than neutral conveyors of information.[22] Over the next several years the administration focused on newspaper editors, indicting twelve for their writings. The editors of the Philadelphia *Aurora* and the Richmond *Examiner,* strong Democratic-Republican supporters, were arrested. Federalists intended these arrests to serve as examples to would-be critics. Even Congressman Matthew Lyon of Vermont was targeted, convicted, fined, and jailed for his speaking out against government policy. But none of the dissidents were silenced for long.[23] A total of twenty-five persons were arrested for what was termed seditious writings, an unprecedented attack on the basic freedoms of speech and the press supposedly protected by the Bill of Rights. Democratic-Republicans were aghast at these government actions to suppress dissident views, and even some Federalists understood that their leaders in Congress had gone too far, although George Washington vigorously supported it. The prosecutions under the Sedition Act and the preparations to equip and deploy the New Army to squelch internal dissent represented the gravest threat to political freedom in the nation's history.[24]

Jefferson was generally an optimistic man, and though he worried about the cast of politics in early 1798, he was not yet truly distressed. He then was still confident that most citizens agreed with his conception of the government and that only the abnormal but understandable veneration of former president Washington allowed the Federalists to rule with what Jefferson interpreted as would-be monarchial tendencies. On June 4 he wrote a moderating letter to John Taylor in which he admitted that "our present situation is not a natural one. the body of our countrymen is substantially republican through every part of the union. it was the irresistable influence & popularity of Genl. Washington played off by the cunning of Hamilton which turned the government over to antirepublican hands." He cautioned against what he called a "scission" of the union, warning that if the southern states broke away from Massachusetts and Connecticut, where would such a separation end? He stated that "an association of men who will not quarrel with one another is a thing which never yet existed," so it behooved men to put up with inconvenience and even mild oppression for the sake of the greater cause, the union. "A little patience," he wrote, "and we shall see the reign of witches pass over, their spells dissolve, and the people recovering their true sight, restore their government to it's true principles.... Better keep together as we are."[25] But as he came to have a better sense of congressional intentions after passage of the Alien Act (June 25) and then the Sedition Act (July 14), along with the development of the so-called New Army with Hamilton at its helm, his concerns about the state of the nation intensified. With one party controlling the legislature, the executive, and the judiciary, and that party seemingly if not vindictively out of control, what recourse did the people have to protect their essential liberties?

Jefferson approached this problem from the context of decades of Virginia attitudes about government. He, like Madison, was a firm constitutionalist, believing that the Constitution set the bounds on legitimate actions by both the central government and state governments. Even in his *Notes on the State of Virginia,* written by late 1784 when he was in France and published in English in 1787, Jefferson had written that when branches of government "transgressed" a constitution, "their acts shall become nullities."[26] During the expansive 1788 ratification debates in Virginia, the concept was repeatedly stated that the central government's legitimate actions were limited by the express language of the Constitution. Thus, reaching back into his memory and his state's traditions, Jefferson after the passage of the Sedition Act began to draft a response to the unprecedented legislation of the Federalist Congress. He at first intended to send his proposed resolution to the Virginia General Assembly, but because of Virginia's legislative calendar and the chance opportunity to send it first to Kentucky by means of John Breckinridge, who stopped by Monticello on his journey to the Blue Grass State, Jefferson's statement became known to history as the Kentucky Resolutions.[27]

Jefferson began by positing that the "several states composing the US. of America are not united on the principle of *unlimited* submission to their general government; but that by a compact under the style and title of a Constitution for the US. and of amendments thereto, they constituted a general government for special purposes, delegated to that government certain definite powers . . . & that whensoever the General government assumes undelegated powers, it's acts are unauthoritative, void, & of no force."[28] Following this foundational principle, he then went through a series of recent congressional decisions, including the Sedition Act and various alien acts, and declared each of them "void and of no force" on the grounds that they exceeded the delegated powers granted the central government by the Constitution.

The resolution then called for the state (he originally meant Virginia) to communicate its decision to each of the other states, precisely because it valued the union "for specified national purposes" and warned against "powers . . . which have not been delegated." In such cases, because the specified powers or acts had not been delegated by the Constitution and were hence unlawful, "a nullification of the act is the rightful remedy."[29] Calling not for the use of force or separation from the union, he asked that the various states, drawing upon their own authority, express their sentiments against such *unconstitutional* acts (although he did not use that phrase). Before the Kentucky Assembly passed the resolution on November 10, 1798, it removed the line containing the word nullification, and Jefferson did not object. Jefferson was here, in effect, calling upon the individual states to declare certain acts of Congress void because they went beyond what was constitutionally permissible. This was before the Supreme Court in 1803 in the case of *Marbury v. Madison* declared in effect that it alone had the right to rule on the constitutionality of legislation. Jefferson was also clearly drawing upon a statement in the Federalist No. 28, written by Hamilton, whose authorship Madison had surely told Jefferson, that argued that in such cases the states should intervene. As Federalist No. 28 stated,

> It may safely be received as an axiom in our political system, that the State governments will, in all possible contingencies, afford complete security against invasions of the public liberty by the national authority. Projects of usurpation cannot be masked under pretenses so likely to escape the penetration of select bodies of men, as of the people at large. The legislatures will have better means of information. They can discover the danger at a distance; and possessing all the organs of civil power, and the confidence of the people, they can at once adopt a regular plan of opposition, in

> which they can combine all the resources of the community. They can readily communicate with each other in the different States, and unite their common forces for the protection of their common liberty.[30]

The Kentucky legislature had passed its resolutions without suggesting their original author. Meanwhile, Madison approached the problem in a slightly different manner in resolutions he anonymously prepared for the Virginia House of Delegates. The reputed father of the Constitution resisted using the word *nullification* and thereby having the legislature explicitly declare the despised acts void. Instead, he wanted Virginia to consult with the other states, and if they agreed, the proper response was for the states' congressmen to take action in the federal Congress. Madison used the ambiguous term *interpose,* by which he meant the states should position their authority between their citizens and the disputed federal law, blocking its effect. Jefferson wished Madison had written a stronger response to the Sedition Act but accepted his wording. In a subsequent report Madison crafted an elegant defense of freedom of speech and the press. In light of how later generations maleficently misused the concept of nullification, it should be emphasized that Jefferson in 1798 was employing the idea to defend the basic civil liberties of the people, not protect slavery.[31]

The effect of the Kentucky and Virginia Resolutions has been difficult to determine with exactitude. Recent research indicates that eight states (the southern states along with Pennsylvania and New Jersey) did not oppose the viewpoints expressed, suggesting that the sentiments of Jefferson and Madison were more mainstream than radical, and although both sets of resolutions were issued anonymously, political insiders quickly guessed the authors.[32] The response did also suggest the increasing sectional division of the nation and the violent partisanship of the age. Hamilton, who had to have recognized the genealogy of the basic principle expressed by Jefferson, nevertheless interpreted the resolutions as further evidence of the dangerous dissent alive in the nation. He wrote to Massachusetts congressman Harrison Gray Otis about the dangers of "internal disorders" that the resolutions indicated and the necessity of military force to restrain them. To Massachusetts senator Theodore Sedgwick, he characterized the resolutions as "a tendency to destroy the Constitution of the UStates," affording "full evidence . . . of a regular conspiracy to overturn the government."[33] The army should, in his view, be ready to crush such opposition.

A small uprising of farmers in eastern Pennsylvania in early 1799 over taxes and other complaints (totally unrelated to the Kentucky and Virginia Resolutions) seemed to overwrought Federalists to herald insurrection, and

Hamilton pushed for an iron-fisted army putdown of the protesting farmers. When troops arrived, they found the rebellion had collapsed. Still, a leader, John Fries, and two others were seized, tried, and convicted of treason, but a sensible President Adams pardoned them, much to the displeasure of hyper-Federalists. Quite clearly, both sides in the national debate saw the other as a fundamental threat to the nation's well-being.

In the midst of these chaotic times, John Adams made a decision that risked his popularity and that of the Federalist Party by deciding to put the interests of the nation above the partisanship threatening to tear the nation apart. The hyper-Federalists in his cabinet excoriated him for it, and Madison and Jefferson, also caught up in the political partisanship, did not recognize Adams's purpose, but what happened was the highpoint of Adams's presidency. With information arriving from his own son, John Quincy Adams, then ambassador to Prussia, that France now wanted to negotiate, President Adams, without consulting or informing anyone in his administration, decided to try diplomacy again. He announced to a surprised Congress on February 18, 1799, that he was sending William Vans Murray (the minister to the Batavian Republic, previously known as the Republic of the United Netherlands) as minister plenipotentiary to France in an attempt to make peace. This shocked his cabinet members; thunderstruck was how Secretary of State Timothy Pickering described their reaction. In fact, all the major Federalists were outraged by this announcement. Peace with France seemed to them out of the question: it would remove the necessity of a strengthened military, and it seemed designed to curry favor with the Federalists' political adversaries. Cautious, level-headed John Marshall defended Adams's decisions, gaining the president's respect. In reality, British admiral Horatio Nelson's dramatic defeat of the French navy at the Battle of the Nile in October 1798 had removed the possibility of France invading either the United States or Britain and eliminated the need for the Federalist military expansion. The more his opponents complained, the more Adams dug in his heels. Finally, though, he added two more delegates, Chief Justice Oliver Ellsworth and North Carolina governor William Davie to form a commission with Murray, and after additional delays, and more evidence that France was serious about negotiation, the commission left in August 1799. Their arrival in France meant that, effectively, the quasi-war with France was over. Negotiations progressed slowly, but in the summer of 1800 the parties reached an agreement and signed the Treaty of Mortefontaine, which Congress ratified in early 1801. Not a momentous treaty, it did ease tensions between the two nations and suspended the 1778 Franco-American treaty that Benjamin Franklin had worked out. It also meant that there was no need for the recently expanded army, much to the chagrin of Hamilton.[34]

Meanwhile Adams hied away to his home in Quincy, Massachusetts, where he remained for seven months. His absence infuriated his enemies within his party who accused him of incompetence and dereliction of duty. Hamilton and his cohorts were beyond furious at the president, and Adams, not a man to take criticism kindly, bristled at every indication of disloyalty from his cabinet. In late March Adams had confided "that he thought Hamilton and a Party were endeavoring to get an army on foot to give Hamilton the command of it & then to proclaim a Regal Government, place Hamilton at the Head of it & prepare the way for a Province of Great Britain."[35] Relations between Adams and Hamilton continued to deteriorate over the next year. Many today characterize the end of the century as a time of animosity between Jefferson and Hamilton, but the truly venomous animosity existed between Adams and Hamilton.

By the late 1790s even Washington, who earlier had imagined himself as above party, had become mired in political infighting. It was for that reason that he successfully urged John Marshall, freshly popular because of his having rejected French diplomatic deception (during the XYZ Affair), to run for election to the House of Representatives.[36] Washington correctly realized that Marshall's balanced stances would allow him to win in a relatively balanced state. Though Jefferson was widely popular in Virginia as a whole, he was far less so in Richmond. A formative era in the nation's history seemed to end in late 1799 when on December 14, 1799, after a long ride across his plantation fields two days before in cold rain and snow, George Washington died at Mount Vernon of epiglottitis, an inflammation and swelling of cartilage at the entrance to his voice box, causing him essentially to smother to death. The nation went into mourning for the loss of the person who, without question, had been the indispensable leader for the era. Eulogies were offered in practically every town of any size, and sermons addressed his life and meaning. Engravings appeared, some of which depicted Washington being wafted to heaven in the arms of angels.

The most famous eulogy was delivered by General Henry "Light Horse Harry" Lee in Washington's German Lutheran Church on December 26, and Lee spoke the line that has ever since been used to sum up Washington's career: "First in war, first in peace, and first in the hearts of his countrymen."[37] Jefferson did not at the time make any remarks, nor did he attend the official funeral. After 1795 or so, the partisan fever of the age, especially the heated atmosphere of 1798 that produced the Alien and Sedition Acts, had driven them apart. Possibly Jefferson had not heard of Washington's death when he departed from Monticello on December 21, but even if he had, he purposefully avoided taking part in any of the memorial services, reasoning that anything positive he might say would be regarded by Federalist partisans as rank hypocrisy. Fifteen years later, after feelings had moderated, Jefferson penned an appropriate characterization of the Father of the Country.

> His mind was great and powerful, without being of the very first order; his penetration strong, though not so acute as that of a Newton, Bacon, or Locke; and as far as he saw, no judgment ever sounder. It was slow in operation, being little aided by invention or imagination, but sure in conclusion. . . . He was incapable of fear, meeting personal dangers with the calmest unconcern. Perhaps the strongest feature in his character was prudence, never acting until every circumstance, every consideration, was maturely weighed; refraining if he saw a doubt, but, when once decided, going through with his purpose, whatever obstacles opposed. His integrity was most pure, his justice the most inflexible I have ever known, no motive of interest or consanguinity, of friendship or hatred, being able to bias his decision. He was, indeed, in every sense of the words, a wise, a good, a great man. . . . On the whole, his character was, in its mass, perfect . . . and it may truly be said, that never did nature and fortune combine more perfectly to make a man great.[38]

Near the end of Washington's illustrious life, he performed an act that surprised many of his contemporaries: he composed a will freeing his 124 enslaved people upon the death of his wife, Martha. She in the meantime controlled some 153 so-called dower slaves, that is, enslaved men, women, and children she had inherited from the Custis estate and who, upon her death, would pass to her grandchildren. This meant that as long as she lived, Martha would continue to benefit from the earnings of her husband's enslaved laborers as well as her own. She, however, felt ill at ease, surrounded by the people her deceased husband had held in bondage, who knew that only her life separated them from their freedom, so on January 1, 1801, she authorized the manumission of her late husband's enslaved people. She herself died sixteen months later. How was it that Washington, who never publicly spoke out against slavery and in his lifetime made no effort to achieve emancipation, became the only major Founder to emancipate his slaves? What did others of similar rank in his situation do?

George Mason had first publicly indicated his displeasure with the institution of slavery in 1765 when he wrote, in a document concerning the recovery of property, on "the ill effects" of slavery "upon the Morals & Manners of our People." In another sentence he referred to the practice as "Evil."[39] Later, in the Constitutional Convention, he had vigorously opposed the counting of the enslaved population in the consideration of representation of the southern states, and he was particularly vocal against the continuation of the slave trade for twenty years. Referring to the "infernal traffic" in humans, he went on to state that "Slavery discourages arts & manufacturers. The poor despise labor when performed by slaves. They prevent the immigration of Whites.... They produce the most pernicious effect on manners. Every master of slaves is born a petty tyrant. They bring the judgment of heaven on a Country."[40]

But most of his concern about slavery was for the bad effect the institution had upon whites, not its impact on enslaved Blacks. And even though he professed to oppose the continuation of slavery, he notably did not manumit his enslaved laborers upon his death on October 7, 1792, leaving to his descendants, along with seventy-five thousand acres of land, personal property worth $50,000, $30,000 in accounts receivable, and a total of three hundred enslaved men, women, and children.[41] Why the discrepancy between his statements and his actions? Probably because Mason had always been extraordinarily concerned about the care and welfare of his numerous children, and whatever his private views, he was unwilling to deprive his own offspring of the economic resources that slavery represented.

Patrick Henry, who died at age sixty-three on June 6, 1799, just six months before Washington did, also never freed any of his enslaved laborers although he on several occasions, private and public, addressed the immorality of slavery. Especially revealing was his response, on January 18, 1773, to a letter from the Quaker abolitionist Robert Pleasant:

> It is not a little surprising that the professors of Christianity . . . should encourage a practice so totally repugnant to the first impressions of right and wrong. . . . Is it not amazing, that at a time, when the rights of humanity are defined and understood with precision, in a country, above all others, fond of liberty; . . . we find men professing a religion the most humane, mild, gentle and generous, adopting a principle as repugnant to humanity, as it is inconsistent with the bible and destructive of liberty? . . . Would anyone believe I am the master of slaves of my own purchase! I am drawn along by the general inconvenience of living here without them. I will not, I cannot justify it.[42]

Henry was an evangelical Christian, so he knew well the immorality of slavery, but still he could not bring himself to free his own enslaved people. He could not imagine how he could support himself and his large and growing family in the agricultural society of the South at the level he found comfortable without resorting to slave labor. He was typical of many slaveholders then except that he freely admitted the gap between his actions and his beliefs. He never saw a way to close the gap.

During the Virginia ratifying convention, one of the reasons Henry opposed the Constitution is because he believed a stronger central government, dominated by northern states, would threaten southern slavery, as morally repulsive as it was. "Slavery is detested," he exclaimed on June 24, 1788, "we feel its fatal effects [and] we deplore it with all the pity of humanity," but he could not see a way to ending the institution. "As much as I deplore slavery," he said, he understood "that prudence forbids its abolition." He continued, "we ought to lament and deplore the necessity of holding our fellow-men in bondage," but he did not see "any humane means to liberate them without producing the most dreadful and ruinous consequences."[43] He could only call for benevolent treatment, not freedom.

Henry may have demagogically emphasized the possibility of racial violence in his effort to thwart the ratification of the Constitution. Probably for him, as for George Mason, the perceived economic necessity of possessing enslaved people to achieve at least a modicum of prosperity was the primary justification for not freeing them. Certainly, for such men with a number of children or grandchildren (and Henry had seventeen children and seventy-seven grandchildren![44]) and other dependents to support, freeing their enslaved laborers seemed impossible if they were to fulfill their presumed role as paterfamilias. This meant that it was far easier for unmarried or childless men to emancipate their enslaved laborers (for example, Edward Coles of Albemarle County and John Randolph of Roanoke).

This brings us back to the example of Washington. Did circumstances allow Washington to do what others felt they could not? Washington had never been outspoken against slavery, had never proposed legislation or any other action to end slavery. But in private, he had often indicated to many his concerns about the institution. He wished slavery could be ended, thought it should be done gradually, and believed enslavers should somehow be compensated. He was a severe taskmaster. And when he had come to believe by the end of his life that slavery was no longer economically profitable, at least at Mount Vernon, he contemplated selling his excess enslaved laborers, not freeing them. In 1796, when a favorite domestic slave named Ona Judge ran away, Washington tried (illegally) to use the manpower of the Treasury Department to track her down, recapture her, and bring her back to Mount Vernon.[45] In short, before the writing of his will in July 1799, less than six months before his death, there was nothing in Washington's public or private life that would lead one to believe he might do something so dramatic. How then do we explain his will, which he wrote entirely on his own, without recourse to lawyers?[46]

After specifying that all his debts ("of which there are but few") should be paid and providing for the support of his wife, he then stated, "Upon the decease of my wife, it is my Will and desire that all the Slaves which I hold in *my own right,* shall receive their freedom." He explained that to free them while his wife still lived would be difficult given that his 124 enslaved people were intermarried with the 153 enslaved men and women she controlled, the so-called dower slaves, and which Washington himself did not have the legal authority to free. Recognizing that the freeing of the totality of his enslaved men, women, and children would involve some who were too old and some too young to support themselves, he provided that the aged individuals should be taken care of during their lifetime, and the children should be taught to read and write and gain a "useful occupation" before being emancipated at age twenty-five. And he wrote, "I do hereby expressly forbid the Sale, or transportation out of the said Commonwealth, of any Slave I may die possessed of, under any pretense whatsoever." He insisted that his executors should follow his express wishes and ordered that his longtime personal valet, William Lee (usually called Billy Lee) be immediately given his freedom, although if he chose he could continue to live as he was at present with his usual support.[47] There followed, in amazing detail, exactly how Washington wished to honor and reward dozens of free people, friends and relatives, with his extensive holdings in land, city lots, and other property laid out in precision.

Washington was able to manumit his enslaved people without concern because not being in significant debt, he did not need to worry about his debtors seizing any of those freed, as a 1792 act permitted.[48] This law, for example, restricted Jefferson's willingness to emancipate his enslaved people because he never escaped the debt he inherited from his father-in-law. Because Washington's enslaved laborers were not to be freed until after his death, obviously their emancipation would not jeopardize his standard of living, and since he could not free his wife's dower slaves because of the technicality of the law, her lifestyle would also not be diminished. Washington had no biological dependents, in contrast to Mason, Henry, and Jefferson, to provide for, so giving up his enslaved laborers would not cause any dependents to face economic hardships or a drop in lifestyle. His wife's dower slaves would descend to her few grandchildren from her first marriage. So in his freeing of his portion of the enslaved laborers at Mount Vernon, Washington did not jeopardize his well-being or that of his wife and her dependents. And because Virginia did not yet require that freedpeople had to leave the state within twelve months or be reenslaved by the state—as it would do in 1806[49]—Washington's wishes in this regard were respected too. The point is not at all to diminish the morally correct decision Washington made at the end of his life but to suggest that his special circumstances may have allowed him to do what other enslavers, such as Henry, might have liked to have done had their situations been different.

Washington's example of manumission did not inspire similar behavior among the Virginia gentry. His death did in a profound way inspire change of a different sort, however. It ended an era, and it had far-reaching consequences. The year 1800 began ominously for Alexander Hamilton, now without Washington. In the spring Adams had pardoned John Fries, the German insurgent of Pennsylvania whose slight rebellion the previous year the army had squelched. Then Adams signed congressional acts that first stopped fresh enlistments in the so-called New Army and then disbanded it. Adams's cabinet officers, loyal not to him but to Hamilton, together with their mentor, were outraged by these actions and believed Adams half mad.

Meanwhile, Hamilton was already thinking ahead to the presidential election later that year. Realizing that a full public break with Adams might give the election to Jefferson, Hamilton began plotting, pushing an informal ticket of Charles Cotesworth Pinckney and Adams. He of course hoped to have some electors drop their votes for Adams, thereby handing the presidency to Pinckney. Adams learned of Hamilton's conniving, and eventually blew up at his cabinet, angrily firing Secretary of State Timothy Pickering and Secretary of War James McHenry, action long overdue. Of course, this simply intensified the anger and disgust swirling among the party leaders. The Federalists approached the election season mired in dissent and intrigue.

In 1796 Thomas Jefferson had played no role in the election and only reluctantly accepted the vice presidency. He had believed as late as mid-1799 that it was best "to wait with patience till those passions & delusions shall have passed over which the federal government have artfully & successfully excited to cover it's own abuses & to cover its designs," but things had worsened.[50] In 1800 Jefferson, clearly the party leader after authoring the Kentucky Resolutions and truly worried about the survival of the nation, believed he now had to act. He decided to eagerly seek the presidency, yet in the mostly passive way thought appropriate at the time, with no active campaigning as we understand it today.

In a letter to John Wise, speaker of the Virginia House of Delegates, Jefferson had described the two "political sects," as he called them, that were warring against each other for control of the government. One "believed that the Executive is the branch of our Government which the most needs support: the other that, like the analogous branch in the English government, it is already too strong for the republican parts of the Constitution, and therefore, . . . they incline to the Legislative powers. the former of these are called Federalists, sometimes Aristocrats or monocrats and Sometimes tories . . . the latter are Stiled Republicans, Whigs, Jacobins, Anarchists, Disorganisers &c."[51] Jefferson and others pressured Madison (retired from the House of Representatives since 1797) to place his name in the contest for election to the Virginia House of Delegates, and he did so. At the moment Jefferson had more trust in the state legislatures than in the federal government.

Fundamentally, Jefferson saw the contest as a battle between a British monarchical style of government and the republicanism of the Constitution. At stake was the true nature of the government. If Democratic-Republicanism was to survive, its proponents had to seize power because the Federalists had shown by their passage of the Alien and Sedition Acts and their ramping up of a standing army that they were willing to crush all opposition to their reshaping of the government into the British form. A civil war did not seem out of question; in the eyes of Madison and Jefferson, the future of the nation was at risk. Jefferson had to get his ideas about governance out to the people, believing that the great mass really supported his conception of government. He did this through writing letters, which he knew would be shared, and by distributing partisan pamphlets written by others. He expected his friends to write letters to individuals and to newspapers and to publish pamphlets, confident that the silent majority of citizens shared his views.

Illustrative of his epistolary campaigning was his letter of January 26, 1799, to Elbridge Gerry, a moderate Federalist who Jefferson (correctly, as it turned out) thought liable to being converted to the Republican ranks. Telling Gerry that the two of them were fellow laborers, Jefferson proceeded to make what he called a "profession of my political faith." Then he summarized his philosophy of government, knowing that Gerry would share Jefferson's views with others. Jefferson sought both to deny charges against himself and to positively express his political ideas: "I do then with sincere zeal wish an inviolable preservation of our present federal constitution," he wrote, "according to the true sense in which it was adopted by the states . . . and I am opposed to the monarchising it's features." He made clear his belief in a frugal government, his reliance on the militia ("till actual invasion"), and opposition to a standing army in peacetime. He wrote of his belief in the "freedom of religion . . . . freedom of the press" and "for encouraging the progress of science in all it's branches." He pointed out that while he initially supported the French Revolution and still hoped it might eventually result in a republican form of government in France, "the first object of my heart," he emphasized, "is my own country. in that is embarked my family, my fortune, & my own existence. I have not one farthing of interest, nor one fibre of attachment out of it, nor a single motive of preference of any one nation to another but in proportion as they are more or less friendly to us." With this he concluded that "these my friends are my principles: they are unquestionably the principles of the great body of our fellow citizens."[52]

Then, after discussing several other topics, including the recent XYZ Affair, Jefferson returned to his general political beliefs and his optimism that the political tides were turning: "The unquestionable republicanism of the American mind will break through the mist under which it has been clouded, and will oblige it's agents to reform the principles & practices of their administration."[53] It was to that task that Jefferson was now committed. Longtime supporters like Madison and Monroe advocated for him, and they were now assisted by a phalanx of newspaper editors. No one, however, at the beginning of 1800 worked the political scene more effectively than Aaron Burr in New York City.

Burr was an enormously able man but more notorious for his burning ambition than for his political principles. The grandson of theologian Jonathan Edwards and the son of a president of Princeton, Burr had lineage and personality aplenty, and he understood that the legislature of New York would choose all twelve of that state's members of the electoral college. Possessed of superior political ability, Burr set about with extraordinary organization and energy to recruit able candidates for the statehouse and then campaigned with a combination of zeal and skill to win enough votes to control the state assembly and hence guarantee the electoral votes for Jefferson.[54] Hamilton was so panicked by the consequences of the election that he quickly urged Governor John Jay to change the state's elective procedure retroactively to deny the votes to Jefferson, but Jay deemed Hamilton's proposal "a measure for party purposes which it would not become me to adopt."[55] The Republicans in effect rewarded Burr for his electioneering prowess by promoting him as Jefferson's running mate later that year even though parties on neither side really presented what is today called a ticket, with presidents and vice presidents so designated.

Hamilton was determined to prevent Jefferson from being elected, so he by mid-1800 was actively supporting Charles Cotesworth Pinckney over Adams as he traveled about New England (in full military regalia). Adams, for his part, hated Hamilton in part at least because he recalled Hamilton's 1796 efforts to have Thomas Pinckney elected. At a meeting in May 1800, Adams finally blew up in a conversation with Secretary of War McHenry, ranting about McHenry, Secretary of State Pickering, and especially Hamilton. The upshot of the meeting, as we have seen, was that Adams fired McHenry and Pickering, which outraged the hyper-Federalists. McHenry sent Hamilton a written account of Adams's verbal explosion, in which he had labeled Hamilton "an intriguer—the greatest intriguer in the world—a man devoid of every moral principle." Just getting started, Adams continued: "Mr. Jefferson is an infinitely better man; a wiser one, I am sure, and, if President, will act wisely."[56] Then, taking a more temperate tack, Adams replaced McHenry and Pickering with Senator Dexter Perkins and John Marshall, whose moderate judgment was gaining recognition. Of course, news of the firing, and Adams's outburst, spread throughout the Federalist universe, and soon even those in the Jefferson camp understood that the Federalists were imploding.

The bickering between the Adams and Hamilton factions almost overshadowed the Federalist attacks on Jefferson, the most extreme of which portrayed him not only as a radical French Jacobin but a raving atheist whose election would strike a fatal blow to Christianity. Jefferson was also depicted as a dreamy philosopher, "fit to be a professor in a college," sarcastically wrote South Carolina Federalist Robert Goodloe Harper, "but certainly not the first magistrate of a great nation."[57] In the midst of the overheated rhetoric, Hamilton began a long letter attacking Adams, which he turned into a pamphlet of some fifty-four printed pages. Published in October under the title of *Letter from Alexander Hamilton, Concerning the Public Conduct and Character of John Adams, Esq., President of the United States,* it was an intemperate, ill-advised, remarkably harsh profile of the sitting president and Federalist candidate, although at the very end, and irrationally, Hamilton claimed not to want to withhold a single vote for Adams.[58] It is difficult to accurately gauge the electoral effect of this tirade, but in addition to deepening the antagonism between Adams and Hamilton, it both dispirited many Federalists and emboldened supporters of Jefferson.

That May, following the adjournment of Congress, the national government moved to the new national capital, Washington, DC, the entire archives of the executive branch packed into only seven crates for the move.[59] There was no nationwide popular vote in 1800. Although several states chose their electors by popular vote, the majority were chosen by the various state legislatures. The candidates did not give campaign-like addresses, did not participate in campaign rallies. Jefferson even once returned to Monticello from Philadelphia by way of Virginia's Eastern Shore to avoid crowds and press coverage.[60] Still, tensions were high throughout the nation. In January, Federalist senator James Ross, seeking to guarantee a Federalist victory in the presidential contest, had introduced a bill in Congress to provide for a special committee to determine the legitimacy of the electoral votes.

He called for the committee to consist of six members chosen by the House, six by the Senate, and the chief justice of the Supreme Court, Federalist Oliver Ellsworth. Since Federalists controlled both houses of Congress as well as the court, this would predetermine the outcome of the election. Fortunately, his proposal was leaked to the press, details were published in the Philadelphia *Aurora,* and the resulting firestorm of opposition killed the bill, with temperate Federalists like John Marshall (who would be appointed chief justice in January 1801) vigorously opposing it because he thought it clearly in violation of the Constitution.[61]

On December 3, 1800, the members of the electoral college met in their respective states and cast their votes, each voting for two men, one of whom could not be a resident of their state. But no vote totals would be known officially until February 11, 1801, when Jefferson, as the sitting vice president but acting in his capacity as president of the Senate, would, as the Constitution then prescribed, unbind the sealed vote certificates submitted by the various states and count the electoral votes.

In the midst of such political turmoil, Jefferson began to worry. What if there was a tie vote between himself and Burr? Had any arrangements been made for one or more electors dedicated to Jefferson and Burr to drop their vote for Burr? Jefferson wrote a subtle letter to Burr, hinting at his concerns, and Burr replied in such a way as to dampen Jefferson's concerns, though he did not state categorically that there was no way he would accept election. If there were a tie and the election thereby went to the House for resolution, and it would be the existing House, not the new one based on the most recent election, what would the Federalist-controlled House do?[62] Would it choose Burr? Or someone else like New York governor John Jay, or Secretary of State John Marshall? Would it attempt to cancel the election and call for another one? Would an apparent Republican victory somehow be thwarted and the president pro tem of the Senate named president?[63]

Meanwhile, some Federalists, fearing Jefferson, began to court Burr, judging that because he was unprincipled, they could buy his support and manipulate him. This in turn frightened Hamilton, who disliked Jefferson but absolutely despised Burr, with the result that Hamilton turned his unquenchable energy toward convincing Federalists in this situation to support Jefferson.[64]

When Jefferson in the Senate, in the presence of all the senators and representatives, tallied the electoral votes on February 11, they were as he expected: 73 votes each for Jefferson and Burr, 65 for Adams, and 64 for Pinckney. As an indication of the increasing party discipline, the electors throughout the nation in 1800 cast votes for only four men, as compared to thirteen in 1796.[65] The result presented a profound dilemma. The nation sensed it was in crisis. In this, the first potential transfer of political power from what we would today recognize as one party to another, would the transition be resisted by the current holders of power? Would there be turmoil and violence? Would the Federalists try to push some new legislation naming an interim president, or some other scheme? Jefferson wrote Monroe on February 15 that if the Federalists tried some unscrupulous means to maintain the presidency, "we thought it best to declare openly & firmly, that the day such an act passed the middle states would arm, & that no such usurpation even for a single day should be submitted to."[66] Would states like Virginia pose armed resistance if they felt the election was stolen? No one knew, and everything now depended upon the action of the House of Representatives, where each of the sixteen states, no matter how many congressmen they had, would cast one vote, and a majority of votes—nine—would be required for a president to be elected. The nation faced a critical moment of decision.[67]

10

A POLITICAL TURNING POINT

Amid fears of violence, even rumors that Thomas Jefferson would be assassinated, the House of Representatives met on February 9, 1801, and made an important decision: it would go into continuous session until the electoral deadlock was broken. No other issues would be considered, and the House proceedings would be conducted in secrecy. On Wednesday, February 11, in the middle of a snowstorm so severe that congressmen had difficulty trudging through it to the Capitol, the voting was to begin. The backdrop was sinister and the stakes high. Alexander Hamilton had written in December that Aaron Burr was "the most unfit man in the U.S. for the office of President" and had warned that if the Federalists succeeded in their unwise plot to get him elected, "the whole responsibility" for the bad measures that would result "will rest with" them. Just how far would diehard Federalists be willing to go to prevent Jefferson's being elected? Every member of Congress understood the significance of the vote that was to begin on that snowy day. Republican congressman Joseph H. Nicholson of Maryland, on his sickbed with what was thought to be pneumonia, arranged to be carried on a litter some two miles to the Capitol so he could vote, his wife staying at his side to nurse him.

At noon, with members of both houses present, Vice President Jefferson had officially counted the electoral votes, which revealed, as expected, that he and Burr each had seventy-three votes. At 1:00 p.m. the House went into session to try to settle the matter.[1] Again, as expected, the vote was inconclusive: eight states for Jefferson, six for Burr, with Maryland and Vermont, their delegates tied, casting no vote. Nine of the possible sixteen state votes were necessary to form a majority and break the tie. Each side believed that the other would give in, but both sides held firm. After seven rounds of votes with the same results, the House members took a break for a quick meal, and then they resumed. Throughout the night, at about one-hour intervals, the voting continued. Some members had blankets and pillows brought in and napped on the floor, others in heavy coats slumped over their desks. By noon on Thursday, after twenty-eight votes, there was still no change. Clearly much talk, maneuvering, and pressure was underway, but no representative as of yet budged. The exhausted members decided to adjourn until the next day. There was a vote on Friday, but no change; four more votes on Saturday; then a recess till Monday. A thirty-fourth vote was taken, and then a thirty-fifth on Tuesday. Meanwhile, rumors of all sorts, some absolutely absurd, were rife.

Finally, on the thirty-sixth vote, the Federalist members from Vermont and Maryland abstained, thereby shifting their states to Jefferson, and James Bayard, the only delegate from Delaware, also abstained, so Delaware cast no vote. The four delegates present from South Carolina abstained as well. This sudden change of events gave Jefferson the votes of ten states; Burr had the four New England states of Massachusetts, Connecticut, New Hampshire, and Rhode Island; and Delaware and South Carolina cast no vote at all. This meant that on the thirty-seventh vote, on February 17, Jefferson won the presidency with a majority of the states voting for him. And not a single Federalist congressman had voted for Jefferson. How had the logjam been broken? Perhaps we shall never know the details of the various conversations that shaped the denouement of the electoral deadlock, but Bayard of Delaware appears to have been key. Because he was Delaware's only representative, he could determine the state's vote. He appears to have initially supported Burr and tried to secure a firm commitment from him that he would accept the presidency if the Federalists could win it for him, but Bayard could not get the agreement he wanted. In the meantime, he had tried to contact Jefferson or at least see if he could extract from Jefferson certain promises. What had Bayard hoped to learn from Jefferson? He approached Congressmen Samuel Smith of Maryland and John Nicholas of Virginia, close Jefferson associates, to see if Jefferson would promise to "support . . . the public credit," maintain the "naval system," and not remove "subordinate public officers . . . on the grounds of their political character."[2] Ultimately Bayard, disappointed in Burr, got from Smith what he took to be a communication from Jefferson agreeing to this demand.

Jefferson later emphatically denied he had made any such agreement, even though Gouverneur Morris had made the same proposition to him. Jefferson said he had made clear to all that he would not submit to any conditions and had never spoken to Smith about such matters, especially in the context of making a commitment to the Federalists. It was possible, he admitted, that in the course of general conversation with friends, Jefferson had indicated what he planned to do, but certainly he had never made any remarks about his proposed positions in the context of meeting Federalist demands. What may have occurred is that Smith had indicated to Bayard what he understood to be Jefferson's positions based on casual conversations with him, and Bayard took Smith's informal reporting to be in fact a Jefferson capitulation to Federalist desires.[3]

On that flimsy ground, and with Burr refusing to cooperate and thereby making himself unelectable, Bayard realized, as he said, that to reject Jefferson would be "at the expense of the Constitution"; *that* he would not do, so Bayard determined to "put . . . an end to the contest," which he in effect could do simply by abstaining, thereby depriving Delaware of a vote.[4] That alone would give the election to Jefferson (eight out of fifteen voting states), and with that information from Bayard, the Federalists from Vermont and Maryland, seeing that Jefferson's election was assured, also abstained, allowing their two states' votes to go to Jefferson. Bayard's simple abstention hence set in train the other votes that settled one of the most disputed elections in US history, a settlement that, in spite of all the rumors and suspicions and plotting, ended quite pacifically, Jefferson winning ten states to four, with two states (Delaware and South Carolina) not voting. Neither contending party questioned the process or result of the congressional resolution of the electoral controversy. The peaceful transition of political power from one party to another would prove to be one of the most important features of the American political tradition, seriously threatened only in 2021.

There was no meaningful communication between Jefferson and Adams to coordinate the transfer of power, no transition team. Jefferson understood that his first task was to defuse the hostile political atmosphere, then to construct a functioning cabinet. He only had about two weeks to prepare his inaugural address before he was to take office on March 4, and, apparently, he did so without consultation. He also wanted to use the inauguration to diminish the aura of a coronation, so, unlike his predecessors who had ridden (at least part of the way) in stately carriages to the event, Jefferson simply walked from his boardinghouse to the Capitol Building where the oath of office was administered in the Senate chamber, with newly appointed Chief Justice John Marshall (who had preferred Burr) swearing him in. No member of Jefferson's family was present, and neither was John Adams, who in a sour mood had left town that morning before daybreak.

But the Senate chamber was full when Jefferson began delivering his inaugural address in a voice so soft that practically no one could hear his remarks. Before he began, he had given a handwritten copy to Samuel Harrison Smith, editor of the *National Intelligencer,* who rushed out a printed version of the address to give to listeners as they left the chamber. In fewer than two thousand words, Jefferson sought both to calm the turbulent political waters and outline the policies his administration would seek to promote. Jefferson stated his total commitment to the key principle of democracy: "Though the will of the majority is in all cases to prevail, that will to be rightful must be reasonable; . . . the minority possess their equal rights, which equal law must protect, and to violate would be oppression."[5] After establishing that bedrock position, he pleaded with his listeners (and readers), "Let us restore to social intercourse that harmony and affection without which liberty and even life itself are but dreary things." After all, he emphasized, "Every difference of opinion is not a difference of principle. We have called by different names brethren of the same principle. We are all republicans, we are all federalists." He here was not referring to the political parties but rather to the concepts of a republican form of government and the federalist sense of a blending of powers between the separate states and the national government, the combination of which he labeled "the world's best hope."[6]

He also outlined what he called "the essential principles" by which he would govern: "Equal and exact justice to all men, of whatever state or persuasion, religious or political"; friendly relations with all nations,

> entangling alliances with none; the support of the State governments in all their rights . . . the preservation of the General Government in its whole constitutional vigor. . . . absolute acquiescence in the decisions of the majority . . . a well-disciplined militia . . . till regulars may relieve them; the supremacy of the civil over military authority; economy in the public expense . . . the honest payment of our debts . . . freedom of religion; freedom of the press, and freedom of person under the protection of habeas corpus, and trial by juries impartially selected. . . . [These] should be the creed of our political faith.[7]

Here, in short compass and memorable eloquence, Jefferson summarized the political values that he and he believed practically every American citizen shared. All in all, it was a call for harmony and common commitment to the fundamental values of the people, a welcome reprieve from the angry language that had so recently been the vocabulary of politics. His generosity of spirit nonplussed many of his former enemies, and hardliners persisted in their animosity toward him and his administration.

Jefferson admired the way George Washington had organized his most intimate advisors, a group that became known as his cabinet, asking the head of each department to share their key correspondence with him, both to keep him advised as to the important issues they faced and so he could help shape their decisions.[8] Jefferson also saw how destructive and dysfunctional had been Adams's relationship with his cabinet. Adams had retained most of Washington's cabinet members, and they were more loyal to Hamilton than to Adams. Jefferson sought to emulate Washington's administrative skill and avoid Adams's troubles as he shaped his own cabinet. Jefferson wanted relatively young, able advisors whose opinions he shared and trusted, and he strove to create and maintain a healthy collaborative relationship with them. Even before the election was settled, Jefferson had asked James Madison to serve as his secretary of state and chosen Pennsylvanian Albert Gallatin, whose knowledge of economic matters was second only to Hamilton's, to be his secretary of the treasury.

Conscious of the importance of having a national, not regional, administration, Jefferson tapped General Henry Dearborn of New Hampshire to be secretary of war and Levi Lincoln of Massachusetts to serve as his attorney general. Robert Smith of Maryland became the secretary of the navy, and Gideon Granger of Connecticut was appointed postmaster general, an important though not cabinet-level position. Jefferson made explicit, via a statement circulated to his cabinet members, how he wished to consult them, drawing on their advice on issues even as he expected to make final decisions. He would throughout his two terms circulate statements and addresses to them, often accepting their advice or subtly revising his words in response to questions they raised. He trusted all of them and proved to have one of the most stable cabinets in US history (only Attorney General Lincoln resigned, and that because of poor health).[9] In short, he made effective the institution of the presidential cabinet.

Jefferson wished in every way imaginable to reduce what he deemed the monarchial aspects of the presidency. Republican simplicity was the new order of the day. Jefferson ceased the stiffly formal weekly levees that Washington had practiced, and he opened the President's House to visitors; he was the first president to live in the official home for the duration of his administration, although John and Abigail Adams had dwelled in the unfinished and barely furnished house for the last months of Adams's term.[10] Eschewing the carriage rides of his predecessors, Jefferson rode about the city on horseback, alone, and casually dressed. He received visitors informally, practically keeping an open house, and once scandalized the British minister Anthony Merry by his purposeful lack of the decorum that the king's representative thought was his due. Jefferson later added to the British minister's aggravation by inviting him to dinner without the rigorous attention to protocol the ambassador believed appropriate. Merry interpreted Jefferson's democratic practices as a studied insult to the Crown, as it may in part have been, but Jefferson practiced democracy daily, on the most intimate level. He often invited congressmen and other office holders to dinner, where they enjoyed good food and Jefferson's friendly conversation. He knew that getting to know one another, a person's needs and interests, was an effective way of earning political support. Not even his Federalist foes could resist his winning personality, which, once experienced up close, made petty politicking less likely. By such means

Jefferson proved to be a highly skilled politician, working to diminish partisan bickering and promoting compromise.[11] He truly believed that absent the iconic attraction of George Washington, most of the nation's citizens would agree with his positions and gradually come to support the Republicans. Indeed, that proved true in 1804.

Washington and Adams had annually delivered what we today call a State of the Union address to Congress. Because Jefferson knew he had few oratorical skills and felt the practice bore too close a resemblance to the British custom of having the monarch deliver an address to Parliament, he simply submitted to both houses a written annual message, which he had carefully worked upon and circulated to his cabinet for their ideas before crafting the final version. (More than a century later, Woodrow Wilson would resurrect the spoken State of the Union address.) His first annual message was delivered to the Congress on December 8, 1801. Jefferson noted that relations with Native Americans in the West were peaceful, as were relations with the nations of Europe, although the pirates of the Barbary States were troublesome. He reported that with good relations now with both France and Britain, commerce would soon so thrive that import duties would pay all government expenses and allow the national debt to be reduced. All other forms of taxes could be eliminated, internal tax officials could be retired, and the government could prosper by such frugality. The size of the regular army could be significantly reduced, and the navy could lay by most of its frigates and depend on smaller gunboats for coastal defense. (Adams had already begun limiting the size of the navy.)

Thus, the Republican ideal could be approached, with the government presence and associated expenses reduced. As Jefferson summarized, "Agriculture, manufactures, commerce and navigation, the four pillars of our prosperity, are then most thriving when left most free to individual enterprise." Then he mentioned, seemingly as an aside, that the "judiciary system of the United States, and especially that portion of it recently erected, will of course present itself to the contemplation of Congress."[12] He meant more than casual contemplation. Jefferson here and elsewhere during his two terms was subtly advancing a policy agenda, unlike his predecessors Washington and Adams who had seen their roles primarily as figureheads for national sovereignty. In a real sense Jefferson reshaped the presidency: not only was he the head of a party but he actively initiated and promoted a program.[13]

Foremost on Jefferson's mind were Adams's so-called midnight appointees. It was clear, certainly after Jefferson's election was ratified by the House on February 17, that the Republicans had won a resounding victory in the election of 1800. In the previous Congress, the Federalists had held a 22-to-10 majority in the Senate and a 60-to-46 majority in the House, but following the election, in the upcoming Congress, the Republicans would hold a 17-to-15 majority in the Senate and a 68-to-38 majority in the House.[14] Before they were to turn over control of Congress, the Federalists on February 27 rushed through the Judiciary Act of 1801 that reduced the membership of the Supreme Court from six to five justices to prevent Jefferson from naming a new justice and created sixteen new circuit courts (each of which would have three judges along with an appropriate number of marshals, attorneys, and clerks). President Adams worked fiercely to make all these judicial appointments, including such hard-line Federalists as Harrison Gray Otis and Oliver Wolcott, along with forty-two justices of the peace, before he left office on March 3, signing the last commission on his final evening.[15]

Jefferson saw these appointments as an outrageous attempt to cancel the effect of the popular vote by stacking the judiciary with Federalists and, as such, he thought these last-minute appointments should be considered inappropriate and void. Jefferson believed the election results truly expressed the will of the people, and their decision, he believed, ought to shape the form and policies of the new administration. He knew he could not remove judges, but he could remove lesser officials, and he could refuse to deliver commissions. And if the new circuit courts were eliminated, then the judges would simply have no function. Following Jefferson's implied wishes, the new Senate and House acted in the spring of 1802 to repeal the Judiciary Act of 1801. That law had also stopped the practice of having Supreme Court justices serve on circuit courts across the nation. The new Congress established a total of six circuit courts and reinstituted the practice of having Supreme Court justices serve on them. It restored a sixth judge to the Supreme Court and changed the practice of having the full Supreme Court sit twice annually in the capital for short sessions and instead directed it to sit for one longer annual session, a gain in efficiency.[16]

Jefferson, meanwhile, had simply declined to appoint lesser officials that the Judicial Act had provided for, such as justices of the peace. Two pieces of old business were addressed in different ways. The hated Alien and Sedition Acts simply expired before Jefferson took office, the Sedition Act on the very last day of Adams's administration. And to prevent a recurrence of a tie for the presidency, Congress in December 1803 approved a constitutional amendment requiring presidential electors to declare one candidate for president and the other for vice president. The amendment received the necessary approval by three-quarters of the states, and ratification became official on September 25, 1804.

William Marbury of Maryland was one of several men Adams had appointed justice of the peace for the District of Columbia, but Marbury's commission had not been delivered to him before Jefferson took office.[17]

Considering Marbury's appointment an affront to democratic principles, Jefferson declared his and similar appointments null. Subsequently, on December 17, 1801, Marbury and three other would-be justices petitioned the Supreme Court to issue a court order, a writ of mandamus, directing Secretary of State Madison to deliver their commissions. Marbury's petition was based on a provision of the Judiciary Act of 1789 that gave the Supreme Court jurisdiction in cases involving writs against officers of the executive branch. A small group of hyper-partisan Federalists promoted Marbury's cause and maneuvered to pressure the Supreme Court to mount an attack on the president. But Chief Justice John Marshall wanted to depoliticize the judiciary and improve relations between the judicial and executive branches, as did Jefferson. Marshall was politically astute enough to realize that the court really had no means to enforce any such order. His brilliant response brought no relief to Marbury but established a lasting principle.

Marshall decreed, in a decision delivered on February 24, 1803, that the 1789 act itself violated the Constitution, so the court had no authority to issue any writs. Nevertheless, Marshall took the opportunity in an obiter dictum to criticize Jefferson and his refusal to deliver the commissions, although this meaningless obiter dictum was probably meant to be just a sop to mollify the most partisan Federalists. The incidental "gratuitous" scolding really annoyed Jefferson, but Marbury and the others did not get their desired commissions. This decision, *Marbury v. Madison,* later became famous for formalizing the precedent that the Supreme Court could declare acts of Congress unconstitutional and hence void. It was not a controversial decision at all. (It was not until the 1807 trial of Aaron Burr that Jefferson and Marshall became confirmed enemies, and retrospectively, Jefferson expressed anger over the *Marbury* decision, which still rankled. But it was the obiter dictum, not the legal ruling, that angered Jefferson.) Rather, the concept of judicial review was understood and accepted by the framers of the Constitution and by prominent Virginia jurists, who had influenced both Jefferson and Marshall.[18] During the 1788 Virginia ratification debates, Marshall had defended the principle of judicial review of legislation, as had, a few years later, the eminent Virginia jurists George Wythe and Edmund Pendleton, so this was by no means a novel doctrine.[19] The Republicans at the time saw the decision as a victory for the administration because the protesting appointees did not get the positions they desired. Beyond the immediate case, this was the first of a long list of important court decisions by Marshall that transformed the role of the Supreme Court and significantly elevated the judiciary's place in the national constitutional system.[20]

Adams's attempt to create new courts and staff them entirely with Federalist judges highlights another problem Jefferson had to face. Because the

Federalists had controlled the government since its inception in 1789, practically every person holding a position in government, not just in the courts, was a Federalist. Thus, Jefferson confronted a government wholly Federalist in makeup. He believed, in principle, that party should not be a factor in government employment, but he also believed that the staff of the government should bear some resemblance to the political sentiment of the nation: there had been a significant increase in voting in the election of 1800, and the Republicans had won a resounding victory.[21] Moreover, those Republicans who supported Jefferson and had worked for his election strongly desired and expected that persons of their persuasion would now find an important role in the national government. As Jefferson soon learned, "Of all the duties imposed on the Executive head of a government, appointment to office is the most difficult & most irksome."[22] The expectations of his supporters only exacerbated the issue of appointments. As a congressman from Virginia wrote him shortly after the inauguration, "A pretty general purgation of office has been one of the benefits expected by the friends of the new order of things," and failure to carry through "would produce general and lasting disgusts in its friends."[23] Jefferson's supporters in Virginia and elsewhere wanted to change the personnel of the government, which at the time was almost exclusively Federalist.

Jefferson fully understood that government agents should not all be from one party, and fair and competent officers and clerks who fulfilled their jobs should not be removed simply because of party affiliation. He was willing to remove those who were incompetent and replace them with persons representing his views, and to similarly replace those who retired or died, but because of the slow pace of turnover, this still meant that for years Federalists would be overrepresented. Of course, every time any Federalist was replaced or succeeded by a Republican, the Federalists complained, and for most Republicans, the continuation in office of any Federalists, even those who did their jobs well, seemed to be a lost opportunity to remake the government. Jefferson ended up trying to split the difference by not removing capable officeholders without cause (except those who fit the category of midnight appointees) and choosing replacements who were from his party. He believed that if he acted magnanimously toward his political opponents, he would gradually attract them to his side. This of course satisfied few partisans of either stripe. At the end of his administration, while there were still many Federalists holding federal office, his appointees were mostly Republican. But at the highest levels, Jefferson did succeed in changing the tone of government and ensured that the total control of all government positions by members of one party was no more. He consciously *appointed* men on the basis of party but did not *remove* them for that reason.[24] Still, the change in the personnel and administration of the government represented most of what Jefferson meant when he later called his election "the revolution of 1800": he had democratized the governance of the nation.

One of the first things Jefferson had called for in his inaugural address was a frugal government. Luckily, international events made possible both a reduction in internal taxation (Jefferson was able to abolish the internal revenue service and dismiss some 40 percent of the Treasury Department's employees outside the capital) and a paying down of the public debt. This was a result of the Treaty of Mortefontaine (signed in 1800 and ratified in December 1801) whereby French privateers stopped preying on US maritime shipping, and the decision, in 1800, of the British Admiralty Court in the so-called *Polly* case to allow American merchantmen to trade with belligerent nations if the goods were first unloaded in a US port city, paid the requisite duties, then reloaded to be shipped to another nation. In the parlance of international trade, such a broken (interrupted) voyage allowed US shippers to trade with both British and French colonies in the West Indies and with their home nations. As a result, international trade boomed in the United States, import taxes and customs duties skyrocketed, and the government found itself with an abundance of revenue, hence it was able to do away with practically all other taxes. Prosperity flourished, taxes fell, the national debt was reduced, the number of government employees declined. On advice of Secretary of the Treasury Gallatin, Jefferson did not move against the national bank, something the Federalists had feared he would do. Meanwhile, state banks proliferated.[25]

From all viewpoints, Jefferson's first administration was an economic and, even more, a political success. His seeking to downsize the role and influence of the national government was a response to his own ideology and an accurate reading of public opinion. The British model of governance was being replaced in the United States by the Jeffersonian model. John Quincy Adams understood the political attraction of Jefferson's policies, commenting in 1802 that "[t]he power of the administration rests upon the support of a much stronger majority of the people throughout the Union than the former administrations ever possessed since the first establishment of the Constitution."[26] Jefferson wanted to lower the involvement of government in American life. The shift in the role of government may have been what prompted Hamilton to remark to Gouverneur Morris in 1802 "that this American world was not meant for me."[27] The election of 1804 validated these viewpoints. The Federalist candidates—Charles Cotesworth Pinckney for president and Rufus King for vice president—proved no match for the Republican ticket of Jefferson and George Clinton. Jefferson won fifteen states (including Massachusetts) to two for Pinckney, with the electoral college vote 162 to 14 for Jefferson.[28]

Perhaps unexpectedly, at least in the context of Federalist jibes against him for being too professorial to be an effective president, Jefferson proved to possess efficacious political skills. Soft spoken in demeanor, on a one-to-one personal level he was disarmingly pleasant. Not a good orator and with a voice that did not carry well, he was instead an expert conversationalist, in part because he was so well informed that he could talk with deftness about practically any issue. He put his conversational skills to use around his dinner table.[29] Two or three evenings a week he invited about a dozen politicians—senators and congressmen from both parties, department heads, and a scattering of other dignitaries (and occasionally their spouses too)—to the President's House for dinner, where invitees sat informally without rank around an oval table. The food was served from two small, movable stands with shelves beside Jefferson's chair. He dished the food himself onto plates and passed them around at the same time as he dispensed verbal pleasantries. He had a knack for reaching out to those who were shy or reticent. He knew how to engage the interests of each person and could move the conversation from person to person without anyone feeling left out or having anyone dominate. The conversation was never narrowly political or obviously partisan; instead, the dinners promoted good feelings, spirited talk, and a sense of well-being on the part of every participant. And the food was superb French cuisine blended with Virginia cooking (at times by three enslaved women Jefferson had brought up from Monticello), supplemented by the finest wine collection in the States—Jefferson served no liquor.

This was a time when Washington, DC, was still only a muddy-street town with none of the comforts or grandeur of European capitals, so most congressmen left their families at home during the congressional sessions and lived in one of fewer than a dozen boardinghouses, eating dreary, monotonous, often greasy boardinghouse food every evening.[30] What a difference was dining with Jefferson. Even political enemies asked, after the end of a pleasant evening, how do we get invited back? The answer, vote the right way. Halfway through his second term, Jefferson wrote a letter to a South Carolina congressman explaining the purpose of his dinners: "I cultivate personal intercourse with the members of the legislature that we may know one another and have opportunities of little explanations of circumstances, which, not understood might produce jealousies and suspicions injurious to the public interest, which is best promoted by harmony and mutual confidence among its functionaries."[31] This form of politics is seldom practiced today.

A perennial issue for Jefferson arose after he had been in office less than two months, when he learned that the bashaw (leader) of Tripoli, Yusuf Karamanli, having raised his demands for additional tribute the previous October, had declared war on the United States on February 26, 1801. The matter of the so-called Barbary pirates had troubled Jefferson since his days in the 1780s as minister to France. Then (as in 1801) pirates from the North African countries of Morocco, Algiers, Tunis, and Tripoli raided maritime commerce in the Mediterranean Sea, capturing ships and sailors and either holding the latter for ransom or enslaving them. John Adams and Jefferson had disagreed over the proper response. Arguing on a cost basis, Adams believed it was cheaper to simply pay the annual tributes the piratical leaders demanded. Jefferson believed doing so was unworthy of a great nation and besides, he argued, the Barbary nations would keep raising their demands. He believed the United States should send a naval force of sufficient size to punish the offending nations.[32] This conflict was seen as a matter of commerce, not a religious dispute between Christian and Muslim nations. In this context, a treaty in 1797 with Tripoli stated explicitly that the United States was not a Christian state.[33] Congress for pecuniary reasons sided with Adams, but as Jefferson predicted, the costs continued to increase. In periodic seizures of US vessels, hundreds of sailors were captured, and the annual tribute paid by the end of the 1790s represented 20 percent of the total US budget.[34] With this background, now that he was president, Jefferson finally saw an opportunity to handle the issue. As he wrote Madison in August 1801, "I know that nothing will stop the eternal increase of demand from these pirates but the presence of an armed force, and it will be more economical & more honorable to use the same means at once for suppressing their insolences."[35]

Jefferson called his cabinet together on May 15, 1801, and asked them, should the small US navy be sent to patrol the Mediterranean? The decision was unanimous: yes. And if the vessels were attacked, they could respond. Consequently, on May 20 the acting secretary of the navy, Samuel Smith (the former congressman), ordered Captain Richard Dale to sail to the Mediterranean, where his forces proved effective.[36] In November the administration received word that the USS *Enterprise* had defeated a Tripolitan vessel and killed twenty of its sailors. Later that year, in his annual written message to Congress, Jefferson explained the crisis underway, and Congress on February 6, 1802, backed his actions, authorizing "all means necessary to defeat the Tripolitans."[37] During the next several years, the US fleet went from victory to victory, but the highpoint came early in the conflict.

In September 1803 the frigate *Philadelphia* ran aground in the harbor of Tripoli. In a daring nighttime raid on February 16, 1804, Lieutenant Stephen Decatur, with seventy volunteers aboard a captured Tripolitan ketch rechristened the *Intrepid,* slipped into the harbor. All but two of the sailors were hidden below deck, but the two above deck were dressed in Turkish clothes, and one of them yelled out to the harbor master, "in the lingua franca of the

Mediterranean," that they were bringing in supplies and, having lost their anchor, needed to tie themselves to the grounded frigate. Attaching themselves to the *Philadelphia,* the sailors from below deck, having practiced just such an activity in darkness with the USS *Constitution,* quickly boarded the *Philadelphia,* scattered combustible materials about, set the ship afire, and escaped back to the *Intrepid.* With the ship ablaze, harbor defenders realized what was underway and began to bombard the *Intrepid,* but just then the gunpowder aboard the *Philadelphia* exploded, and amid the smoke and confusion the American sailors escaped with no injuries or deaths. The pirates would not be able to use the *Philadelphia* against US forces! This courageous exploit generated great praise in the United States and an eruption of nationalism. Even British naval hero Admiral Horatio Nelson labeled Decatur's raid "the most bold and daring act of the age."[38]

Following this success, Jefferson sent a larger squadron of American forces to the region, now commanded by Samuel Barron. On the advice of William Eaton, a former consul to Tunis, the US forces combined with the ragtag supporters of Hamet, the older brother of the bashaw of Tripoli, Yusuf Karamanli. Hamet, having had the throne stolen from him by Yusuf, now sought to take it back. Captain Eaton's marines joined forces with Hamet in Egypt and together with five hundred men they marched westward some four hundred miles to attack the Tripolitan port of Derne at the same time the US naval vessels bombarded the port city of Tripoli. Both attacks were successful, and the Tripolitan government signed a treaty even before the battles were over.[39] This treaty did not settle all the problems in the region, but by demonstrating that, like Britain and France, the United States was a powerful state that the various Barbary kingdoms would have to respect, it changed the maritime calculus and protected subsequent commerce in the Mediterranean. It also led to a huge outpouring of nationalism in the United States, increasing the popularity of the Republicans.

Jefferson made a number of other decisions in his first administration that also bore fruit, for example the establishment of the Library of Congress and the founding of the US Military Academy at West Point, New York. But his most significant achievements resulted from unanticipated developments. The first arose after the president learned from private correspondence in August 1801 that Spain had re-ceded Louisiana to France, news that confirmed an earlier rumor picked up by the American minister to England. This intelligence presented a crisis situation for Jefferson, who for more than a decade had considered control of Louisiana and hence New Orleans a key concern of the nation. A substantial portion of the nation's trade, practically all of it west of the Appalachians, flowed down the Ohio and Mississippi Rivers and thence, via the port of New Orleans, to the larger world. As long as relatively powerless

Spain had controlled the region, Jefferson had few concerns; in fact, he expected eventually the United States would quietly absorb the region without significant resistance. But control by powerful France was another matter, especially because rumors persisted that France intended to actively colonize the region again.

Jefferson had at the beginning of his administration named Robert R. Livingston, the longtime chancellor (highest ranking judicial officer) of New York, as minister to France. They had served together on the committee in 1776 to write the Declaration of Independence, and Livingston had administered the oath of office to George Washington in 1789. Jefferson and Secretary of State Madison sent letters to Livingston and Charles Pinckney, whom Jefferson had named the minister to Spain (Pinckney, cousin to Charles Cotesworth Pinckney, was a former governor of South Carolina and a senator from that state), to consult on what should be done. Together they concluded to try to convince France that ownership and colonization of Louisiana was not in its best interest.[40] France's Caribbean colonies could easily purchase needed supplies from the United States in peacetime, but if war should break out, that trade would immediately end. The gunboats of the (admittedly small) US navy could defeat any threatened French invasion. Yet Jefferson, as usual, turned first to diplomacy.

He sought to convince France to sell the United States a portion of the east bank of the Mississippi below New Orleans, where what was called a port of deposit could be established for the temporary storing of goods before they were reloaded onto ocean-going vessels for shipment elsewhere. He so informed Livingston in a letter to be delivered by his friend Pierre Samuel Du Pont de Nemours, purposely left open so Du Pont could read it too. It was a thinly veiled warning to Napoleon, whom Jefferson abhorred. Importantly, it contained words pregnant with meaning for the future. "If France considers Louisiana however as indispensable for her views, she might perhaps be willing to look about for arrangements which might reconcile it to our interests. if any thing could do this it would be the ceding to us the island of New Orleans and the Floridas."[41] In Washington, both Madison and Jefferson went out of their way to cozy up to the British chargé d'affaires, knowing that his French counterpoint would notice and inform his superiors. Du Pont, before he left for France with the letter, wrote Jefferson that he hoped the United States would try to buy Louisiana, to which Jefferson replied that the United States wanted only New Orleans and Florida. For months there was no reply from France. Suddenly the stakes were raised.

On or about November 25, 1802, the administration learned that the acting Spanish intendant of New Orleans, Juan Ventura Morales, had closed the port to US trade, suspending the traditional right of deposit for commerce via the Mississippi River. After questioning the Spanish minister to the United States, Carlos Martinez de Yrugo, who professed to know nothing of the matter, Jefferson decided it was the action of a wayward minor official, not royal policy from Spain (much later it turned out the order did come from the king). The news, though, produced an uproar in the West, and western farmers began to raise threats about seizing New Orleans. Jefferson made sure French officials knew of this opposition. To calm those in the United States who wanted instant action, he repositioned some military forces near Natchez and quickly arranged to send James Monroe (both liked and trusted in the western states and popular in France from his prior service as US minister in the 1790s) to assist Livingston in Paris. Expressing much confidence in Livingston, whom he now nominated as minister plenipotentiary, and with Monroe labeled minister extraordinary & plenipotentiary, this move was intended both to "tranquilize" those protesting in the western states and to indicate to the French just how important the United States considered the negotiations underway.[42] Congress approved the appointment of Monroe on January 11, 1803, and on March 2 authorized the expenditure of a total of $11.375 million for any successful territorial transactions. When Monroe arrived in Paris, it was clear that negotiations were at a standstill. As Livingston had confided to Secretary of State Madison, "There never was a government in which less could be done by negotiation than here. There is no people no legislature no counselors one man [Napoleon] is everything—he seldom asks advice and never hears it unasked."[43]

Unbeknown to Jefferson or his ministers, Napoleon was in the midst of changing his mind. He had once had dreams that Saint-Domingue / San Domingo could continue as a wealthy sugar island, and to assist its prosperity, he had desired Louisiana as a provisioning colony to support his projected sugar empire. But a successful slave rebellion had broken out on San Domingo, led by François-Dominique Toussaint Louverture. Toussaint Louverture's troops repeatedly defeated the French army sent in to put down the rebellion. Then a devastating yellow fever epidemic swept through the French forces, and by late 1802 the French had lost twenty-four thousand men, including the commanding general, Charles Victory Emmanuel Leclerc, Napoleon's brother-in-law. Meanwhile, a French fleet, intended to establish a colony in Louisiana, was iced in at the Dutch port city of Hellevoetsluis during an unusually severe winter. The combined news of Leclerc's death and the frozen status of the fleet led to Napoleon's reputed cry of frustration, "Damm sugar, damm coffee, damm colonies."[44]

Giving up on San Domingo and thus having no need of Louisiana, and instead casting his eyes to the eastern Mediterranean and the Middle East, Napoleon realized he both needed additional money and a possible ally against

England. Therefore, the increasing hostility from the United States concerned him. Napoleon's solution: sell Louisiana to the United States at such a bargain price as to purchase its friendship. Napoleon instructed his foreign minister, Charles Maurice de Talleyrand-Périgord, to tender such an offer to Livingston just the day before Monroe arrived. Monroe would write to Madison several months later that "a desire to place us at repose with respect to France, to establish a solid peace between the two nations, and prevent our connection with Engld., by a liberal policy, were among the strong motives which had induc'd the cession of Louisiana."[45]

On April 12, 1803, in what appeared casual conversation, Talleyrand had asked Livingston if the United States would like to have "the whole of Louisiana." In his letter describing the occasion, Livingston said he had replied that no, the United States only wanted to buy the island of New Orleans, as the city on the eastern bank of the Mississippi was called, and the Florida territories. Talleyrand persisted, asking what they might offer for all of Louisiana. A nonplussed Livingston said perhaps 20 million francs, which Talleyrand thought was too little. At that point Livingston pushed for a delay, saying that his colleague Monroe would soon be there and they would need to discuss the matter. Then Talleyrand backed off, saying this idea had just come to him, that he was not making a formal offer. He pretended the next day that Louisiana was not really France's to sell anyway.[46]

That afternoon Livingston noticed that Napoleon's minister of the treasury, the Marquis François Barbé-Marbois, was wandering through his garden. Napoleon had recognized that Talleyrand did not like Livingston (and probably knew that Talleyrand opposed selling Louisiana), so he asked Barbé-Marbois to take over the transactions. Barbé-Marbois spoke flawless English, liked Americans, had married an American woman, and had lived in Philadelphia (it was he who prepared the list of questions that led to Jefferson's *Notes on the State of Virginia*). Barbé-Marbois assured Livingston that Napoleon was serious and wanted 100 million francs ($18.75 million) for the territory. Livingston said that was too much. Barbé-Marbois agreed and offered 60 million francs ($11.25 million), with another 20 million francs ($3.75 million) to reimburse Americans for claims against the French government. Napoleon had helpfully suggested the Americans could borrow money from English and Dutch bankers so that France could be paid up front. After conferring among themselves, Livingston and Monroe agreed to accept the deal before Napoleon changed his mind, recognizing that in so doing they were far exceeding the terms of their instructions from Jefferson. Livingston quickly wrote President Jefferson, proactively defending their decision.[47] As if one letter were not enough, Livingston wrote the president again on May 2, essentially restating that "I trust the acquisition we have made will be satisfactory to our country tho in obtaining it we have exceeded our powers."[48]

For several days the three men negotiated, and the two Americans worked hard to fulfill the transaction, discussing the details of financing, deciding on the price of $11.25 million for the territory, and another $3.75 million to settle the claims of US citizens on France. Barbé-Marbois insisted that the treaty include a provision that

> The inhabitants of the ceded territory shall be incorporated into the Union of the United States and admitted as soon as possible according to the principles of the federal Constitution to the enjoyment of all these rights, advantages, and immunities of citizens of the United States, and in the mean time they shall be maintained and protected in the free enjoyment of their liberty, property [including enslaved people] and the Religion which they profess.[49]

Then the three negotiators worked out the financial loans from the banks and handled the transfer of funds. At the conclusion, the three shook hands and Livingston remarked, "We have lived long, but this is the noblest work of our whole lives. . . . From this day the United States take their place among the powers of the first rank."[50]

Livingston and Monroe then prepared a copy of the treaty (its official language was in French) and supporting legal and financial documents to send back to the United States, conveyed by a private citizen to Jefferson. When the president learned the details of the purchase on July 3, he was overjoyed. The treaty guaranteed US control of the Mississippi—long a major concern of Jefferson's—and effectively guaranteed that the nation would be free of potentially hostile European nations to its west, making possible its eventual rise to a great world power. And at the cost of about four cents an acre!

Still work had to be done. The treaty had to be formalized, and then American governmental institutions had to be imposed upon the territory, part of which of course was home to thousands of persons who had previously identified with Spanish (and before that, French) governance, along with an extensive Indigenous population. Was such a purchase even constitutional? Jefferson initially believed an amendment to the Constitution was required—after all, had not he been an advocate of so-called strict construction in the debate over Hamilton's proposal for a national bank? Jefferson also contemplated holding off white settlement in the region, keeping the territory north of the settlements near New Orleans as a preserve for Native Americans. Like most leaders of his time, Jefferson shared the common Enlightenment viewpoint that societies over time progressed through four stages, ranging from what they considered primitive to most advanced. These stages were labeled hunting, pasturage, agriculture, and commerce. As did other contemporaries, Jefferson believed that Native Americans had to change their hunter-gather economies because of the pressure of growing population and the exhaustion of wild game and switch to a farming economy if they were to survive. He thought that a protected zone like Louisiana would allow them time to make such a transition. But then word arrived from France that the mercurial Napoleon was having second thoughts. Livingston wrote that "I hope in God that nothing will prevent your immediate ratification & without altering a syllable of the terms. . . . The slightest pretense will lose you the treaty."[51] Jefferson had already been backing away from the idea of proposing and working to ratify an amendment; such strict adherence to principle would risk a great loss. Now the nation had to act. By the end the treaty was pared down to "Louisiana, as ceded by France to the US. is made a part of the US."[52]

Jefferson asked the Congress to convene earlier than usual to consider the treaty, so on October 3, 1803, the session opened. The Senate debated the issue for two days before approving, despite almost total opposition from diehard Federalists. Subsequently, on October 20 Jefferson exchanged the ratification agreement with the French chargé d'affaires in Washington, Louis-André Pichon, with whom he was on excellent terms. Two months later, on December 20, 1803, the would-be French governor of Louisiana, Pierre Clément Laussat, whose territory had been sold out from under him, met the American, William C. C. Claiborne, whom Jefferson had just named governor of the Territory of Orleans, at the Cabildo (City Hall) in New Orleans. There, in a small ceremony in the Place d'Armes in front of the Cabildo, the transfer occurred. In the plaza now known as Jackson Square, the French tricolor was lowered and the US flag raised. The American nation had just doubled in size. The generous availability of ample land would, it was assumed, allow the idealized commercial agricultural economy to thrive for many generations into the future.

Opportunities, like troubles, often come in bunches, and as with the Louisiana Purchase, the positive can emerge from what at first appears a negative. Shortly after Jefferson began receiving evidence in 1801 that Spain might have ceded Louisiana to powerful France, thereby jeopardizing the US future in the whole Southwest and West, he learned of another territorial threat to what he saw as the nation's destiny. About mid-1802, he purchased a copy of a book published in 1801 by a Scottish explorer, Alexander Mackenzie, that told the story of his 1793 journey across Canada, through the Rocky Mountains, to the Pacific Coast. In the final chapter of *Voyages from Montreal . . . through the Continent of North America, to the Frozen and Pacific Ocean,* Mackenzie called for the British to establish a settlement in the northwestern portion of the continent and from that development they could obtain "the entire command of the fur trade of North America," promote fisheries, and have access to "the markets of the four quarters of the globe."[53] Jefferson was apparently shocked. Just as France was threatening to settle the Southwest, here was England being tempted to develop permanent settlements in the Northwest. This must have been when Jefferson began to plan an exploration up the Missouri River in the hope of finding a mostly water route to the Pacific, linking that vast ocean to the mighty Mississippi.

In Jefferson's papers there is an undated memorandum, presumably prepared before the end of 1802, concerning a cost estimate for a small exploratory party to the West. It was doubtless prepared by Jefferson's private secretary, Meriwether Lewis. Jefferson had hired Lewis at the beginning of his administration. Lewis was from Albemarle County, so Jefferson knew him and his family. He chose Lewis in large part because the twenty-six-year-old had served in the army since 1795 and had broad familiarity, as a regimental paymaster, with the US officer corps. Jefferson intended to reduce the size of the military forces and desired an assistant who could advise him on manpower needs, the qualities of various officers, and the extent of fortifications. Lewis actually lived with Jefferson in the commodious President's House, as Jefferson described it to his daughter Martha, "like two mice in a church."[54] Jefferson trusted Lewis, understood that he was extraordinarily skilled as a woodsman, knowledgeable of the flora and fauna of Virginia, and a close observer of nature. As the exploration developed in Jefferson's mind, he settled on Lewis as its commander.

Following the sage advice of Secretary Gallatin, Jefferson had on January 18, 1803, forwarded a confidential message to Congress ostensibly seeking funding to send an exploratory expedition up the Missouri to examine commercial possibilities with the Native Americans of the region. He suggested that an "intelligent officer with ten or twelve chosen men, fit for the enterprise" could perform the mission, and by selecting them from among soldiers already serving in the region and already on the payroll, with a slight additional cost for supplies (and trade goods for Indigenous peoples they would encounter), the total expense would be minimal. He asked for an appropriation of $2,500. He added that incidentally the explorers could "advance the geographical knowledge of our own continent."[55] The latter was of course Jefferson's true aim, but he knew that he could only get congressional funding if he presented the so-called enterprise as an attempt to promote commerce, a recognized constitutional function of Congress. With such disingenuous phrasing, and by lowballing the projected expense, Jefferson persuaded Congress on

February 28 to approve the funds "for the purpose of extending the external commerce of the United States."[56]

After choosing Lewis to lead the expedition, he sought to elevate his skills and knowledge. Toward that aim, Jefferson asked a series of experts—surveyor Andrew Ellicott, botanist and naturalist Benjamin Smith Barton, physician Benjamin Rush, and mathematician Robert Patterson—if they would tutor Lewis in their respective spheres of expertise. Lewis was both a dedicated and a quick learner, so Jefferson in effect provided him a crash course in the science and medicine of the era. He also began to prepare a letter to Lewis that would constitute a statement of his mission. After drafting the letter, Jefferson, as was his practice, circulated it among his cabinet members, adapting some of their suggestions. Then he sent a preliminary copy to Lewis, asking him to share it with the mentors Jefferson had arranged. The finalized letter was given to Lewis on June 20, 1803, setting out a stunningly broad program of desired areas for investigation.

The letter began by mentioning the variety of instruments and tools that would be provided, indicated that the ministers of France, Spain, and England had been informed (though before the Corps of Discovery actually set forth, the Louisiana Purchase was approved and they would be in effect examining territory the nation had just acquired), and then laid out the key objective: "to explore the Missouri river, & such principle stream of it, as, by it's course & communication with the water of the Pacific Ocean may offer the most direct & practicable water communication across the continent, for the purposes of commerce."[57] Jefferson instructed Lewis and his team to make precise measurements of latitude and longitude for all significant landmarks and observe the soils, climate, mineral deposits, and flora and fauna encountered, especially those not known on the Eastern Seaboard (even to record such details as the temperature of the water in hot springs they came upon). He also asked for a wide range of questions about the Native Americans they would encounter: their languages, traditions, relations with other Indigenous nations, their food, agricultural and hunting practices, their diseases, clothing, medical practices, religions, laws, and finally, what "articles of commerce they may need or furnish & to what extent."[58] That of course met the stated congressional purpose of the mission, but in the long list of objectives Jefferson laid out, it ranked in interest far behind scientific and anthropological investigations. Understanding that as a soldier, Lewis might be prone to risk danger to fulfill his mission, Jefferson urged him "to err on the side of your safety, & to bring back your party safe, even if it be with less information."[59]

So instructed, Lewis, after completing his period of study, began to gather supplies of every sort—canned soup, lead for bullets, gifts for the Native

Americans, medicines, tools—and had several boats constructed, including a fifty-five-foot-long keelboat that, loaded with tons of supplies, the Corps of Discovery would float down the Ohio River from Pittsburgh and then, after spending the winter of 1803–4 near St. Louis, they would, beginning on May 14, 1804, push the keelboat and their smaller boats up the Mississippi to its quick junction with the Missouri, and then up that turbulent river to the north. Earlier, Lewis had persuaded William Clark to join him as cocaptain, and having signed up a group of almost forty men—soldiers, hunters, fur trappers, translators competent in several Indigenous spoken languages in addition to the sign language known almost universally among Native nations—the expedition was underway.

Known to history as the Lewis and Clark Expedition, or more officially the Corps of Discovery, the crew included an enslaved man named York belonging to Clark, and eventually a teenage Shoshone Indian woman named Sacagawea, the "wife" of a hired French interpreter named Toussaint Charbonneau, who would subsequently demonstrate her bravery and skill to the leaders of the expedition. They would complete a journey of exploration across a third of the continent and over the daunting Rocky Mountains.[60] During their first frigid winter among the Mandan Indians in present-day North Dakota, Sacagawea gave birth to a son, Jean Baptiste, nicknamed Pomp or Pompey by Clark, who would become a great favorite of the men, his childish antics brightening spirits after many an exhausting day. As that terrible winter drew to a close, on April 7, 1805, the corps (after sending the keelboat back to St. Louis loaded with animal skins and artifacts, along with seven men), now numbering thirty-three members including the infant, set forth to the West. They thus began the most storied exploration in US history, the participants over the next seventeen months surviving incredible dangers and hardships but managing to get all the way to the Pacific and back to St. Louis on September 23, 1806. Over the journey of several thousand miles, Sacagawea carried her infant son on her back across mountains, along narrow ridges, and aboard canoes, an accomplishment that today seems hardly believable.

As it was underway, Jefferson heard nothing of the journey. No doubt he would have exulted if he had known, on July 4, 1805, that some 1,800 hundred miles to the west near present-day Great Falls, Montana, on the banks of the Missouri River, the Corps of Discovery celebrated the Declaration of Independence with a hearty meal, fiddling and dancing, and the last of their grog, "in short," as Lewis recorded in his journal, "we had no just cause to covet the sumptuous feasts of our countrymen on this day."[61] Both Lewis and Clark kept journals, as did several of the sergeants, and these journals included detailed scientific data of every imaginable sort. After more than a year of no communication with the corps, finally, on October 20, 1806, Jefferson received "with unspeakable joy" a letter postmarked September 23, 1806, from Lewis in St. Louis: the corps had returned![62]

Three months later Lewis visited Jefferson in Washington, and on January 1, 1807, with Clark's composite map spread out on the floor of the President's House, Jefferson and Lewis got down on their hands and knees to inspect Clark's work and discuss their remarkable trip. Jefferson was, however, eventually to be disappointed because the scientific results of the expedition were not published in his lifetime. Lewis was assigned the task of preparing the voluminous journals and notes for publication, but the onset of an interminable writer's block prevented him from making any progress on the project and contributed to a depression that led to his suicide in 1809. Clark then took over and arranged for a Philadelphia polymath, Nicholas Biddle, to prepare the papers for publication. Biddle thought the writing insufficiently graceful, so he essentially rewrote their journals, omitting most of the valuable scientific observations and data and transforming the journals into a mere adventure tale, and published them in two volumes in 1814. Unfortunately, not until the end of the century was a more complete version published, and not until the 1980s was a scholarly, accurate version prepared and published under the auspices of the University of Nebraska Press.[63]

The bulk of the scientific contributions was lost because of this century-plus delay—for example, most of the place names they ascribed to geographical features disappeared on later-drawn maps—but the story of the courageous explorers and the role of Sacagawea, exaggerated into a mythical pathfinder, helped create the romantic image of the West in the American imagination. The journals now provide valuable ethnographical information (but of course from the perspective of the members of the Corps of Discovery) about the Native Americans the corps encountered, along with vivid depictions of the landscape and wildlife as they existed more than two centuries ago. Unfortunately, Jefferson, who is credited with promoting the expedition and loved travel accounts, never read the entirety of their journals and must have considered the expedition in some ways at least as a profound failure.[64] Nevertheless, the Lewis and Clark Expedition stands as one of the signal accomplishments of Jefferson's first administration. There had been several highpoints for Virginians, from the first of many important Supreme Court decisions by Marshall, and Monroe's helpful negotiations in France to acquire the Louisiana Territory, to Meriwether Lewis's setting forth to explore the West. The second administration would find few such successes.

11

JEFFERSON, MADISON, AND JOHN BULL

President Thomas Jefferson had quickly demonstrated that he could employ his political skills to achieve his purposes in the Congress. A good listener and mediator whose weekly dinner parties helped persuade congressmen, Jefferson both wrote bills that legislators would introduce and managed to have his various cabinet members meet with congressional committees to advance positions he desired. Neither of his predecessors had actively pursued political agendas in Congress, and not until the election of Andrew Jackson in 1828 would another president take such effective legislative initiatives. But Jefferson found the judiciary to be resistant to his influence. He understood that judges, and they were all Federalists when he took office, were by the Constitution guaranteed appointment for life assuming good behavior, but it was unclear what constituted bad behavior.

In 1803 Jefferson was confronted with a federal judge who quite obviously was incompetent, but what was the remedy? He did not want to provoke a conflict with the judiciary as a whole. John Pickering earlier in his career had been a respected jurist in New Hampshire, but shortly after appointment as the state's chief justice, he became ill, began to deteriorate mentally, and succumbed to alcoholism. After the citizens of New Hampshire got rid of him by convincing George Washington to appoint him to the state's federal district court, he only worsened. His judgeship was characterized by profanity and drunkenness. Once Jefferson became president, Pickering became his problem. Albert Gallatin asked Pickering to resign, and when that did not work, both he and Jefferson pressured several Federalist senators to attempt to convince Pickering to resign.[1] Nothing worked. Jefferson subsequently sent letters and affidavits to the House, pushing them to begin impeachment proceedings. The Federalists recognized Pickering's liabilities but did not want to allow Jefferson a judgeship to fill, so they resisted; were drunkenness, profanity, and mental instability sufficient to merit removal, or were they only symptoms of bad behavior but not legally impeachable offenses? Eventually Pickering was removed after a strictly partisan vote without a precise charge ever being listed. He was, thus, the first federal judge impeached, and the Federalists saw the episode as proof of Jefferson's antipathy toward the judiciary.[2]

In the midst of this imbroglio, another judicial controversy emerged, and this one involved an associate justice of the Supreme Court, Samuel Chase. Chase was an immensely talented jurist with an ego to match, and his partisanship only increased when he was appointed to the Supreme Court in 1796. Even from the bench he was stridently partisan and eager to speak his mind. Long a foe of Jefferson, at a trial on the Baltimore circuit court in May 1803, he had harshly attacked the current political scene, including the Republicans in general and the president in particular. Jefferson at this time hoped to moderate whatever animosity might exist between his party and the courts, but in a private letter to a Maryland congressman he commented on what he termed "the extraordinary charge" of Chase to the Baltimore jury and wondered, should such "seditious" attacks "go unpunished"?[3] Apparently Jefferson was just venting, took no more actions against Chase, and played no role in what happened next. In fact, the congressman to whom he wrote did not act, either, nor did the Speaker of the House, Nathaniel Macon, but hyper-partisan John Randolph decided to lead the charge against Chase.

There is no evidence that Jefferson really wanted to mount a campaign against Chase—he knew the Federalists already believed he had a vendetta against the court—and if he had, he certainly would not have chosen the contentious and unpredictable John Randolph to lead the effort.[4] Randolph was an ultra-Republican who was angry at Jefferson for his moderation and his failure to remove all Federalists officeholders. He would soon lead a splinter group that called themselves the Tertium Quid (Latin for "the third other") to distinguish them from either the Republicans or Federalists. Randolph was a flamboyant personality and a master of vitriol as a speaker, but he was no lawyer and no match for Chase. Nevertheless, on January 4, 1804, Randolph insisted that the House investigate Chase, and he chaired the committee that rushed out a set of charges.[5] These charges were never acted on by the House because the case shifted directly to the Senate, and Randolph headed a select committee that prepared articles of impeachment, bringing charges related to behavior on the circuit court, not the Supreme Court. The trial began on February 9, 1805, in the Senate. Randolph's lack of legal expertise was instantly clear, and Chase made a meticulous and learned legal defense of himself.

So persuasive were the rebuttals to Randolph that Chase was acquitted on every single charge despite there being enough Republican senators to have convicted him without a single Federalist vote. Apparently, most of the senators felt the charges were unproven if not unfair. Many, like Jefferson himself, probably did not want to exacerbate the tensions between the judiciary and the other branches of government, and at least some of the Republicans did not want in any way to support the irascible Randolph who was proving himself to be an intemperate enemy of Jefferson. John Marshall was called as a witness in the case, and he spoke carefully and judiciously. In fact, though he supported Chase in the trial, he did not himself approve of the kind of language Chase had used in the past. And Chase, although acquitted, thereafter controlled himself in court and never again interjected his Federalist opinions in such stark fashion from the bench.[6] The outcome of the trial established two precedents, one moderating the behavior of judges in trials and the other protecting judges from partisan attempts at impeachment. Both Jefferson and Marshall could take some satisfaction from the conclusion.

Jefferson as president understood that, with the government's fiscal situation so improving, it was possible to contemplate a series of internal improvements, so he took occasion in several of his annual messages to Congress to suggest that the Constitution should be revised to authorize the federal government to undertake efforts to benefit the nation. For him it was not a question whether such improvements were needed but rather that the Constitution, strictly interpreted, did not allow such expenditures. In such cases he believed it wise to revise the Constitution to adapt it to fit the needs and capabilities of the nation. In his second annual message, delivered to Congress on December 15, 1802, Jefferson had mentioned the need to "cultivate peace and maintain commerce and navigation," "foster our fisheries," and "protect the manufactures adapted to our circumstances," meanwhile "keep[ing] all things within the pale of our constitutional powers."[7] He went further in his fourth annual message on November 8, 1804, urging Congress that "in the discharge of the great duties confided to you by our country, you will take a broader view of the field of legislation. Whether the great interests of agriculture, manufactures, commerce, or navigation, can, within the pale of your constitutional powers, be aided in any of their relations."[8] He continued in this vein in his sixth annual message on December 2, 1806, noting the surplus of funds that peacetimes were producing in the national government. "To what other objects shall these surpluses be appropriated" in addition to continuing to pay down the national debt: "to the great purposes of the public education, roads, rivers, canals, and such other objects of public improvement as it may be thought proper to add to the constitutional enumeration of federal powers." He particularly emphasized the importance of promoting education. Then he made clear his recommendation: "I suppose an amendment to the constitution, by consent of the States, necessary, because the objects not recommended are not among those enumerated in the constitution, and to which it permits the public moneys to be applied."[9]

Clearly, Jefferson here demonstrated that he was not so narrowly devoted to the promotion of agriculture as to be indifferent to other aspects of modern economic development. In 1816 he made his views even more explicit in a letter to Benjamin Austin, a former merchant in Boston then serving as federal loan commissioner in Massachusetts. Jefferson acknowledged that, when he wrote *Notes on the State of Virginia* in 1784, he had been highly critical of manufacturers, but subsequent events had forced him to change his mind. "An opinion founded in the circumstances of that day" cannot be "fairly applied to those of the present . . . . We must now place the manufacturer by the side of the agriculturist." He continued, "experience has taught me that manufactures are now as necessary to our independance [*sic*] as to our comfort. . . . In so complicated a science as political economy, no one axiom can be laid down as wise an expedient for all times and circumstances."[10]

Jefferson was making an important point and one that is essential for understanding his evolving positions on a number of issues over time that are often used to accuse him of inconsistency. This man who attacked cities in *Notes* had become a connoisseur of cities by the 1790s when he and Washington were planning the new capital for the nation, and he admitted in 1805 that he wished he had time to thoroughly revise what he had written about cities two decades before.[11] While Jefferson believed that the federal government's actions were limited to what the Constitution explicitly allowed, he simultaneously believed the Constitution should be periodically revised to fit changing times. He explained his attitude toward the nation's foundational document in a letter in 1816.

> Some men look at Constitutions with sanctimonious reverence, & deem them, like the ark of the covenant, too sacred to be touched. . . . I am certainly not an advocate for frequent & untried changes in laws and constitutions. . . . But I know also that laws and institutions must go hand in hand with the progress of the human mind. as that becomes more developed, more enlightened, as new discoveries are made, new truths disclosed, and manners and opinions change with the change of circumstances, institutions must advance also, and keep pace with the times.

By no means did he disparage the wisdom of the past, but he was open to new ideas. "Let us," he wrote, "avail ourselves of our reason and experience to correct the crude essays of our first and unexperienced, altho' wise, virtuous, & well meaning councils. And lastly, let us provide in our constitution for it's revision at stated periods."[12] Of course, sometimes a president would be presented with dangers so imminent, or opportunities so great, that time did not allow the seeking of a constitutional amendment; in such cases, executives had to act boldly, "risking themselves like faithful servants," and afterward "throw themselves on their country" for forgiveness for doing what the people themselves would have done "had they been in a situation to do it."[13] That is how he had justified to himself accepting the Louisiana Purchase.

Jefferson had another controversial court case, this one involving Chief Justice Marshall in the federal circuit court in Richmond and revolving around Aaron Burr. Following the disputed election of 1800 and Burr's evident willingness to serve as president had the Federalists attempted to choose him by a vote in the House of Representatives, Jefferson never fully trusted him. In the spring of 1804 Republican caucus, only one congressman voted to retain Burr as vice president on the forthcoming ticket; all the other votes were for George Clinton, then governor of New York. Realizing he had no future in the administration, Burr decided to run in the New York election to replace Clinton. In that election Burr met the spirited opposition of Alexander Hamilton. The two had long been opponents. After what Burr took to be an unacceptable insult, he challenged Hamilton to a duel.

Why Hamilton did not simply find a way to apologize, or somehow avoid a showdown, is unclear. His own life had taken a dive too. He was in debt, he had personal problems and family tragedy, and he had lost much of his political effectiveness after his break with Adams. Did he see this as an honorable form of suicide, or did he think standing for a duel was a way of recouping his former political fortunes?[14] We cannot know. But early on the morning of July 11, 1804, near Weehawken on the New Jersey side of the Hudson River, Burr and Hamilton faced each other, pistols in hand. Who fired first is not certain. Did Hamilton purposely miss? Again, we cannot know. We do know that Burr's shot hit Hamilton in the torso above his right hip, and thirty-one hours later, after excruciating pain, Hamilton died. The outpouring of sympathy for Hamilton astonished many, perhaps especially Burr, who quickly fled the scene for fear of arrest. Hamilton's physical life was over, and Burr's normal political life ended too.

Desperately in debt, Burr began another phase of his life. He spent months touring the western territories, inspecting locations for settlement, sizing up the political situation, contemplating raising forces for a raid on Spanish-held Latin America, collecting a flotilla of flatboats at Blennerhassett's Island in the Ohio River, perhaps plotting to gain political support to create a dominion out of the western territories and break away from the United States, becoming himself the leader of a new nation. He sent offers to England, proposing with their support to lead the breakaway nation; he put out feelers to Spain. He said different things to different people, promoting a variety of schemes, some really harebrained. Or was he simply planning to purchase land on the Washita River in present-day Oklahoma? Even today Burr's ultimate motives are unclear.[15]

Beginning in the early autumn of 1805, Jefferson started hearing rumors of Burr's activities in the West. Jefferson received an anonymous letter that suggested an improper relationship with Britain, then a letter from the US attorney for Kentucky, Joseph H. Daviess, that claimed information of a plot with a group of prominent men, all Republicans, to break away from the union and found a rival nation. Because Daviess was the brother-in-law of Chief Justice Marshall, Jefferson discounted the letter as an attempt to smear Republicans.[16] Throughout 1806, several Federalist newspapers carried stories about nefarious plots in the West involving Burr, but again Jefferson dismissed the accounts as partisan slander. However, later in 1806 Jefferson began hearing from reputable Republicans tales of western intrigue, of Burr attempting to raise funds and gather men and supplies, and Jefferson had to take seriously the authenticity of this news.

Jefferson now took alarm. He convened his cabinet and released a proclamation on November 27, warning persons in the West against "conspiring & confederating" "against the dominions of Spain" and calling upon them "to cease all further proceedings."[17] Jefferson then asked Secretary of State Madison to look into the constitutionality of using US regular army forces to put down internal insurrections. (The attorney general had died, so Jefferson turned to Madison for his advice.) Jefferson wrote out a bill authorizing such use of the army and asked a trusted congressman to introduce it. Soon it was law. Then Jefferson presented his annual message to Congress on December 2, 1806, making clear the actions he had taken to suppress illegal militaristic escapades in the West.[18] Yet still information continued to trickle in, all of it sounding dangerous and most of it implicating Burr.

Jefferson learned that men had assembled, put together a flotilla of flatboats at Blennerhassett's Island in westernmost Virginia, and were preparing to float down the Ohio River into the Mississippi. Burr was arrested but available information and witnesses were insufficient to allow an indictment. Two supposed accomplices, Erich Bollman and Samuel Swartwout, were arrested and put on trial. Rumors upon rumors flowed eastward, and newspapers repeated and probably exaggerated the threat, but various details about Burr's supposed activities became commonly known.

Many authorities were understandably worried, and John Randolph, now a clear enemy of Jefferson, pushed through Congress a resolution calling upon Jefferson to give the House of Representatives any information he had about individuals reputed to be plotting against the nation. Jefferson sent a special message to Congress on January 22, 1807, laying out such evidence as he had.

In this message, Jefferson spelled out how difficult it was to discover the truth of what had happened. He explained, "little [of the evidence] has been given under the sanction of an oath," much of it is a "mixture of rumors, conjectures, and suspicions," but on the basis of what he could determine, it was clear that "the prime mover" was Aaron Burr, "whose guilt is placed beyond question."[19] This frankness proved to be a mistake. Jefferson in effect, before a trial had been held, declared Burr guilty. Trained in the law, why did Jefferson make such a damaging mistake? Probably because in the midst of the widespread public controversy, Burr was constantly mentioned as being the lead conspirator, and if in a report to Congress to tell what he knew, Jefferson omitted mentioning Burr, it would suggest his report was incomplete or purposefully misleading.

Burr was arrested on February 18, 1807, in the Mississippi Territory and eventually brought under military escort to Richmond, where he would stand trial in the US Court for the Fifth Circuit and the District of Virginia, with John Marshall presiding. Marshall had ruled the previous month, when the Supreme Court had overturned a district court conviction of Bollman and Swartwout, that "if a body of men be actually assembled for the purpose of effecting by force a treasonable purpose, all those who perform any part, however minute, or however remote from the scene of action, and who are actually leagued in the general conspiracy, are to be considered traitors."[20] The government prosecutors at Richmond took that wording as the basis for developing their case against Burr. However, because Attorney General John Breckinridge had recently died and his replacement, Caesar A. Rodney, the only (and part-time) member of the Justice Department, was barely involved because of family illness, Jefferson had to play a larger role than he would have wished in forwarding evidence to the court and trying to arrange the appearance of witnesses. The government's case would be argued by George Hay as assisted by William Wirt. Burr, himself an accomplished lawyer, had hired the state's leading defense lawyer, John Wickham, and he obtained, gratis, the cooperation of the incomparable master of courtroom invective, Luther Martin of Maryland.

Almost instantly it was apparent that the case would not go well for the government. Marshall appointed Jefferson's enemy, John Randolph, to be foreman of the grand jury, and Marshall soon attended a dinner, hosted by Wickham, where Burr was the guest of honor. Present-day notions of judicial neutrality did not then obtain. Without the assistance of an operative Justice Department, Jefferson from afar tried to assist the local lawyers gather evidence, but he was greatly distracted in the midst of the trial by both the murder of his mentor George Wythe and by an explosive foreign policy emergency, the attack on the USS *Chesapeake* by the British ship HMS *Leopard.*

Meanwhile, Marshall demanded that Jefferson promptly provide evidence but agreed that the president himself would not have to appear in court. Jefferson tried to collect all the desired evidence but was hampered by the absence of staff assistance.

Though the level of courtroom argument and oratory in Richmond was remarkably high, Marshall's decisions were key. For the actual jury trial, he named his brother-in-law Edward Carrington foreman, and Carrington skillfully explained Marshall's view of treason to the jury. Wickham and particularly Martin excoriated Jefferson for having declared Burr guilty in his message to Congress and described the present trial as a charade, while Wirt—in a declamation that became famous—demonized Burr as the snake in the American Eden. But it was Marshall's redefinition of treason that determined the outcome of the trial, not the arguments or evidence. In the *Bollman* decision, he had borrowed from an older British definition of treason, but now he ruled that "levying war" (the constitutional phrase) meant the actual use of armed force, not planning or intending to do so. Since Burr did not commit real violence against the nation—he was stopped before he could do anything—there was no war, and with no war, no treason.

This was a definition of treason perhaps more appropriate to American concerns about liberty, but in effect it meant that whatever Burr's ambitions might have been, since he had been prevented from putting any plan into operation, he could not be guilty of treason. Accordingly, the jury, with the instructions from Marshall about precisely what treason meant made clear by foreman Carrington, decided that "Aaron Burr is not proved to be guilty under this indictment," not exactly a ringing endorsement of his innocence.[21] The general public, even most members of Congress, and certainly Jefferson, believed that Burr in fact was guilty, despite the ruling of the court. Even Marshall seemed to have no affection for Burr, and Burr lived out the remainder of his life under the specter of opprobrium. Though Jefferson had now fully broken with Marshall as a result of his handling of the trial, and they would thereafter be enemies, he could take some comfort from the fact that the mass of the people in the West had not succumbed to Burr's allurements and instead had steadfastly supported the union, justifying Jefferson's expressed conviction, in his first inaugural address, that this was the "strongest Government on earth . . . . where every man, at the call of the law, would fly to the standard of the law and would meet invasions of the public order."[22]

Just as Jefferson was most involved in the Burr trial, the British ship HMS *Leopard* attacked the USS *Chesapeake,* on June 22, 1807. It was the result of a series of events, both local and international, and it in turn initiated a train of further events that eventually led to Jefferson's disastrous embargo and the War of 1812. Following the Jay Treaty of 1795, the British had allowed US ships to carry goods to and from the French and Spanish islands in the Caribbean and from there to European destinations as long as the ships landed temporarily in a US port, paid a minimum customs duty, and then re-exported the goods to the Continent. This prosperous maritime trade by means of the so-called broken voyage—the United States was the largest neutral carrier in the Atlantic World—had generated the customs duties that produced budget surpluses. But in 1805, a British admiralty court changed the law and reverted to the so-called Rule of 1756 that said that trade prevented in peacetime was also now to be prevented in wartime. And in 1803, Britain and France had gone to war.

So suddenly, in 1805, the British navy began stopping US merchant ships on the high seas. After British admiral Lord Horatio Nelson's fleet destroyed the combined fleets of Spain and France off the Cape Trafalgar coast of Spain in October 1805, the British navy commanded the seas, and that same year, Napoleon's victory over the combined Austrian and Russian armies at Austerlitz (in the modern-day Czech Republic) gave France uncontested control of the Continent. Now France and Britain were engaged in a titanic war, with both nations willing to run roughshod over the rights of any minor nations in order to further their cause against the other. The United States, with its large merchant fleet but practically nonexistent military forces, simply got in the way.[23]

Britain began stopping all US ships and usually determined that they were engaged in now-banned trade. What troubled the Americans even more was the rise in the British practice of impressment, or the seizing of supposedly British sailors who had abandoned the Royal Navy and were now serving in the US merchant fleets. Britain held that its citizens could not expatriate themselves and become US citizens, so they felt justified—in the midst of their fierce war with the French—to stop American ships, board them, and seize whichever English-speaking sailors they wanted and put the so-called impressed sailors back into the service of the hugely expanded Royal Navy. By this time, the British navy consisted of more than nine hundred ships, with crew members totaling between 130,000 and 140,000, a total needing constant augmentation. These high-handed seizures, totaling about ten thousand, enraged Americans, indicating as they did complete repudiation of US nationhood and a collective slap in the face of all Americans.[24] Impressment of men was seen as a greater outrage than the taking of cargoes, or even Britain's declaring a blockade of the northwest European coast in 1806, obviously a blow to US shipping.

Britain's intention, of course, was to deprive Napoleon of much-needed resources from both France's Caribbean colonies and the United States. Napoleon responded with the Berlin Decree of 1806 that placed a French blockade on Britain, outlawing any neutral ship that stopped in a British port from continuing on to a European port. Britain followed up with a decree that any ship headed for the Continent had to stop first in Britain. Napoleon then issued his Milan Decree that authorized seizure of any vessel that even submitted to a British search in international waters. This combination of orders and decrees obviously thwarted every kind of American commerce at sea. But because of British naval superiority, it could more effectively interfere with US trade in international waters (the French simply confiscated cargoes seized in French ports), and that, combined with Britain's practice of impressing sailors, made it seem the far more serious enemy.

What could the United States do? In September 1805, Secretary of State Madison wrote to Jefferson suggesting the use of economic pressure, a weapon employed against Britain in the lead-up to the revolution. "The efficacy of an embargo . . . cannot be doubted," he wrote, remembering perhaps what he had learned about the British repealing of the Stamp Act in 1765. "Indeed, if a commercial weapon can be properly shaped for the executive hand, it . . . can force all the nations having colonies in this quarter of the globe, to respect our rights."[25] Madison had been an advocate of using trade restrictions to effect change since his pushing of discriminatory tariffs in the First Session of Congress in 1789. Would that it were so easy to persuade or pressure other nations to revise their policies! In 1806, Jefferson sent William Pinkney, a moderate Federalist from Baltimore, to join James Monroe, since July 1803 the US minister to Britain, to open negotiations, with explicit instructions to focus on the issue of impressment. (Monroe took the appointment of Pinkney as a slight.) But the British, absorbed in their war with Napoleon and desperately in need of additional sailors, would not budge on that issue. The best Pinkney and Monroe could do was to get a minimalist agreement that more caution would be exercised when searching for supposed runaway British sailors, along with several minor concessions. Jefferson was so disappointed in the inability of Pinkney and Monroe to get stronger assurances from Britain that he did not even submit the resulting treaty to Congress. British confiscations and impressment continued, heightening tensions between the two nations. In his annual message for 1806, Jefferson called for strengthening defensive positions in port cites, a gradual readying of military forces, and stepping up vigilance.

In the spring of 1807, there were rumors that three British sailors had jumped ship and joined the crew of the US naval frigate, the USS *Chesapeake,* which had been in the Norfolk Harbor in Virginia for repairs. Meanwhile the British admiral in Halifax sent orders to the British sea captains to be on the lookout for the *Chesapeake,* which on the morning of June 22 raised anchor and began to sail, unsuspectingly, into the broad entrance of the harbor. There it met a patrolling British vessel, the HMS *Leopard,* which maneuvered into position and demanded to let its men come aboard the *Chesapeake* to search for the missing British sailors. The American captain denied that they were aboard, but he seemed not to understand the conversation that followed from the *Leopard.* Suddenly the *Leopard* fired a warning shot, and then proceeded for ten bloody minutes to bombard the *Chesapeake,* which had not even had time to open its gunports. The stricken *Chesapeake* lowered its flag, British troops boarded it and seized four men, and the damaged US vessel, taking on water, thereupon limped back to port, having in addition suffered three of its men killed and sixteen injured.

The resulting American outrage was unprecedented: mobs in Norfolk destroyed supplies intended for British ships, British sailors with the bad fortune of being on shore leave were assaulted, and there were widespread calls for retaliation that reached all the way to Congress, which, had it been in session, might have summarily declared war. As Jefferson wrote a few weeks later, "Never since the battle of Lexington have I seen this country in such a state of exasperation as at present."[26] He knew the US was in no position to make effective war against Britain, but he hoped he could harness the outrage to motivate Congress to make preparations for war should it come.

Jefferson issued a proclamation saying that perhaps in its response the United States could teach a lesson to the European powers—he had in mind a temporary but total elimination of trade. He sent a sharp message of protest to England, called upon all British ships to leave American ports forthwith and forbade others from entering; and he called upon Americans to cease providing any provisions to British ships. He sent word for all US merchant ships in the Mediterranean to return home as a defensive measure to prevent their being seized by the forces of the Royal Navy. He then called for the new session of Congress to meet early, on October 26, 1807, and he prepared his annual message of 1807 to be ready by the next day. That message was decidedly hostile toward Britain; he referred to the "many injuries and depredations committed on our commerce and navigation upon the high seas for years past." Although he did not call for war, he acknowledged Congress's role in such a decision and promised to forward it whatever relevant evidence he possessed.[27]

In November, Jefferson got word that British foreign secretary George Canning had brushed off his protests and refused to reconsider the policy of impressment. In Jefferson's mind, the options were either to do nothing, to go to war, or to declare an embargo, that is, recall all American ships to their home ports and withdraw from international maritime commerce at least for the time being. His greatest fear was that public outrage over seized ships would lead to an unstoppable demand for war, and he knew that would be catastrophic for the young nation. After all, Republican ideology meant opposition to having a standing army and a strong navy, with reliance instead on militia forces and small gunboats for protecting the coastline—no match for the powerful British navy with its many hundreds of warships. In December, Jefferson forwarded to Congress the most recent dispatches from London showing Britain's refusal to budge on impressment. Less than two weeks later, he submitted to Congress a recommendation stating that given "the great and increasing dangers with which our vessels, our seamen, and merchandise, are threatened on the high seas," he urged Congress to pass "an inhibition of the departure of our vessels from the ports of the United States."[28] He did not provide additional information but only suggested a total embargo on all shipping to ports outside the United States. Neither did he provide a recommended end date for the embargo, but he expected it to be temporary, a buying of time necessary for diplomacy. In his mind, it safeguarded US shipping and seamen. He had not consulted any members of Congress before formulating this policy, deeming such matters solely in the purview of the president's powers, and he failed to provide a rationale for such drastic action to the public. These two mistakes would eventually help to undermine the decision, but for the moment, the Senate approved the policy the very day it received the message from Jefferson, as did the House three days later.

Jefferson signed the embargo law on December 22, 1807, stopping all international exports from the United States. In a series of anonymous editorials in the *National Intelligencer,* Secretary of State Madison laid out the rationale: the embargo would keep US ships safe in their harbors and "have the collateral effect of making it the interest of all nations to change the system which has driven our commerce from the ocean."[29] Of Jefferson's cabinet members, Madison was the most supportive of the embargo. Secretary of the Treasury Albert Gallatin was the most skeptical of its efficacy: either it worked immediately, he believed, or it became almost as destructive as war itself. At least, Jefferson thought, the embargo would prevent the taking of ships and sailors, and he believed there was a chance that peace would soon be achieved in Europe, thereby ending the need to prohibit maritime trade.

But Jefferson quickly found out that maintaining an effective embargo required an unprecedented degree of governmental interference: searching ships; patrolling the Canadian border to prevent the smuggling of trade goods; surveilling every port city, navigable river, and bay. Subsequent acts had to be passed to authorize enhanced enforcement of the embargo, and each act made it more unpopular. Near the end of his term Jefferson even signed draconian legislation authorizing the use of local militias to enforce it. A boycott merely meant refusing to purchase imported goods from a foreign nation, while an embargo meant forbidding US vessels from transporting any goods to other nations, a significantly more complicated and far-reaching endeavor.

Sentiment regarding the embargo turned out to be based as much or more on ideology than on economic impact. While it did cause a harmful economic slowdown, the lurid tales of grass growing on wharves and ships rotting in their berths, though often repeated in textbooks, was more the result of partisan rhetoric than reality. The maritime-oriented New England states that had most ships at risk were ideologically pro-British and considered the embargo more a result of Jeffersonian animosity toward Britain than a realistic response to the threat merchants faced. Many New Englanders excoriated Jefferson, hinted to the British that the policy would soon fail, and flirted with secession from the nation. The southern states, whose export-based agricultural economy was actually more harmed by the embargo, were ideologically pro-French and supported the embargo longer and more energetically than any other part of the nation. But slowly opposition grew everywhere till finally it was clear that the effort required to make it truly effective was financially, logistically, and politically unacceptable.

Jefferson had already begun seeking additional ways to justify the embargo: it would promote American manufacturing, and by showing the power of commercial boycotts, it could demonstrate an alternative to shooting wars. In the final months of his second administration, as sentiment turned ever stronger against the embargo, Jefferson stubbornly refused to revise his policy, and neither would he advise Congress as to how it should meet the challenge. Nor did others offer effective policy choices. Jefferson became uncharacteristically passive, and he in effect withdrew from governance before the end of his office. Perhaps, as he said, he wanted to leave all options open for his successor, James Madison, or perhaps he actually could see no acceptable options and hence was unable to make a decision. His inaction frustrated his closest supporters, Gallatin and Madison, and Congress in general despaired over his uncharacteristic lack of leadership. Finally Congress decreed that the embargo should end on March 4, 1809, the day Jefferson left office, but to save face, it enacted on March 1 a Non-Intercourse Act that opened up all trade with nations other than Britain and France while authorizing the president to lift the trade restriction on either or both of those nations if they stopped their infringements upon US commerce.

Yet despite the growing unpopularity of the embargo, in the election of 1808, essentially a plebiscite on Jefferson's two administrations, his handpicked successor, James Madison, won a resounding electoral college victory, 122 electoral votes to Federalist candidate Charles Cotesworth Pinckney's 47. In the congressional caucus, James Monroe, still irked by the president's failure to forward to Congress the treaty he and Pinkney had worked out with the British, passively let his name be promoted by John Randolph, who hated Madison and Jefferson both, but Madison overwhelmingly won the caucus's approval. (Much of the caucus support for Madison may have been the result of the increasingly popular dinner parties hosted in his home by his wife,

Dolley, whose political skills turned out to rival her reputation as a hostess.[30]) Recent econometric research indicates that in fact the embargo was having a significant impact on the British economy, and the British might have been pressured to change their most antagonistic policies had the United States maintained the embargo a while longer.[31] But there was no way for those in Washington to know this in 1808.

Jefferson had been counting the hours until he could take leave of the presidency. In early 1809 he had written James Monroe, "Five more weeks will relieve me from a drudgery to which I am no longer equal, and restore to me a scene of tranquility, amidst my family and friends, more congenial to my age and natural inclinations."[32] He had begun preparing for this day more than a year in advance, pushing hard to get the renovations on Monticello that had begun in 1794 finished at last. He had also taken the opportunity in 1806 to advocate a measure he felt immensely important for the future. He had long worried about the consequences of slavery on the nation, for both whites and Blacks, and had long hoped to find some practical solution to the presence of the institution.

In 1793, learning of a deadly slave insurrection on the island known as San Domingo in the West Indies (an insurrection that turned out to be the first successful uprising by enslaved peoples that would eventually lead to the founding of the country of Haiti), he had written to his son-in-law that "What is to take place in our Southern states will depend on the timely wisdom and liberality of their legislatures," and he expressed hope that enslaved people in the United States would be set free and then be colonized in a nearby island such as San Domingo.[33] Jefferson had seen the killing of whites who held enslaved people in San Domingo as a horror, but he never advocated that the United States attempt to suppress Black efforts there to escape their bondage, and he as president accepted US trade with the Black government. From the 1790s to his death, Jefferson saw Haiti as the best destination for colonized freedpersons.[34] But in the intervening years none of the southern states had made a concerted move to free and colonize their enslaved populations, although in Virginia about ten thousand had been manumitted for a variety of reasons in the decade and a half after 1785.

The danger came home when, in September 1800, while at Monticello, he received a letter from Governor James Monroe reporting an aborted slave insurrection apparently intended to take over Richmond. Led by an enslaved man named Gabriel, the planned insurrection was thwarted both by two enslaved Blacks leaking the plan to authorities and a drenching thunderstorm that made creeks impassable. Monroe, like Jefferson a philosophical opponent of slavery even as he profited from holding men, women, and children in bondage, called forth the militia to capture the insurrectionists and calm public fears. Eventually some twenty-seven Blacks, following trials before a special court, were found guilty and condemned to hang. The public clamored for more reprisals, leading Monroe to write Jefferson questioning, "Where to arrest the hand of the Executioner?" When debating "whether mercy or severity is the better policy," especially when culpability was difficult to determine, Monroe felt "it is best to incline to the former."[35] Jefferson replied that "there is a strong sentiment that there has been hanging enough. the other states & the world at large will for ever condemn us if we indulge a principle of revenge, or go one step beyond what is absolutely necessary."[36] Both men knew there was popular support for much harsher reprisals, and Jefferson recommended expatriation rather than hanging. The possibility of a far worse Gabriel-like revolt lingered in Jefferson's mind. How might slavery be ended, the threat of insurrection lessened, the number of enslaved persons in the nation reduced?

He understood that by the explicit terms of the Constitution, US participation in the transatlantic slave trade could not be ended before 1808 (but such prohibition after that date was not actually mandated by the Constitution). Accordingly, in his annual message of 1806 Jefferson wrote to Congress:

> I congratulate you, fellow citizens, on the approach of the period at which you may interpose your authority constitutionally, to withdraw the citizens of the United States from all further participation in those violations of human rights which have been so long continued on the unoffending inhabitants of Africa, and which the morality, the reputation, and the best interests of our country, have long been eager to proscribe. Although no law you may pass can take prohibitory effect till the first day of the year one thousand eight hundred and eight, yet the intervening period is not too long to prevent, by timely notice, expeditions which cannot be completed before that day.[37]

The Senate, acting promptly, on January 13, 1807, passed a bill "to prohibit the importation of slaves into any port or place within the jurisdiction of the United States, from and after the first day of January, in the year of our Lord, one thousand eight hundred and eight."[38] Most previous congressional efforts to limit in any way the operation of slavery had met powerful opposition, but because of his political finesse, and the increased cultivation of wheat with its lessened need for enslaved laborers, Jefferson was able to get this act passed. Some slaveholders also calculated that the per capita value of their present enslaved people would increase if new imports were ended. This act halted almost two centuries of legal importation of enslaved persons from Africa and as such was one of the most important if almost totally overlooked achievements of his presidency. However, it had little impact on the institution of slavery in the nation. This would be his last effort to address the problem as president, and his subsequent attempts to confront the issue could be termed aspirational at best.

The effects of the embargo lingered long after Jefferson, following days of packing, finally left the president's house on March 11, 1809, never to return to Washington. Now another president, James Madison, had to deal with the problems of British attacks on American commerce and the continuing national embarrassment of having to put up with impressment of its sailors. Madison had been inaugurated on March 4, 1809, and by then the new chamber for the House of Representatives had been completed. His brief address in that room was so softly delivered that few heard it, but Madison pledged always to support the Constitution and always to seek peaceful accommodations instead of war. That evening a ball was held in celebration, with Dolley Madison as usual wowing everyone with her fashionable gown, a turban on her head, beautiful eyes, and disarming grace, and everyone, including Jefferson, seemed to enjoy the occasion except the obviously exhausted new president.

Within days a generous Congress authorized twenty-five thousand dollars to pay for improvements to the President's House and buying new furnishings. Working with architect Benjamin Henry Latrobe, Dolley redecorated the largest downstairs hall (today called the State Dining Room) into an elegant drawing room, furnished with handsome chairs and fancy sidebars and the walls covered in yellow satin. She soon began hosting elaborate affairs on Wednesday afternoons, complete with delicious pastries and other snacks, along with music. Members of Congress, ranking government officers, diplomats, and anyone else important and known by the Madisons were invited, with the attendance often exceeding two hundred. The convivial occasions, called Drawing Rooms, were presided over by Dolley—she was universally called by her first name and sometimes labeled the presidentess—and quickly became the social phenomena of the era. Here people came to meet others, share secrets, make bargains, discuss issues, seal friendships, settle disagreements, create alliances, in effect to animate governance. Dolley transformed the President's House symbolically into the nation's home. James Madison, who had few of the personal charms of his predecessor, needed and came to depend upon the social attractions of the irrepressible Dolley and her Drawing Rooms to make the gears of government work.[39] For all his brilliance, Madison possessed few political skills, and fortunately the politically adept Dolley came to play a large role in maintaining a semblance of party loyalty. Tall for a woman at the time, and easily visible at her receptions because the feathers or plumes she wore in her turban made her stand out even more, Dolley was a force to be reckoned with. She created the role of First Lady in a variety of ways: her winning personality earned support for her husband, her hospitality eased personal tensions between political actors, and she had the kind of political instincts that Madison himself lacked.

Madison in particular needed this assist because friction was mounting in the Congress. John Randolph tried to throttle everything Madison proposed, and another group of dissidents, led by Senators William B. Giles and Samuel Smith and labeling themselves the Invisibles, disliked Gallatin and opposed much that Madison supported. Moreover, some northern Republicans began to take umbrage at the continuing power of Virginians in the administration. Madison wanted to name the talented Gallatin his secretary of state, but because of the vociferous opposition of the Invisibles faction, he kept Gallatin in Treasury and reluctantly appointed to the State Department Robert Smith, Senator Smith's brother, who proved to be so incompetent that Madison had, in effect, to be his own secretary of state, even writing official letters for Robert Smith. All together, Madison's cabinet was subpar.

By an act of Congress, the embargo ended on the day Madison took office, with the newly imposed Non-Importation Act cutting off trade to England and France but opening it to other nations; should either England or France cease their commercial restrictions, the United States would trade with them but not the other. In April the young British minister to the United States, David Erskine, perhaps misinterpreting his instructions, told Madison that Britain would withdraw the hated Orders in Council limiting trade if the United States would, as the Non-Importation Act suggested, open commerce to Britain. Madison, eager to believe it proved the efficacy of economic coercion, jumped at this apparent diplomatic break, and announced that the United States would renew trade with Britain on June 10. The announcement was met with praise and acclaim, only to be squashed when officials in London repudiated the agreement on the grounds that Erskine had exceeded his instructions. Erskine was recalled, Madison was embarrassed, and in August he reversed his opening of trade to Britain, just before the unrepentant British sent a new minister. Francis James Jackson was a hard-liner, known for his 1807 naval attack on neutral Copenhagen, a preemptive terroristic assault using the newly developed Congreve rockets to rain down incendiary bombs on the city to prevent Denmark's potential cooperation with France.[40] Arrogant and contemptuous of Americans, Jackson's presence rubbed salt in the wounded pride of the United States, and Madison essentially refused to deal with him. This showing of backbone accrued to the diminutive president's public approval.[41] But Madison now certainly believed he could not trust what Britain said or intended.

Obviously, the Non-Importation Act was ineffectual, so, along with futile urging that Congress support some increase in military preparations, Madison pushed ahead with what was called Macon's Bill, which would open commerce to both Britain and France, but if either continued to prohibit US shipping, then Madison would stop trade with the offending nation. However, the Senate opposed this measure. The next effort was labeled Macon's Bill No. 2, which called for opening US trade to Britain and France, and if either one then ended their measures against US shipping, the United States would give the other nation three months to do similarly and if not, would then cease trade with the uncooperative nation. Madison doubted this bill would effect change in either nation's policies, but then in August 1810, Napoleon directed the Duc de Cadore to send a letter to Secretary of State Smith stating that the Berlin and Milan strictures against US trade with the Continent would be ended on November 1 if Britain repealed her Orders in Council or the United States would put into practice what Macon's Bill No. 2 announced. Madison ill-advisedly accepted Napoleon's proposal, and three months later suspended all trade with Britain, only to discover that Napoleon's offer (and the Cadore letter) were false promises. Madison at last understood that he could trust neither France nor Britain. Was war the only option other than completely caving in to the European powers?

Complicating Madison's dilemma was the ineptitude of Secretary of State Smith. Finally, by early spring of 1811 Madison had enough; he called in Smith to push him to resign, but the conversation went badly.[42] Madison offered Smith the ambassadorship to Russia so he could save face, but Smith resisted, even after Madison bluntly accused him of incompetence. Before Smith could reply, Madison wrote his old friend James Monroe, just elected governor of Virginia again, offering him the position of secretary of state. He knew Monroe was competent and highly respected. Monroe had been hurt by Jefferson's repudiation of his and Pickney's negotiations with Britain over the issue of impressment, and he suspected Madison's hand in that, with the result that their relationship had cooled. After some communication, however, the two smoothed over their differences and Monroe accepted Madison's invitation. Meanwhile Smith rejected the offer of the ambassadorship. Madison, infuriated, bluntly fired him, but Madison was helpless to dampen the anger of Smith and his supporters.

In the midst of the controversy over maritime trade, one longtime controversy was settled. The negotiations with France in 1803 had not produced a precise agreement on the boundary of Louisiana, and Jefferson and Madison had for several years maneuvered to try to include Texas and both East and West Florida in the purchase and determine the exact northern boundary between the two Floridas and the southernmost part of the territories of what became Mississippi and Alabama. Repeated efforts to deal with Spain produced no agreement. At the time West Florida was deemed more important than Texas because of Mobile Bay and the south-draining rivers that ran through the territory to the north into the Gulf of Mexico. US settlers also hungered to establish farms and plantations in the Floridas. In early 1810 the small population in West Florida, egged on by American authorities in Louisiana, revolted against anemic Spanish control, and Madison announced on December 5 that the United States had taken possession of the territory. So at least the problem of West Florida was solved, less by diplomacy than by stealth and seizure.[43] Neither Spain nor France was in a position to protest. Yet this small triumph did not negate the problems with international commerce, which was more an issue of national pride than it was economics. Monroe's predilection was to strongly pursue efforts for peace with Britain, but national sentiment was strongly opposed to the erstwhile mother country. Continuing impressments rankled most Americans, although New Englanders mostly held to their anglophile beliefs and associated Jefferson, Madison, and all Virginians with intemperate affection for France. In the spring of 1811, vessels of the British navy still patrolled the northeast coastline, irritating American nationalists.

Then in the evening of May 16, 1811, American commodore John Rogers, commanding the frigate USS *President,* after a long sea chase caught up with a British ship off the Virginia Capes. Rogers hailed the vessel but got no reply, and in the failing light, Rogers thought it was a major warship, the man-of-war *Guerriere.* Apparently, the British ship fired first, perhaps not recognizing the disparity in size and armaments, because the British vessel was in fact a small, single-masted sloop, HMS *Little Belt,* less than a third the size of the American frigate. The *President* attacked in return, and being the far larger, better armed ship, it quickly defeated *Little Belt,* killing nine British sailors and wounding twenty-three, and badly damaging the smaller ship. The incident infuriated the British just as it thrilled Americans, happy to interpret the encounter as just revenge for the attack on the *Chesapeake* four years before. Relations between the two nations worsened still further.[44]

Furthermore, US relations with American Indians also worsened. Settlers from the United States had been steadily moving west since the revolution, squeezing Native Americans from their traditional territories and exacerbating tensions and conflict. In early 1801, outgoing president John Adams had appointed William Henry Harrison governor of the Indiana Territory. Born at the stately Berkeley Plantation on the James River between Richmond and Jamestown and educated in the classics, Harrison was an intrepid foe of Native Americans and steadily used a combination of whiskey, bribes, and the threat of military force to obtain concessions of land in the Midwest. Responding to these depredations, two Shawnee brothers, Tecumseh and Tenskwatawa, began a two-pronged Indigenous counteroffensive.[45]

Tecumseh was a marvelous orator and political and military leader, and advocating complete rejection of all the ways of white settlers, from clothing style to alcohol, he succeeded in creating a confederation of like-minded supporters across the region and even stretching far into the South. His brother, after a powerful religious conversion in 1805 that included revelations about reviving traditional Indigenous culture, emerged as a powerful spiritual leader known as the Prophet. Together the two brothers, combining politics and religion, produced a growing rebellion that threatened white settlements. Governor Harrison and others believed that, as in the 1790s, the British were arming the Indians and supporting their movement. In the fall of 1811, having cobbled together a force of about a thousand men consisting of regular soldiers, militia, and volunteers, and learning that Tecumseh was on a recruiting trip to the South, Harrison moved toward his village called Prophet's Town at the juncture of the Wabash and Tippecanoe Rivers. But before Harrison could launch his raid, the Prophet led a surprise attack on the US forces during the early dawn of November 7, inflicting severe casualties but suffering grievously as well. Tenskwatawa and his forces abandoned their town and fled, leaving it open for Harrison's troops to capture and burn all the houses. Harrison called the sacking of the abandoned town a military victory, and "Tippecanoe" would be the sobriquet associated with him ever after. Unopened boxes of British rifles found in the captured town confirmed the Americans' view that the British were behind all Indian raids. Headlines from newspapers as far away as the East Coast screamed out about an "ANGLO-SAVAGE WAR," and the Lexington, Kentucky, paper wrote that "[T]he SCALPING KNIFE and TOMAHALK [*sic*] of British savages, is now, again, devastating our frontiers."[46]

This anti-Indian and anti-British sentiment enflamed the rhetoric of an ardent group of about a dozen younger politicians, mainly from the West and South, who had been elected to Congress in 1810, taking office in 1811. Strongly nationalistic, these new voices in Congress, the so-called War Hawks—men like Henry Clay and Richard M. Johnson of Kentucky, Felix Grundy of Tennessee, and John C. Calhoun of South Carolina—were quick to blame Britain for every hint of trouble with Native Americans and eager to stand up to defend the nation's pride, even to the point of invading Canada. There was no actual need for more territory in the United States, but the War Hawks assumed the lightly populated region would be easy to capture and then could be used as a bargaining chip in negotiation with the British.[47] Clay, another Virginia transplant, was smart, articulate, and immensely personable, and he had a knack for politics. Quickly named Speaker of the House, he turned that position into one of genuine power, organized the House to make it more effective (for example, putting fellow War Hawks in charge of major committees), and provided the kind of leadership that body had not seen before. As an example of his take-charge attitude, Clay for the first time demanded that the exotic John Randolph, who was accustomed to entering upon the floor of the House accompanied by his hound, remove his dog from the halls of Congress.

Except in the New England states, public sentiment for military measures against Britain was on the increase. Normally a peaceful man who always preferred diplomacy, by the middle of 1811, Madison had reluctantly concluded that war was probably inevitable.[48] Although Secretary of State Monroe was widely thought to be more positively inclined toward Britain than was Madison, Monroe too by now believed war probably unavoidable. The British minister to the United States, Augustus J. Foster, misreading the situation, thought war unlikely.

Against this background, Madison called for Congress to assemble earlier than usual, on November 5, and sent them his annual message. While it briefly criticized the policies of France, it was markedly hostile to Britain. The primary concerns were the Orders in Council that interfered with free trade and the continuing problem of impressment. As Madison wrote, "our Coasts and the mouths of our harbours, have again witnessed scenes, not less derogatory to the dearest of our national rights, than vexatious to the regular course of our trade."[49] Britain's actions "have the character, as well as the effect, of war on our lawful commerce. With this evidence of hostile inflexibility in trampling on rights which no Independent Nation can relinquish," Madison continued, "Congress will feel the duty of putting the United States into an armour [*sic*], and an attitude demanded by the crisis, and corresponding with the national spirit and expectations."[50] After that prologue, he recommended that "adequate provisions be made" for supplying regular troops, militia, the manufacture of cannon and small arms, and limited augmentations to the naval force. In closing his message, Madison stated his "confidence in a wise and honorable result to your deliberations . . . invoking, at the same time, the blessing of Heaven on our beloved Country, and on all the means that may be employed, in vindicating its rights, and advancing its welfare."[51] With that, he left the critical matter to the constitutionally prescribed role of Congress.

Congress, though, was rent by division. In December John C. Calhoun brought from the Foreign Relations Committee resolutions to increase the size of the standing army, but this led to dispute. There were differences of opinion over the precise size, others thought enlarging naval forces would be ineffective given the power of the British navy, and there were seemingly endless disagreement over how military preparations were to be paid for. After all, Republican ideology had long argued against both standing armies and an enlarged debt, and internal taxes were anathema. Secretary of State Monroe had sufficient influence in the House to get military forces augmented, but he had less sway in the Senate, and there opposition senators both pushed for a larger military and against taxing measures. Madison was vexed both by

British policy and the confusion manifested in Congress. He wrote to Jefferson in February that the information he had from Britain "indicates an adherence to her mad policy towards the U.S.," while "the Newspapers give you a Sufficient insight into the measures of Congress." Jefferson replied twelve days later that he had "much doubted whether, in case of a war, Congress would find it practicable to do their part of the business. That a body containing 100. lawyers in it, should direct the measures of a war is, I fear, impossible."[52] Finally in early March, a reluctant Congress passed several tax measures, prompting Madison to write his mentor Jefferson that the House "have got down the dose of taxes. It is the strongest proof yet . . . that they do not mean to flinch from the contest to which the mad conduct of G. B. drives them."[53]

In an attempt to neutralize the opposition of congressmen from the New England states, Madison and Monroe conspired to show their political opponents the nefarious interference of Britain in American affairs. In January, Elbridge Gerry had written to introduce Madison to a supposed British count who was visiting Massachusetts. He was accompanied by a man named John Henry, who had served briefly in the US army and then in 1809 had been sent by the governor of Canada to essentially spy on New Englanders to determine the extent of pro-British sentiment; in theory, the British might use such intelligence to foment secessionist feelings or, in the case of war, some form of cooperation.[54] Feeling that he had been inadequately paid for his services, Henry, in cahoots with the alleged count, subsequently offered to sell to the United States letters that revealed British activities and incriminated certain New Englanders. Thinking such evidence could be used to squelch a secessionist movement and generate support for war measures, Monroe, acting for the president, offered an astounding fifty thousand dollars for the letters—the totality of money in the State Department's contingency funds. But Henry had redacted names from the letters, and they in truth offered little information not available in the press other than that the British had sought to interfere. Nevertheless, on March 9 Madison delivered the batch of letters to Congress, stating that they proved that "a secret Agent . . . was employed in certain States . . . in fomenting disaffection to the constituted authorities of the nation."[55] But the effect of the letters was underwhelming, and though they produced a momentary uproar, and may have embarrassed some New Englanders, the whole episode suggested a degree of desperation on the part of the administration.

Later that month Madison learned that Britain had no intention of repealing the offensive Orders in Council or repudiating impressment. Consequently, believing war imminent and wanting to prevent US shipping from risk at sea, on April 1, 1812, Madison sent a confidential message to Congress recommending that a general embargo be placed "on all vessels now in port or hereafter arriving, for the period of sixty days."[56] This was widely seen as preparation for war. In the midst of these troubled days, Vice President George Clinton died, and the Republican caucus, meeting a month later, in addition to renominating Madison for president, after some squabbling appointed the elder statesman Elbridge Gerry of Massachusetts as vice president. John Adams had earlier written on behalf of Gerry to Madison, and probably Gerry's age, sixty-seven, also played a role, for Madison obviously understood that Gerry by seeming superannuated, would not be put forward by the 1816 caucus to be his successor, opening the way for Secretary of State Monroe to eventually win the nomination.

So Madison's political situation was settled, and his backbone was stiffened both by the presence of the War Hawks in Congress and the intransigence of the British government. Accordingly, on June 1, 1812, Madison delivered a fateful message to Congress, asking it to declare war. In contrast to Jefferson's embargo message that contained minimal explanation as to cause or implementation, Madison took pains to lay out the history of bad relations with Britain, emphasizing her disrespect for the United States as a nation. With his third sentence he stated that "British cruisers have been in the continued practice of violating the American flag on the great high way of nations, and of seizing and carrying off persons sailing under it," the old issue of impressment. "[T]housands of American Citizens, under the safeguard of public law, and of their national flag, have been torn from their county, and from every thing dear to them."[57] At the time, perhaps a quarter of US seamen were British.

Then he moved to the depredations of the Orders in Council. "British cruisers have been in the practice also, of violating the rights and peace of our Coasts. They hover over and harass our entering and departing Commerce. To the most insulting pretentions, . . . they have wantonly spilt American blood within the sanctuary of our territorial jurisdiction."[58] At this point everyone recalled the deadly attack on the *Chesapeake*. Continuing, Madison wrote that "the great staples of our Country have been cut off, from their legitimate markets; and a destructive blow aimed at our agricultural and maritime interests."[59] These British interruptions of commerce were not really intended primarily to cut off goods from the Continent so much as to promote "the monopoly which she covets for her own commerce and navigation."[60]

But that was not all. "In reviewing the conduct of Great Britain towards the United States, our attention is necessarily drawn to the warfare just renewed by the Savages . . . a warfare which is known to spare neither age nor sex, and to be distinguished by features peculiarly shocking to humanity." Here, Madison's mischaracterization of Indigenous resistance to white settler encroachment reflected popular white attitudes. In summing up, he stated that "Such is the spectacle of injuries and indignities which have been heaped on our Country: and such the crisis which its unexampled forbearance and conciliatory efforts have not been able to avert."[61] Then the hard truth: "We behold, in fine, on the side of Great Britain a state of war against the United States; and on the side of the United States, a state of peace towards Great Britain." "Whether the United States shall continue passive under these progressive usurpations, and these accumulating wrongs; or, opposing force to force in defence of their national rights . . . is a solemn question, which the Constitution wisely confides to the Legislative Department of the Government."[62] The Father of the Constitution had laid out the rationale for declaring war but stopped short of doing so himself because he understood that such action was the sole province of Congress, as prescribed in Article 1, Section 8 of the Constitution. Now it was up to Congress to decide the course of the nation.

12

MR. MADISON'S WAR

Tensions had been rising between the United States and Britain for years, and though France's interference with American commerce was also maddening, the size and power of the British fleet made its actions far more demeaning to the nation's pride. And that was the central point. Outside of New England, many Americans still harbored resentment against their revolutionary foe and felt Britain had not yet fully accepted the United States as an independent nation. That alone made British naval interference with US trade, especially on the high seas, more upsetting than French incursions that usually took place in French seaports. Because the huge British navy needed so many sailors to man its ships, it constantly intercepted US vessels to press members of their crews into service on His Majesty's ships. This impressment was interpreted as more an attack on US honor than on its trade. White Americans believed that the British also instigated the Native American raids on western settlements, and thus they were further examples of how Britain failed to respect the American nation. The various US diplomatic efforts to change British behavior were ineffective because Britain's focus was on its battle against France. American events, American protests, American issues were hardly more than a distraction to the government officials in Whitehall, but they loomed large in Washington City, as the capital was called. Consequently, Congress turned quickly to President James Madison's war message.

Madison did not enjoy the influence over Congress that Thomas Jefferson had cultivated, but Speaker of the House Henry Clay of Kentucky, one of the strongly nationalistic new members who possessed good political skills, did know how to lead, and Secretary of State James Monroe also worked the House to good effect. Within four days of Madison's delivering his war message, the House, after vigorous debate behind closed doors, by a vote of 79 to 49 declared war on Great Britain. Monroe had less power in the Senate, and there were several factions of senators who either had broken ideologically with the Jefferson-Madison center of the party or simply felt the Virginians in general possessed too much political power. And of course in both houses of Congress, the New England Federalists to a man opposed the war. The result was a closer vote in the Senate of 19 to 13. The following day, June 18, 1812, Madison signed the measure into law, announcing it on June 19 by proclamation.[1]

The vote had both sectional (the South and West favoring a declaration, the North and Northeast opposing it) and partisan cleavages, with the section most involved in international maritime commerce, New England, paradoxically being most opposed. In part this was because New Englanders remained staunch anglophiles and suspected the war party of simply favoring French interests, maybe even taking orders from France. Meanwhile in staunchly Republican Baltimore, a mob ransacked the offices of antiwar Federalist editor Alexander Hanson, whose newspaper the *Federal Republican* had strongly opposed the declaration of war. New England opposition to France had grown even more intense after the rise to power of Napoleon. So the United States did not enter the war united, nor was it even remotely prepared in terms of armed or naval forces. In fact, the disparity in military strength between Britain and the United States was astonishing: the British had a standing army of about 250,000, while US forces numbered fewer than 10,000. However, what gave Madison and others hope was the belief that Britain was so entangled in its war with France on the Iberian Peninsula that it would have neither the will nor capacity to turn its military might to a ground war on the North American continent. American strategists assumed the US forces could easily take Canada (where there were only 6,000 regular British troops stationed) and thereafter bargain with Britain for a satisfactory peace. So a woefully underprepared young nation declared war against a military superpower.

While Congress debated what kinds of trade restrictions the nation should continue to impose on its maritime commerce, tried to hammer out some means of financially supporting the war, and argued, for example, over the pay of soldiers, Secretary of War William Eustis was a miserable administrator who never mastered either gathering the necessary military supplies or choosing effective military commanders—too many were elderly veterans of the revolution or fresh graduates of West Point with no military experience. Having forgotten one essential lesson of the revolution, he still tended to depend far too heavily on militia, who were usually ill trained, poorly armed, and sometimes refused to fight outside their home state much less across the national border. As the nation's first wartime president, Madison in 1812 found that his stable of officers was very sparse, there was no effective War Department to offer advice and information, and Republican party ideology was still opposed to a large standing army, a strong navy, and raising taxes. Despite his brilliance as a political theorist, Madison made poor choices in putting together and maintaining his cabinet and in appointing military commanders.

Against this inauspicious background, US military strategy began with what was intended to be a three-pronged invasion of Canada: one aimed at Fort Detroit (held by the British), the second at Niagara, and the third at Montreal, blithely assuming the population there would forsake the Crown and join the US side. That did not happen, and when Native Americans joined their Canadian allies, the poorly equipped US forces proved ineffective.[2] About the only success was the taking of the small provincial capital of York (today's Toronto) after a hard fight in April 1813, burning all the government buildings there. This minor victory would later come back to haunt the Americans when the British in 1814 captured Washington and, in memory of York, torched most of the federal buildings.

A young Commodore Oliver H. Perry achieved the only significant American success when he led his small naval squadron of gunboats to a well-fought victory over British ships near "Put-in-Bay" on Lake Erie on September 10, 1813, reporting back to General Harrison that "We have met the enemy and they are ours."[3] This victory emboldened Harrison to prepare an attack on British and Indigenous forces near the western end of Lake Erie. Richard M. Johnson commanded troops in a daring raid that led US forces to a major victory, and apparently Johnson himself fatally wounded Shawnee chief Tecumseh at the Battle of the Thames (River) on October 5, 1813.

But despite these two victories in the fall of 1813, the American effort in western Canada in 1812–13, where Americans thought they had the advantage and expected quick success, must be considered a major disappointment. Critics of Madison abounded, especially among Federalists. No sitting president before him had been subjected to such virulent attacks.[4] Interestingly, on the high seas, freelancing US naval vessels, seeking British naval ships not in protective convoys, won a number of single-ship sea battles. These skirmishes occurred off the coasts of Africa and Brazil, in the middle of the Atlantic and in the Pacific. Although these US triumphs frustrated British government officials and outraged the British public at the same time that they heartened American military planners, they had no strategic value. The British navy was so huge that random American successes were only irritants, not significant factors in the war. Actually, more damaging to British commerce were the raids of US privateers, many of them operating out of Baltimore. They took hundreds of British ships as prizes. One privateer alone, the *Rossie,* based in Baltimore, captured eighteen ships worth approximately $1.5 million.[5]

In late 1812 Madison, hoping to solve the problem of the incompetency of Secretary of War Eustis, sought a replacement. Secretary of State Monroe contemplated accepting that lesser position at least temporarily or in tandem with his present role but ultimately decided otherwise. Madison then made a fateful choice, picking the former US minister to France, John Armstrong, who would turn out to be widely unpopular, arrogant, and shockingly lazy. Meanwhile, Czar Alexander I of Russia, fearing a French invasion in 1812 and wanting to make sure that Britain did not weaken its ability to resist Napoleon by engaging in a war in North America, offered to mediate a peace between the United States and Britain. Alexander's offer reached Madison in early 1813, and the president accepted the proposal in principle in March of that year, but the whole effort collapsed when later that summer Britain officially declined Russia's offer.[6] US forces stumbled from fiasco to fiasco in their attempts to subdue Canada, for example, with repeated attempts to take Montreal.

Meanwhile, responding to the charismatic leadership of Tecumseh and the Prophet several years earlier, the Creeks in the Southeast, led by young warriors who called themselves Red Sticks, were resisting the encroachment of white settlers in the region, and throughout 1813 and 1814 the western frontier was aflame with conflict. The disorganized War Department struggled to meet this threat from Native Americans in the Southeast at the same time that the Canadian offensive to the north was stumbling. Eventually Andrew Jackson, cobbling together regular troops and volunteers, began to make headway against the indominable Red Sticks, and on March 27, 1814, at Horseshoe Bend on the Tallapoosa River in Alabama, he inflicted a devastating defeat on Creek forces, essentially ending the Indigenous threat to white settlements and setting underway the process that would eventually lead to the forced exodus of the Creeks and other Native Americans in the Southeast to what later was known as the Oklahoma Territory. But this shameful chapter of US history in most ways was incidental to the major battle between the young nation and the British imperial forces.[7]

Events far away from the American theater would have a significant impact on the conflict with Britain. In October 1813, on the plains near Leipzig, the combined forces of Russia, Prussia, Austria, and Sweden defeated the French army led by Napoleon in a battle fought by 600,000 contestants that produced approximately 100,000 casualties. Napoleon, though severely weakened, persisted, but by April 1814 he was forced to abdicate and was sent into exile on the island of Elba off the coast of Italy. With Britain's years-long nemesis now seemingly eliminated, would it turn the full power of its huge war machine on its North American foe? Britain did succeed in placing a naval blockade—doubling the number of its patrol ships—along the Atlantic Coast south of New York, though it left New England free to trade and thereby hoped to promote regional opposition to what was known locally as Mr. Madison's War. This blockade devastated US commerce.

Nevertheless, with Napoleon fading, President Madison began the new year somewhat hopeful, though he still faced internal political opposition and turmoil amid his cabinet. The resignation in February 1814 of the immensely talented Treasury Secretary Gallatin was an especially serious blow. Out of necessity, Madison became more flexible and learned from experience, changing some of his earlier positions. For example, he now supported a reauthorization of a national bank in 1814. The first Bank of the United States, whose authorization had expired in 1811, had proved its utility and justified its constitutionality by default. In late 1813 Madison had succeeded in getting another embargo approved by Congress. Never having given up on the principle of economic coercion, he sought to pressure Britain by preventing the departure of ships and banning the importation of certain British goods.[8] He also sought, with little success, to halt the continued smuggling of goods across the Canadian border, to Spanish markets via Amelia Island off the coast of Florida, and to English merchants courtesy of pirates operating out of Lake Barataria south of New Orleans. The profits to be gained in such trade simply overwhelmed any commitment to US law.

Madison, at the same time, had the perennial problem of recruiting troops, financing the war, and countering New England Federalists who insisted on fighting only a defensive war, and even that half-heartedly. At the beginning of 1814 came surprising news when Britain suggested that it and the United States should enter into negotiations for peace, meeting for that purpose in Sweden. Britain, tired of war, was to a degree perhaps seeking to curry favor with Russia, whose peace overtures it had rejected in 1813. Madison jumped at the offer, naming John Quincy Adams, Henry Clay, Jonathan Russell, James Bayard, and Albert Gallatin as negotiators. Madison was skeptical of the proposal but open to its possibility. Before anything could get underway, however, the complete collapse of Napoleon resulted in a toughening of Britain's attitudes toward the United States, while military planners in the US were seeking, once more, victories in Canada. Military success on either side could influence whatever negotiations might eventuate.

As the European war wound down and Britain started sending more troops to North America, the US forces began another campaign into Canada but found little more success than before. Britain now determined to take the fight to the Americans, emphasizing controlling Lower Canada and invading the United States. Having sent more than thirteen thousand troops to Canada, British officials instructed the governor-general of the territory, Sir George Prevost, to go on the offensive. Accordingly, on August 14, 1814, Prevost, with ten thousand troops under his command, invaded New York, marching along the western bank of Lake Champlain on the way southward toward Plattsburgh. US general Alexander Macomb had about a third that number of troops to resist the invasion. Prevost planned to coordinate his invasion with a naval squadron on Lake Champlain led by Captain George Downie, who would be challenged on the water by a smaller US fleet led by Lieutenant Thomas Macdonough.

The larger British ships had the advantage in long guns, but the Americans had a slight edge in short-range guns. Moreover, Macdonough had his fleet gathered in Plattsburgh Bay awaiting attack, with his ships' anchors dropped. The geography of the bay took away the advantage of the long guns, and with Macdonough's ships at anchor and thereby able to easily pivot, their improved maneuverability gave them a significant advantage over their British adversaries in close-quarter combat. In less than three hours, the Americans claimed victory. Meanwhile, the British invaders had been unexpectedly slowed by General Macomb's defenders at the Saranac River during the first week of September, forcing the British to await the outcome of the naval fight. When Prevost learned on September 11 that the British fleet in Lake Champlain had been defeated and his supply line thereby compromised, he panicked and withdrew his large army. This was a stunning, actually shocking, defeat for the British. After two years, both nations had basically fought to a draw in the Canadian theater.

Throughout 1813, British ships had marauded along the East Coast, particularly afflicting Maine and wreaking havoc with quick raids to seize supplies and enslaved people up and down Chesapeake Bay. Altogether about 3,400 enslaved people had fled to the British ships by mid-1814, most of them eventually settled as free in Nova Scotia.[9] (Although this number represented less than 1 percent of the enslaved population of Virginia and Maryland, it was enough to both frighten and outrage the white population along the riverbanks and shores of the Chesapeake.) But so far, no large-scale invasion had been attempted. This was to change, dramatically so, in 1814.

At first British general Robert Ross was ordered to create a divergence in the Chesapeake region to assist British efforts in Lower Canada, but then, in one of his last actions, General Prevost asked Admiral Alexander Cochrane to retaliate harshly against earlier American raids into Canada. The result was that Ross and Cochrane decided to combine their efforts in the Chesapeake, with both the city of Washington and the major seaport of Baltimore—the nation's third most populous city and a center of US privateering activities—offering tempting targets, the latter for its economic importance and the capital for its symbolic significance.

Both cities were lightly defended, and US Secretary of War Armstrong believed that the small capital city was of such slight strategic value that it was not at risk. Madison found himself exasperated by Armstrong to the point of instructing him in writing that "the Secretary of War . . . [must] act under the authority & subject to the decisions & instructions of the President," and he followed this with a list of directives. Madison also, pushed by Monroe, finally created a special military district that contained both cities, placing General William Winder in charge of their defense. Winder had no meaningful military experience, but as the nephew of the Federalist governor of Maryland, Madison hoped the appointment would lessen Federalist foot-dragging and energize the Maryland militia.[10]

In mid-August, Cochrane and Ross, with twenty warships and thousands of British regulars, had made their way up the Patuxent River that ran between Baltimore and Washington. On August 19 and 20, they landed over four thousand troops and were in Upper Marlboro, Maryland, two days later. Stopping in Upper Marlboro to consider his options, Ross decided to march his troops to Bladensburg, from where he could quickly cross the Eastern Branch of the Potomac and attack Washington. Unsure of the enemy's exact location and its intentions, Winder was preoccupied with preparing defenses for Baltimore. With Armstrong disengaged, only Secretary of State Monroe seemed duly alarmed about the capital's military situation, so ahead of a small force of about two dozen dragoons on August 20, he rode on horseback toward the British encampment to reconnoiter for himself. He repeated his efforts to scout out the British position the following day. On August 22, he wrote ominously to Madison that "You had better remove the records."[11]

That morning Madison himself, who had absolutely no military experience, rode into the field to inspect the situation. For two days he rode within a few miles of enemy forces, by now sending notes to General Winder urging maximum efforts. Monroe, for his part, began trying to put into effect some sort of defense as Secretary of War Armstrong sulked and did nothing. On August 24, Madison realized that the capital was at risk. He had sent Dolley a hurried message the day before to "be ready at a moment's warning to enter my carriage and leave the city."[12] (He could not know then that the intrepid Dolley was already busy—assisted by enslaved workers—packing up valuable papers, silver, and managing to save a portrait of George Washington to be carted away from the President's House while menacing British troops were just miles away.[13]) On the morning of the twenty-fourth, Madison and Monroe were both near Bladensburg when a military scout warned them to leave. Just after noon, with the temperature at 100 degrees, hostilities began.

The battle turned into a rout, with the US militia fleeing for their lives, and the whole American defense turned into a carnival of ineptitude. It was really all over by four o'clock in the afternoon. From a distance, Monroe attempted without success to mount a defense. Trying to avoid the onrush of runaways, Madison and Attorney General Richard Rush struggled to make their way back to the capital city.[14] Madison reached the President's House just minutes after Dolley had left.[15] After a short rest, he mounted his horse and fled across the Potomac to safety in Virginia.

General Ross allowed his troops a couple of hours to rest before they marched to Washington itself, where they found confusion and panic but no defenders, not even anyone officially authorized to surrender the capital. So with methodical care the British soldiers began to burn the government buildings, but they carefully avoided doing harm to private structures. After briefly admiring the architecture of the Capitol, the soldiers began chopping up furniture to produce kindling, even tossing into the pile, along with drapes and rugs, the several thousand books that composed the Library of Congress, sprinkling gunpowder on it all, then setting the whole afire. From there they marched from one federal building to the next, putting the torch to each one. The retreating US forces had set the naval yard on fire, and now flames across the city could be seen from miles. Even people on rooftops in Baltimore could see the glow on the horizon. When British troops got to the President's House, they found the dining room table had been set for dinner, complete with food and drink. Helping themselves to a quick meal, they mocked President Madison with a toast to His Majesty, then again broke the furniture into kindling and set the mansion afire.

The Patent Office Building alone was saved because Dr. William Thornton, superintendent of patents, confronted the British officer readying to burn it and convinced him that because it was filled with inventors' models that were private property, it should be spared. Amazingly, the officer relented and spared the building. Later in the night a violent thunderstorm struck and extinguished many of the other fires (and blew down some buildings), but the next day the British troops set more fires to finish their work of destruction, later justifying the barbarity of their activity by recalling the Americans' burning of York's public buildings in April 1813.[16] Their destructive task completed, on August 25 they left the smoldering capital city and prepared to move northward to the more valuable target, Baltimore.[17]

Monroe, more confident in military matters than was Madison, was trying to arrange a defense of Baltimore, and General Winder was busy gathering soldiers and supplies. Madison and Monroe also believed it was important to return to Washington now that the British had left and reestablish some semblance of government. When Madison arrived at the capital, he found, amid the smoking embers, a scene of confusion. A force of British ships had sailed up the Potomac, originally to reinforce Ross, but Washington City was of no interest to them. However, when the city fathers of Alexandria, fearing it was at danger of being burned too, surrendered the city and the ships and supplies at its docks, the British were only too happy to oblige the defeatist city fathers.

Madison appointed Secretary of State Monroe, not Secretary of War Armstrong, to take command of Washington City and develop a strategy for its defense. Monroe was eager to do so, and he quickly thwarted the city of Georgetown from following Alexandria's example of surrendering. Madison had a frank conversation with Armstrong and suggested that Armstrong voluntarily retire for a while to visit family in New York. Armstrong tarried several days in Baltimore, then angrily resigned. Madison promptly appointed Monroe acting secretary of war.

Meanwhile Dolley had returned to Washington to find a burned-out and smoke-blackened President's House. For several days she and the president stayed at the home of her sister, Anna Cutts, but soon they rented Octagon House, at Eighteenth Street and New York Avenue. They lived there for two months until they rented a townhouse at the corner of Pennsylvania Avenue and Nineteenth Street, where they resided for the rest of Madison's presidency.[18] But in his quiet way Madison took pains to reestablish normal government in Washington, and on September 1, 1814, he issued a proclamation condemning the British for "invading the capital of the nation . . . during the possession of which . . . they wantonly destroyed the public edifices having no relation in their structure to operations of war . . . monuments of taste and of the arts . . . public archives." He called on the "good people" of the nation "to unite their hearts and hands . . . to chastise and expel the invader." Seeking to inspire the citizens further in this moment of national distress, he spoke of "the high destinies which await it" and referred to "the glory acquired by their fathers, in establishing the independence which is now to be maintained by their sons."[19] He quickly held cabinet meetings, in part to demonstrate the resilience of the city, and later that year he had to rebut calls from some Philadelphians that the capital be moved back to their city. A nonbinding resolution to that effect narrowly passed in the House on October 6—with the New Englanders voting in a bloc for the move, but on October 17, after word of the victories at both Plattsburgh and Baltimore, the House solidly passed a resolution to keep the capital at Washington.[20]

The British had long been more focused on Baltimore, a city known to dislike British policies and a hotbed of privateering. Accordingly, after their punishing raid on Washington, British forces moved northward, where they expected to mount a ground and naval assault on Baltimore. The governor of Maryland, having little confidence in the military prowess of his nephew General Winder, had appointed Senator Samuel Smith to the rank of general and given him responsibility to protect the city. Smith worked diligently, constructing shore fortifications, building up his military forces, and making repairs to Fort McHenry, the star-shaped fort that sat in the middle of the Baltimore Harbor and was commanded in the fall of 1814 by Major George Armistead.

Before dawn on September 12, General Robert Ross began to land his army of 4,500 men at North Point, about twelve miles east of Baltimore. While his men were marching toward the city, they stumbled upon a slightly smaller defensive force. In the sharp battle that ensued and that eventually led US forces to retreat, General Ross was fatally wounded. The British, demoralized by his death, paused to consider their options, with their land forces now led by Colonel Arthur Brooke. They decided to await the results of a naval attack on Fort McHenry, which they expected to be followed by the landing of additional British troops. Accordingly Admiral Cochrane, holding back his transport ships, moved his frightening array of "bomb" ships to within almost two miles of Fort McHenry—just beyond the range of the fort's guns—and had them arranged in the form of a half circle. On hand were five bulky bomb ships, like giant barges, armed with huge mortars that could loft two-hundred-pound explosive ball-shaped shells up to two and a half miles, and each ship could fire at the rate of forty-five to fifty shells an hour. Along with the bomb ships was the rocket ship *Erebus,* capable of firing Congreve rockets.

On the morning of September 13, the bomb ships began firing, a mighty fusillade of explosive firepower no American had ever seen before. For hours, mortars and rockets rained down on sturdy Fort McHenry, although many of the shells fell short or went long, or failed to explode on time. Still, the shelling inside the fort was fearsome, but miraculously, despite over two thousand mortar shells and rockets launched at the fort, only four men within were killed and twenty-four wounded.

An America lawyer, Francis Scott Key, watched the bombardment from aboard a small truce ship sent out to the fleet where he was attempting to arrange the release of an elderly prisoner. Throughout the night, Key paced the deck, watching the shelling by bombs and rockets, until finally, at the first light of dawn, via his handheld telescope, he could see that the large American flag still waved over the fort, meaning that Fort McHenry had not surrendered.[21] (Key, an amateur poet, recorded his experiences in a poem intended to be the lyrics set to a well-known British song, "To Anacreon in Heaven," and though as "The Defense of Fort M'Henry," it quickly became popular, it did not become the official national anthem until 1931. Already by October 1814, however, it was being called "The Star-Spangled Banner."[22])

Soon the American defenders were surprised to see the British begin to withdraw, in part at least because Admiral Cochrane did not want to risk ships and men now that he realized how difficult an invasion of Maryland would be. Looking ahead, he expected to be part of a major invasion planned months later for New Orleans. Importantly, the British failure to take Baltimore meant that, after the almost simultaneous failure to take Plattsburgh, two major British military initiatives had failed, much to the disappointment of the war-wearied administration at Whitehall and the British public. Many Americans were weary of the war, too, especially in New England where the conflict with Britain had never garnered public support. The New England states opposed the use of their militias, especially when they were called upon to attack Canada, and they opposed any kind of federal command of their forces. That disaffection grew, and by such men as Congressman Daniel Webster, who at the time was a strong partisan of New England interests, not at all the powerful spokesman for the union he would later become as a senator. Many New Englanders saw the war as simply a pro-French continuation of the policies they had long associated with Jefferson.[23]

Moreover, they opposed the now more than twelve years of Virginians' holding the presidency. Firm believers that New Englanders possessed the most virtue, the most talent, the superior politics, and the greatest ethnic uniformity of any place in the nation, they resisted the rising influence of the South and West, the increasing democratization of the nation, and the possibility of additional states in the West, all of which portended a decline of their influence in the nation.[24] This hostility to the war boiled over in 1814 after Britain expanded its blockade to include the New England states and occupied portions of Maine, which was then still part of Massachusetts. With the end of hostilities in Europe, it was easy to imagine Britain turning to a punishing full-scale invasion of the US. Federalist politicians and Congregationalist ministers continued to vilify Madison, the so-called Virginia Dynasty, and every aspect of the war.

In this context, with Massachusetts almost in a state of rebellion, its governor called for a special legislative session to consider what should be done. A committee led by influential Harrison Gray Otis proposed that the New England states send delegates to a special convention to propose possible amendments to the US Constitution to protect New Englanders' rights. Subsequently, twenty-six delegates from the five New England states convened in Hartford, Connecticut, from December 5, 1814, to January 5, 1815, meeting in secret to discuss the issues.[25] While some in the region had called for secession from the union (many newspapers did) and hotheads bandied about the concept of nullification and refusing to obey federal legislation, the convention named moderate George Cabot president, and passions were kept under control.

Madison was filled with apprehension over the attitudes in New England, believing they gave hope to the British. In late November 1814 he revealed his worries to Governor Wilson Cary Nicholas of Virginia, writing that "the conduct of the Eastern States [is] the source of our great difficulties in carrying on the war; as it certainly is the greatest, if not the sole, inducement with the enemy to persevere in it."[26] Even before the results of the convention in Hartford were known, it is most important to note that Madison made no effort to squelch the convention in advance or intimidate radical newspaper editors or publicists, in dramatic contrast to the Federalists of the 1790s who wielded the Sedition Acts against dissenters and secretly at least contemplated using the army to crush political opponents. Madison took no political retaliation because he truly believed in the First Amendment principles and trusted the good sense of the populace.[27]

Throughout his administration Madison hoped to avoid or defuse the kind of poisonous partisanship that had erupted in the late 1790s. Among other things, he had wanted to lessen the tension between the presidency and the federal judiciary, and surely it was at his suggestion or at least his approval that Monroe, when Congress had declared war against Britain in 1812, had sent Chief Justice Marshall all the documents relevant to Madison's decision to advocate such a vote. Marshall did not approve of the war, but neither did he actively oppose it.[28] Seeking to promote national unity, Madison signed a presidential proclamation promoting a resolution passed by both houses of Congress on November 3, 1814, that recommended a day of "Public Humiliation and Fasting, and of Prayer to Almighty God, for the safety and welfare of these States, his blessing on their arms, and a speedy restoration of peace." Madison added a supplication to the "Great Sovereign of the Universe" that he "inspire the Enemy with dispositions favorable to a just and reasonable peace."[29]

As it turned out in late 1814, not opposing the Hartford Convention was politically wise. The convention served as a mechanism for flaring off the angriest ideas of the antiwar dissenters and resulted in a series of relatively moderate proposed amendments: to prohibit any trade embargo of more than sixty days; require a two-thirds Congressional vote for approving a declaration of war, admitting a new state, or interdicting foreign commerce; end the three-fifths compromise rule on counting enslaved population when assessing southern congressional representation; and limit future presidents to one term and not allow their successor to be from the same state. Every one of the amendments was intended to bolster New England's position in the nation. Massachusetts, Connecticut, and Rhode Island officially adopted the report, and Massachusetts sent three commissioners to Washington City to lobby for the amendments, but events far beyond the capital, and the nation, conspired to make the recommendations moot and the whole Federalist counteroffensive seem silly. It came to be seen as a disloyal harbinger of later southern secession and effectively ended the Federalist party.[30]

President Madison himself had long been open to negotiating a peaceful conclusion to the conflict with Britain. Indeed, within a week of the declaration of war, he had invited the British minister to the United States, Augustus J. Foster, to the President's House, to suggest terms for a treaty. But nothing had come of these early probes, nor of the Russian offer in 1813 to mediate negotiations for peace. Britain had itself suggested negotiations, as we have seen, in early 1814. Because of slow communications and uncertainty on both sides as to the intentions of the other, and because both sides jockeyed to gain a military advantage, progress was slow. Finally, given the increasing collapse of Napoleon, Britain became more interested, so the negotiations were moved from Sweden to the more convenient city of Ghent, in present-day Belgium, and the five American diplomats (John Quincy Adams, named to preside over the American group, Henry Clay, James A. Bayard, Albert Gallatin, and Jonathan Russell) began talks with their three British counterparts in August 1814. The US contingent was far more skilled, in large part because British Foreign Secretary Viscount Castlereagh and his top staff were in Vienna, where the Congress of Vienna was set to open in November. The delegates from all the powerful European nations had arrived in the Austrian city in late September and had begun preliminary talks to establish the post-Napoleonic order in Europe that ended up preventing a major continental war for almost a century.[31] The Ghent discussions were held in the shadow of talks in Vienna.

The British delegates at Ghent began confidently because they expected British military successes were imminent with planned raids on Plattsburgh and Washington and Baltimore, so they made radical demands for establishing a buffer state to the west of Lake Michigan to protect both Native Americans and the Canadian provinces from American expansion, and they demanded a demilitarized Great Lakes. According to John Quincy Adams, the British wanted "submissions to disgraceful conditions, and sacrifices little short of Independence itself."[32] The Americans instantly rejected the British proposals, and Madison revealed the British demands to the US public, which created an outrage at British audacity. The skilled American delegates simply overmatched their diplomatic opponents, who, having exceeded their instructions and overreached, quickly backed down. The negotiations continued, and Clay thought the British negotiators were trying to buy time awaiting news of military successes in America. But by early November, word arrived that the British had been defeated in trying to take both Plattsburgh and Baltimore. British citizens were thoroughly weary of war by this point, and British merchants clamored for a return to the prosperity of peacetime maritime commerce.

As a result, British Prime Minister Lord Liverpool agreed that peace was needed. The plodding British delegates at Ghent asked their American colleagues to draw up the terms, and both sides signed off on the agreement on December 4, 1814. Now that Britain was no longer at war with France, it had no need to either interfere with neutral commerce or impress sailors from US ships, the two main irritants to the United States. Neither topic was even mentioned in the Treaty of Ghent. Issues like fishing rights in the Atlantic, navigation of the Mississippi, and precise boundary disputes were left to future committees to settle. Likewise, it was agreed that both sides would endeavor to end the traffic in humans. In essence, however, the Treaty of Ghent left relations between the two nations where they had been in 1812, *status quo ante bellum,* minus the matters of impressment and the Orders in Council, which had now gone away.

Britain ratified the treaty on December 28, 1814, and it was sent across the Atlantic, arriving in New York City on February 11, 1815, and delivered to Washington City two days later. Madison submitted the document to the Senate on February 15, where it was unanimously ratified the next day. After ratifications were exchanged on February 17 with the British agent who had brought the treaty from England, the war officially ended. Yet another development that occurred between the signing of the treaty on Christmas Eve in Ghent and its ratification in Washington on February 16 would shape how Americans interpreted the end of the war. Before the summer of 1814, Admiral Cochrane had proposed to his superiors that a relatively small force could take New Orleans, which offered access to the interior of the continent, could stop a significant proportion of US commerce, and could take pressure off the military situation in Canada. Officials had approved this plan by July, and soon Cochrane, commanding his fleet from Jamaica, began to make preliminary preparations for the invasion he imagined.[33] Anticipation of this operation had led Cochrane to be cautious at the battle for Baltimore in September. He plotted sending his fleet toward Mobile, and from there, with an army of perhaps four thousand to be led by General Robert Ross, move toward the Crescent City.

But these plans changed drastically. First, Ross was killed during the attempted Baltimore invasion, to be replaced for the New Orleans campaign by Lieutenant General Sir Edward Michael Packenham (brother-in-law to Britain's famous war hero, the Duke of Wellington). Second, Andrew Jackson, fresh from his victory over the Creeks at Horseshoe Bend, had solidified his rule of the South's Gulf Coast, controlling Pensacola and Mobile by the fall of 1814. Revising his plans, Cochrane decided to invade New Orleans directly from the east, entering through Lake Borgne and crossing the flat Plain of Gentilly that lay between it and Lake Pontchartrain to the north. Jackson learned of Cochrane's plans and rushed his forces from the vicinity of Mobile to New Orleans on December 1; he quickly began to prepare defensive positions, augmenting his forces by accepting the assistance of two battalions of Free Black militia and perhaps a thousand pirates from Barataria Bay. Jackson recruited volunteers from Tennessee and Kentucky, amassed supplies, studied the topography of the region below the city. A stern disciplinarian and inspirational leader with intuitive military skill, he began to develop a strategy for defending the city.[34]

Both sides made preparations for the major battle they knew was coming. General Packenham arrived from England on Christmas Day with three thousand more troops. A quick reconnoiter revealed that his position was not advantageous, but he decided he had no viable alternative to attacking here and now. The men of both sides performed simply astonishing feats of labor, the British arduously dragging heavy cannons from ships through knee-deep mud into position, and the American forces building a massive earth-and-log parapet reaching from the Mississippi River eastward to impenetrable cypress swamps; the embankment was just north of a canal, which acted as a moat. There were preliminary skirmishes, and the British regulars, fresh from victories over Napoleon's armies, were surprised at the accuracy of the American sharpshooters and their fortitude in the face of British shelling.

Finally, on January 8, the morning darkness was interrupted when a solitary Congreve rocket lit the sky to signal the British assault. But the frontal onslaught against the Americans defended by their earthen embankment and moat-like canal was a catastrophe: artillery fire, including musket balls fired by a thirty-two pounder directly into the British ranks, was devastating, and as the morning fog lifted and a slight breeze blew away some of the smoke, American sharpshooters with rifles and muskets raked the oncoming redcoats in what one veteran from the wars against Napoleon called "the most murderous [fire] I ever beheld."[35] The brunt of the battle was over in a half hour, the crack British army suffering more than two thousand casualties to Jackson's army taking about seventy. Packenham himself was fatally wounded, as were two other generals and dozens of lesser officers. In terms of the number of troops engaged and casualties, this was the greatest battle of the War of 1812, and it proved to be a humiliating loss for the British. Admiral Cochrane was loath to give up the invasion, but after several more weeks of minor skirmishes in the swampy vicinity and a belated attempt to take Mobile on February 14, his forces received word that a treaty had been signed in December at Ghent and that his own government had ratified it before the end of the month. Reluctantly, Cochrane ceased hostilities and sailed away.

Victorious General Jackson was instantly hailed as a hero in New Orleans and beyond, becoming an American icon and eventually turning his military fame to political success in Tennessee and all the way to the presidency in 1829.[36] News of his victory brought joy to the face of President Madison, when on February 3, Secretary of State Monroe forwarded a letter from Jackson bringing the first news of the stupendous victory, which Monroe called "truly glorious."[37] That news, combined with the information that came ten days later of success in Ghent, climaxed a triumphant February for the beleaguered president.[38] Newspapers across the nation excitedly spread the news, and the one-two arrival of the information—first of the military victory, then the peace treaty—made it seem as though the battle success had brought forth the diplomatic triumph. People everywhere of whatever political persuasion were jubilant: the war had ended, and on such a note that it was widely interpreted as a second War of Independence from Britain, a repeat of the glorious victory of the revolution that indisputably established the independence of the United States as a full-fledged nation equal to any of the storied nations of Europe. A generous Madison even issued a presidential proclamation pardoning from any prewar law-breaking those pirates and freebooters from Barataria who had fought so bravely in defense of New Orleans, demonstrating, in the president's words, "unequaled traits of courage and fidelity."[39]

Madison demonstrated uncharacteristic political acumen in his message to Congress on February 18, laying before it copies of the treaty. He began by congratulating both the Congress and the nation's citizens "upon an event which is highly honorable to the nation, and terminates, with peculiar felicity, a campaign signalized by the most brilliant successes." "The late war," he continued, "although reluctantly declared by congress, had become a necessary resort, to assert the rights and independence of the nation." Here again he referred to the theme of national honor that had been the driving motif in the initial call for war. He claimed that the success was the "natural result of the wisdom of the Legislative Councils"—which was a wild stretch—"of the patriotism of the people, of the public spirit of the militia"—again an exaggeration—"and of the valor of the military and Naval forces of the country." He understood this was not the moment for prolonging grudges or settling scores. Speaking magnanimously, he heaped praise upon "the gallant men, whose achievements, in every department of military service . . . have so essentially contributed to the honor of the American name."[40]

Then turning to the lessons taught by the last few years and looking ahead, Madison both indicated how his ideas had evolved and how classical Republican ideology had matured as a result of the exigencies of wartime. Despite his earlier paean to the militia forces, he was not unaware of just how inadequate they could be in a real national emergency. Accordingly, he now argued that "a certain degree of preparation for war, is not only indispensable to avert disaster in the onset, but affords also the best security for the continuan[ce] of peace." Here he was breaking with decades of American bias against standing armies. "The wisdom of congress will therefore I am confident provide for the maintenance of an adequate military force; for the gradual advance of the naval establishment; for improving all the means of Harbour defence; for adding discipline to the distinguished bravery of the militia; and for cultivating the military art, in its essential branches under the liberal patronage of the Government."[41] A cautious Madison was not calling for the kind of military might that Hamilton had wanted and that rivaled the standing armies of Europe, but he was moving beyond the colonial-era dependence on ill-trained and poorly supplied voluntary militia.[42]

Madison also wanted to defend the manufacturing capabilities of the nation that had emerged during the times of embargo and war. He stated that with peace and the restoration of maritime commerce would come a resurgence of prosperity, and hence "there is no subject, that can enter, with greater force & merit into the deliberations of congress, than a consideration of the means, to preserve and promote the manufactures which have sprung into existence, and attained an unparalleled maturity, throughout the U. States during the period of the European wars. This source of national independence & wealth, I anxiously recommend, to the prompt & and constant guardianship of Congress."[43] This represented closely the evolving political opinion over the last several decades of both Jefferson and Madison, who were never dogmatic opponents of commerce and manufacturing, which they believed should work in consort with agriculture to bring national prosperity. And then Madison concluded with a sharp poke at the secessionist threat and ignoring of federal laws he had weathered from New England dissenters: "And while we accord in grateful acknowledgements for the protection which Providence has bestowed upon us, let us never cease to inculcate obedience to the laws, and fidelity to the Union, as constituting the Palladium of the national independence & prosperity."[44]

No doubt one reason Madison supported a modest military and naval presence was the continuing interference of the Barbary pirates with US trade in the Mediterranean. With British support, corsairs from Algiers had begun once more to interfere with what little US shipping there was in the region in 1812, and the ruling dey raised the amount of tribute demanded from the United States. A US ship was promptly captured and its crew held for ransom. Throughout the duration of the war with Britain, pirates from Algiers, Tripoli, and Tunis harassed American shipping. Madison who, like Jefferson before him, hated any form of annual tributes to them, was infuriated by the actions of the various Barbary States, and within a week of the signing of the Treaty of Ghent ending hostilities with Britain, he sent to Congress on February 23, 1815, a message asking it to declare the "existence of a state of war between the United States and the Dey and Regency of Algiers; and of such provisions as may be requisite for a vigorous prosecution of it to a successful issue."[45] Congress followed his direction and voted to declare war on March 3. Almost incongruously, the very next day Madison issued a presidential proclamation thanking "Almighty God" for restoring peace. "No people," he declared, "ought to feel greater obligations to celebrate the goodness of the Great Disposer of events, and of the destiny of nations, than the people of the United States."[46]

Madison wanted a flotilla of US navy ships to arrive in the Mediterranean with a massive display of force to overawe the marauding forces. Accordingly, on March 20, Captain Stephen Decatur led a squadron of ten warships, the largest squadron yet assembled by the navy, toward the region, followed several months later by a still larger squadron led by Captain William Bainbridge.[47] Now a total of twenty-seven US warships were available in the Mediterranean, and they instantly began to overwhelm the Barbary ships they encountered; after all, this was not the British navy they faced. Within a period of months, Decatur captured two Algerian ships and successfully demanded capitulation by the Algerian dey, ending tribute payment and obtaining the return of American personnel and supplies. Then Decatur sailed to Tunis, where in addition to a treaty that ended the payment of tribute, the Tunisians reimbursed the United States for vessels they held. After Tunis, Decatur and his squadron went to Tripoli, where they held similar negotiations.

The United States was extracting provisions from the region that even the most powerful European nations had not achieved, and the US naval presence of the combined squadrons of Decatur and Bainbridge so impressed Barbary officials that they agreed also to release various European prisoners. In total, the American naval forces achieved astonishing success along the Barbary coast of North Africa, and although Europe was too caught up in celebrating the final defeat of Napoleon at Waterloo to pay much attention initially, gradually the European powers took due notice. These victories, after the obvious success marked by the Treaty of Ghent, helped establish the United States as a nation worthy of some respect. At home, Decatur and Bainbridge were saluted as great heroes, and their naval successes, combined with the victory over the British at New Orleans, resulted in a surge of national pride.

Not until September 1815 did Madison learn of the victories of US naval forces in the Mediterranean, but as early as late spring he could also take pleasure in another piece of good news, namely that the US capital city of Washington was recovering from its wartime devastation. Bibliophile Jefferson had been appalled when he learned that the rampaging soldiers had used the books of the infant Library of Congress to help start the conflagration that burned the Capitol Building, one of a series of "acts of barbarism which do not belong to a civilized age," as he put it. Jefferson wrote to his old newspaper friend Samuel Harrison Smith, now commissioner of revenue in the Treasury

Department, not quite a month after the sacking of Washington City to say that he presumed, among other tasks, that Congress would want to "recommence" its library. Jefferson then made a remarkable offer: his personal library as a replacement. Of course, it was far more than a simple replacement. As he confided to Smith, "you know my collection, it's condition and extent. I have been 50. years making it, & have spared no pains, opportunity or expence to make it what it is. While residing in Paris," he recalled,

> I devoted every afternoon I was disengaged, for a summer or two, in examining all the principal bookstores . . . and putting by every thing which related to America, and indeed whatever was rare & valuable in every science. besides this, I had standing orders, during the whole time I was in Europe, in it's principle book-marts, particularly Amsterdam, Frankfort, Madrid and London, for such works relating to America as could not be found in Paris. . . . Such a collection was made as probably can never again be effected.

He estimated he had between nine and ten thousand volumes. He then asked Revenue Commissioner Smith to offer his book collection, complete, to the library committee of Congress, at whatever price and on whatever terms they chose. He only wished them to keep the collection complete and together.[48]

At Jefferson's suggestion, Congress sent a person to examine the quality of his collection and count the titles (6,487), and Congress agreed upon the price of $23,950, an incredible bargain. Despite Federalist opposition (his library had too many foreign-language books, they argued, too many of a deistic or atheistic nature, too many philosophical tomes), Congress had the good sense to acquire Jefferson's library, and Madison signed the bill making the purchase on January 30, 1815.[49]

Throughout 1815, Madison was consumed with making new appointments to his cabinet; working to slightly downsize the army and strengthen the Department of the Navy; helping reestablish international commerce, especially a commercial treaty with Britain; dealing with the financial needs for funding the government; considering new tariff policies; working to fulfill all the requirements of the Treaty of Ghent (such as prisoner exchange); and beginning to try to engage diplomatically with various Native Americans groups, who of all parties involved had come out the worse as a result of the war. The death of Tecumseh in the North and the devastating attacks on the Creeks by Andrew Jackson in the South, accompanied by massive cessions of territory, changed the whole course of Native American history in that part of the nation east of the Mississippi River. In March, Madison also normalized diplomatic relations with Britain by appointing John Quincy Adams as minister and communicating "our sincere desire to cultivate and strengthen the friendship and good correspondence between us." King George III sent an equally fulsome letter in July, stating his desires of "Having nothing more at Heart than to cultivate and improve the Friendship and good Understanding now so happily restored between the Two States."[50] Meanwhile, Congress appropriated funds to begin the repair of the federal buildings in Washington, with architect Benjamin Henry Latrobe hired to supervise the redesign and rebuilding of the US Capitol.[51] By September 1817, the fire-blackened exterior walls of the President's House were cleaned and whitewashed, and thereafter it was known as the White House. Now with the rebuilding of public buildings in Washington City underway, the restoration of commerce, and the flowering of nationalistic pride, the state of the nation must have seemed quite auspicious to Madison as he drafted his annual message to Congress for delivery on December 5, 1815.[52]

"I have the satisfaction," he began, by reporting on the "successful termination of the war" with the Barbary powers. Likewise "another source of satisfaction" was the opening of a convention on commerce following the Treaty of Ghent. Then he reported guarded success with effecting treaties with Native Americans, developing means to reduce the national debt, "fixing an efficient military peace establishment," and the necessity of targeted tariffs to support new manufacturing interests that had emerged during the war. Assuming the continuing improvement in the nation's finances, he wrote that "the occasion is a proper one for recalling the attention of Congress, to the great importance of establishing throughout our country, the roads and Canals which can best be executed, under the national Authority." Here, like Jefferson, Madison was using the occasion of his annual message to suggest to Congress action he thought advisable.

He praised internal improvements for their obvious contribution to the economy and also for their "political effect . . . for intercommunication, in bringing and binding more closely together, the various parts of our extended confederacy." This was a theme that both George Washington and Thomas Jefferson had emphasized in their support of constructing canals and building locks around river impediments. Then Madison added an important disclaimer: "And it is a happy reflection, that any defect of constitutional authority, which may be encountered, can be supplied in a mode [the amendment process], which the constitution itself has providently pointed out." He still believed that government power was limited by the words of the Constitution, though, like Jefferson, Madison believed the founding document should be regularly updated. Continuing on the theme of national improvements, Madison then heartily supported the establishment of a "national seminary of learning within the District of Columbia," again something his predecessors had recommended. He concluded by noting that the "nation finds itself possessed of a growing respect abroad, and of a just confidence in itself."[53]

Madison enjoyed 1816 as a triumphant year: the economy was improving and his desired candidate to replace him, James Monroe, won the support of the Republican caucus (though there was some opposition to the continued dominance of Virginians). Madison's support that year for the rechartering of a national bank, a modest standing army and strengthened navy, and internal improvements (although only after a constitutional amendment to enlarge government authority) represented less a rejection of traditional Republican orthodoxy and more a series of moderate revisions of policy appropriate to changed circumstances. Hamilton had always pushed his proposals in maximal fashion while Madison was fundamentally moderate in all measures. The public recognized this about him. For example, he was not as associated with fervent pro-French positions as Jefferson had been, and he took measures to ease conflicts between the executive and judicial branches. The Federalists looked like the extremists in the aftermath of the successful conclusion of the War of 1812. The presidential vote in 1816 ratified Madison's approach when Monroe then easily defeated his opponent, Federalist Rufus King of Massachusetts, 183 to 34 in the electoral college, and won sixteen of nineteen states.

In many ways, Madison saw his final annual message to Congress, sent on December 3, 1816, as his valedictory, not unlike Washington's Farewell Address. He began by pointing out some problems that required attending to, for amid the "general invigoration of industry among us and . . . the extension of our commerce," the "excess of imported merchandise" was causing a "depression . . . in particular branches of our manufactures." Such imbalances needed to be corrected by what we today would call protective tariffs—Madison was not a dogmatic proponent of free trade in every situation.[54] Even former War Hawk John C. Calhoun supported a tariff to support American manufacturing because it would help free the nation of dependence on other powers.

Madison also called for strengthening the enforcement of the prohibition of the transatlantic slave trade and for augmenting the judicial department and the office of the attorney general. He went on to call for a reorganization of the nation's various militias, the development of a uniform system of weights and measures throughout the nation, and the creation of a standardized medium of currency for the country.

In his conclusion the retiring president turned to the nation's system of government, which had been his life's work. Speaking of the nation, he wrote, "I behold it blessed with tranquility and prosperity at home and with peace and respect abroad. I can indulge the proud reflection that the American people have reached in safety and success their 40th year as an independent nation; that for nearly an entire generation they have had experience of their present Constitution, the off-spring of their undisturbed deliberations and of their free choice."[55] It was a government, he said, that reconciled "public strength with individual liberty," and he praised the "character of the American people" and "their devotion to true liberty and to the Constitution which is its palladium. . . . a Government which watches over the purity of elections, the freedom of speech and the press. . . . a Government, in a word, whose conduct within and without may bespeak the most noble of ambitions—that of promoting peace on earth and good will to man." So judged President Madison the historical outcome of those struggling days of discussion and drafting in Philadelphia almost three decades ago, contemplation of which he knew would "sweeten . . . the remnant of my days."[56]

But one more trial would test Madison's principles. Congressmen had heard his support for roads and canals but ignored his caution to first amend the Constitution and accordingly had passed, in early February of 1817, a bill authorizing federal expenditures for internal improvements. Madison got the bill just days before leaving office, and sure that Monroe would follow his decision, on March 3, in his last formal act as president on his final day in office, Madison sent to Congress a veto message. Here he remained true to a central conviction, held since the opening months of the new government and the debate over a national bank, that the national government's powers were closely restricted to those specified in the Constitution. "I am constrained," he stated, "by the insuperable difficulty I feel in reconciling the bill with the Constitution." Then he went through and refuted the several justifications offered. He made clear that he was "not unaware of the great importance of roads and canals and the improved navigation of water courses." But he "cherish[ed] the hope that its beneficial objects may be attained by a resort for the necessary powers" through the process of amendment.[57] To the very end, Madison stuck to his foundational principles. Although his presidency is little remembered today, in 1817 crusty John Adams wrote Jefferson, with whom he had recently reconciled, that "notwithstand[ing] a thousand Faults and blunders, [Madison's] Administration has acquired more glory, and established more Union, than all his three Predecessors, Washington Adams and Jefferson, put together."[58] Quite a testimonial from one usually sparing in praise.

13

A MATURING NATION

March 4, 1817, was a gloriously warm and sunny day, and an unprecedented crowd of eight thousand gathered in Washington, DC, for James Monroe's inauguration, the first to be held since the Capitol Building had been so ignominiously burned by the British army in 1814. A hurriedly built brick building adjacent to the original Capitol now housed the legislative functions, but Speaker of the House Henry Clay, angry because Monroe had not named him secretary of state, refused to allow the senators to bring their plush red-velvet chairs into the temporary House chamber for the inaugural. This ridiculous spat meant that Monroe had to take the oath of office outside, standing on a platform just east of the replacement Congress hall. Shortly after noon, James Monroe approached the lectern on the platform and, with childhood friend and now chief justice John Marshall officiating, took the oath of office. Dressed as was his usual wont in a short coat, knee britches, and silk hose—often all black, but on formal occasions such as this a blue coat and buff-colored knee britches—with buckles on his shoes, Monroe visually harkened back to the revolutionary era. Then in a low voice he proceeded to give his inaugural address.

He began by humbly acknowledging that he was "deeply affected by the strong proof" the citizens had given of their confidence in him. Then, as had already been established as a feature of such addresses, he proceeded to praise the state of the nation. "To whatever object we turn our attention," he stated, "we find abundant cause to felicitate ourselves in the excellence of our institutions." He went on to laud the nature of the governance system, the natural resources of the nation, and the virtue and patriotism of the people. But with the memory of the late war visible behind him in the still-not-fully-usable Capitol Building, he reminded the people that the nation "may be again involved in war." From his perspective of having served as the secretary of war, he was quick to emphasize the importance of military preparation. "To secure us against these dangers, our coast and inland frontiers should be fortified; our army and navy . . . be kept in perfect order; and our militia be placed on the best practicable footing."

Shifting from preparations for defensive warfare, President Monroe made clear that "other interests of high importance will claim attention; among which is the improvement of our country by roads and canals, proceeding always"—and no one could miss his point here—"with a constitutional sanction." These transportation sinews "shall bind the Union more closely together," a point previous presidents had made. Then, pushing beyond the earlier pronouncements of his party, he stated that "our manufacturers will likewise require the systematic and fostering care of the Government." Pointing to its abundance of raw materials, along with the skill and industry of its people, the nation should not be so dependent as before upon "supplies from other countries." Almost incidentally, he mentioned the importance of cultivating friendly relationships with various Indigenous nations and persevering "in our efforts to extend to them the advantages of civilization," by which of course he meant to lay out a colonial agenda of westward expansion of white settlers while compelling Native Americans to cede their territories and pressuring them to abandon their own culture for his own.[1]

In conclusion he turned to a central concern of his, the political affairs of the nation. "Equally gratifying is it," he said, "to witness the increased harmony of opinion which pervades our Union. Discord does not belong to our system. . . . To promote this harmony . . . will be the object of my constant and zealous attentions."[2] Here he had in mind ending the partisanship that had marked the nation's politics for its first two and a half decades. Like Jefferson, Monroe truly believed that most Americans believed in the same principles and, when not led astray, shared political sentiments. Monroe's ideal of a common body politic, not rent by faction—the Republican party, properly conceived, in his view encompassed all elements of American society—was a goal he believed worth striving for. As he had written Andrew Jackson in December, the president "ought not to be the head of a party, but of the nation itself."[3]

In the weeks that followed his inauguration Monroe worked to complete his cabinet. He asked William H. Crawford to continue as secretary of the treasury, reached out to John Quincy Adams to become secretary of state (Adams had switched his allegiance to the Republican party in 1807 and had extensive diplomatic experience), and later in the year appointed John C. Calhoun, then a strong nationalist, as secretary of war, and William Wirt as attorney general. Crawford was irritated that he had not been named secretary of state and harbored resentment against Monroe thereafter, and Clay was angry for the same reason. Andrew Jackson had written Monroe the previous fall recommending that he appoint a firm Federalist to his cabinet, but Monroe, though he wanted to diminish the role of party, still feared the monarchial tendencies he had long associated with the Federalists and instead hoped to unify the nation by governing in a moderate, open manner, in that fashion attracting former Federalists and weaning them to his position.[4] He wanted to be the president of all the people, not a regional or ideological subset of them.

To further his goal of promoting national unification (and remembering the successful national tours that George Washington had undertaken as president), Monroe planned to make a tour of the northern portion of the nation at the beginning of his administration, hoping to heal the anti-administration views in the region that had led to the Hartford Convention during the War of 1812. His stated object was to travel unofficially, more as a citizen than as president. A private secretary and General Joseph Smith, the army's chief engineer and the head of West Point, would accompany him. Monroe planned to inspect various military and defensive fortifications, and he would undertake the trip at his own expense. But no sooner had he set forth by carriage on June 1, 1817, and approached Baltimore than Monroe was met by throngs of people. They gave speeches, made toasts, rang church bells. It turned out that in an age before television and photography, most people had never seen their president; as a result, a visit by him was a stupendous event. Almost instantly Monroe realized the magnitude of what he had begun. This could not be a low-key inspection of military facilities but instead would be a significant national unity tour that generated a succession of parades, speeches, and spontaneous displays of affection and patriotism.[5]

This scene repeated itself day after day, destination after destination. Traveling by stage, mail coach, and steamboat (the new technological invention), Monroe met acclaim in city after city. Neither an accomplished speaker nor a gifted writer, in plain language Monroe spoke democratic commonplaces to the crowds, but they loved his down-to-earth, comfortable presentations. From Baltimore to Philadelphia, to Trenton and on to New York City, to West Point, New Haven, Hartford, and Providence, and then to Boston for five days, where upward of forty thousand people stood in the Boston Commons to hear the president speak. Who could have imagined this? He attended a dinner hosted by John Adams, received an honorary degree from Harvard, and read in the pages of the Boston *Columbian Centinel* that his administration represented an "era of good feelings," a phrase that inadvertently became the label for the age.[6] Monroe found the trip utterly exhausting, but he soldiered on.

He traveled up to Portsmouth, New Hampshire, on to Portland and Kennebunk, Maine, then over to the northern region of New York, down Lake Champlain, stopping at Plattsburg on his way to Sackett's Harbor. From Plattsburg, renowned for the battle there in September 1814, Monroe reflected on his tour in a letter to Thomas Jefferson. Everywhere he had seen huge crowds of people making "manifest [their] respect, for our Union, & republican institutions." He acutely did not take the popular demonstrations as a tribute to him personally but rather to the nation. "I have seen enough," he wrote, "to satisfy me, that the great mass of our fellow-citizens, in the Eastern States are as firmly attached to the union and to republican govt. as I have always believ'd or could desire them to be."[7] Eventually he got to Buffalo, Detroit, down through the state of Ohio, stopping at Sandusky, Chillicothe, and Zanesville, then he headed eastward to Pittsburgh, thence through western Pennsylvania and northern Maryland, finally arriving back in Washington on September 17, after a journey of three and a half months. By now the President's House was ready for occupancy, so Monroe and his family moved in. Monroe had summarized the purpose of his trip, as he saw it, in early August: "I wish to bring about a union of the whole population of our country . . . which can only be done by a union of parties on republican principles."[8] That was to be a central theme of his presidency.

The reoccupation of the President's House in September 1817 (the front portico so familiar to us today was not added until 1824)—now popularly being called the White House—occasioned both a decorative and social reset of the house. Of course, practically all its furnishings had been destroyed, although Dolley Madison had saved the Gilbert Stuart painting of George Washington, so it would be up to the Monroes to refurnish. Thankfully, on the last day of Madison's term, Congress had appropriated twenty thousand dollars to pay for furniture and other necessities. By October 1818 the Monroes were actively engaged in restoring the White House to private and most importantly to public use. They essentially sold to the government the wonderful collection of Empire furniture they had purchased in France in the 1790s while Monroe served as the US minister to France; in the midst then of the revolutionary disruption of aristocratic families and their mansions, there had been available a huge amount of superb furniture at bargain-basement prices. Of course, it was not nearly enough to furnish the White House, so they proceeded to purchase from France other items of furniture, tableware, table linens, carpets, draperies, clocks, candleholders, all of sufficient quality to merit use in the nation's house. Congress in fact appropriated another thirty thousand dollars to complete the desired purchases.

James Monroe also wanted to reshape the social role the White House (and he and his family) played in the national capital. He began by reopening the house to the public on January 1, 1818, with a New Year's Day reception, but this festive occasion was limited to the members of the diplomatic corps, who were required to wear full court dress. Jefferson had practiced an aggressively democratic informality during such events—and in fact diplomats could drop in on him anytime in the President's House to chat—but both Monroe and Secretary of State Adams believed this informality had lessened the diplomats' respect for the nation. Monroe had served as US minister to both France and Britain, and Adams, the nation's most experienced diplomat, had served as the US minister to the Netherlands, Portugal, Prussia, Russia, and Britain, so both were accustomed to the European style of protocol and wished to incorporate that formality into American practice, thereby, they believed, adding an enhanced dignity to the nation's foreign relations.

Monroe also cut back extensively on the frequency of dinners at the White House and on the popular "drawing room" receptions that Dolley Madison had hosted with such éclat. This was because of economy. Congress did not allow the president's office any entertainment expenses, and with new states (and thus additional congressmen), Monroe simply could not afford such generous sociability. Like Jefferson and Madison before him, he discovered that serving as president was a gradual form of going bankrupt. Monroe in fact considered selling some of his land but finally just went deeper in debt. Also, the Monroes were simply a more private family than had been their predecessors, and they were trying to live more frugally. Even at White House dinners for members of Congress and formal state dinners, guests noted that the fare was not as abundant as in former days. Few understood the begrudging support Congress provided for the staffing and operation of the White House and its occupants.

Because of Monroe's experience and skill as a diplomat, it should be no surprise that significant diplomatic successes came during his administration. The first was one he had himself actually negotiated with British foreign secretary Lord Castlereagh while finishing up his term as secretary of state in the Madison administration, but because the formal version was not signed until April 1817 by Monroe's then-acting Secretary of State Richard Rush (John Quincy Adams had not arrived yet from his current posting as minister to England to accept his new post as secretary of state) and the new British minister to the United States, Charles Bagot, the resulting treaty came to be known as the Rush-Bagot Agreement. In a way it represented a tweaking of the Treaty of Ghent that ended the War of 1812: The agreement demilitarized the Great Lakes, thereby preventing a possible arms race and resulting in a significant saving of funds. It also suggested a normalization of relations with Britain.[9] Meanwhile Rush was instructed to negotiate with British authorities to attempt to restore American fishing rights off the coasts of Newfoundland and Labrador that the British had revoked during the recent war.

On October 20, 1818, both sides signed an Anglo-American Convention that restored most of the Americans' desired fishing rights, and Britain made some concessions on the old issue of impressment. And most importantly, the nations reached an agreement on a boundary line along the 49th parallel between the United States and Canada west of the Lake of the Woods all the way to the Rocky Mountains, thus putting a northern cap on the hitherto vaguely defined Louisiana Purchase. They could not reach an agreement on extending the boundary to the Pacific, so both nations agreed that for ten years the Oregon territory would be jointly open to settlers from both nations.[10] The United States' claim to the region was loosely tied to the discovery in May 1792 by Captain Robert Gray of the mighty river pouring into the Pacific that he named after his ship the *Columbia,* and the winter stay in 1805–6 of the Lewis and Clark expedition members along the coast of Oregon. All in all, the Anglo-American Convention was a remarkably positive agreement from the American position, and the Senate quickly approved it.

The precise southern and western boundaries of the Louisiana Purchase had also not been established by the purchase agreement in 1803, and Thomas Jefferson, for example, had tried to expand the land transfer to include all of Florida and even Texas. Of course Spain pushed back, and although in 1810 during the Madison administration the United States, in response to a questionable mini-rebellion in the region, simply seized and absorbed West Florida, the rest of Florida, much less Texas, remained under Spanish control. Monroe, who had been passionately interested in the Louisiana Purchase since those heady days in Paris in 1803, wished to, in his mind, complete the land transfer. He realized that the major rivers of Alabama and Georgia flowed through Florida on their course to the Gulf of Mexico. Aware of the political implications of acquiring Texas as a putative additional slave state, he focused his attention on the portion of Florida south of Alabama and Georgia. Andrew Jackson, who had no qualms subjugating and killing Indigenous peoples and hated all perceived enemies of the United States, became an unwitting catalyst in the evolving diplomatic maneuvers of Monroe and Secretary of State Adams.

Spanish-held Florida was very minimally governed from Madrid because Spain had still not recovered from the Napoleonic Wars and was preoccupied with the problem of various colonial nations in Latin America declaring their independence and fighting against Spanish authority. In this power vacuum, Florida became a problem for the United States because a motley variety of pirates, outlaws, and rebels of all sorts gathered there, even including some Latin American rebels who were leading raids against Spanish forces.[11] From the US perspective, the Creeks who had been expelled from their ancestral lands sought refuge in the region, runaway slaves fled there and sometimes joined with Seminole Indians, and random criminals escaped from southern legal authorities by running to Florida. At Amelia Island, just off the coast at the Georgia-Florida border, pirates, smugglers, slave traders, and Latin American revolutionaries threatened US interests. In response to this combination of perceived threats, Monroe had in 1817 ordered General Edmund Pendleton Gaines to pacify Amelia Island.

Meanwhile American settlers continued to complain of attacks from Seminoles, so Monroe asked Andrew Jackson to move troops into Florida to punish the Seminoles and stop their raids into US territory. At this point the record becomes unclear. Jackson later claimed that Monroe authorized him to basically take charge of the situation as Jackson saw fit—and Jackson's hatred of both Indians and Spaniards guaranteed he would apply a heavy hand—but Monroe denied ever giving Jackson unrestricted authority. This controversy later exploded in Congress, but for the moment, Jackson's forces invaded Florida with a vengeance, attacked the Seminoles and burned their villages and crops, captured Spanish towns and forts, and generally gave no quarter. At St. Marks, he captured two hapless British citizens, a Scots merchant named Alexander Arbuthnot, and an adventurer named Richard Ambrister who was reputedly giving military advice to Seminole warriors. After a makeshift trial, Jackson, wanting to make an example of them, overturned their relatively mild sentences and summarily put both men to death. In the face of all of this, Spanish control over the region was nonexistent.

Complicating affairs in Florida was both the domestic controversy in Congress over Jackson's high-handed actions and the intense diplomatic wrangling with Spain to acquire Florida and settle the western boundary of the Louisiana Purchase. In Congress, Secretary of War John C. Calhoun was outraged over Jackson's expansion of his role without authorization, and Secretary of the Treasury Crawford was equally upset. Monroe tried to thread the needle of not infuriating Jackson's many supporters but also not seeming to approve of actions that on the surface were contemptuous of Spain. For example, he demanded that the fort at St. Marks and the town of Pensacola be returned to Spanish authorities. Only Secretary of State Adams openly approved Jackson's scorched-earth campaign in the Florida, but his position, like Monroe's, was also shaped by his diplomatic tactics. Adams had already been in talks with the Spanish minister to the United States, Don Luis de Onís, to settle the outstanding issues between the two nations.

This was why Monroe had been publicly reluctant to support the independence aspirations of the various Latin American nations that were revolting against Spanish control. Monroe did not want to further infuriate Spain but understood that Jackson's ability to have his will within the Florida territory clearly indicated to Madrid its incapacity to govern there. Adams, a hard-nosed and skilled negotiator, made sure that Onís was aware of this good-cop-bad-cop approach, with Monroe withholding support of the rebellious colonies and Adams pressing hard for Spain to relent on Florida and the western boundaries.[12] Adams argued that since Spain could not maintain order in Florida, it should give it up. Onís sensed that the Spanish position in Florida was tentative at best, and he was much more determined to hold on to Texas as a buffer to keep the United States away from Mexico proper.

The negotiation was protracted. Onís's opening gambit was to claim the Mississippi River as the western boundary of the Louisiana Purchase. Adams's response was to advocate for the Colorado River in central Texas, with a line drawn northward from its source to the Arkansas River, and from there westward to the Rocky Mountains. Adams then proposed to shift the boundary eastward to the Trinity River, and from its source northward to the Arkansas. More haggling, more examination of maps. Finally, giving up Texas, Adams proposed the western bank of the Sabine River north to the 32nd parallel, then due north to the Red River, thereafter following its course to the 100th meridian, and from that point a line due north to the Arkansas River; then, following the westward course of the Arkansas to the 42nd parallel, and from that point due west to the Pacific Ocean. Adams understood the trade potential with China, and merchants from New England had long wanted access to the fur trade via Oregon.

To keep pressure on the Spanish, US forces meanwhile remained in Florida. Onís was skilled, but he had no strong hand to play. Finally, with Adams relentlessly pushing for his position, the two agreed on February 22, 1819, to what has become known as the Transcontinental Treaty (though sometimes called the Adams-Onís Treaty), establishing the Sabine River as the western boundary between Texas and the United States and accepting the proposed boundary all to the way to the Pacific. Spain renounced all claims to Florida and the upper Northwest, as did the United States to Texas, and the US agreed to assume the claims (amounting to $5 million) of its citizens against Spain.

At last Adams had achieved his longtime goal: the United States was now a transcontinental nation, striding the continent from the eastern seaboard to the Pacific coast of Oregon, with the land of the far Northwest to be shared for a decade with Britain, though Adams and his expansionist colleagues all assumed Oregon would in short time become a part of the United States. The treaty was formally approved by the Senate on February 19, 1821. Adams recorded in his diary the next day that this signing was "the most important event of my life," and even more than twenty years later, in a moment of reflection, he wrote that "The Florida Treaty was the most important incident in my life and the most successful negotiation ever consummated by the Government of this Union."[13] That might be a slight exaggeration, but not by much. Together Monroe and Adams had achieved a momentous diplomatic triumph for white Americans. And in the following year, the United States became the first nation to begin recognizing the independence of the former Spanish colonies in Latin America.

Monroe had taken office in March 1817 with a sense of optimism about the nation, fresh off its victory over Britain. "To whatever object we turn our attention," he stated in his inaugural address, "we find abundant cause to felicitate ourselves in the excellence of our institutions. During a period fraught with difficulties . . . the United States have flourished beyond example."[14] At the end of the year, he prepared his first annual message to Congress, summing up, from his perspective, the state of the nation. "At no period of our political existence had we so much cause to felicitate ourselves at the prosperous and happy condition of our country. The abundant fruits of the earth have filled it with plenty. An extensive and profitable commerce has greatly augmented our revenue."[15]

Presidents might be expected to put a positive spin on events, but there was evidence for Monroe to draw upon. As a measure of expanding commerce, the New York Stock Exchange had opened that year, and it was announced that the first regularly scheduled packet ships would begin sailing twice a month between New York City and Liverpool. Already the newly perfected steam-powered paddle boats were revolutionizing commerce on the western rivers.[16] The Second Bank of the United States went into operation in January 1817, and state and local banks mushroomed across the nation. One of the unintended consequences of the embargo that had preceded the War of 1812 had been an increase in American manufacturing, and that process had continued during the war. The so-called factory system was still new, and much manufacturing occurred in homes via the putting-out system, with individual households assembling pieces that were then gathered up for sale. Along with an increase in manufacturing came a rise in both the scale and sophistication of marketing. Even typical farmers now usually produced something to sell, and they increasingly bought ready-made products instead of trying to make everything necessary for everyday life. These developments were accelerated by the proliferation of corporations, which allowed an increase in funds raised for investment at the same time that it decreased the risk to individual investors. With the larger sums of money came investments in manufacturing and such infrastructure projects as turnpikes and bridges, which were expected to pay for themselves via tolls collected. No one precisely foresaw how this variety of developments would gradually transform the nation, but in total a process of modernization was underway, and at a far more rapid rate in the northern states than in southern ones. The absence of modern data gathering, modeling, and statistical concepts meant that even the president was barely conscious of the cumulative effect of the changes underway.[17]

Following the destruction and economic dislocations in Europe after years of Napoleonic Wars, the demand for American grains was high in 1815 and 1816, so corn and wheat exports from the United States soared. This contributed mightily to the population growth in western and midwestern states; US population increased by a third between 1810 and 1820, and the fastest growing states were west of the Appalachians, where Native Americans had their lands seized by white settlers. The cost of public land fell to fifty cents per acre, and land could be bought in 160 acre increments, with payment spread out over five years.[18] The resulting land rush gave rise to the expression "doing a land office business" as millions of acres were staked. The proliferating banks had eased their loan requirements, allowing farmers to finance the purchase of lands and equipment, facilitating the population shift westward. No one seemed to question if this kind of expansion could continue forever. Monroe in his annual message for 1818 continued to state that "commerce has flourished," and he went on to exult in the addition of another state, Illinois (making twenty-one now overall), which he said by "increasing the number of the States the confidence of the State governments in their own security is increased and their jealously of the National Government proportionally diminished.... The General Government," he predicted with optimism, "will no longer be dreaded."[19]

But by the final months of 1818 the boom had already ended in some sections and an economic decline was creeping across the nation. The European demand for grains had slacked off, following bumper crops there in 1817, leading to a collapse of export receipts for American agriculturalists. Farmers who had borrowed to purchase land saw their income plummet and many of them defaulted on their loans. Banks that had overextended credit, especially the for-the-time enormous Bank of the United States, began to call in loans, caused in part by the federal government's need to acquire bullion to pay back the long-term loans from British banks to finance the Louisiana Purchase.[20] Both honest depositors and reckless speculators lost money. Bankrupt farmers lost their lands.

Thomas Jefferson was also affected. Wilson Cary Nicholas, a former governor of Virginia and prominent Richmond banker, had often come to Jefferson's assistance when Jefferson needed loans. The two were friends, and after Nicholas's daughter married Jefferson's grandson Thomas Jefferson Randolph, he became family. Then in 1818, Nicholas got into what he thought was a temporary financial bind. He came to Jefferson and asked him if he would cosign two loans of ten thousand dollars each that the banker had taken out, assuring Jefferson, "This request wou'd not be made but under the most entire confidence, that you can never suffer the slightest inconvenience from complying with it." How could Jefferson refuse this request for help from an old friend and now member of his family? But later crop failures and other problems led Nicholas to default, leaving Jefferson with an unexpected additional twenty thousand dollars in debt, with annual interest payments of twelve hundred dollars. This ended Jefferson's hope that he could somehow emerge from his longtime affliction of debt. As he confided to Madison some years later, "Our friend W.C.N. gave me the *coup de grace.*"[21] Multiply such cases and a multitude of others, and it becomes clear why enmity arose toward the Bank of the United States.

The contraction of loans and the shortage of funds struck many businesses hard, leading them to cut wages or lay off employees. British manufacturers flooded the United States with underpriced goods, hoping both to unload their surpluses from prior years and simultaneously to undercut American manufacturers and try to hamper their success. Congress did eventually respond to this threat by passing a tariff that, by increasing the cost of imported goods, protected smaller and less efficient American manufacturers. Thousands of jobs were lost and the unemployment rate rose to as high as 20 percent, a level not reached again for more than a century. The nation found itself in what today would be called a depression, and the economic collapse came to be known as the Panic of 1819.

Monroe's third annual message, issued on December 7, 1819, was the first to address the growing economic problems. No longer did he find reason to use the word *felicitate.* Instead he now referred to "a derangement . . . in some of our moneyed institutions which has proportionally effected their credit." He spoke of "pecuniary embarrassments," of diminished public receipts, of a "great reduction in the price of the principle articles of domestic growth," a "fall in the price of labor," of blows to the "commercial interests of the nation" and "the manufacturing establishments." He mentioned the "reductions" of the currency banks could provide, to the "loss of individual confidence."[22]

It was evident that no one knew exactly what had caused the economic problem, what could be done about it, or what the government's role should be if indeed it had one. Oddly from today's perspective, no one blamed the administration or called upon the government to solve the problem. There was no federal effort to support the unemployed, although several states passed stay laws to delay repayment of bank loans. Monroe had become far more aware of the nation's economic conditions in his second major national tour, this one to the southern states. Setting forth from the capital in late March 1819, accompanied by Secretary of War Calhoun, his private secretary and an aide, the presidential party first reached Edenton, North Carolina, and worked its way south through New Bern and Wilmington, to Charleston, where there were great festivities heralding Monroe's arrival. He spent a week in that lovely city, then via Beaufort on to Savannah. Traveling by steamboat and stage, the presidential party journeyed into the interior, to Augusta, through the Cherokee Nation on to Nashville, where Monroe stayed with Andrew Jackson at his plantation. Jackson accompanied the president as he toured Kentucky, visiting Louisville, Frankfort, Lexington, and smaller towns en route. Deciding not to push on to St. Louis, Monroe began to head back east, arriving, completely exhausted, at his Highland estate near Charlottesville on August 2.[23]

As Monroe traveled throughout the South, the nation was just entering a long season of political turmoil of an intensity that had not been witnessed before and would reshape the political landscape for the next four decades or more. The controversy caught even seasoned political observers by surprise, in part because it arose as a result of a process the nation had frequently experienced with hardly a murmur: the admission of a new state. Although, in 1818, several muted protests had been made in Congress about the slight chance of slavery becoming accepted in Illinois despite the prohibition outlined in the Ordinance of 1787, or the admission of new states with slavery. Since 1791, eight new states had entered the union uneventfully, most of them after a steady growth of population, and, despite the hint of antislavery expressed in Congress in 1818, no opposition had been raised when preparations began for the territory of Alabama to be organized into a state. Accordingly, in December 1819 Alabama was admitted as the twenty-second state, and given its location between Mississippi and Georgia, where slavery flourished, no politician questioned the acceptance of slavery in the new state.

Against this background, when Speaker of the House Henry Clay and John Scott, the delegate from the territory of Missouri, drew up plans early in 1818 to authorize that territory to draft a constitution and organize a state government preparatory to requesting admission as a state, they expected no difficulties, although Congress adjourned before progress could be made on the request. In December 1818, when the new session began, Clay formally presented to the body the petition from the Missouri Territory for statehood. But Missouri was carved out of the massive Louisiana Purchase, hence was in a way precedent-setting, and most of it lay just west of the presumptively free state of Illinois. Missouri seemed geographically more like a midwestern than a southern state. (Louisiana had been admitted as a slaveholding state in 1812, but slavery had existed in that portion of the Louisiana Territory for almost a century, and the purchase agreement had specified that the current inhabitants maintained all their property rights, which included their enslaved men, women, and children.)

On February 13, 1819, as the House members prepared to consider the enabling legislation in response to the Missouri petition, Congressman James Tallmadge Jr. of New York took the floor and offered an amendment barring the introduction of new enslaved people into the proposed state (there were already about ten thousand there) and requiring that children born to enslaved women in the state after its admission would be freed upon reaching the age of twenty-five. With Tallmadge's unexpected proposal, the issue of slavery's expansion, if not its continuation, exploded in the halls of Congress at it had not since the brief flare-up in 1790. Most northern supporters of the amendment highlighted the immorality of slavery, with Congressman Arthur Livermore of New Hampshire arguing that now was the time, "if not to diminish, at least to prevent, the growth of a sin which sits heavy on the soul of every one of us."[24] Southern congressmen strongly repudiated such views, with Virginia congressman Thomas Cobb charging Tallmadge with having "kindled a flame which all the waters of the ocean cannot put out, which seas of blood can only extinguish."[25]

While the immorality of slavery dominated the arguments of those favoring the amendments, with claims that the outcome would "decide the destiny of millions," southern opponents at first did not mount a defense of slavery.[26] Instead, they critiqued Tallmadge on narrow constitutional grounds, arguing that the issue of slavery in a state was a matter for the people of that state to decide: emancipation could not be imposed by Congress. They recognized that the Constitution gave Congress authority over territories, but, they insisted, not over states, which would in effect preempt the citizens' decision-making right in the process of accepting the territory's request for statehood.

The vote in the House was purely sectional, with Tallmadge's amendment being divided into two parts (no additional slave imports and eventual emancipation of new-born enslaved children) with both passing, but when the decision came to the Senate, statehood was approved but not the antislavery amendments. Because neither the House nor the Senate could agree, the proposal to accept Missouri as a state lapsed when the session ended on March 4. The deadlocked Congress left the issue unresolved for the moment, but the debates continued and intensified throughout 1819. At stake, many believed, was the survival of the union. Support for the Tallmadge amendments grew in the North as antislavery forces organized meetings, published articles in newspapers, and mounted a variety of protests against slavery. Remnants of the defunct Federalist Party also saw the occasion as an opportunity to whittle away at the political power of President Monroe and the Virginians, both for genuine reasons of abolitionist principle and because they understood that by reason of the three-fifths rule, slavery benefited the political power of the South and the party founded by Jefferson and continued by Madison and Monroe. The prominent role of former Federalist presidential candidate Rufus King in opposing slavery in Missouri only confirmed the opinion of many southerners that the primary purpose of Tallmadge's amendment was to revivify the Federalist party.

As the debates pro and con roared, it became clearer that the southern position was more strongly based on proslavery sentiment than the initial opposition had suggested. Few were yet actually defending slavery as a positive good, but fewer still were expressing the kinds of antislavery views that had been common two decades earlier. Southern defensiveness solidified as northern determination grew: as one distinguished scholar has written hyperbolically, "In a sense, the Tallmadge Amendment . . . summoned the South into being."[27] In early December Jefferson wrote John Adams, mentioning the economic crisis, the bank issue, and other concerns, but, he penned, "These are occurences [*sic*] which like waves in a storm will pass under the ship. But the Missouri question is a breaker on which we lose the Missouri country by revolt, and what more, God only knows. From the battle of Bunker's hill to the treaty of Paris we never had so ominous a question."[28] Jefferson feared the controversy over slavery could destroy the union of states, which he considered the greatest imaginable calamity.

Just days before Jefferson's letter, the new session of Congress opened on December 6, 1819. This was its first meeting in the splendid new House chamber, and the first real business after organizing was a petition from Maine, a district of Massachusetts, asking to be admitted as a separate state. The matter was referred to a select committee to be chaired by Congressman John Holmes, who had introduced the petition. Then petitions were presented by John Scott again seeking admission of the Missouri Territory as a state, and he was asked to chair a committee to consider the issue. Immediately afterward, James Strong of New York put the House on notice that he would soon ask permission to propose a bill to stop the extension of slavery into any of the nation's territories but would defer for the moment. Both statehood issues proved divisive, and Congress appointed a special committee to seek a resolution, but with no solution in sight the committee gave up and asked to be discharged on December 28. Congress was at an impasse.

President Monroe was fully aware of the gravity of the situation and by early January had an intimation that a possible compromise might be devised by combining the admission of the two states and possibly adding, as a gesture to those opposed to slavery, a territorial ban of some sort. Monroe was secretive about his own role, but evidence suggests that he believed a compromise must and could be achieved to save the union from dismemberment. He was evidently active behind the scenes, writing letters and conferring with close associates. Although he had at times expressed opposition to the institution of slavery, he held men, women, and children in bondage himself, and he felt that the preservation of the union was more important than limiting the expansion of slavery. Like Jefferson and Madison, he also believed that the diffusion of enslaved people over a broader territory would simultaneously improve their condition and possibly make eventual emancipation more feasible. This idea seems farfetched today, but for men who had witnessed in their lifetimes the putting into place of processes to end bondage in northern states with low concentrations of enslaved laborers, it seemed possible.[29]

Monroe and Clay—Clay openly, Monroe more clandestinely—were busy trying to gather the votes for a compromise solution, seeking to find some way to avoid sectional disruption. But could the immediate Missouri issue be peacefully resolved? Speaker of the House Henry Clay bemoaned on January 22, 1820, that "The words, civil war, and disunion, are uttered almost without emotion."[30] Monroe, in his typically convoluted language, confided to Jefferson that "The Missouri question, absorbs by its importance, & the excitement it has produc'd, every other & there is little prospect, from present appearances of its being soon settled. The object of those, who brought it forward, was undoubtedly to acquire power."[31] Henry Clay about the same time also complained that "the Missouri subject monopolizes all our conversation, all our thoughts and for three weeks at least to come will all our time."[32]

Many southern congressmen—especially a faction from Virginia self-labeled the Richmond Junto who, long at odds with the moderate nationalism of Monroe, opposed any action by the national government to limit slavery—were adamant that no restrictions regarding slavery be imposed on Missouri (or on any of the territories).[33] Finally Senator Jesse B. Thomas of Illinois proposed a restriction on slavery more limited than that originally floated by James Strong back in December. Thomas proposed prohibiting slavery only in that portion of the Louisiana Territory that lay to the north of the southern boundary (36°30′) of Missouri, hence allowing slavery in that portion of the purchase south of Missouri. But after multiple votes the House and the Senate could not agree on the status of Missouri. Yet slowly the outlines of a solution emerged from the work of a conference committee put together for that purpose.

On March 2, Holmes of Massachusetts presented the committee's report: the joint admission of Maine and Missouri (with no restrictions as to slavery within its bounds), and the prohibition forever of slavery in that portion of the Louisiana Territory north of latitude 36°30′. Votes were cast, with the slavery restrictions on Missouri removed by a close margin of three votes. The next day, March 3, the Senate accepted the settlement. Forebodingly, nineteen of the forty-two votes in the House opposing the proposed slavery dividing line came from Virginia. Three days later, an act authorized the territory of Missouri to draft a constitution without any limitations on slavery and form a state government. Monroe assembled his cabinet and, with the assistance of

Secretary of War Calhoun, worked out a unanimous acceptance of the compromise (including the approval of Secretary of State Adams). On March 6, 1820, Monroe signed the bills that Congress had so meticulously crafted.

But the Missouri controversy did not end there because of the intransigency of the proslavery forces within the legislature of the new state-to-be and its disapproval of free Blacks. The second phase of the Missouri crisis began after the state convention, meeting in St. Louis, adopted on July 19, 1820, a constitution that contained a provision requiring the new state legislature to pass whatever laws necessary to ban free Blacks and persons deemed "mulattoes" from ever entering and settling in the state. Many outside Missouri were outraged by this provision, especially considering that in several northern states free Black Americans were legally citizens. Did the Missouri legislators really expect to be able to ban certain citizens from entering the state? Many beyond the state, including southern legislators, understood that these mandated laws flew in the face of the federal Constitution's provision (Article 4, Section 2) that "The Citizens of each State shall be entitled to all the Privileges and Immunities of the Citizens of the Several States." In response to Missouri's constitution, there arose a powerful demand that Congress not allow the admission of the state with this flagrant discrimination against Black citizens. Protesting congressmen insisted that the state constitution be rescinded, although others simply noted, as did Monroe in a letter to Madison, that because the federal Constitution nullifies "all parts of State Constitutions repugnant to it, then . . . it will nullify any part of the Constitution of a new State which may be admitted."[34]

The controversy over the offending provision of the state constitution threatened to undo the compromise that had been so painstakingly worked out earlier in the year. Henry Clay now threw his immense energy and skill into the effort to solve this problem. One aspect of it was in counting the electoral votes for the election of 1820. Because the Federalist Party had earlier collapsed and had in fact not regained strength as a result of the Missouri controversy, Monroe, with no opposition candidate, had swept to virtual unanimous electoral victory in the least contested presidential election in US history. The only debate was whether the votes of Missouri, its status as a state not yet determined, should be counted. Clay's solution was to announce two results, one including, the other excluding Missouri's electoral votes. Monroe easily won either way, with all but four electoral votes (there were three abstentions and one vote for John Quincy Adams).

Meanwhile, Clay, with consummate political skill, finally, after a series of congressional votes, committee meetings, and other efforts, persuaded Congress on March 2, 1821, to conditionally accept Missouri as a state *provided* that the state legislature promise never to actually pass laws that would abridge the privileges and immunities clause of the federal Constitution. The state reluctantly agreed to this requirement on June 26 (although it complained that Congress had no power to demand such a promise), and on August 10, President Monroe proclaimed the admission of Missouri as the twenty-fourth state.[35] Clay's indispensable role in the final resolution merited his gaining the reputation as the Great Compromiser, but Monroe's significant role in implementing the first phase of the so-called Missouri Compromise has not been sufficiently appreciated.

With the immediate controversy settled, the union was saved. Southerners claimed a victory with the admission of Missouri with no restrictions on slavery, and its entry, combined with that of Maine, preserved the balance of slave and free states—twelve of each—in the Senate. That balance was particularly important to southerners because the faster population growth in the North guaranteed ever-increasing free state domination in the House of Representatives. While many in the North saw the compromise as a defeat, in the long run more free states would be formed out of the Louisiana Purchase territory than slave states, although in truth, climate more than political compromise limited the growth of slavery in the northern portion of the territory. But the whole controversy had made the slavery issue a critical factor in American politics.

Conditions external to the actual issue of Missouri greatly exacerbated the effects of the controversy. The economic collapse that came to a head in 1818–19 and particularly the drastic calling in of loans by the Bank of the United States, disproportionately damaged the economy of the southern states, and they interpreted the bank's actions as sectionally discriminatory. Moreover, a major Supreme Court decision in 1819, *McCulloch v. Maryland* (examined in more detail in the following chapter), contained language by Chief Justice John Marshall that struck fear among many southerners, especially those influenced by the reactionary Richmond Junto, because its justification of expanding the powers of the federal government raised worries that among those expanded powers could someday be a threat to the continuation of slavery.

Amid these economic and legal concerns, Tallmadge's 1819 amendment had fallen like a bombshell, igniting southern fears of a concerted northern effort to limit or end the institution of slavery. A possible slave revolt planned by Denmark Vesey, a free Black man, in Charleston in 1822, further enflamed southern white fears, especially as it became known that in part Vesey had been inspired by a powerful antislavery speech and pamphlet by Federalist Rufus King. Decades earlier, leaders such as Jefferson, Madison, and Monroe had primarily been concerned over a split between the western and the seaboard states—that is what had made so controversial the debates over the proposed Jay-Gardoqui treaty and the Jay Treaty in the 1780s and 1790s, respectively, that threatened to close western commerce via the Mississippi River.

After 1819, the fear was over a split based on slavery that divided the southern and northern states. The South had become a defensive, self-conscious section quick to sense multiple threats.

Monroe continued to engage the affairs of his administration head on. Not as intellectual as either Jefferson or Madison, and no prose stylist, Monroe was hardworking and politically astute. Unlike modern presidents, he did not use patronage, or appeals to the public, to pressure congressional leaders, although he did hope the members of his cabinet would use their personal contacts to advance his administration policies. And he often employed his annual messages to shape legislative initiatives.[36] Monroe carefully considered the issues, domestic and international, he met in his role as president, and he deeply believed in the moral stance of the nation vis-à-vis the world community.

In that context, he had felt for years that the nation should support the independence aspirations of the South American nations that were declaring their freedom from Spain in a wave of revolutions sweeping the continent. He had initially hesitated to promote US recognition of them because he did not want to complicate the ongoing negotiations with Spain over the Florida territory and finalization of the western boundary of the Louisiana Purchase. However, the Senate confirmed the Transcontinental Treaty in February 1821. So in March 1822, Monroe sent a message to Congress recommending recognition of the various South American nations that had proclaimed their independence. Monroe himself did so—making the United States the first nation to recognize the new states—without consultation with Spain or any other European nations and without giving them advance notice. It was a bold international move, but Monroe felt confident in the realm of diplomacy and believed the United States was riding the arc of history.[37]

That is one of the reasons he got along so well with his sometimes difficult secretary of state, the brilliant John Quincy Adams. Adams fervently shared Monroe's belief in the nation's special role in the world as the exemplar of liberty and democracy. Perhaps because earlier in his career Adams had been the first US minister to Russia, he was especially alert to Czar Alexander I's increasing desires to promote Russian interests along the Pacific coast of North America, particularly after Alexander issued a decree in 1821 claiming exclusive trading rights along the coastline (and there already was a Russian fort on Bodega Bay in California). Spying a threat to the United States in the czar's ambitions, Adams on July 17, 1823, sent a strongly worded message to the Russian minister in Washington warning that "we should contest the right of Russia to *any* territorial establishment on this continent, and that we should assume distinctly the principle that the American continents are no longer subjects for any new European colonial establishments."[38] Adams shortly after sent essentially the same message to the British ambassador. Adams's missives had little effect other than irritating both Russia and Britain, but neither responded to his firm stand.

Adams could not know that George Canning, the British foreign secretary, was simultaneously worried about possible French involvement in South America, for at the moment a French army was in Spain putting down a popular rebellion against the Spanish monarchy. British officials worried that France (or other European powers, the so-called Holy Alliance, who were similarly determined to strengthen the regimes of monarchs) might be contemplating interference in South America either to help restore the former Spanish colonies or gain them for themselves. In order to create a united front against such European expansionism, Canning had informally proposed in writing to the American minister to Britain, Richard Rush, that the United States join his nation in proclaiming a set of principles declaring that henceforth no European powers should become involved with any of the former Spanish colonies. Canning's principles also included one stating, "We aim not at the possession of any portion of them ourselves," which may have reflected British fears that the United States might have eyes on Cuba.[39]

Rush instantly realized that this stunning proposal—that the United States and its former enemy unite in opposition to theoretical actions by other European powers, the United States obviously depending on the power of the British navy to enforce any such policy—was a matter for the president to decide. Accordingly he sent Canning's note to Washington, where it arrived on October 9, 1823. The proposal immediately raised profound issues, for central to US policy for decades had been the commitment, articulated in both Washington's Farewell Address and Jefferson's first inaugural, of having, with regard to other nations, "entangling alliances with none."

Monroe had a strong consultative relationship with his cabinet members and with his presidential predecessors. On October 17, he sent Jefferson a letter, along with two documents outlining Canning's proposal, stating, "My own impression is that we ought to meet the proposal of the British govt. & to make it known, that we would view an interference on the part of the European powers . . . as an attack on ourselves."[40] He asked Jefferson to forward the letter along with the documents on to Madison because he wanted his opinion also. Jefferson replied a week later, beginning by restating what he took to be the bedrock of US policy. "Our first and fundamental maxim should be, never to entangle ourselves in the broils of Europe. Our second, never to suffer Europe to intermeddle with cis-Atlantic affairs." That said, "One nation, most of all, could disturb us in this pursuit; she now offers to lead, aid, and accompany us in it. By acceding to her proposition, we . . . bring her mighty weight into the scale of free government, and emancipate a continent at one stroke. . . . I could honestly, therefore, join in the declaration proposed."[41] Reversing years of antipathy toward Britain, Jefferson now approved its proposal. Madison later agreed, writing Monroe on October 30, that with Britain's cooperation the United States had "nothing to fear from the rest of Europe" and "with it the best reliance on success to our just & laudable views. There ought not to be any backwardness, therefore, I think, in meeting her in the way she has proposed."[42] Madison commented to Jefferson that, with Britain's support, "in the great struggle of the Epoch between liberty and despotism, we owe it to ourselves to sustain the former in this hemisphere at least."[43] Monroe was no doubt heartened by the support of Jefferson and Madison, but he did not need their advice to know what he wanted to do, and as he gathered his cabinet to consider his response, he did not share with them the letters he had received from his predecessors.

The discussion was spirited. Monroe, reflecting Secretary of War Calhoun's views, was genuinely worried about French interference, but Secretary of State Adams dismissed this possibility. Monroe did not want to respond in such a way that suggested a dependence on Britain, a view Adams strongly agreed with. As Adams put it, he did not want the United States to appear "as a cock-boat in the wake of the British man-of-war."[44] Monroe wanted to make the announcement unilaterally as a bold statement of American resolve. Monroe also wished to, in effect, lecture Europe about the virtues of the US system of government and offer support to the freedom rebels of Greece, but Attorney General William Wirt successfully argued against unnecessarily antagonizing European governments.

Adams most vigorously argued in support of the United States declaring its defense of the right of this hemisphere to be free of European interference, but this was already Monroe's view. For him, the statement had to communicate the moral purpose of the US position. While Monroe accepted a great deal that Adams wrote, he insisted on maintaining much of his own language. Adams's important role has often been exaggerated because scholars have so depended upon his extensive diaries for documentation. His advice was essential and formative, but Monroe's own positions were determinative, especially the decision to make the policy public by means of his annual message to Congress on December 2, 1823.[45] In that format it did not require congressional approval.

The annual message discussed a wide range of topics, everything from internal improvements to a characterization of the African slave trade as piracy, and the paragraphs outlining what eventually became known as the Monroe Doctrine are separated from one another by many pages. Early in the text, after a brief reference to negotiations with Russia over trade interests in the far Northwest, came these words, obviously borrowed from Secretary of State Adams:

> The occasion has been judged proper for asserting, as a principle in which the rights and interests of the United States are involved, that the American continents, by the free and independent condition which they have assumed and maintain, are henceforth not to be considered as subjects for future colonization by any European powers.[46]

After this forthright announcement followed a rather routine discussion of various topics, then a statement of hope on behalf of the current Greek struggle for independence but no indication of any action to help them achieve that event. "In the wars of the European powers in matters relating to themselves we have never taken any part, nor does it comport with our policy so to do." But, and this was the crux of the statement, "With the movements in this hemisphere we are of necessity more immediately connected, and by causes which must be obvious to all enlightened and impartial observers."

> We owe it, therefore, to candor and to the amicable relations existing between the United States and those powers to declare that we should consider any attempt on their part to extend their system to any portion of this hemisphere as dangerous to our peace and safety. With the existing colonies or dependencies of any European power we have not interfered and shall not interfere. But with the Governments who have declared their independence and maintained it, and whose Independence we have, on great consideration and on just principles, acknowledged, we could not view any interposition for the purpose of oppressing them, or controlling in any other manner their destiny, by any European power in any other light than as the manifestation of an unfriendly disposition toward the United States.[47]

These two extracts from Monroe's annual message of 1823 would after 1850 become known as the Monroe Doctrine, and they were instantly greeted throughout the nation with pride and self-confidence even as they rankled the European powers. But they observed the warning to keep their hands off the American hemisphere—in actuality, British naval power enforced the concept—and the doctrine shaped US foreign policy for the next century. As the leading scholar of the topic has written, "the message was a brilliant diplomatic document," and it remains the major accomplishment of Monroe's presidency.[48]

Four of the nation's first five presidents had been Virginians, and Monroe was the third in a row. Their instincts had been fundamentally nationalistic, they had developed a workable and financially solvent government, seen the country expand to the Pacific, weathered a severe economic crisis, and established a stable diplomatic policy vis-à-vis Europe, but underneath their feet the political landscape was shifting in Virginia. They did not fully comprehend that the country had entered the beginning of a sectional conflict that would shape the coming decades and, temporarily at least, disrupt their nation-building project. A small but influential group of state politicians called the Richmond Junto that had earlier in the century largely backed Jefferson's policies and the mild nationalism of his successors had gradually become disenchanted with various central government decisions and the evident growing influence of the Supreme Court. Over time these leading Virginia politicians, focusing narrowly upon the state's perceived interests, broke with Monroe and the tradition he represented, and year by year they became increasingly more states-rightist in orientation, more hardened in their views, and less willing to accept change in any form. A dark cloud was gathering on the horizon, barely noticeable at first.

14

INSTITUTION BUILDERS

Perhaps the chief irony of the presidency of James Monroe was that this man who did not believe in political parties and hoped they would disappear found out that without the discipline that opposition parties imposed, political factionalism metastasized. Early in his second term, when every politically ambitious man knew Monroe would not break what was already the tradition of only serving two terms, backbiting and jousting for possible electoral advantage began within his administration. Secretary of State John Quincy Adams, aware that his position had often been a stepping-stone to the presidency, assumed it was his right, but Secretary of War John C. Calhoun was equally ambitious. Secretary of the Treasury William H. Crawford, from Georgia but a favorite of the conservative Virginia power bloc, thought he deserved the position, but so did Speaker of the House Henry Clay. And then there was military hero Senator Andrew Jackson from Tennessee. Unlike the previous transitions in 1808 and 1816, no dominant Virginia statesman stood in line to follow Monroe. In fact, the era of Virginia dominance was ending.

Monroe faced bickering and maneuvering almost nonstop. As he wrote James Madison in mid-1822, "I have never known such a state of things as has existed here during the last Session, nor have I personally ever experienced so much embarrassment and mortification. . . . The approaching election . . . excites greatest interest. . . . There being three avowed candidates in the administration is a circumstance which increases the embarrassment. The friends of each endeavor to annoy the others."[1] And he was talking here only about the three rivals in his cabinet, not counting Clay and Jackson on the outside. This competition made a mockery of the characterization of the age as the "era of good feelings." For those reasons the president looked forward even more than most Americans, in late summer 1824, to the celebratory visit of Revolutionary War hero Marquis de Lafayette, who Monroe had first met in 1777.

The fabled general was on a year-long tour to all twenty-four states as the "nation's guest," and as he traveled about the United States, he was feted with unabashed affection. The whole journey was a combination of nationalism and patriotic reminiscence that, at least for intervals, banished the partisanship that broiled the political scene. Arriving in Staten Island on August 15 with his son and a private secretary named Auguste Levasseur, Lafayette first traveled about New England and then worked his way south through Pennsylvania and Maryland, arriving in Washington on October 12 for the first of two visits, this initial one of only five days before traveling southward.

The night of his arrival, Lafayette and his entourage came to the White House. At his entrance into the large room where Monroe and other public officials were seated, the president, in the words of Lafayette's secretary, "advanced eagerly to meet him, embraced him with fraternal tenderness, then came to us and shook us kindly by the hand." Monroe said he knew the general was in Washington as the city's guest and so they had a room for him at a hotel and a grand dinner planned, but he extended an offer to the general to "consider my house as your own; you will always find your places ready at my table, and I wish whenever you have no engagements with the citizens, that you will dine with me."[2]

The next day at the festive public dinner for the general, Monroe brought his wife, two daughters, and sons-in-law to greet the visitors, and Levasseur noted, "We found throughout the family, the same cordiality and simplicity, which distinguished the president."[3] The Monroes had first met Lafayette and wife Adrienne socially in France in the 1790s, and amid the political turmoil and violence of the French Revolution, they had saved the lives of Adrienne and her three children, with Elizabeth Monroe risking her own safety to get Adrienne released from prison. So the affection and friendship between the Monroes and Lafayette were genuine and long-standing.[4] Monroe regretted that he could not travel to Charlottesville on November 8 to attend the banquet at the soon-to-be-opened new university where both Thomas Jefferson and James Madison would honor General Lafayette.

Before the nation's guest returned to Washington, the election results of 1824 had begun the post-Monroe era. In an age before there was active campaigning, Monroe was determined to be scrupulously neutral amid the political maneuvering, though he privately felt Adams to be the most qualified. Calhoun, sizing up the crowded field, had withdrawn from the presidential race and was seeking the vice presidency. During the year, Crawford suffered a debilitating stroke, effectively eliminating him from real consideration by those who were well informed, but not the voting public. Adams of course was strong in New England (then called the East), while Clay and Jackson divided the West.

Jackson had more popular votes than any of the other candidates, and when the electoral votes were tabulated, Jackson had 99, Adams 84, Crawford 41, and Clay 37. (Calhoun had easily won the vice presidency.) Since no one had a majority of the electoral votes, the contest shifted to the House, which would choose the winner from the top three candidates, with each state having one vote. Clay, whose nationalism synched with that of Adams and with whom he shared diplomatic experience, favored the New Englander, especially since Clay worried about Jackson's militarism. Clay and Adams talked several times before the House decision, but almost certainly no "bargain" was sought. Those in favor of various candidates had conferred and cajoled, but on the first vote, Adams won the approval of 13 states, Jackson 7, and Crawford (though disabled) 4.

It was a stunning upset for Jackson, and when Adams promptly chose Clay to be his secretary of state, an angry Jackson was quick to charge Adams and Clay with having engaged in a "corrupt bargain."[5] It soon became clear that a new age of political intrigue had begun, with Jackson looking ahead to the election of 1828. This was the beginning of the so-called second party system, and it also saw the House being eclipsed in importance by the Senate, where for the next three decades senatorial giants like Daniel Webster, Jackson, Clay, and Calhoun would dominate the political scene. Monroe's active career was over.

In his last annual message to Congress, on December 7, 1824, Monroe reported that "the situation of the United States is in the highest degree prosperous and happy. There is no object which as a people we can desire which we do not possess or which is not within our reach." He spoke here, of course, only with reference to the white population. He continued, "Blessed with governments the happiest the world ever knew. . . . Our institutions form an important epoch in the history of the civilized world."[6] He took comfort in having spent much of his life in service to the cause of the nation. He would be gratified too, three months later, when John Quincy Adams generously praised him and acknowledged his contributions in his augural address. And then on August 6, 1825, President Adams, accompanied by the visiting General Lafayette, journeyed the thirty-seven miles outside Washington to visit Monroe at his home plantation, Oak Hill, in Loudon County, where they reminisced and celebrated Monroe's life and accomplishments over the course of a long dinner.

A few weeks later Monroe traveled with Lafayette to Monticello for a final visit with the ailing Jefferson, who proved to be too weak to attend a dinner planned for him that evening.[7] Jefferson somehow regained his strength and lived almost another year. He died on July 4, 1826, as did John Adams; it was the fiftieth anniversary of the Declaration of Independence. It was evident that Virginia's time of prominence in the life of the nation was over.

In addition to the praise Monroe received from President Adams in August 1825, Chief Justice John Marshall also provided a warm encomium to the retiring president.[8] Of the prominent men, and certainly Virginians alive who had been active since the revolution, Marshall was the most vigorous in 1825 and the only one still in government service. His contribution to the nation's development equaled that of his distinguished Virginia presidential colleagues. Marshall and Monroe had known each other almost their entire lives, from their schoolboy days together at the Reverend Archibald Campbell's academy in Westmoreland County; bunking in the same cabin at Valley Forge; participating (on opposing sides) at the Virginia Ratification Convention, at the time as up-and-coming lawyers; then as members of Congress, with Monroe a committed Jeffersonian and Marshall just as firm a Federalist. Later as chief justice of the Supreme Court, Marshall had administered the oaths of office to presidents Jefferson, Madison, and Monroe.[9]

Marshall had briefly studied law in 1780 at the College of William and Mary with the legendary George Wythe, who had been Jefferson's mentor, and at Wythe's direction Marshall became intimately acquainted with William Blackstone's *Commentaries on the Laws of England,* a 1775 compilation of immense influence. Marshall soon passed the bar and entered practice in Richmond, where the city's leading lawyer and Virginia's attorney general from 1776 to 1778, Edmund Randolph, took him under his wing, making him essentially a junior partner. Ironically, Randolph's career had been accelerated in 1774 when Jefferson, deciding to leave the active practice of law, handed all his cases over to Randolph. Then in 1786, when Randolph was elected governor, he turned all his cases over to Marshall.

That proved a boon to the young Marshall, who also benefited from the fact that his father-in-law, Jaquelin Ambler (Marshall had married Polly Ambler in January 1783), was the treasurer of the state and one of the leading citizens of Virginia. The combined mentorship and patronage of Randolph and Ambler ensured Marshall quick prominence at the bar of Virginia and a sure—and rapidly growing—income. Marshall often argued before the Virginia Court of Appeals, where the senior judge was Edmund Pendleton, whose style of decision writing, short on legal citations but well-grounded in legal principles and logic, later characterized Marshall's decisions. It would be from Pendleton that Marshall adopted the practice of having the senior judge write for the entire court rather than having the individual judges issue separate decisions.[10] Unlike many of his contemporaries who were planters first and lawyers second, Marshall was a pioneer of the occupation of professional lawyer.

As Marshall's case load grew and his income soared, he became a leader of the Virginia establishment. Marshall, like George Washington, was an extremely aggressive land speculator, and he bought as many acres as he could afford. His total purchases in Kentucky, aided by his father having moved to the state as a land surveyor, totaled more than two hundred thousand acres, and between the late 1790s and 1806, through his legal acumen and persistence, he managed to acquire thousands of acres of land in northern Virginia that had originally been part of Lord Fairfax's colonial estate. He also regularly bought enslaved people during these years.[11] Marshall's immense holdings in land and people would later support his comfortable lifestyle after he gave up the practice of the law to serve on the Supreme Court. But despite his ample income, Marshall never lost the common touch and his congeniality, and he quickly rose in the ranks of the Federalist Party even in the heart of Jefferson country.

Washington especially came to like him. Consequently Marshall, with his ability, connections, and political astuteness, by the mid-1790s was a rising star in national politics, a status cemented by the good judgment he had demonstrated in 1797–98 as a member of the aborted mission to France that collapsed as a response to the so-called XYZ Affair. That experience led John Adams on May 7, 1800, to appoint Marshall as secretary of state and then, on January 20, 1801, to the position of chief justice of the Supreme Court. He was confirmed a week later, taking the oath of office on February 4. For the next thirty-four years, Marshall held that position, transforming the Supreme Court into a true equal partner of the other two branches of the government. The length of his tenure and the significance of his legal decisions make Marshall one of the leading figures in American history.

Several factors help explain Justice Marshall's towering influence, and one is the obvious physical hardiness that allowed him to sit on the court for more than three decades. Unlike presidents, who could serve only eight years because of the unspoken rule that they step down after two terms, justices serve as long as good behavior and physical competence allows. Had Marshall, for example, been required to step down after eight years, he would be known only for one important case, *Marbury v. Madison,* delivered in 1803. Instead, he served the equivalent of eight presidential terms, into the administration of Andrew Jackson. In addition, presidents have to handle every issue that arises, from international controversies and wars to domestic problems and economic depressions. The justices of the Supreme Court confront a much narrower range of issues and to some extent pick those they wish to engage, though during Marshall's tenure they had less control over their cases then than they do now.

The Supreme Court at the beginning of Marshall's term had, in addition to him, only five members, a number that increased to six in 1807 when another circuit court was established comprising the states of Kentucky, Ohio, and Tennessee. The early Supreme Court considered surprisingly few cases, only sixty-three in the years 1790–1800 combined, though its case load grew significantly over the next decades.[12] Before Marshall's arrival, the various judges tended to issue separate decisions seriatim even when they basically agreed. Marshall, following the practice of Judge Pendleton of the Virginia Court of Appeals, determined to meld the various decisions into one unified opinion, and he wrote most of the important ones for three decades. He understood that one unified decision, *the opinion of the court,* representing the voice of the entire court, carried more weight—seemed more authoritative—than a variety of individual arguments even if they came to the same effect.

The court met for about two months in Washington annually, and at Marshall's insistence, the judges (who did not bring their families with them) all lived together in the same boardinghouse, where they read the court documents, discussed the cases in detail, and worked out their decisions. In this comfortable, clubby atmosphere, living and dining together, the contours of the cases were discussed, complicating issues examined, differences overcome, arguments perfected. Then Marshall, employing the strength of his personality, the power of his mind, and the perspicuity of his writing, always performed with a quill pen, shaped the court's unitary decision.[13]

The judges had no interns, and they were without the use of a strong law library. The court had such a low status in 1801 that it met in a single, undistinguished room on the first floor of the Capitol Building, with no offices adjacent and no secretary. (A more handsome courtroom was provided after 1810.) The judges on the whole were moderate, especially after the death of Samuel Chase in mid-1811, and none of the justices appointed by Jefferson, Madison, and Monroe represented ideological extremes. They worked together harmoniously in a deliberative, judicious, and nonpartisan fashion. Marshall did not force uniformity, and in fact he sometimes changed his own opinion in the midst of conferring with his colleagues, or even muted his opposition to a position in order to achieve a compromise common agreement. And after Madison named Joseph Story to replace the combative Chase in early 1812, Marshall gained a particularly congenial colleague whose moderation and legal acumen matched his own.

Marshall possessed the vision and skill to mold the court into an effective institution for the first time. Writing 49 percent of the court's majority opinions during his long career, 59 percent of the constitutional law decisions, and practically all the important ones, he in effect made the Supreme Court a coequal branch of the US government.[14] Yet the court during the Marshall years rendered no famous decisions dealing with the contentious issue of slavery, and in no case did it address directly the constitutionality of the institution. In the fourteen relatively unknown cases concerning Black freemen, Marshall wrote seven of the opinions, and in each case the freed people lost. Here as elsewhere he always ruled in favor of property rights.[15]

The first major decision rendered by the Marshall court, *Marbury v. Madison,* we have already discussed in chapter 10. This famous case, known because it gave the widely accepted concept of judicial review the imprimatur of the Supreme Court, did not represent an original legal doctrine, and in fact the results of the case—the overturning of an act of Congress on the basis of its unconstitutionality—was the first and *only* time the Marshall court so ruled. The great bulk of the court's decisions supported or even expanded upon congressional legislation. It worked primarily to limit the impact of state legislation and enhanced the role of the national government, which is what ultimately caused the court's decisions to threaten conservative, states' rights advocates such as the members of the Richmond Junto. It is ironic that the sole decision the Marshall court made to strike down congressional legislation should for many later observers be seen as emblematic of his legacy. If Marshall's reputation rested on that single famous decision, he would be relatively inconsequential. But, to emphasize the point, he wrote almost half the total decisions during his tenure and most of the important ones, and in that larger record is to be found his significance to US constitutional history.

The next landmark case, *Fletcher v. Peck* (1810), in contrast to *Marbury v. Madison,* nullified the legislation of a *state,* the first of several important cases to do so. It had its origin in an act perpetrated by a corrupt Georgia legislature (every legislator save one had accepted a bribe) to sell some thirty-five million acres of the state's western lands—basically the territory that makes up Alabama and Mississippi today, the so-called Yazoo lands—to four New England land companies for one and a half cents an acre.[16] The corruption of the original deal was so stark that outrage quickly mushroomed in the state, and the following year, 1796, a completely new legislature rescinded the act. But in the meantime, the New England land companies had quickly sold hundreds of thousands of acres of their newly purchased lands to dozens of innocent purchasers. The New England Mississippi Land Company, for example, of which John Peck was a director, had busily been offering smaller plots for sale, and one of the early purchasers was Robert Fletcher of New Hampshire, who had bought fifteen thousand acres from Peck.

In 1803 Fletcher sued Peck on the grounds that his ownership was now questionable. Had the 1796 rescinding act invalidated Peck's title to the land that he had subsequently sold to Fletcher? Because of this uncertainty, Fletcher demanded his money back. Almost certainly this was a prearranged suit, the two having colluded because they wanted to legally establish their land titles in the aftermath of the rescinding act. Both sides in 1803 hired high-powered lawyers, the able, but often inebriated, Luther Martin arguing for Fletcher (once Martin was so drunk that Marshall adjourned the court until he sobered up) and Robert Goodloe Harper and Joseph Story for Peck. The circuit court ruled for Peck in 1807, but the case was appealed to the Supreme Court in 1809, set aside because of a technicality, and re-appealed in 1810. It is somewhat puzzling that the court agreed to hear an almost certainly put-up case, but Marshall, who was a land speculator at heart, may have bent over backward to have a decision made that privileged the interests of private speculators over a state and thereby protected land titles. Marshall wrote the final decision, and it is clear that he had had to employ all his persuasive skills to meld a unanimous opinion from among his court brethren. The result was a resounding victory for the sanctity of contracts to the benefit of private property interests.

In the *Peck* decision, Marshall deftly handled a series of controversial issues.[17] First he reasoned that there was nothing in the Georgia state constitution that limited the authority of the Georgia legislature to sell state acreage to the New England companies. He said whether there was corruption involved in the original legislative act was a matter for politics, not the court, to decide. (He ignored the fact that politics *had* decided the matter with the result that a new legislature in 1796 voided the 1795 land sales.) Then he came to the matter of the presumably innocent third-party land purchasers. Their interests had, for the sake of fairness, to be protected, and Marshall did this by enlarging the meaning of a clause in the federal Constitution. Part of a sentence in Article 1, Section 10, reads that "No State . . . [may] pass . . . [a] Law impairing the Obligation of Contracts." Hitherto it had been assumed that this referred to contracts between private individuals. But, borrowing from Blackstone, Marshall reasoned that the 1795 grants of land had been in effect contracts, and that these original public contracts, which underwrote the purchase agreements that private individuals made subsequently, were also protected by the Constitution. Hence the 1796 legislation, intended by the Georgia legislature to correct the fraudulent 1795 land sales, in fact had damaged the implied contracts involving the original land sales, and in doing so had violated the constitutional prohibitions against impairing contracts.

On that ground, he declared the 1796 Georgia legislation unconstitutional, giving a major victory to the land speculators. Here Marshall, speaking with the authority of the Supreme Court, put the sanctity of contracts beyond state legislative reach, protecting individual property rights, and he dissolved the legal differences between public and private contracts: both were protected by the Constitution. He was seeking to create what might be called a legal environment in which title deeds were secure and, by extension, so were a wide range of commercial negotiations. In fact, as a leading scholar has written of the case, Marshall "spent his professional life making law serve those who had property and wanted to get more or keep what they had."[18] But this was not a controversial position. James Madison and most of his fellow Republicans also believed that property was an essential part of the "foundation of civil liberty and a free society."[19]

Marshall never missed a court session over the course of his long career, and he wrote dozens of decisions of varying degrees of significance. But in the year 1819 he wrote three opinions of monumental influence, though their import may not have been fully realized at the moment. *Dartmouth College v. Woodward,* delivered on February 2, was the first, and its origins lay in the colonial past. Dartmouth College had been granted a charter by King George III in 1769 as a private educational institution in New Hampshire, and it was governed by a self-perpetuating board of trustees. Over time the board became completely Federalist even as the state, after 1800, became dominated by the Republicans. In 1816 a newly elected Republican governor, deciding the college no longer reflected the state's values, pushed the legislature to pass an act establishing a board of overseers, to be appointed by the governor, that would have control of the trustees and in effect change the private Dartmouth College into a state-run Dartmouth University.

The trustees, understandably upset, took the matter to the state courts, and their able lawyers, including Daniel Webster, argued, among other things, that their 1769 act of incorporation was in effect a contract and therefore could not, by reason of the contract clause of the Constitution, be overturned. In the eighteenth century, corporations had usually been for specific, mostly economic enterprises and subject to a good bit of government regulation. The counsel for the trustees argued that their corporation had been intended for private and charitable (or "eleemosynary") purposes and hence should be seen as protected from interference (or "impairment"), as the Constitution put it. The state court ruled against the trustees, and the case eventually came before the Supreme Court in 1818, where, in an impassioned oration that brought the judges to tears, Webster famously argued on behalf of the trustees that "It is, Sir, as I have said, a small college. *And yet there are those who love it.*"[20]

In 1818 there still was some disagreement on the court, so Marshall decided to hold the decision over to the next year. Marshall was able in the meantime to shape a majority opinion (although two judges wrote concurring opinions and there was a silent dissent), surprising court watchers when he announced a decision on February 2, 1819, at the very beginning of the next session. The lower court had accepted the lawyers' argument that the charter constituted a contract, but since the purpose of the college affected the public, the court ruled the contract was a public one, not a private matter, and hence was subject to state regulation. Marshall began his argument modestly, declaring "in no doubtful case, would it [the Supreme Court] pronounce a legislative act to be contrary to the constitution."[21] Then in what was essentially a long essay, with only two incidental citations, he proceeded to assert that clearly the charter was a contract, and although it involved the citizens of the state, it was without doubt a "private eleemosynary institution"; the contributions to it "were made not indeed to make a profit for the donors or their posterity, but for something in their opinion of inestimable value." Hence this was no public corporation but rather a private charity institution, whose founding charter met the definition of private contract as meant by the plain words of the Constitution. The act of the state of New Hampshire to change the nature of the institution, accordingly, was—in Marshall's phrase—"repugnant to the constitution of the United States."[22] But in the process of coming to this conclusion, Marshall argued in a more general sense that a corporation possessed "immortality," was "a perpetual succession of individuals . . . capable of acting for the promotion of [a] particular object." "It is no more a state instrument, than a natural person exercising the same powers would be."[23]

This is why the decision was so important. The court, by declaring corporations to be perpetual and inviolable by state governments, made them safe instruments for the aggregation of private investment, with, as successive legislative enactment provided, limited individual liability. As such, the corporation became the favored mechanism for economic development, and within a decade thousands of corporations were founded for an incredible variety of purposes. Marshall doubtless did not foresee this subsequent development, but the *Dartmouth College* case unleashed decades of unparalleled economic growth in the nation.[24]

Two weeks later the court issued another opinion, this one carefully calibrated to meet the economic crisis at hand that saw many thousands of people destitute and companies in ruin. While the Constitution, in Article 1, Section 8, gave Congress the power to establish "uniform Laws on the subject of Bankruptcies throughout the United States," no such law had been passed except one valid temporarily for the period 1800–1803. At the current moment, in the midst of the Panic of 1819, no national bankruptcy law was in effect. But it was not clear legally if that meant that no state could pass bankruptcy laws, which did exist in England and had been enacted in the colonial period. In this situation of legal uncertainty, New York in 1811 had passed a law that allowed debtors to declare bankruptcy, assign their existing property to their creditors, and thereafter be free of their obligations. As it turned out, just *before* the act passed, a merchant, Richard Crowninshield, had borrowed a little over fifteen hundred dollars from one Josiah Sturgis (whose name would be misspelled in the official court records). Several months later, Crowninshield's business failed, whereupon he declared bankruptcy according to the 1811 act, handed over his assets, which did not fully cover his debts, and thus released from other penalties, moved to Massachusetts and subsequently prospered. When in 1816 Sturgis sued Crowninshield to recover the remainder of his debt, Crowninshield claimed that he had met his obligations according to New York law. The case came to the Supreme Court amid the economic collapse of 1818–19 when many financially devastated men faced a similar dilemma.

Marshall's written decision in *Sturges v. Crowninshield* actually concealed the difference of opinion among his judicial colleagues. Marshall ruled that in the absence of a national bankruptcy law, it was permissible for the states to legislate for such exigencies. Marshall here compromised his own principles because, given the economic plight of the nation, bankruptcy laws were simply convenient if they were not absolutely necessary. Pragmatism had triumphed. But while he would bend on the permissibility of bankruptcy laws, he would not on the sanctity of contracts. Any law that compromised the validity of a contract, he wrote, was impermissible, but the decision was narrowly "confined," as Marshall wrote, "to the case actually under consideration."[25] That is, the court ruled against bankruptcy acts when applied to contracts written *before* the act was passed.

The court did not explicitly prohibit bankruptcy acts' application to contracts drawn up *after* passage of such acts, so there still was some ambiguity about their legitimacy. But over the next few years, lower courts and state legislatures, enmeshed in the economic trauma of the Panic of 1819, pushed to more regularly accept bankruptcy laws when explicitly applied prospectively. Marshall had grudgingly accepted the ambiguity in order to forge a unanimous decision in 1819, but he still in his heart of hearts believed in the inviolability of contracts. Eight years later, in a related case, *Ogden v. Saunders,* the court ruled four-to-three explicitly in favor of bankruptcy laws when applied to contracts written after the particular act was passed, and here, for the first time in his entire judicial career, Marshall dissented. Nevertheless, the availability of bankruptcy laws, like the new understanding of corporations, helped make possible the growth of the American economy.

Then on March 6, 1819, Marshall announced a blockbuster court opinion, *McCulloch v. Maryland,* one of the most significant in his career, and it ignited a firestorm of opposition. The charter of the original Bank of the United States, whose beginning had initiated such controversy in the first Washington administration, had elapsed in 1811, but over the next few years its financial utility to the operation of the government had become obvious. Eventually, with the strong support of President Madison (who had so opposed the first bank), a Second Bank of the United States was chartered by Congress in 1816 and opened the following year. Soon there were eighteen branch banks in various cities, and this bank, in truth not carefully administered, freely dispensed loans to underwrite an expansionist flurry throughout the nation. Then, when the economic bubble began to deflate in 1818, the bank, in a rush, began to call in its loans to dozens of businesses and state banks, particularly in the South and West, a contraction that exacerbated the economic disaster and created great anger in those regions toward the "monster" bank.

A hostile Maryland legislature responded by slapping a tax on the activities of the Baltimore branch of the Bank of the United States. When William M'Culloch (the actual spelling of his name, but the court reporter misspelled it *McCulloch*), the cashier of the Baltimore bank, issued notes without paying the tax, the state of Maryland sued him. The state won at the first court level, then the decision was appealed to the Maryland Court of Appeals, and from there it went to the Supreme Court. Everyone recognized the importance of this case, and both sides lawyered up with the best counsel money could hire. In fact, the case may have been manufactured because the business and merchant class of Baltimore strongly supported a national bank that could stabilize the currency and control the issuance of loans, and they desired to have the bank backed by the mandate of the Supreme Court.

The case was argued for nine days before the court, beginning on February 22, 1819, with the old but still effective Luther Martin representing the state and Daniel Webster, William Wirt, and the talented William Pinkney defending the bank. After the uncommonly high level of legal disputation was finished, in only three days, on March 6, Marshall announced his lengthy decision. He must have begun writing it before the court hearings were finished even though much of his argument was shaped to counter the state's presentation. The result, delivered in vivid prose and completely clear of legal citations, was a powerful defense of the legality of the bank, the primacy of the federal government, and an expansive view of federal power, with phrases, sentences, and paragraphs that became famous in American legal discourse.

Marshall quickly dismissed the questioning of the bank's constitutionality, pointing out that it had twice been approved by Congress (in 1791 and 1816) and signed by two presidents. He also had little patience for the state's position that the Constitution was originally the product of the action of the several states. Marshall replied that it had been approved by the people of all the states in various ratifying conventions, and the document itself began with the phrase, "We the people." Marshall emphasized that "The government proceeds directly from the people; is 'ordained and established' in the name of the people."[26] Moreover, though the government is one of only "enumerated powers," "it is supreme within its sphere of action." Consequently, "its laws, when made in pursuance of the constitution, form the supreme law of the land, 'any thing in the constitution or laws of any state to the contrary notwithstanding.'" But the Constitution does not attempt to outline every last detail of the actual process of governing, otherwise it would be outrageously prolix.

So in their wisdom, the drafters of the nation's foundational document had left it to Congress to work out the "necessary means for the execution of the powers conferred on the government." Laws "necessary and proper for carrying into execution" the legitimate powers of government were foreseen by the drafters to have to be enacted by later legislators, but, drawing on the writings of Alexander Hamilton during the first debates over the national bank, Marshall elaborated on the meaning of *necessary*.[27] It did not mean *absolutely essential* but rather *useful or convenient,* giving a wide range of authority to the national government to enact laws "beneficial to the people." "Let the end be legitimate, let it be within the scope of the constitution," Marshall wrote, "and all the means which are appropriate, which are plainly adapted to that end, which are not prohibited, but consist with the letter and spirit of the constitution, are constitutional."[28] No one had ever defined the principle of implied powers more forcefully or more broadly.

With the bank's legitimacy established, Marshall then turned to define a state's authority to levy taxes, which he said was obviously appropriate but only as regards the people and property of that state. No state could tax property in another state, and certainly no state would submit to another state's taxing its people. No state's authority extended beyond its bounds. "The sovereignty of a state . . . does not extend to those means which are employed by Congress to carry into execution powers conferred on that body by the people of the U. States."[29] Because the Bank of the United States was chartered for the nation, representing all its people, it was therefore not subject to being taxed by any one state. Moreover, "the power to tax involves the power to destroy." In excess, taxation can be destructive, can be an abuse, can interfere with the operation of a government entity. If accepted, a state could tax the mail, or the mint, or the patent office, or the judicial process, "to an excess which would defeat all the ends of government."[30] Marshall elaborated upon how wayward state taxation could prove vexatious to national purpose. To allow such would not be reasonable. "The result is a conviction," he wrote, "that the States have no power, by taxation or otherwise, to impede, burden, or in any manner control the operations of the constitutional laws enacted by Congress to carry into execution the powers vested in the general government."[31]

Marshall was not expanding the powers of the general government but rather protecting them from hindrance by the various state governments. Speaking for the court, Marshall wrote that "We are unanimously of opinion, that the law passed by the Legislature of Maryland, imposing a tax on the Bank of the United States, is unconstitutional, and void."[32] The thrust of the statement was a ringing endorsement of the supreme power of the national government, strengthened by the principle of implied power. In one stunning session in 1819, the Supreme Court had protected corporations from state interference, allowed bankruptcy laws, and defended by an expansive view of implied powers a national bank that theoretically could regulate loans and stabilize the currency. While these decisions pleased the entrepreneurial class, they—particularly the expansive bank opinion—outraged conservative southerners who saw the bank as an enemy and a strong national government as a potential threat to slavery. As such, *McCulloch v. Maryland* contributed mightily to a rising sense of southern defensiveness and a corresponding belief that the South had important interests at odds with the rest of the nation. These ideas would ultimately ripen into the state of mind that led to national disintegration.

No sooner had the *McCulloch* decision been announced than a prominent Richmond judge, William Brockenbrough, under the name of "Amphictyon," began to publish a series of critical essays in the Richmond *Enquirer* attacking the opinion, essays so biting toward the court and promotive of states' rights dogma that Marshall himself felt moved to reply to them in the Philadelphia *Union,* using the pseudonym "A Friend of the Union." In response to Marshall, an even more distinguished Richmond judge, Spencer Roane of the Virginia Court of Appeals, writing as "Hampden," published four essays in the *Enquirer.* Marshall replied with nine essays in the Alexandria *Gazette,* now writing as "A Friend of the Constitution." Neither side convinced the other, and Marshall in particular was not satisfied with the states' rights sentiment growing in Virginia.[33]

It was against this backdrop of newspaper controversy that the court's next major case arose, and Marshall maneuvered to get the case on the docket even though, technically, it did not meet the guidelines for such attention. But he saw an opportunity to make a statement on behalf of the national government and rebut the Virginia jurists. Two brothers from a distinguished Baltimore family, operating the Norfolk branch of the family's firm that marketed lottery tickets across the nation, were charged on June 1, 1820, with selling tickets for a National Lottery (authorized by Congress to raise funds for the District of Columbia) even though the state of Virginia had passed a law in January 1820 outlawing the sale of out-of-state lottery tickets. After Philip and Mendes Cohen were convicted by a local Virginia court, they appealed their case to the Supreme Court on the grounds that the state courts had no regulatory power over a lottery authorized by the national government. Virginia authorities, instructed by the legislature, and with a states' rights agenda, protested that the Supreme Court had no jurisdiction over a state law even though the Cohens' lawyers claimed so by virtue of Section 25 of the Judiciary Act of 1789. The issue of jurisdiction loomed as far more important than the actual merits of the Cohens' case. The Cohens engaged two eminent lawyers, David Ogden of New York and William Pinkney of Baltimore, to represent them.

The case, known as *Cohens v. Virginia,* was argued on February 18, 1821, and two weeks later, on March 3, Marshall delivered the court's unanimous opinion (which he had written), focusing entirely on the jurisdictional issue. In one of his most quotable decisions, Marshall refrained from legalistic citations to other cases and actually spent little time on Section 25, putatively the source of the government's position. Instead he based his argument on a minute, detailed analysis of the Constitution, in the process shaping an eloquent defense of the union and the national authority of the Supreme Court. Marshall here emerged as the most effective articulator of US nationalism. The opinion was a full-bore attack on the supremacy of states' rights. Marshall practically ridiculed the position that the applicability of the national government's laws should be left up to the opinion of the various states, suggesting that would produce as many "constructions" of the "constitution, laws, and treaties" "as there are states." Marshall's key points came through forcefully: "The American states as well as the American people," he wrote, "have believed a close and firm Union to be essential to their liberty and to their happiness. They have been taught by experience, that this Union cannot exist without a government for the whole." This unity of purpose extended to the judicial department. "It is authorized to decide all cases of every description, arising under the constitution of the laws of the United States. . . . No exception is made of those cases in which a state may be a party." He acknowledged that controversies could arise within the dual system of state governments and the national government. Even though "The people made the constitution, and the people can unmake it," such a drastic decision could only be an act of "the whole body of the people; not in any subdivision of them."[34]

Marshall was building up, by page after page of careful argument, to what reads like a paean to a nation whose authority was indivisible and unquestionable:

> That the United States form, for many and for most important purposes, a single nation, has not yet been denied. In war, we are one people. In making peace, we are one people. In all commercial regulations, we are one and the same people. In many other respects, the American people are one, and the government which is alone capable of controlling and managing their interests in all these respects, is the government of the Union. It is their government, and in that character they have no other. America has chosen to be, in many respects, and to many purposes, a nation; and for all these purposes, her government is complete; to all these objects, it is competent. They have

> declared, that, in the exercise of all powers given for these objects, it is supreme. It can, then, in effecting these objects, legitimately control all individuals or governments within the American territory. The constitution and laws of a state, so far as they are repugnant to the constitution and laws of the United States, are absolutely void. These states are constituent parts of the United States. They are members of one great empire—for some purposes sovereign: for some purposes subordinate.[35]

It is important to note here, as the editor of the Marshall papers has written, that "the constitutional vision that inspired Madison in the 1780s was essentially the same one that animated Marshall as the chief justice of the United States."[36] The nation carefully balanced the authority of the central government and the various state governments. It came as no surprise that by a unanimous decision the Supreme Court ruled that it had jurisdiction to rule in the *Cohens* case. What may have been a surprise was the court's decision, several days later, that on the matter of the actual merits of the case, the National Lottery law was intended to support a lottery only for the residents of the District of Columbia, so the Virginia municipal court decision prohibiting the Cohen brothers from selling District tickets in Norfolk was upheld. But of course that was a matter of little consequence. What was significant was the jurisdictional decision that defended the supremacy of the union. Although Judge Roane disliked it and took up his pen again, outside of Virginia the decision was applauded.[37]

Marshall issued one last truly transformative court decision, announced in 1824, the final year of Monroe's administration and at the end of the era of the Virginia Dynasty's political dominance. This case had its origins in the development of the steamboat in New York at the end of the eighteenth century, and although John Fitch had pioneered the steamboat, it had been Robert Fulton with his *Clermont* who in 1807 really proved the efficacy of this new mode of water transportation. Influential New York statesman and financier Robert Livingston formed a partnership with Fulton, and in 1811 they received a thirty-year exclusive right from the state to navigate with steam-powered boats on the Hudson River and other waters surrounding New York City. One Aaron Ogden obtained a license from the monopoly to operate a steam-powered ferry connecting New York City with Elizabethtown, New Jersey.

Then, in 1818, a competitor arose. Thomas Gibbons, armed with a license based on the Federal Coastal Act of 1793, began to operate two steam-powered ferry boats. Ogden promptly sued Gibbons, the New York state court upheld his monopoly, and eventually Gibbons took his case to the Supreme Court in 1824, backed by the legal team of Daniel Webster and William Wirt. Beginning on February 4, the legal arguments went on for five days, and Webster and Wirt put on remarkable demonstrations of legal reasoning and stirring oratory. Webster grounded his argument on the commerce clause in the Constitution, Article 1, Section 8, which gives Congress the right "to regulate commerce with foreign nations, *and among the several States,* and with the Indian tribes" (emphasis added). He posited that the congressional act of 1793 took precedence over the state granting of monopoly rights to Livingston and Fulton.

Here was a case just perfect for Marshall. From reading his long opinion it is clear what Marshall understood his tasks to be. Regarding the commerce clause of the Constitution, he needed to fully define the meaning of the word *commerce,* he needed to explicate the degree to which Congress could employ its regulatory powers within the separate states, he needed to determine whether this regulatory power was exclusive to Congress or shared with the states, and he wanted to discuss how broadly the commerce power (and by implication other powers) should be construed. How he met these various needs is what elevated his opinion in *Gibbons v. Ogden* to one of his greatest decisions, with significant impact on the subsequent economic growth of the nation.

Marshall began by reminding his readers that the Constitution "contains an enumeration of powers expressly granted by the people to their government. It has been said, that these powers ought to be construed strictly. But why ought they to be so construed. Is there one sentence in the Constitution which gives countenance to this rule?" Some who so advocate "would deny to the government those powers which the words of the grant, as usually understood, import, and which are consistent with the general views and objects of the instrument, for that narrow construction . . . would cripple the government, and render it unequal to the objects for which it is declared to be instituted."[38] Rather, Marshall insisted that the essence of the Constitution was to be found in its very words, understood plainly in their common, everyday meanings. Neither here nor elsewhere did Marshall try to conjure the original intention of the drafters. In the everyday sense, "commerce" means not narrowly just "buying and selling," but rather all aspects of commercial intercourse, including transportation of goods and people.[39] After all, the topic of transportation relating to commerce was the very issue that had instigated the 1786 meeting at Annapolis that put underway the chain of events that led to the writing of the Constitution in 1787. The commerce clause used the phrase "among the several States," and Marshall clarified that *among* meant "intermingled with," or between, two or more states.[40] It meant that commerce subject to congressional regulation was only that commerce that involved several states, which is to say that commerce confined to interactions between people in the same state or between different regions of the same state were not subject to congressional regulation, a slight nod to states' righters. Regarding commerce within a single state, that state within its borders had what we would today call police powers to issue regulations concerning the health and safety of its residents. Even commerce originating in another state, upon entry into a second state would be subject to the health and other regulations of the receiving state—or even subject to tolls on local roads—because such regulations were not primarily an issue of trade but of local police powers.

In other words, congressional regulation of trade was not exclusive and on many occasions operated alongside residual state regulations. And regulated commerce was not a matter of whether the ship or boat was wind or steam powered, or whether it carried goods or people. In other words, the commerce clause gave Congress broad power to regulate interstate commerce of every kind, without meaning to completely remove states from legal involvement with commerce within their own boundaries. But states did *not* have the authority to regulate or interfere (or limit, as with bestowing monopoly rights on a means of navigation) with commerce that originated outside their boundaries or that flowed through, as on a river, or around their bounds. Still, after all this, the court unanimously ruled that the New York act was void not because it was unconstitutional but because it came into "direct collision with" an act of Congress.[41]

Nevertheless, the court's general opinion struck a powerful blow against local monopolistic legislation that hindered commerce and transportation. While some, especially in the conservative hotbed of Virginia, objected to the court's strident nationalism, the almost universal opposition to monopolies made this a popular decision. It allowed a phenomenal increase in steam-powered water transportation (and later trains) that produced what became known as the "transportation revolution" linking much of the nation together. In *Gibbons v. Ogden,* as elsewhere, Marshall's major decisions elevated the Supreme Court to a coordinate level with the other two branches of government, a position it occupies today. He in effect *made* the institution of the Supreme Court. But it did not become an institution that attempted to devise a means to end slavery.

Thomas Jefferson spent much of the last two decades of his life creating an enduring institution in another sphere, higher education.[42] In 1778 he had proposed a public system of elementary education for white boys and girls through grade three (the state refused to fund the proposal), and in 1779 had proposed modernizing the College of William and Mary, turning it into a university, with far more instruction in the sciences, but the legislature failed to act on this proposed bill also. Years later, on Christmas Eve, 1804, he received a letter from a member of the Virginia General Assembly alerting him that perhaps there would soon be sufficient funds in the state treasury to think again about creating a new university in the state.

This set Jefferson's mind to working, and on January 5 of the new year he sent the delegate a long letter musing about the role of education, both secondary and higher, in the state and laid out his current ideas. He noted that consideration had to be given to the optimum location, to having a governing "board of visitors" who would establish all the requisite academic policies, and to having, as soon as possible, ten professorships cover the necessary disciplines, and the salaries should be such as would allow them to hire a faculty of true distinction. He especially was concerned with the design of campuses, opposing the common practice of having all the students and faculty in one large building, like Nassau Hall at Princeton or the Wren Building at the College of William and Mary. "Large houses are always ugly, inconvenient, exposed to the accident of fire, and bad in cases of infection. A plain small house for the school & lodging of each professor is best. These connected by covered ways out of which the rooms of the students should open would be best. These may then be built only as they shall be wanting. In fact an University should not be an house but a village."[43] But the hoped-for funds did not materialize, so no progress was made on establishing a new university. Clearly though Jefferson liked mulling over in his mind the best way to organize a university, and a letter in 1810 showed that he was elaborating his ideas of campus design into what he now labeled "an academical village."[44]

At the time, Jefferson was retired and had no official involvement with academic planning in his home state, but his commitment to higher education was abiding. Suddenly, and for no apparent reason, five prominent citizens of Jefferson's Albemarle County met in 1814 to see if they could breathe life into a dormant Albemarle Academy that had been chartered by the state's General Assembly in 1803 but never opened. They decided to enlarge the number of trustees, and among those chosen was Jefferson.[45] He was placed on a committee to draft regulations for the academy and later draft a petition to the General Assembly for funding. But in the midst of the War of 1812, nothing happened. In September 1814, Jefferson took it upon himself to write a long letter to his nephew Peter Carr, now the president of the academy's board, laying out his ideas about the role of education in the state, from elementary schools to university with appropriate professional schools. He listed the subjects he thought worthy of study, with a strong emphasis on science and technology.[46] For almost two years Jefferson and other friends of education wrote letters advocating for the college, and finally, on February 14, 1816, the General Assembly created Central College by law—on its board of trustees sat Jefferson, Madison, Monroe, and other prominent Virginians such as Joseph C. Cabell and John Hartwell Cocke.

This was not yet the state university, but Jefferson busied himself with moving ahead to purchase a site for the campus just west of the town of

Charlottesville (the land had once been part of a farm owned by James Monroe) and began drawing up architectural plans. On October 6, 1817, Jefferson, along with his plantation manager, his most skilled carpenter, and ten enslaved workers, staked out the foundation for the proposed college's first building and began to level the site. Meanwhile Cabell and others lobbied the General Assembly and the governor to create a capstone university. Finally, in February 1818, the General Assembly passed a bill instructing the governor to form a committee of leading men, including Jefferson, to meet that August at Rockfish Gap, thirty miles west of Charlottesville, to determine the best location for a new university and recommend its structure and curriculum. Jefferson had already worked carefully on a document outlining his recommendations for a state university, revising it through several drafts, and had shared it and discussed its contents with James Madison and several others before the meeting.[47] When he was asked to speak, he used a map and census data to demonstrate that Charlottesville was the location nearest to the center of the state's white population, and the committee accepted his previously written document, with almost no changes, as their official report.[48] Central College was about to become the University of Virginia.

The report laid out Jefferson's innovative architectural ideas, with the professors' houses called pavilions, and the student dormitories linked to them by covered walkways, and now with a larger building (later called the Rotunda) proposed at the eastern end of the two rows of pavilions. Then Jefferson discussed the various purposes of higher education. The report continued, describing all the subjects to be taught, with an emphasis on modern languages and sciences, and later medicine and law. Because of the principle of religious freedom, there would be no state-funded professor of religion, although many of the principles of religion would be relevant topics for the professor of philosophy and ethics. The report ended with a detailed discussion of methods of student and faculty administration, including student self-discipline grounded in character and honor, which eventually (1842) evolved into an honor code covering academic and personal behavior.[49]

The proposed curriculum was a completely open and unstructured elective system whereby each student could choose precisely the courses that fit his (and only *his;* women were not admitted at Jefferson's university or any other in the nation at the time) interests and ambitions, unlike other universities then with rigidly prescribed courses of studies the same for every student. Following Jefferson's earlier thoughts, the professors would teach by means of lectures, not enforcing students to undergo hours of monotonous recitation, and there were rigorous written examinations. As Jefferson wrote in a private letter in 1820, "This institution will be based on the illimitable freedom of the human mind. For here we are not afraid to follow truth wherever it may lead, nor tolerate error so long as reason is left free to combat it."[50] Throughout the final decade of his life, Jefferson continued to worry about the lingering influence of the Federalists—which he associated with antiscience and pro-monarchialism—on the political life of the nation, and he wanted his university to be a bulwark against such pernicious attitudes.[51]

Obtaining sufficient funding from the state government was extremely difficult. In addition, the shortage of money and skilled laborers caused delays in the construction of the buildings, which were, by Jefferson's plans and at his insistence, more ornate and substantial than anything else built in the state. Although many of the craftsmen and laborers building the campus structures were enslaved, the university, a creature of its time, would be open only to white males.[52] Last, finding faculty of sufficient distinction to please Jefferson proved more difficult than the planners imagined, with eminent faculty from Harvard turning down the new institution, and the planners turned to recruiting younger scholars from England.[53]

Jefferson deployed most of his energies over his final years on planning and pushing for the completion of his dream of a university. As it took physical form, his hopes for the new institution grew. When the touring General Lafayette visited Monticello in November 1824 and was feted at a dinner within the not-quite-completed Rotunda, Jefferson, after praising Lafayette's contributions to the American Revolution and their comradeship in Paris in the 1780s, turned to his own final years of working to make the university a reality. "And could I live to see it once enjoy the patronage and cherishment of our public authorities with undivided voice, I should die without a doubt of the future fortunes of my native State, and in the consoling contemplation of the happy influence of this institution on its character, its virtue, its prosperity, and safety." He added an invocation in this, his final public address, "to heaven for [the] indissoluble union . . . [of the country]."[54] Alas, as we will see, his native state at the moment was sinking into a morass of ultra-conservatism while he was trying to create a progressive university. Virginia would eventually secede from the Union.

Finally, on March 7, 1825, the University of Virginia opened with about thirty students present, though another fifty drifted in by May. Not all the faculty members were yet on hand, three of the pavilions were still incomplete, and the library was almost nonexistent. And most of the students were not as Jefferson had envisioned. Jefferson wanted young men of intellectual curiosity and intellectual ambition, like a young him, but the students who enrolled were the spoiled, unruly sons of planters, who found academic rigor and professorial lecturing not to their liking. Some of them on occasion mistreated the enslaved laborers working to prepare their food and clean their rooms. The students were mostly academically unprepared and unaccustomed to being held subject to discipline. Ugly student riots resulted, classes were disrupted, and faculty assaulted, leaving the aging Jefferson aghast. (Such student unrest and violence was common among northern and European universities at the time also. Harvard even expelled its entire sophomore class in 1818.) Jefferson was distressed, but he nevertheless every Sunday invited small groups of students to Monticello for dinner and discussion, and he learned every student's name.[55]

Gradually the faculty restored order, the university grew over time, and by 1860 it had become one of the largest in the nation. However, it never in these years became an incubator for emancipationist ideas. The political climate of the state turned conservative after Jefferson's death, and the student body reflected this shift in public opinion, not the hopes of its founder.[56] Mr. Jefferson's University, as it is often called today, did eventually become in this century one of the finest public universities in the nation, and as Jefferson could not even have imagined, it is now coeducational and multiracial. In 1976, a poll of the members of the American Institute of Architects revealed that the overwhelming choice for "the proudest achievement of American architecture over the past 200 years" was the original campus of the University of Virginia, and it and Monticello were two of the first World Heritage Sites designated in the United States.[57]

The opening of the University of Virginia in 1825 was one of the last achievements of the Virginia Founders. Monroe issued his pronouncement 1823 that the western hemisphere was no longer open to European colonialism, and Marshall, in a series of decisions, had created the legal environment for economic growth, promoted a national consciousness, and elevated the status of the Supreme Court. But there would not be another president elected from Virginia for decades. The state had become increasingly hidebound in its political views, and states-rightism was now the dominant political philosophy. Massachusetts-born John Quincy Adams's inauguration in 1825 signaled not just a change in administrations but the end of an era.

15

LEGACY DEFERRED AND THE END OF A DYNASTY

With the exception of Patrick Henry, the seven men who so largely shaped the history we have been examining left such an extensive body of correspondence and other writings that we feel that we can know them intimately, understand what they thought and why. But that is a conceit of historians. It is difficult to truly know ourselves, much less those who lived two centuries ago. Things we take for granted, like the germ theory of disease or the concept of biological evolution, were foreign to them. The intricate even if unwritten laws of etiquette and demeanor of the past that governed the closest relationships between the elites and the plain folk, and between white and Black Americans, to a degree elude us. Much they accepted simply because of when and where they were born. The same of course is true for us. And yet we cannot fail to regret what we acknowledge as the moral failures of those who came before us.

Nothing today stands forth more disappointing about the seven men here highlighted than their attitudes toward people of African ancestry and the institution of slavery. Probably they would have thought and acted differently had they been born and come of age in Massachusetts or New York, but they did not. Only slowly and incompletely did they come to see the wrongness of slavery. They could not see how to correct this flaw in their society. Their failure to do so does not invalidate their better principles and higher actions in other arenas, nor does it mean they deserve only condemnation. But it complicates efforts to come to terms with the men who constituted this dynasty and reflects a tragic dimension of our national history.

Thomas Jefferson, who wrote most eloquently about liberty and the promise of democracy, demonstrates the problem in its full dimensions. His teacher, the Reverend James Maury, may have first introduced him to the idea that slavery was evil, around 1760, but Jefferson lived with slavery his entire life.

Jefferson's first memory was of having been carried as a toddler, cradled in a pillow on a horse, by an enslaved person when his parents moved, for several years, to a friend's plantation. More than eight decades later, another personal slave, Burwell Colbert, recognized Jefferson's last attempt at communication on his deathbed and adjusted his pillow. We do know that shortly after Jefferson had first been elected in 1768 to the House of Burgesses, one of his initial acts was to have his much older cousin, Colonel Richard Bland, introduce a bill to make it easier for slaveholders to legally free their enslaved people, but Bland was harshly attacked for doing so and the bill failed. The next year Jefferson voluntarily argued for the freedom of an indentured servant whose term had been unfairly overextended, and in the process he stated that "Under the law of nature, all men are born free," a statement that so outraged the judge that he promptly ruled against the servant.[1]

Jefferson would many times write and speak against slavery: in his pamphlet titled *A Summary View of the Rights of British America* (1774); in the draft of the "Declaration of Independence," though Congress excised the long passage attacking slavery; in a new constitution proposed for the state of Virginia in 1783 that called for the end of slavery in 1800; in his 1784 committee report to the Congress of the Articles of Confederation recommending that the new territory acquired in 1783 (from the Appalachians to the Mississippi River) be divided up into a number of states in which slavery would cease to exist after 1800 (the proposed bill failed by one vote); in a famous passage in *Notes on the State of Virginia* (1787); in numerous personal letters; and in his successful call to Congress in 1806 to end the Atlantic slave trade, effective January 1, 1808. Jefferson called for the end of slavery more often and more publicly than did any other of the Founding Fathers from the southern states, all to no avail. But, and this is an important *but,* he never freed the great bulk of his own enslaved people, nor did he move as president to end slavery by proclamation, and *Notes on the State of Virginia* contains an equally infamous passage on the supposed inferiority of Blacks.[2] How do we square these apparent contradictions? That he wrote so eloquently about liberty makes it all the harder to understand.

It is not enough simply to condemn those in the past for their moral failures; we need to try to understand why they acted as they did. Jefferson, for example, was constrained both by laws and by social expectations. When his father-in-law, John Wayles, died in 1774, Jefferson's wife inherited some ten thousand acres of land and over one hundred enslaved people, which by the laws of the time, meant that this inheritance became property of Jefferson. At the same time he inherited Wayles's immense personal debts, which even by trying to sell the land, Jefferson could not settle. Never throughout his life was Jefferson able to escape the burden of this inherited debt. And when, in 1792, the General Assembly passed a law allowing creditors to seize their debtors' manumitted enslaved people, it effectively prevented Jefferson, even if he wanted to, from freeing his enslaved laborers. Had he tried, toward the end of his life, to free them and distribute his Monticello farmland to them, he was deterred by an 1806 Virginia law that required freedpeople to leave the state within a year or bear the penalty of being reenslaved by the state.[3] George Washington, by contrast, being debt free, had not been so restrained by the 1792 legislation, and he manumitted his enslaved people in his 1799 will, before the removal law (but only upon the death of his wife, whom they still had to serve).

To a degree that we do not share today, Jefferson really believed that in the system of government under which he lived, all important decisions had to receive the approval of the citizens as expressed through elections or legislative action. His strong antipathy toward monarchical government made him reject rule by fiat: even could he have waved a magic wand and done away with slavery, he believed that would be repugnant to the rule of democracy. He understood that most white citizens were not yet ready for such a decision, and for that reason he believed education—as at the proposed University of Virginia—was necessary to train up citizens who would by their votes help abolish slavery. He had, at least in his earlier years, great hope that the coming generation would be willing to do what his would not. This hope soon crashed against the emerging reality that after the invention of the cotton gin and the spread of cotton culture, slavery became more firmly established, not less.[4]

Jefferson believed that with the ending of fresh imports of enslaved men, women, and children from Africa in 1808 and the dispersion of the enslaved population across the expanded acreage offered by new territories and states, their reduction in population density would embolden southern and western states to gradually end slavery as the northern states had done after 1780. But of course this did not happen. Jefferson and nearly all his white contemporaries believed that white prejudice and understandable Black resentment meant that in order for emancipation to be become widely accepted, freedpeople would need to be colonized abroad—he believed ideally in Haiti—and be provided with funds, tools, draft animals, and support of all kinds until they prospered as an independent nation. This point deserves emphasis: it was practically a national consensus that emancipation had to proceed hand in hand with colonization. Obviously, there was insufficient white political support for this, and freedpeople showed little desire to leave the land of their birth.

Famously, Jefferson had a longtime intimate relationship with an enslaved woman named Sally Hemings, the half sister of his deceased wife, and with her he had several children. One might ask, why did Jefferson not marry her? Virginia law prohibited whites from marrying an enslaved person, and it also prohibited a man from marrying the sister of his deceased wife, so even had Hemings been free and white, he could not have legally married her. And Martha Jefferson on her death bed had asked Jefferson to promise never to remarry. By all appearances the relationship between Jefferson and Hemings was based on at least a degree of mutual affection, but the power imbalances at play meant that she had almost no other choice.[5] As Jefferson sank ever deeper into bankruptcy in his final years, his enslaved laborers suffered the largest tragedy by being sold after his death, with families torn asunder. This tragedy is multiplied a thousandfold across the course of early American history. In manifold ways the history of this nation *is* a story of courage, creativity, principle, even freedom and opportunity for many, but running throughout is the pernicious sin of slavery.

We see it everywhere. James Madison also lived with slavery his entire life, and whatever pangs of conscience he may have suffered, he never emancipated his enslaved people. In private letters he condemned slavery, and he took pains to ensure that the words *slave* and *slavery* did not stain the Constitution because he, like many, thought slavery would die out and he did not want the remnant of the nation's founding sin to afflict the fundamental law of the land. Although he never wrote in detail about the supposed inferiority of people of African descent as did Jefferson in *Notes on the State of Virginia,* when, for example, he mentioned "the physical and lasting peculiarities" of Blacks, he did not do so to praise them.[6] Madison knew intellectually that slavery was wrong, but so conditioned was he to living in a slave society and so dependent was he on the income produced by his enslaved labor that he never found the will to end his engagement in the institution. Like Jefferson, he sank into near bankruptcy, confessing to Jefferson in early 1826, "Since my return to private life . . . I have made but one tolerable crop of Tobacco, and but one of wheat. . . . And having no resources but in the earth I cultivate, I have been living very much throughout on borrowed means."[7] His debts were greatly increased by his having to constantly support Dolley's wastrel son Payne Todd, who could never hold on to a position and drank and gambled heavily, expenses into the thousands of dollars that Madison silently paid and tried to protect his beloved Dolley from having to face.

As though he wanted to hide the ugly reality of slavery, Madison had three model slave cabins constructed near the rear of his Montpelier home, complete with wooden floors, glass windows, and fireplaces, although most of his enslaved people lived in far more primitive cabins nearer the tobacco fields.[8] His young friend and former secretary, Edward Coles, urged him, as he had Jefferson, to free his enslaved people, but Madison never did, seeing the income they produced as necessary to support his wife, Dolley. There were some rumors that he privately asked her, upon her death, to manumit their enslaved people, but if so—despite her Quaker background—she never did. She lived another thirteen years in genteel poverty after the June 28, 1836, death of her husband. Coles, on the other hand—who had no debts, was unmarried, and had no biological descendants—did buy land in Illinois, freed his handful of enslaved people, and moved them to that free state and gave them land to farm.[9]

James Monroe, like his two presidential predecessors, had been born in Virginia ensconced in a slave economy, owned enslaved people his entire life, and depended upon them for his income beyond government salary, which was never enough to cover expenses. Like most educated southerners of his time, Monroe in private correspondence expressed repugnance toward slavery, but he depended upon the profits of his enslaved property throughout his life. He, like Jefferson and Madison before him, came to see colonization as a prerequisite for gradual emancipation, a belief that was strengthened during his term as governor of Virginia when Gabriel's Revolt occurred. As governor, Monroe had called out the militia to ensure public safety and calm fears, and he submitted to the executive council's authorization of the hanging of twenty-seven supposed slave insurrectionists (after minimal trials). Yet Monroe had felt uneasy about the harshness of that response and agreed with Jefferson's advice to rein in retaliatory violence on the part of white authorities. Expatriation would be the more humane solution, Jefferson had written. After the American Colonization Society was formed in December 1816, Monroe became a member, and when it subsequently established a colony on the western coast of Africa, its capital Monrovia was named after him.[10]

In part because the government never properly paid him for his diplomatic service in the 1790s, Monroe's financial plight worsened throughout his presidential years and retirement. He sold his lands near Monticello and lived at Oak Hill on a plantation site he had inherited in the 1790s, but he could only eke out a living. He was never able to persuade Congress to reimburse him for his expenses, with Virginia congressmen, resentful of his turn toward nationalism, being among those who did not vote to repay him. Near destitution, after his wife Eliza died in 1830, he closed down his home and moved to New York to live with his younger daughter, where, on July 4, 1831, his quietly died. He never reconciled his life with his antislavery sentiments.[11]

The only one of the last four Virginians who made up the Virginia Dynasty to avoid financial disaster, John Marshall, was the only one who did not attempt to operate a plantation. Income from his lucrative law practice helped him establish himself, and rental income from his extensive land holdings in Kentucky and his various plantations in Virginia supported his comfortable lifestyle.[12] Like George Washington, land rentals were the secret to his economic well-being, but unlike Washington, Marshall only held about a dozen enslaved domestics to serve his household in Richmond. Yet he had as many as two hundred enslaved people, or perhaps more, working on plantation lands he owned. A portion of the income from the enslaved labor on these lands came to him as rent, though he was not personally involved in actually operating any of these plantations. Thus he did not consider himself a planter but rather an urban lawyer.[13]

Like others of his social class in Virginia, Marshall understood intellectually that slavery was wrong, but this knowledge did not produce a moral passion to end the institution. He had grown up and prospered in its midst, and ownership of enslaved domestics brought comfort and convenience. Yet he came to realize that in various ways slavery threatened the security and economic well-being of his state. For those reasons, not moral persuasion, he supported colonization as a means of ending slavery and draining away from the state those who were freed. Like other prominent Virginians, he was a member of the American Colonization Society, and he was head of the auxiliary of the national organization in Richmond. In 1827 he helped found the Virginia Society for Colonization explicitly for transporting freedpeople abroad. In none of these attitudes did Marshall differ from most of his white contemporaries. He simply accepted the reality of slavery in his society and saw no practical solution to ending the institution and no moral requirement to do so. He could not foresee, even imagine, a society in which people of the two races intermingled as equals, and his commitment to the sanctity of private property put a powerful damper upon any contemplation of abolition without ample compensation.

With regards to his enslaved domestic servants, he apparently was considered a "benevolent owner," a phrase that to our ears sounds contradictory.[14] But by the terms of his several wills, he did not free his enslaved people upon his death on July 6, 1835. In fact, for all seven of the men who dominate our story, from Washington to Marshall, the survival of the union was their ultimate political concern. Issues of race generally and slavery specifically were deemed of lesser importance, especially because all of them believed the institution to be somehow on the decline at least before the beginning of the nineteenth century. The central tragedy of the nation's history is that these otherwise able leaders did not see the basic flaw in their worldview and act to address it.

Political observers everywhere but particularly in Virginia realized that the Virginia Dynasty had ended with the conclusion of the Monroe administration, a finality marked soon afterward by the death on July 4, 1826, of Thomas Jefferson (and, that same day in Massachusetts, of John Adams). Thus it represented more than just a turn in Virginia politics but to a degree in national politics. As the eminent Massachusetts orator Edward Everett said in a joint eulogy, "Providence seems to have appointed that the revolutionary age of America should be closed up."[15] But the sense that an era was over in Virginia was reflected in population figures as well, data that pointed out a decline in the state's size and hence congressional influence. Having ranked first in population in 1800, by 1830 the state had dropped to third, and it would fall to seventh by 1860. While the state's population had grown by 29 percent between 1800 and 1830, the national growth had soared 140 percent. During the next decade the state's population actually sank while that of the nation increased by 33 percent. Amazingly, by 1850 almost four hundred thousand people born in the Commonwealth of Virginia had moved out of the state to other states. Not only that, but within Virginia itself, population was shifting away from the Tidewater and Piedmont—the traditional power centers—and toward the Valley and especially the Trans-Allegheny West.[16]

The population drain was felt especially hard in the older settled portion of the state. The sense of decline could be seen everywhere in the region. Land values collapsed—for example, Jefferson's executors only got a fraction of what they expected from the sale of his Monticello acreage—and the value of total state exports between the years 1817 and 1829 fell by two-thirds. Correspondents noted with sadness and despair the economic decline, and even popular fiction commented on the said state of affairs. "Nostalgia, pessimism, and malaise" was in the air everywhere.[17] One planter, James Mercer Garnett, having toured the state in 1827, wrote "Virginia—poor Virginia . . . the Education of her youth either neglected or perverted . . . her Agriculture nearly gone to ruin . . . her general politics degenerated into a scuffle almost universal for office and emolument." "What times have we fallen upon," lamented William Wirt in 1828; and a few years later he added, "I am a disappointed man, . . . disappointed in my country and the glory that I thought awaited her."[18] Thousands of acres of soil were exhausted from many decades of tobacco planting, with abandoned fields overrun with sedge grass, and houses and outbuildings stood in decay.

There was a decided decline in the quality of political leadership as well. With the increasing democratization of politics, the older leaders drawn from the elite, men of education and nationalist in outlook, were being replaced by men of a more localistic orientation who won elections less because of their ability but because of their oratorical prowess on the hustings, where attention to provincial and immediate needs was more attractive to voters than commitment to national interests. Older leaders like Washington, Jefferson, and Madison had been elected for other than their speaking abilities, but their like had scant chance for electoral success now.[19] It was easier in the new political environment to attack scapegoats like the Bank of the United States or northern interests or abolitionists; a defensiveness in outlook came to dominate, and the ideals of Washington, Jefferson, Madison, and even Monroe were scorned. Rather than really addressing the issues pressing upon society, narrow politicians harkened back to a rigid, narrow interpretation of the political ideas of the ratification period. The Jeffersonian era was over in more ways than one. Four of the nation's first five presidents hailed from Virginia, but since the final election of Monroe in 1820, not again has a single Virginia politician headed a major party's presidential ticket.[20]

Nearly everyone knew that slavery, at least in some way, was at the heart of the decline of Virginia. For example, Jefferson's favorite granddaughter, Ellen Randolph, had married Joseph Coolidge Jr. of Boston in April 1825, the marriage taking place in the parlor of Monticello, and during the summer she traveled to Boston with her new husband. Ellen Randolph Coolidge was astonished at the difference she saw in the evidence of prosperity in the northern states as compared to Virginia. She wrote her beloved grandfather about the "flourishing" situation she witnessed in New England.

> It has given me an idea of prosperity and improvement, such as I fear our Southern States cannot hope for, whilst the canker of slavery eats into their hearts, and diseases the whole body by this ulcer at the core. . . . I should judge from appearances that they are at least a century in advance of us in all the arts and embellishments of life; and they are pressing forward in their course with a zeal and activity which I think must ensure success.[21]

Her grandfather agreed: "One fatal stain deforms what nature has bestowed on us of her fairest gifts," he sadly replied.[22] Madison and Monroe would have also agreed, but none of them could see a solution to the dilemma of Virginia. Perhaps in part the remedy, they believed, was political.

It was that sentiment that lay behind the state's decision, in 1829, to elect delegates to a convention to consider revising the Virginia's 1776 constitution. Political leaders from the western section of the state had been pushing for such a convention for years and in 1816 had met in Staunton asking for one, only to be repulsed. They asked again in vain in 1824. Finally the General Assembly session of 1827–28 put the issue to the voters, who approved a convention and called for an election of delegates in early 1829. Each of the state's twenty-four senatorial districts would be allowed four delegates, and the convention was scheduled to open on October 5, 1829, meeting in the impressive quarters of the Jefferson-designed Capitol Building in Richmond. The push for reform came primarily from the thirty-six delegates from the west of the Blue Ridge, meaning that the more conservative delegates from the Piedmont and Tidewater were in control. Over three-quarters of the delegates from the latter two regions were either planters or planter-lawyers, while less than an eighth of those from the western regions were.[23]

The ninety-six delegates were a distinguished group. James Madison and James Monroe were elected, as was John Marshall. Every significant political leader was present: cranky John Randolph of Roanoke, former Speaker of the House Philip P. Barbour, up-and-coming stars like Littleton W. Tazewell, Benjamin Watkins Leigh, and Abel Upshur, and the stalwart western reformer, Philip Doddridge. The delegates gathered in Richmond on October 4. That evening, Marshall had James and Dolley Madison, along with James Monroe and his daughter Eliza Hay, over for dinner. The next day the three men walked to the Capitol, with Madison, the eldest delegate, taking the chair. Then by prearrangement he nominated Monroe to be elected president of the convention, Marshall seconded the nomination, and Monroe was elected by acclamation. Though the youngest of the three most distinguished delegates, he was the feeblest, but presiding was not expected to be an especially arduous role. Yet the most notable presence that opening day was the deceased Thomas Jefferson. His ideas, first elaborated in a letter of July 1816 written to Samuel Kercheval in Frederick County, established the agenda for all the key items under discussion. Jefferson had asked Kercheval to keep his views private, but Kercheval quickly showed Jefferson's letters (including a second letter written in September) to others, had them published in a local newspaper, and in 1829, following Jefferson's death, published them in a pamphlet.[24] Jefferson's views about the Virginia constitution and the nature of republican government had evolved and matured since his earlier proposed drafts of constitutions for the state in 1776 and 1783. His views on a variety of topics often changed with additional reading and experience of more than three decades of state governance. Most of what he wrote to Kercheval were intended as revisions needed to the existing state government. Fundamental was the principle that "a government is republican in proportion as every member composing it has his equal voice in the direction of it's concerns." That is, the flagrantly disproportional representation of the Tidewater and Piedmont regions in the state government was an affront to republican government.

Not only should the various sections of the state be equally represented, but Jefferson called for practically universal suffrage, without property requirements. He proposed that the governor be popularly elected, not appointed by the legislature; the governor should not be restrained by an unelected council; judges should be elected, not appointed for life; justices of the peace and sheriffs, the self-perpetuating courthouse oligarchies that were the arm of local government, should be elected by the people, not self-appointed; counties should be subdivided into smaller, self-governing districts called wards; and he strongly supported the idea of periodic amendment of the constitution.[25] For example, by explicitly authorizing expenditures for internal improvements and the advancement of education and science, the national government could promote economic diversification and prosperity. Each of these ideas was anathema to the eastern conservatives in the state. When the convention began, all the delegates knew Jefferson's idealistic prescription for reform had to be addressed. As the reform leader Philip Doddridge proclaimed from the floor on November 27, "Every principle for which we contend, is supported by the deliberate opinions of Mr. Jefferson."[26]

Because of the regional distribution of delegates, it was clear from the beginning that the advocates of reform would have an uphill struggle, and they could be successful only if they could attract some delegates from the Piedmont and Tidewater who were at least moderately open to change. The reformers tended to emphasize the ideals of democracy, which argued for equal representation and a broadened franchise. Natural rights, republican virtue, and popular sovereignty were their key words. Virginia at this moment was only one of two states (North Carolina being the other) that insisted that only freeholders—that is, property holders—could vote, a restriction that denied the franchise to about half of all white males. The reformers found much to fault in the existing state constitution, which had no provision for amendment. They also advocated infrastructure and transportation improvements, which of course would necessitate additional taxes. The conservative delegates from the Piedmont and Tidewater attacked all these ideas. On October 9, Littleton W. Tazewell of Norfolk praised the existing constitution, asking could anyone "name one practical evil it has brought upon us? Can more be said? A Government, born of wisdom and virtue, . . . it must surely be rash, to cut it at once to pieces; scatter all its parts; and then see if we cannot make something out of them, that may peradventure do better."[27]

Three weeks later, another of the Tidewater defenders, Abel P. Upshur of Northampton County, raised the specter of danger to the institution of slavery and the threat of rising taxes because of the different nature of society in the western counties. "[T]he course of industry in the west," he said, "does not require slave labour; slaves will always be found in the grain-growing and tobacco country alone. This is not now the character of the western country, nor can it be, until a general system of roads and canals, shall facilitate their access to market. And when that time shall arrive, the worst evils which we apprehend will have been experienced; for it is to *make* these very roads and canals, that our taxes are required."[28] Two days later, Richard Morris of Hanover County, just north of Richmond, described the effect on slaveholders that high taxes would bring, because such taxes would be laid on their human property, leading to some having by "compulsion" of the government to free their enslaved people. This could only produce violence on the part of the freed Blacks: "and soon a sword will be unsheathed, that will be red with the best blood of this country, before it finds the scabbard."[29]

On November 3, skilled orator Benjamin W. Leigh of Chesterfield County, across the river from Richmond, argued that his region, already overtaxed because of the levy on their enslaved property, would be doubly burdened to pay for all kinds of internal improvement schemes should it lose control of the General Assembly by reason of reapportionment. "I doubt whether there is a people on earth, more heavily taxed than the slave-holding planters of Virginia."[30] After that absurdity he went on to defend slavery: "In every civilized county under the sun, some there must be who labour for their daily bread, either by contract with, or subjection to others, or for themselves. Slaves, in the eastern part of this State, fill the place of the peasantry of Europe—or of the peasantry of day-labourers in the non-slave-holding States of the Union. . . . who earn their daily bread by the sweat of their brow."[31] He must have instantly realized he had just insulted the plain folk of the western counties, so he immediately began to say how much regard he had for such common men, but the damage had been done. His aristocratic condescension was palpable.[32] Against this backdrop of fear of change by the majority of eastern delegates and their defense of their privileged position in the state, the reformers had no chance of achieving meaningful reform.

The reformers grounded their arguments in republican ideology—for example, delegate Briscoe G. Baldwin from the Valley posited that "Our Republican Institutions rest for their support upon the virtue and intelligence of the people; and if they should not be sufficient to ensure a faithful and wise administration of the Government, the best hopes of human liberty and happiness which we have cherished must be disappointed, and we shall be compelled to abandon the scheme of self-government, and yield up the many to the protection of the few."[33] But the eastern delegates disparaged philosophical and idealistic language for the hard reality of self-interest: protection of their enslaved property and low taxation, which obviated the potential of significant internal improvements.

One of the dominant tropes of conservative disputation was ridicule of Jeffersonian idealism, a line of argument spearheaded by the shrill-voiced John Randolph of Roanoke. Speaking for "practical men—not theorists and visionary speculators," he attacked those who would impose a "monstrous tyranny" upon the state by writing a new constitution.[34] Several weeks later he was even more personal. "I have not much deference for the opinion of Mr. Jefferson. We all know he was very confident in his theories—but I am a practical man and have no confidence *a priori* in the theories of Mr. Jefferson, or of any other man under the sun." The majority of eastern Virginia delegates now rejected the political ideals that had undergirded the revolution and the development of the national government, and the delegates retreated instead to a narrow defense of their self-interest.

On the key issues, Madison at first supported apportioning delegates simply on the basis of the free white population, which would give additional representation to the West, but that position faced instant opposition. Several eastern delegates proposed white population combined with some method of determining taxable property, which would heavily favor the slaveholding regions. Others supported white population augmented by the three-fifths accounting of the enslaved population, what was called the federal number. Still others suggested an averaging of these various means of apportionment, and when the soft-spoken Madison rose from his desk to address the issue, delegates rushed to surround him so as to hear. But realizing the intransigence of eastern opinion, and fearing that the state would break apart if representation were solely on the basis of white population, Madison backed down. Monroe, whose opinions reflected those of Madison, accepted representation based on the use of the three-fifths rule. The result, of course, continued the domination of the state government by the planter class.

Reformers also pushed to broaden the franchise so that every white male citizen could vote, not just those who owned property, but this too failed, with conservatives complaining vituperatively about universal suffrage posing a threat to the well-being of the propertied class. Again, the elderly Madison and Monroe compromised, and Marshall never was a strong supporter of an expanded voter class. As we have seen, Marshall had always put property interests first, so with no regrets he sided with the eastern slaveholding class. At least the franchise was extended to leaseholders and housekeepers, but even after passage of the new constitution, one-third of white male citizens still could not vote.[35] The secret ballot was also rejected, so voting remained by voice as it had been in colonial times. Madison pushed to have the governor popularly elected instead of being chosen by the legislature, but this democratic measure also failed. Both he and Monroe did successfully labor to lengthen the governor's term of office to three years, and the size of the executive council was reduced. The judicial structure and the nature of county governance was left essentially unchanged, and, in complete repudiation of Jeffersonian principles, the new constitution made no provision for amendment. When this topic had arisen in the convention on December 30, Randolph had raged against the very idea of a changeable constitution, practically spitting out his contempt for what he called "this *maggot* of innovation," which was a harsher version of a prior complaint on November 28 against the "lust of innovation" that he said had been "the death of all Republics."[36] His outburst stopped cold the discussion of amendments. The convention finished writing the new constitution on

January 14, 1830, and after the voters ratified it the following April, the reform impulse in Virginia was defeated if not quite dead. (As Madison and Monroe had feared, a little over three decades later, in the midst of the Civil War, fifty western counties broke away from the Old Dominion and founded the free state of West Virginia.)

For decades, Washington, Jefferson, Madison, Marshall, and Monroe had in the broadest sense worked together, in a nationalistic and optimistic fashion, to help create a new nation characterized by political and religious freedom for its white citizens, but they ended up losing Virginia and eventually the South. As they had feared but could see no way to prevent, the issue of slavery did destroy the union, at least temporarily. A mighty Civil War, with three-quarters of a million deaths, ensued, and only that horror ended the scourge of slavery, but it left a wide vein of racism that has not yet been removed. The last gasp of Jeffersonian liberalism was expressed by Thomas Jefferson Randolph, the president's grandson, now a member of the Virginia House of Delegates, in a special meeting called by that body for December 1831–January 1832 in response to the Nat Turner slave revolt of August 1831. That event, plus the founding of a more aggressive form of abolitionism by William Lloyd Garrison, who had begun publishing the antislavery newspaper *The Liberator* on January 1 of that year, very significantly changed the terms of debate about the South's so-called peculiar institution. The topic of the special session was to be the place of slavery in the future of the state.[37] Prominent in the House was a new generation of leaders, not only Jefferson's grandson but the grandson of Patrick Henry and the son of John Marshall. Various proposals were made, and spokesmen described the immorality of slavery and its deleterious influence on the state. Thomas Jefferson Randolph even offered a revised version of his grandfather's plan, that all enslaved people born after 1840 were to become the property of the state, and when they became adults, the state would hire them out, using the funds received to pay for their eventual emancipation and colonization outside the state. (Although Virginia, by his plan, could sell its enslaved people to other states; only those remaining in Virginia would ultimately be free.)[38]

But the defenders of slavery were in the majority, and they rejected all criticisms of the institution and all proposals, even partial ones, to emancipate and colonize them. In fact, the final decision of the legislature was that it "was *inexpedient* for the present legislature to make any legislative enactments for the abolition of slavery."[39] (This in a state where in 1785 the College of William and Mary had bestowed an honorary degree on British antislavery activist Granville Sharp and in 1816 the House of Delegates had officially endorsed colonization in Africa.) No longer did the agonizing over slavery that had characterized the attitudes of the Founding Fathers prevail among the legislators. It remained for a young professor of political law at the College of William and Mary, Thomas R. Dew, to write the valedictory for the older viewpoint and shape an updated and comprehensive defense of slavery for the state. At a crucial fork in the road, Virginia took a catastrophically wrong turn.

Dew's long essay was first published under the title of "Abolition of Negro Slavery" in the *American Quarterly Review* in September 1832, and then it appeared in an expanded version in pamphlet form several months later as *Review of the Debate in the Virginia Legislature of 1831 and 1832*.[40] In this wide-ranging essay, Dew argued that "every plan of emancipation and deportation . . . is *totally* impractical." He stated that such beliefs as "'all men are born equal,' that 'slavery in the abstract is wrong,' that 'the slave has a natural right to regain his liberty,' . . . are inapplicable and mischievous."[41] He demonstrated the demographic and financial difficulties of trying to colonize all freed Blacks to Africa and pointed out the horrific disease environment there. Next he turned to a biblical defense of slavery. "The children of Israel themselves were slaveholders," he wrote, "and were not condemned for it." And "When we turn to the New Testament, we find not one single passage at all calculated to disturb the conscience of an honest slave-holder."[42] Here of course Dew was drawing from a long train of biblical defenses of slavery that reached far back into the colonial era.

Then he turned to those famous passages in Jefferson's *Notes on the State of Virginia* in which the former president had described the deleterious moral consequences on whites of slaveholding. Dew went to great length to deny every aspect of Jefferson's arguments. Dew wrote that masters were normally kind to their enslaved people, that their benevolent actions taught their own children, by example, principles of kindness and generosity. Dew insisted that enslaved people loved their enslavers, that they were their masters' best friends, that the institution promoted the republican spirit, that there was only slight risk of insurrection. The recent Nat Turner revolt was not the result of general unrest but rather the consequence of one demented enslaved man misled by wild and fanatical religious views.[43] Dew also argued against the common idea that slave labor was less productive than free labor; if the South were less wealthy than the North, it was because of unfair policies of the federal government. He concluded that "the time for emancipation has not yet arrived, and perhaps it never will."[44] Actually nowhere in his survey of proslavery arguments did Dew come up with anything that had not been said often before, even in the 1790 legislative debates, but he did offer an encyclopedic summary of defenses of slavery and a critique of efforts to abolish the institutions. Absent in his discussion were the kinds of laments or moral concerns about slavery that had infused the private and sometimes public comments of the former leaders of the Virginia Dynasty.

That era was over; a conservative, antidemocratic, proslavery attitude of self-serving, hard-nosed realism—not idealism—was now the dominant tone of Virginia political life. Dew's essay helped capture and promote the increasingly hegemonic support of slavery as the defining feature of Virginia, and southern, life. It was a tragic denouement to the daring adventure in nation-making engaged in by Washington, Mason, Henry, Jefferson, Madison, Monroe, and Marshall and others over the course of the previous century. Yet the seeds of the ideals they planted would over time have impacts they could not have foreseen, leading to the eventual demise of slavery and the slow, halting advance toward that more perfect union, the ideal of which still motivates the nation when it adheres to its founding vision. The institutions they established have weathered the adversities of a Civil War, two world wars, a great depression, natural calamities, and pandemics; they have undergirded our ability, so far, to escape—even if barely—succumbing to authoritarianism. They have allowed, even though far too slowly, the increasing diversity in race and gender of our national leadership. The goals of political and religious freedom, the hope for the achievement of equality of all humankind, and the pursuit of happiness remain fundamental to the nation they did so much to create two centuries ago.

NOTES

Abbreviations

DHRC — *Documentary History of the Ratification of the Constitution, Virginia.* Edited by John P. Kaminski and Gaspare J. Saladino. 14 vols. Madison: State Historical Society of Wisconsin, 1988.

GWW — *George Washington: Writings.* Edited by John H. Rhodehamel. New York: Library of America, 1997.

PAH — *Papers of Alexander Hamilton.* Edited by Harold C. Syrett and Jacob E. Cooke. 27 vols. New York: Columbia University Press, 1961–87.

JMW — *John Marshall: Writings.* Edited by Charles F. Hobson. New York: Library of America, 2010.

PGM — *Papers of George Mason, 1725–1792.* Edited by Robert A. Rutland. 3 vols. Chapel Hill: University of North Carolina Press, 1970.

PGWConS — *Papers of George Washington, Confederation Series.* Edited by W. W. Abbot and Dorothy Twohig. 6 vols. Charlottesville: University Press of Virginia, 1992–97.

PGWCS — *Papers of George Washington, Colonial Series.* Edited by W. W. Abbot, Dorothy Twohig, and Philander D. Chase. 10 vols. Charlottesville: University Press of Virginia, 1983–95.

PGWPS — *Papers of George Washington, Presidential Series.* Edited by Dorothy Twohig, W. W. Abbot, and Philander D. Chase. 21 vols. Charlottesville: University of Virginia Press, 1987–2020.

PJM — *Papers of James Madison.* Edited by William T. Hutchinson, William M. E. Rachal, and Robert Allen Rutland. 18 vols. Chicago: University of Chicago Press, 1962–2000.

PJMar — *Papers of John Marshall.* Edited by Herbert A. Johnson et al. 12 vols. Chapel Hill: University of North Carolina Press, 1974–2006.

PJMPS — *Papers of James Madison, Presidential Series.* Edited by Robert A. Rutland et al. 11 vols. Charlottesville: University of Virginia Press, 1984–2020.

PJMSSS — *Papers of James Madison, Secretary of State Series.* Edited by David B. Mattern et al. 12 vols. to date. Charlottesville: University of Virginia Press, 1986–.

PTJ — *Papers of Thomas Jefferson.* Edited by Julian P. Boyd, L. H. Butterfield, Charles T. Cullen, and John Catanzariti. 44 vols. to date. Princeton: Princeton University Press, 1950–.

PTJRS *Papers of Thomas Jefferson, Retirement Series.* Edited by J. Jefferson Looney. 19 vols. to date. Princeton: Princeton University Press, 2004–.

RL *The Republic of Letters: The Correspondence between Thomas Jefferson and James Madison, 1776–1826.* Edited by James Morton Smith. 3 vols. New York: W. W. Norton, 1995.

TJW *Thomas Jefferson: Writings.* Edited by Merrill D. Peterson. New York: Library of America, 1984.

WJM *Writings of James Monroe.* Edited by Stanislaus Murray. 7 vols. New York: G. P. Putnam's Sons, 1898–1903.

Introduction

1. John Adams to Hezekiah Niles, February 13, 1818, published in *Niles' Weekly Register,* 2 (March 7, 1818), *Founders Online,* National Archives, https://founders.archives.gov/documents/Adams/99-02-02-6854.
2. See Mayo, *Myths and Men,* 1.
3. Morgan, *American Slavery, American Freedom,* 301; Kolchin, *American Slavery,* 252.
4. See Billings, Selby, and Tate, *Colonial Virginia,* 260.
5. Quoted in Henriques, *Realistic Visionary,* 2–3.

1 The First Rumblings

1. For good descriptions of the youthful Washington, see Ellis, *His Excellency,* 7–12; and Chernow, *Washington,* 10–28.
2. Chernow, *Washington,* 50–51.
3. Thomas Jefferson to William Wirt, August 5, 1815, in *PTJRS,* 8:641–45 (645 qtd).
4. For Washington's Mount Vernon expenditures, see Ellis, *His Excellency,* 49. These expenditures dwarf those of George Mason and Thomas Jefferson, who also had constructed for themselves handsome mansions.
5. The best account of this feeling of unease remains Wood, "Rhetoric and Reality in the American Revolution," 3–32.
6. Breen, *Tobacco Culture.*
7. Billings, Selby, and Tate, *Colonial Virginia,* 285.
8. Broadwater, *George Mason,* 29.
9. Holton, *Forced Founders,* 6–8.
10. For a succinct description of the Revenue (Sugar) Act, see Morris, *Encyclopedia of American History,* 72–73.
11. Otis, *The Rights of the British Colonists,* 65.
12. See the description of the Stamp Act in Morris, *Encyclopedia of American History,* 73–74.
13. A convenient summary of Bland's main points is provided in Kukla, *Patrick Henry,* 49–51.

14. The five resolutions are quoted in Beeman, *Patrick Henry,* 35–36 (36 qtd). The final two resolutions (along with the first five), may be found in Meade, *Patrick Henry: Patriot in the Making,* 171 (first five on 170).
15. "Autobiography," in *TJW,* 6.
16. These words are quoted in every biography of Henry; see, for example, Beeman, *Patrick Henry,* 37.
17. "Journal of a French Traveler," 726–47 (745 qtd).
18. Quoted in Kukla, *Patrick Henry,* 70.
19. Morris, *Encyclopedia of American History,* 74–75.
20. Quoted in Kukla, *Patrick Henry,* 96.
21. Jefferson, "Autobiography," in *TJW,* 36.
22. "To the Committee of Merchants in London," June 6, 1766, in *PGM,* 1:65–72 (66, 67, 68, 71–72 qtd).

2 The Fateful Step

1. Chernow, *Washington,* 144–46.
2. Mason, "The Virginia Nonimportation Resolutions of 1769," in *PGM,* 1:109–12 (109, 110 qtd). There has been some question as to Mason's authorship, but see Broadwater, *George Mason,* 49–53.
3. Washington to Bryan Fairfax, July 4, 1774, in *PGWCS,* 10:109–11.
4. Quoted in Boswell, *The Life of Samuel Johnson,* 2:420.
5. See Boles, *Jefferson,* 46–47.
6. "Association of Members of the Late House of Burgesses," [May 27, 1774], reprinted in *PTJ,* 1:107–9 (107, 108 qtd).
7. "Fairfax County Resolves," [July 18, 1774], in *PGM,* 1:201–9 (201–2 qtd).
8. My discussion here is adapted from Boles, *Jefferson,* 50–54. A facsimile of the pamphlet is sold today in the printmakers shop in Colonial Williamsburg.
9. Jefferson, "Autobiography," in *TJW,* 3–101 (10 qtd).
10. "Draft of Instructions to the Virginia Delegates in the Continental Congress," [the text of *A Summary View of the Rights of British America*], in *PTJ,* 1:121–35 (121 qtd).
11. Ibid., 125.
12. Ibid., 130, 134.
13. Ibid., 134.
14. Ibid., 135.
15. Ibid., 121.
16. For visitors to London, see Chervinsky, *The Cabinet,* 99.
17. Quoted in Meade, *Patrick Henry: Practical Revolutionary,* 29.
18. See Hayes, *Mind of a Patriot,* 56–62.
19. Mason to Martin Cockburn, May 26, 1774, in *PGM,* 1:190.
20. Quoted from the excerpts from Wirt's account as printed in Meade, *Patrick Henry, Practical Revolutionary,* 33–35.

21. Washington to Joseph Reed, March 7, 1776, quoted in Selby, *Revolution in Virginia,* 50.
22. Quoted in ibid., 66.
23. Quoted in Boles, *Jefferson,* 61.
24. "First Draft of the Virginia Declaration of Rights," in *PGM,* 1:277–78 (277 qtd).
25. See the explanation in ibid., 289n.
26. Ibid., 277, 278.
27. Ibid., 290–91n; and Ketcham, *James Madison,* 72–73. I have found Broadwater, *George Mason,* 70–91, an excellent guide to the shape and import of Mason's Virginia Declaration of Rights.
28. Both quotes are from John Quincy Adams, *The Jubilee of the Constitution,* 111.
29. Jefferson to Thomas Nelson, May 16, 1776, in *PTJ,* 1:292.
30. Edmund Pendleton to Jefferson, in ibid., 296.
31. The various drafts, along with extremely helpful explanatory notes, are provided in ibid., 329–65; see also Boles, *Jefferson,* 64–65.
32. "First Draft by Jefferson," in *PTJ,* 1:337–45 (339 qtd).
33. Ibid., 344.
34. Ibid., 347–54 (353 qtd).
35. Mason's first draft of a constitution for Virginia, and the final draft as approved by the General Assembly, are reprinted in *PGM,* 1:299–302 and 304–9, respectively.
36. Broadwater, *George Mason,* 99.
37. Jefferson to Henry Lee, May 8, 1825, in *TJW,* 1501.
38. "A Declaration by the Representatives of the United States of American, in General Congress Assembled," in ibid., 19–24 (22 qtd). The Declaration is obviously widely available, but I am citing this version because it indicates the additions and omissions made by Congress, much to Jefferson's annoyance.
39. Ibid., 19.
40. Ibid., 19.
41. Ibid., 23–24.

3 Winning Independence

1. See the wide variety of bills written by Mason as printed in *PGM,* 1:317–467, passim.
2. Cheney, *James Madison,* 68.
3. "Autobiography," in *TJW,* 46.
4. "Resolutions Urging Recruitment and Conferring Emergency Powers on the Governor and Council," in *PGM,* 1:325–26 (326 qtd).
5. "Bill for Establishing a Land Office . . . ," in *PTJ,* 2:139–47 (139 qtd). The text of the bill may also be found in *PGM,* 1:399–408.
6. Ibid., 140.
7. "Bill for the Revision of the Laws," [October 15, 1776], in *PTJ,* 1:562–63 (563 qtd).
8. Quoted in Broadwater, *Jefferson, Madison, and the Making of the Constitution,* 31.
9. For Bill 55, see *PTJ,* 2:476–77 (477 qtd); for Bill 64, see ibid., 492–504.
10. "A Bill Concerning Slaves," in ibid., 470–72; "Autobiography," 44.

11. "A Bill for the More General Diffusion of Knowledge" is reprinted, with very helpful editorial scaffolding, in *PTJ,* 2:526–35.
12. "A Bill for Establishing Religious Freedom," in *PTJ,* 2:545–47 (545, 546 qtd). There is no truly satisfactory comprehensive study of Jefferson's personal religion. Gaustad's *Sworn on the Altar of God* is insufficiently rigorous, and Kidd's more recent *Thomas Jefferson: A Biography of Spirit and Flesh* is too relentlessly hostile in tone.
13. See Rakove, *Beyond Belief,* 68.
14. For Henry's opposition to Jefferson's bill and his support of a general religious tax for the support of religion, see Kukla, *Patrick Henry,* 277–82.
15. Ammon, *James Monroe,* 13–14.
16. There are many biographies of Washington, including the comprehensive recent one by Chernow, *Washington,* but no one is more successful in capturing Washington's accomplishments than Ellis, *His Excellency,* especially chapters 3 and 4.
17. Chernow, *Washington,* 354–56.
18. Washington to Mason, March 27, 1779, in *PGM,* 2:491–94 (492 qtd).
19. Henry to Jefferson, February 15, 1780, in *PTJ,* 3:293–94 (293 qtd).
20. Madison to Jefferson, March 27, 28, 1780, in *RL,* 1:135–37 (136 qtd).
21. An excellent account of the end of the Battle of Yorktown is Chernow, *Washington,* 417–19.

4 Unresolved Problems

1. Quoted in Boles, *Jefferson,* 115.
2. Jefferson to Washington, April 16, 1784, in *PTJ,* 7:105–8 (106–7 qtd).
3. Chernow, *Washington,* 409. My discussion of Washington in retirement is based on this biography and Ellis, *His Excellency.*
4. Chernow, the leading modern biographer of Washington, says that he was "habituated to profligate spending and a baronial lifestyle." Chernow, *Washington,* 490.
5. Washington to Hamilton, March 31, 1783, in *GWW,* 504–5 (505 qtd).
6. "Circular Letter to State Governments," June 8, 1783, in ibid., 516–26.
7. Ibid., 516.
8. See "Marriage Agreement with Sarah Brent," in *PGM,* 2:620–21.
9. "In Opposition to Direct Election of the Chief Executive," July 17, 1787, in ibid., 3:925.
10. Mason to Henry, May 6, 1783, in ibid., 769–73 (770 qtd).
11. Mason to William Cabell, May 6, 1783, in ibid., 768–69; for Jefferson's proposed new constitution, see Boles, *Jefferson,* 110–11.
12. My discussion of Henry is based on Kidd, *Patrick Henry,* uncritically pro-Henry; Kukla, *Patrick Henry,* more balanced; and the definitive two volumes by Meade: *Patrick Henry: Patriot in the Making* and *Patrick Henry: Practical Revolutionary.*
13. Even John Paul Jones, the revolutionary naval hero, was surprised at Henry's conservative attitude with its emphasis on the states. See Meade, *Patrick Henry: Practical Revolutionary,* 271.
14. Cheney offers the best analysis of Madison's mild epilepsy in *James Madison,* 51–52.

15. Madison to Jefferson, *PTJ,* 9:332–36 (332–33 qtd).
16. Jefferson to Madison, Dec. 12, 1784, in ibid., 353–55 (354 qtd).
17. Jefferson to Monroe, May 20, 1782, in *PTJ,* 6:184–86 (185, 184 qtd).
18. The text of Jefferson's proposed new constitution is printed in *PTJ,* 6:294–305, and the material regarding ending slavery is on 298.
19. Quoted in Boles, *Jefferson,* 120. My discussion of Jefferson is adapted from this book, where all statements of fact are documented.
20. See the beautifully written account by Schiff, *A Great Improvisation.*
21. Every aspect of Jefferson's relationship with Sally Hemings is discussed in marvelous detail and insight by Gordon-Reed in *The Hemingses of Monticello,* 153–391.
22. For Jefferson's racial views in context, see Curran, *The Anatomy of Blackness;* and for Jefferson's *Notes,* see Rogers, "Jefferson's Changing Audiences," 171–208.
23. Jefferson to Washington, May 2, 1788, in *PTJ,* 13:124–28 (128 qtd).
24. Van Cleve, *We Have Not a Government,* 70. Consult also Klarman, *The Framers' Coup,* 11–125, who sees the writing of the Constitution as a decidedly anti-populist move to safeguard the interests of the economic and political elites.
25. Klarman, *The Framers' Coup,* 75.
26. For the economic plight of the nation in this period, see Van Cleve, *We Have Not a Government,* 49–52, and passim.
27. The most succinct treatment of these legislative abuses is in Wood, *Empire of Liberty,* 15–20.
28. Madison to Jefferson, October 24, 1787, in *PTJ,* 12:270–85 (276 qtd).
29. Washington to Benjamin Lincoln, November 7, 1786, in *PGWConS,* 4:339.
30. Washington to Henry Knox, February 3, 1787, in ibid., 5:7–9 (7–8 qtd).
31. Marshall to James Wilkinson, January 5, 1787, in *PJMar,* 1:199–201 (201 qtd).
32. John Jay to Washington, June 27, 1786, in *PGWConS,* 4:130–32 (131 qtd).
33. Washington to Jay, August 15, 1786, in ibid., 212–13.
34. Jefferson to Madison, January 30, 1787, in *PTJ,* 11:92–97 (92 qtd).
35. Jefferson to Abigail Adams, February 22, 1787, in ibid., 174–75 (174 qtd).
36. Madison to Pendleton, February 25, 1787, in *PJM,* 9:299.
37. Jefferson to Madison, January 30, 1787, in *PTJ,* 11:92–97 (93 qtd).
38. I have found most useful on this entire issue the treatment in Van Cleve, *We Have Not a Nation,* chapter 6 (161–85), although there is a large literature on the Jay-Gardoqui controversy.
39. Quoted in Rakove, *Revolutionaries,* 354.
40. Quoted in Beeman, *Plain, Honest Men,* 19.
41. "Answers to Demeunier's First Queries," January 14, 1786, in *PTJ,* 10:11–20 (14 qtd).
42. Madison to Jefferson, March 19, 1787, in ibid., 11:219–23 (219 qtd). Jefferson received the letter on June 16 when back in Paris.
43. Franklin to Jefferson, in ibid., 301–2 (302 qtd).
44. See Madison to Jefferson, April 23, 1787, in ibid. 307–10; Carrington to Jefferson, April 24, 1787, in ibid., 310–12 (311 qtd); Jay to Jefferson, April 24, 1787, in ibid., 312–14 (313 qtd).

45. Madison to Jefferson, June 6, 1787, in ibid., 400–402 (401, 402 qtd).
46. Jefferson to Edward Carrington, August 4, 1787, in ibid., 678–80 (679 qtd); Jefferson to Adams, August 30, 1787, in ibid., 12:66–69 (69 qtd).

5 Creating a New Government

1. The document is reprinted in *PJM,* 9:348–57.
2. This summary is drawn from the text cited above. Madison actually listed a twelfth vice, "impotence of the laws of the States" but did not elaborate it. Two excellent analyses of the entire document are Feldman, *Three Lives of James Madison,* 95–101, and Rakove, *Revolutionaries,* 359–65.
3. Madison to Jefferson, March 19, 1787, in *PTJ,* 11:219–23 (219, 220 qtd).
4. Jefferson to Madison, June 20, 1787, in ibid., 11:480–84 (480–81 qtd).
5. Madison to Washington, April 16, 1787, in *PJM,* 9:382–87 (383 qtd).
6. Ibid. 383, 385.
7. For Jackson's limitations, see Beeman, *Plain, Honest Men,* 70, 84–85. This is the best single book on the convention.
8. Jefferson to John Adams, August 30, 1787, in *PTJ,* 11:66–69 (69 qtd).
9. My description of the meeting room and the delegates is drawn from Bowen, *Miracle at Philadelphia,* 4, 23–24; and Beeman, *Plain, Honest Men,* 61–68. For an excellent account of every aspect of the Constitution—why the convention was called, its deliberations, and the whole ratification process—see Klarman, *The Framers' Coup.*
10. See Madison, *Notes of Debates in the Federal Convention,* 24. Hereinafter cited as *Madison's Notes.*
11. Ibid., 25–28 (28 qtd).
12. "Notes of Major William Pierce," 310–34 (332 qtd). Hereinafter cited as "Notes of William Pierce."
13. *Madison's Notes,* 30–33.
14. Ibid., 30.
15. Ibid. 31, 33.
16. Ibid., 34.
17. Ibid., 39.
18. "Notes of William Pierce," 326.
19. *Madison's Notes,* 39, 40.
20. Ibid., 46.
21. Ibid., 56.
22. Ibid., 84, 87, 88.
23. Ibid., 95–97 (97 qtd).
24. Ibid., 103.
25. See Wilentz, *No Property in Man,* for a persuasive analysis of the Founders' determination to keep slavery from being a permanent feature of the Constitution. Oakes, *The Crooked Path to Abolition,* traces out the abolitionist potential of the nation's founding document.

26. See Waldstreicher, *Slavery's Constitution.*
27. *Madison's Notes,* 115–17.
28. Patterson's plan is printed in ibid., 118–21.
29. Hamilton's speech (as Madison recorded it) is in ibid., 129–39 (134, 135, 136 qtd).
30. Ibid., 159.
31. Ibid., 209–11, 226–27.
32. Ibid., 237–38.
33. Rakove, *Revolutionaries,* 374.
34. "Notes of William Pierce," 325.
35. *Madison's Notes,* 286, 295.
36. For the passage of the Northwest Ordinance, see Beeman, *Plain, Honest Men,* 215–18.
37. The compromise that led to the acceptance of the revised Grand Committee report is often called the Connecticut Compromise because Roger Sherman, Oliver Ellsworth, and William Samuel Johnson of Connecticut argued so effectively for it.
38. McCoy, *The Elusive Republic,* 131n.
39. *Madison's Notes,* 308.
40. Ibid., 331, 332.
41. Ibid., 331.
42. The entire document is reprinted in ibid., 385–96 (385, 390 qtd).
43. Ibid., 390.
44. Farrand, *Records of the Federal Convention of 1787,* 3:327, 1:392, 2:268.
45. *Madison's Notes,* 502 (Rutledge's comments), 503 (Pinckney's comments).
46. Ibid., 532.
47. Ibid., 552.
48. Broadwater, *George Mason,* 207.
49. *Madison's Notes,* 569.
50. Ibid., 58, 393, 605.
51. "The Federalist No. 65 [64]," in Cooke, *The Federalist,* 439–45 (439–40 qtd).
52. Madison quote in Beeman, *Plain, Honest Men,* 346.
53. *Madison's Notes,* 653–54.
54. Ibid., 659.
55. Washington to Lafayette, February 7, 1788, in *PGWConS,* 6:95–97 (95 qtd).
56. Madison to Jefferson, September 6, 1787, in *PTJ,* 12:102–4 (103 qtd).

6 The Virginia Ratification Debate

1. James Madison to Thomas Jefferson, October 24, 1787, in *PTJ,* 12:270–84 (280 qtd).
2. Quoted in Maier, *Ratification,* 58.
3. George Washington to the Marquis de Lafayette, September 18, 1787, in *DHRC,* 8:12; and George Washington to Thomas Jefferson, September 18, 1787, in *PTJ,* 12:149. Three of the *DHRC* volumes, 8, 9, and 10, cover events in Virginia, and they are the indispensable source for understanding ratification in the state.
4. Washington to Henry, Harrison, and Nelson, September 24, 1787, in *DHRC,* 8:15.

5. Alexander Donald to Jefferson, November 12, 1787, in *PTJ,* 12:345–48 (345 qtd).
6. "George Mason's Objections to the Constitution of Government formed by the Convention," in *DHRC,* 8:43–46 (45 qtd).
7. See Washington to Madison, October 10, 1787, in *DHRC,* 8:49–50; and Madison to Washington, October 18, 1787, in ibid., 8:76–77, in which both express uncertainty about Henry's position.
8. Henry to Washington, October 19, 1787, in *DHRC,* 8:79.
9. *DHRC,* 8:114.
10. Madison to Washington, October 28, 1787, in ibid., 126–27 (126 qtd).
11. Madison to Jefferson, December 9, 1787, in ibid., 226–28 (226 qtd).
12. My discussion of the ratification conventions in states other than Virginia is based on the following three books: Maier, *Ratification;* Rutland, *The Ordeal of the Constitution;* and especially Beeman, *Plain, Honest Men.* These books obviously cover Virginia as well, but for more on ratification in Virginia, see the valuable study by Glover, *The Fate of the Revolution.*
13. For the Federalists' advantage in general, see Klarman, *The Framers' Coup,* 405–17. Klarman is good for the Constitutional Convention also.
14. Again, my discussion largely summarizes Maier, *Ratification,* and Beeman, *Plain, Honest Men.*
15. The pamphlet is reprinted in *DHRC,* 8:262–74 (274 qtd).
16. See Maier, *Ratification,* 155, 160–62.
17. For reaction of Madison and Washington, see Klarman, *Framers' Coup,* 443–44; Edward Carrington to Henry Knox, March 13, 1788, in *DHRC,* 8:491.
18. Edward Carrington to Madison, January 18, 1788, in *DHRC,* 8:308–9 (309 qtd).
19. Madison to Jefferson, December 9, 1787, in *PTJ,* 12:408–12 (410 qtd).
20. Madison to Washington, February 20, 1788, in *DHRC,* 8:601–2 (602 qtd).
21. Mason to John Francis Mercer, May 1, 1788, in *PGM,* 3:1039–41 (1040 qtd). For concerns that Henry aimed as disunion, see Madison to Jefferson, April 22, 1788, in *PTJ,* 13:98–99; and Edward Carrington to Jefferson, April 24, 1788, in *PTJ,* 13:100–103.
22. Jefferson to David Humphreys, March 18, 1789, in *PTJ,* 14:676–79 (678 qtd). For a more thorough narrative of Jefferson's evolving position on the Constitution than is possible here, see Boles, *Jefferson,* 189–96.
23. Washington to Jefferson, May 30, 1787, in *PTJ,* 11:385–90 (389–90 qtd).
24. Madison to Jefferson, June 6, 1787, in ibid., 400–402 (401 qtd).
25. Jefferson, "Answers to Demeunier's First Queries," January 24, 1786, in ibid., 10:14; Jefferson to Edward Carrington, August 4, 1787, in ibid., 11:678. He mentioned the necessity of reforming the executive position to a variety of correspondents.
26. Jefferson to C. W. F. Dumas, September 10, 1787, in ibid., 12:113.
27. Jefferson to Adams, November 13, 1787, in ibid., 349–51 (350–51 qtd).
28. Madison to Jefferson, September 6, 1788, in ibid., 12:102–4, and Madison to Jefferson, October 24, 1788, 12:270–84.
29. Jefferson to Madison, February 6, 1788, in ibid., 568–70 (569 qtd), and the very similar letter to Alexander Donald, on the same day, in ibid., 570–72.

30. Carrington to Jefferson, May 14, 1788, in ibid., 13:156–57.
31. See Koch, *Jefferson and Madison.*
32. Jefferson to Carrington, May 27, 1788, in *PTJ,* 13:208–9 (208 qtd).
33. Jefferson to Edward Rutledge, July 18, 1788, in ibid., 377–79 (378 qtd).
34. Jefferson to Madison, July 31, 1788, in ibid., 440–43 (443 qtd); and Jefferson to William Carmichael, August 12, 1788, in ibid., 502–3 (502 qtd).
35. *DHRC,* 9:911.
36. Ibid., 914. For a detailed account of Madison's role in the convention, see Feldman, *Three Lives of James Madison,* 198–241.
37. *DHRC,* 9:917–31 (930 qtd).
38. Ibid., 931–36 (933 qtd).
39. Madison to Washington, June 4, 1788, in *DHRC,* 10:1574.
40. *DHRC,* 9:945.
41. Ibid., 951–68 (963, 968 qtd).
42. Klarman, *Framers' Coup,* 467.
43. *DRRC,* 9:971–89 (971, 988 qtd).
44. Ibid., 989–98 (995 qtd).
45. Ibid., 989.
46. Ibid., 1035–47 (1046 qtd).
47. Ibid., 1050–72 (1050–51, 1059, 1066 qtd).
48. *DHRC,* 10:1476.
49. My sketch of Monroe's early career in based upon Ammon, *James Monroe,* 1–70.
50. Monroe's remarks are reprinted in *DHRC,* 9:1103–15 (1115 qtd).
51. My sketch of Marshall's background is based upon Smith, *John Marshall,* 21–168.
52. Marshall's remarks are reprinted in *DHRC,* 9:1115–27.
53. Ibid., 10:1431.
54. Nicholas's remarks are reprinted in ibid., 10:1249–52 (1252 qtd).
55. Ibid., 1367.
56. The comment about Mason is based on Broadwater, *George Mason,* 234.
57. Madison to Hamilton, June 16, 1788, in *DHRC,* 10:1630; Madison to Hamilton, June 20, 1788, in ibid., 1656–57 (1657 qtd).
58. Ibid., 1425.
59. Madison to Washington, June 23, 1788, in ibid., 1668.
60. Ibid., 1474.
61. Ibid., 1506.
62. Ibid.
63. Ibid., 1530–34 (1533, 1530, 1534 qtd).
64. Ibid., 1519–24 (1524 qtd).
65. Ibid., 1534–37 (1537 qtd).
66. Glover, *Fate of the Revolution,* 147.
67. Mason to Washington, June 19, 1789, in *PGM,* 3:1157–61 (1160–61 qtd).
68. Mason to Jefferson, in ibid., 1216–18 (1218 qtd). There is no evidence Jefferson ever tried to intervene with Madison.

69. Madison to Washington, June 27, 1788, in *DHRC,* 10:1688–89 (1689 qtd).
70. Madison to Washington, August 24, 1788, in *PJM,* 11:240–42 (241 qtd).

7 Launching the New Nation

1. James Madison to George Washington, June 27, 1788, in *PJM,* 11:182–83 (183 qtd). Hereafter cited as *PJM.*
2. Henry is quoted in *DHRC,* 10:1762.
3. Washington to Madison, September 23, 1788, in *PJM,* 11:261–62; Madison to Edmund Randolph, November 2, 1788, in ibid., 328–30 (329 qtd).
4. See Morris, *Encyclopedia of American History,* 120.
5. Madison to Washington, August 24, 1788, in *PJM,* 11:240–42 (241 qtd).
6. Henry Lee to Madison, November 19, 1788, in ibid., 355–57 (356 qtd).
7. The common charge, then by Madison's contemporaries and now by present-day historians, that Henry conspired to gerrymander the district, appears to be unfounded. See Hunter, "The First Gerrymander?," 781–820; and Risjord, *Chesapeake Politics,* 326.
8. Madison to Jefferson, December 8, 1788, in *PJM,* 11:381–84 (384 qtd).
9. See George Lee Turberville to Madison, December 14, 1788, in ibid., 396–98; Hardin Burnley to Madison, December 16, 1788, in ibid., 398–99; Madison to George Washington, January 14, 1789, ibid., 417–18; Madison to George Eve, January 2, 1789, in ibid., 404–5 (404 qtd).
10. See Jefferson to Madison, December 20, 1787, in *PTJ,* 12:438–42 (440 qtd).
11. "To a Resident of Spotsylvania County," January 27, 1789, reprinted from the Fredericksburg *Virginia Herald* in *PJM,* 11:428–29.
12. I have found the most useful account of the election to be that of Feldman, *Three Lives of James Madison,* 247–57.
13. For the concern over monarchism, see Wood, *Empire of Liberty,* 74–75.
14. For a first-hand account, see Maclay, *The Diary of William Maclay,* 13.
15. "Address of the President to Congress" [Washington's first inaugural address], April 30, 1789, in *PJM,* 12:121–24 (123 qtd).
16. Washington to Madison, May 5, 1789, in ibid., 131–32 (132 qtd).
17. "Address of the House of Representatives to the President," May 5, 1789, in ibid., 132–33 (133 qtd).
18. Madison to Jefferson, June 30, 1789, in ibid., 267–72 (268 qtd).
19. Renamed the Department of Defense in 1947.
20. Wood, *Empire of Liberty,* 61.
21. The essential book for understanding this relationship is Leibiger, *Founding Friendship,* especially chapters 4 and 5.
22. "Import and Tonnage Duties," [a proposed bill], in *PJM,* 12:64–69 (65 qtd).
23. See "Editorial Note," in ibid., 53–55; Feldman, *Three Lives of James Madison,* 259–62; and Bordewich, *The First Congress,* 38–42, 72–77, 93–95.
24. "Amendments to the Constitution," [June 8, 1789], in *PJM,* 12:196–209 (199 qtd). See also Washington to Madison, ca. May 31, 1789, in ibid., 191.

25. The amendments are spelled out in *PJM,* 12:200–203 (202 qtd).
26. Washington to Richard Peters, August 19, 1789, in ibid., 346–48 (347 qtd).
27. My discussion of the adoption of the Bill of Rights is based on Feldman, *Three Lives of James Madison,* 267–77; Bordewich, *The First Congress,* 84–93, 115–28; Leibiger, *Founding Friendship,* 120–22; Editorial Note, *PJM,* 12:57–59; and Elkins and McKitrick, *The Age of Federalism,* 58–62.
28. See Bordewich, *The First Congress,* 105–12; Elkins and McKitrick, *Age of Federalism,* 62–64; and Wood, *Empire of Liberty,* 408–15.
29. Madison to Samuel Johnston, July 31, 1789, in *PJM,* 12:317–18 (317 qtd).
30. The size of the court has varied over time: the number of justices dipped to five in 1801, was returned to six in 1802, increased to seven in 1807, to nine in 1837, and then to ten in 1863. Then it was reduced to nine in 1866 and to eight in 1867, but restored to nine in 1869. It has stayed at that number ever since.
31. Washington to Catharine Macaulay Graham, January 9, 1790, in *GWW,* 751–54 (753 qtd).
32. The standard biography of Hamilton is now Chernow's *Alexander Hamilton,* which is very favorable toward the secretary of the treasury.
33. Chernow, *Washington,* 608–13, presents an excellent account of Washington's northern tour.
34. James Madison [Jr.] to James Madison Sr., February 27, 1790, in *PJM,* 13:66–67 (66 qtd).
35. See McCoy, *The Elusive Republic,* 148–52.
36. Ibid., 58–59, 153, 164.
37. See Burstein and Isenberg, *Madison and Jefferson,* 211–24 generally, but especially 224.
38. See Chervinsky, *The Cabinet,* 6, 7, 194.
39. See Gordon-Reed, *The Hemingses of Monticello,* 647–48. See also Reed and Onuf, *"Most Blessed of the Patriarchs,"* 316.
40. Washington to Jefferson, January 21, 1790, in *PTJ,* 16:116–18 (117 qtd).
41. For a fuller account of Jefferson's appointment and the delay in accepting it, see Boles, *Jefferson,* 206–10.
42. Jefferson's account, probably put in writing in 1792, is reprinted as "Jefferson's Account of the Bargain on the Assumption and Residence Bills," in *PTJ,* 17:205–7 (205, 207 qtd). See also the editorial note in *PJM,* 13:243–46.
43. Maclay, *Diary of Maclay,* 293.
44. Bowling, *Creating the Federal City,* 7, 23.
45. Elkins and McKitrick, *Age of Federalism,* 155–61.
46. Madison to Monroe, July 24 [25?], 1790, in *PJM,* 13:282–83.
47. [Maclay], *Diary of Maclay,* 202.
48. This whole event is best described by Newman in "Prelude to the Gag Rule," 571–99.
49. [Maclay], *Diary of Maclay,* (entry for March 22, 1790), 226.
50. Jefferson, "Answers to Demeunier's First Queries," January 24, 1786, in *PTJ,* 10:11–20 (18 qtd).

51. As a pronounced Hamilton enthusiast says about the slavery issue in this context, "this man [Hamilton] of infinite opinions grew mute on that all important matter." Chernow, *Alexander Hamilton,* 307. Based on Chernow's depiction (p. 6) of Hamilton as a "staunch abolitionist"—a gross exaggeration—the Broadway hit entitled *Hamilton* by Lin-Manuel Miranda also misrepresents Hamilton's abolitionism. For a corrective, see Romano and Potter, eds., *Historians on Hamilton,* and especially Scherr, "Alexander Hamilton and Slavery," 130–70.
52. Washington to Stuart, March 28, 1790, in *GWW,* 756–58 (757–58 qtd).
53. Ona Judge successfully escaped to freedom in May 1796.
54. For the enslaved people in Washington's house, see Chernow, *Washington,* 633–40, and Ross, *Slavery in the North,* 121–52.
55. For the funding and uses of the Bank of the United States, see Elkins and McKitrick, *Age of Federalism,* 226–27; Chernow, *Alexander Hamilton,* 348–61; Leibiger, *Founding Friendship,* 134–36. Bordewich, *The First Congress,* 284–300, provides an excellent account of the entire bank issue.
56. For the more recent criticism of Hamilton's bank, as compared to the uncritical praise of its modernity by scholars such as Chernow, *Alexander Hamilton,* above, see Appleby, *Capitalism and a New Social Order,* and Wood, *Empire of Liberty,* 99, 110.
57. That clause contains the following statement: "The Congress shall have Power . . . To Make all Laws which shall be necessary and proper for carrying into Execution the foregoing Powers, and all other Powers vested by this Constitution in the Government of the United States, or in any Department or Officer thereof."
58. Sharp, *American Politics in the Early Republic,* 39.
59. [Jefferson], "Opinion on the Constitutionality of the Bill for Establishing a National Bank," in *PTJ,* 19:275–80 (276 qtd).
60. Ibid., 280.
61. Quoted in Chernow, *Alexander Hamilton,* 354.
62. Bordewich, *The First Congress,* 297–99.
63. For the southern tour, see Chernow, *Washington,* 651–55.

8 Political Fissures

1. The Postal Service Act had been signed by Washington on February 20, 1792.
2. "Memoranda of Conversations with the President," March 1, 1792, in *PTJ,* 23:184–87 (185 qtd).
3. Jefferson to Washington, May 23, 1792, in ibid., 535–40 (537, 538, 539 qtd).
4. Hamilton to Washington, August 18, 1792, with enclosure, in *PAH,* 12:228–58 (251, 253, 254 qtd).
5. Washington to Jefferson, August 23, 1792, in *GWW,* 815–18 (817–18 qtd).
6. Washington to Jefferson, October 18, 1792, in ibid., 825–26 (825 qtd).
7. "Notes of a Conversation with George Washington," [October 1, 1792], in *PTJ,* 24:433–35 (435 qtd).

8. An excellent brief account of the so-called Genet affair is in Sharp, *American Politics in the Early Republic,* 78–91. The definitive study is Ammon, *The Genet Mission.*
9. Jefferson to Madison, August 11, 1793, in *PTJ,* 26:651–53 (652 qtd).
10. Jefferson to Benjamin Rush, January 16, 1811, in *PTJRS,* 3:304–8 (305 qtd).
11. For a brief account of the "Whiskey Rebellion," see Wood, *Empire of Liberty,* 134–39. For a more thorough treatment, see Slaughter, *The Whiskey Rebellion.*
12. Washington, "Proclamation Calling Forth the Militia," August 7, 1794, in *GWW,* 870–73 (870 qtd).
13. Sharp, *American Politics in the Early Republic,* 85–87, 100–101.
14. Washington to Burgess Ball, September 25, 1794, in ibid., 17:39–40 (723 qtd); Washington to Henry Lee, August 26, 1794, in *PGWPS,* 16:600–604 (602, 601 qtd).
15. Quoted in Hofstadter, *The Idea of a Party System,* 95.
16. Madison to Jefferson, November 30, 1794, in *PTJ,* 28:211–13 (211, 213 qtd).
17. Jefferson to Madison, December 28, 1794, in *PTJ,* 28:228–30 (228 qtd).
18. Wood, *Empire of Liberty,* 138.
19. Sharp, *American Politics in the Early Republic,* 97.
20. Hamilton to Angelica Church, October 23, 1794, quoted in ibid.
21. Washington, "Sixth Annual Message to Congress," November 19, 1794, published in *GWW,* 887–95.
22. Washington to Jefferson, January 1, 1794, in *PTJ,* 28:3.
23. For Washington's complete estrangement with Madison, once his most trusted advisor, see Leibiger, *Founding Friendship,* chapters 9 and 10.
24. Washington to Arthur Young, December 12, 1793, in *GWW,* 851–58 (852 qtd).
25. "Jefferson Note," November 29, 1790, in Jefferson, *Thomas Jefferson and the National Capital,* 30–36.
26. See "Commissioners to the President," November 25, 1791, in ibid., 78–79; Jefferson to L'Enfant, December 1, 1791, in ibid., 80–81; and "Jefferson's Opinion on L'Enfant's Letter of December 7," December 11, 1791, in ibid., 82–86 (83 qtd).
27. For L'Enfant's firing, see Jefferson to L'Enfant, February 27, 1792, in ibid., 100; for the naming of the city and territory, see "Commissioners to L'Enfant," September 9, 1791, in ibid., 74–75.
28. See Reps, *Washington on View,* 29–30, 40.
29. Ibid., 30; Jefferson to Daniel Carroll, February 1, 1793, in Jefferson, *Thomas Jefferson and the National Capital,* 71.
30. Ellicott to Jefferson, January 9, 1793, and Ellicott to Jefferson, January 12, 1793, in ibid., 167–68.
31. Jefferson to Madison, October 17, 1792, in *PTJ,* 24:493–94 (494 qtd).
32. Quoted in Cheney, *James Madison,* 249.
33. Feldman, *Three Lives of James Madison,* 444–45.
34. Kukla, *Patrick Henry,* 383.
35. The classic study of the treaty is Bemis, *Pinckney's Treaty,* but the still older study by Whitaker, *The Spanish-American Frontier,* remains useful.
36. See Combs, *The Jay Treaty.*

37. Washington to Hamilton, July 29, 1795, in *GWW,* 914–16 (914 qtd).
38. Jefferson to Edward Rutledge, November 30, 1995, in *PTJ,* 28:541–42 (542 qtd).
39. Benjamin Rush to James Currie, July 26, 1796, in Butterfield, *Letters of Benjamin Rush,* 2:779–80 (779 qtd).
40. An incisive brief account of this controversy between Washington and Madison may be found in Feldman, *Three Lives of James Madison,* 395–406.
41. Washington to Jefferson, July 6, 1796, in *GWW,* 951–54 (952 qtd). For the partisan nature of the Farewell Address, see DeConde, "Washington's Farewell," 641–58; Hofstadter, *Idea of a Party System,* 96–99; Chernow, *Washington,* 756; and even Elkins and McKitrick, *The Age of Federalism,* 493–96, although they cannot quite bring themselves to admit it forthrightly.
42. Cunningham, *The Jeffersonian Republicans,* 107–8.
43. Washington's Farewell Address, in *GWW,* 962–77 (964 qtd).
44. Ibid., 965.
45. Ibid., 966.
46. Ibid., 967.
47. Ibid., 968.
48. Ibid. 969, 970.
49. Ibid., 972.
50. Ibid., 973.
51. Ibid., 973.
52. Ibid., 974–75.
53. "First Inaugural Address," March 4, 1801, in *TJW,* 492–96 (494 qtd).
54. Washington's Farewell Address, in *GWW,* 977.
55. Madison to Monroe, September 29, 1796, in *PJM,* 16:403–4 (403 qtd).

9 Political Crisis

1. Jefferson to Madison, December 28, 1794, in *PTJ,* 28:228–30 (230 qtd).
2. Madison to Jefferson, March 23, 1795, in ibid., 315–16 (315 qtd).
3. Jefferson to Madison, April 27, 1795, in ibid., 338–40 (339 qtd).
4. A succinct account of Hamilton's plan is in Sharp, *American Politics in the Early Republic,* 147–48.
5. Quoted in ibid., 149.
6. See Burstein and Isenberg, *Madison and Jefferson,* 312, for Jefferson's non-campaign, and, in general, Pasley, *The First Presidential Contest.*
7. Madison to Jefferson, December 10, 1796, in *PTJ,* 29:218; Jefferson to Madison, December 17, 1796, in ibid., 223–24 (223 qtd); Madison to Jefferson, December 19, 1796, in ibid., 226–27; Madison to Jefferson, December 25, 1796, in ibid., 227–28.
8. Quoted in Smith, *John Adams,* 2:908.
9. Jefferson to Adams, December 28, 1796, [not sent], in *PTJ,* 29:235; and Jefferson to Madison, January 1, 1797, in ibid., 247–48 (248 qtd).
10. Quoted in Sharp, *American Politics in the Early Republic,* 165.

11. Jefferson to Philip Mazzei, April 24, 1796, in *PTJ,* 29:81–83 (82 qtd). For the whole Mazzei letter affair, see Boles, *Jefferson,* 278–79.
12. A detailed and judicious account of all this is provided in Elkins and McKitrick, *The Age of Federalism,* 549–79 (573 qtd).
13. See Halperin, *The Alien and Sedition Acts,* 35–38.
14. See Malone, *Jefferson,* 3:334–37.
15. For Hamilton's militaristic ambitions, see Wood, *Empire of Liberty,* 264–65. See also Chernow, *Alexander Hamilton,* 563–68, who calls the South American scheme "one of the most flagrant instances of poor judgment in Hamilton's career" (568).
16. Jefferson to Thomas Mann Randolph, May 9, 1798, in *PTJ,* 30:341.
17. For opposition and the effect of the act, see Wood, *Empire of Liberty,* 250 and 260; and Halperin, *Alien and Sedition Acts,* 60.
18. Quoted in Kraut, *Threat of Dissent,* 21.
19. Ibid., 16.
20. For full text of the act, see Smith, *Freedom's Fetters,* 435–42.
21. Jefferson to James Madison, June 7, 1798, in *PTJ,* 30:393–94 (393 qtd).
22. On the rise of newspapers and their change in tone, see Pasley, *"The Tyranny of the Printers."*
23. For the results of the Sedition Act, see Halperin, *Alien and Sedition Acts,* 72–96.
24. For Washington's support, see Cheney, *The Virginia Dynasty,* 185–86.
25. Jefferson to Taylor, June 4, 1798, in *PTJ,* 30:387–89 (388, 389 qtd).
26. Jefferson, *Notes on the State of Virginia,* 129.
27. For the drafting of Jefferson's resolution, see the editorial note in *PTJ,* 30:529–35, and the classic article by Koch and Ammon, "The Virginia and Kentucky Resolutions," 145–76.
28. "Jefferson's Fair Copy" [of the Kentucky Resolutions], in *PTJ,* 30:543–49 (543–44 qtd).
29. Ibid., 547.
30. "The Federalist No. 28," in Cooke, *The Federalist,* 176–90 (179–80 qtd).
31. For a more extensive discussion of Jefferson's motivation and views on this point, see Boles, *Jefferson,* 291–96.
32. See Bird, "Reassessing Responses," 519–51; and Boles, *Jefferson,* 295.
33. Hamilton to Harrison Gray Otis, December 27, 1798, in *PAH,* 20:393–95 (394 qtd); Hamilton to Theodore Sedgwick, February 2, 1799, in ibid., 452–53 (452 qtd).
34. See Rohrs, "The Federalist Party and the Convention of 1800," 237–60; Lyon, "The Franco-American Convention of 1800," 305–33; and Coleman, "'A Second Bounaparty?' A Reexamination," 183–214.
35. Quoted in Elkins and McKitrick, *Age of Federalism,* 617.
36. See Chernow, *Washington,* 782, 797–98. In Chernow's words, "Fiercely opinionated, even strident, Washington was now avowedly partisan in private, fulminating against the Republicans as pawns of the French" (782).
37. Lee, "Funeral Oration on the Death of General Washington," 17.
38. Jefferson to Dr. Walter Jones, January 2, 1814, in *TJW,* 1317–21 (1318–19 qtd).

39. "Scheme for Replevying Goods and Distress for Rent," December 23, 1765, in *PGM,* 1:61–64 (61–62 qtd).
40. Comments in Constitutional Convention, August 22, 1787, in ibid., 965–66.
41. Broadwater, *George Mason,* 245.
42. Quoted in Ragosta, *Patrick Henry,* 37. Every biography of Henry quotes these words.
43. *DHRC,* 10:1476, 1477.
44. Ragosta, *Patrick Henry,* 155.
45. Ona Judge's dramatic story is told in Dunbar, *Never Caught.* For Washington's attitudes toward runaways in general, see Chernow, *Washington,* 116–17.
46. The best account of Washington and slavery, and the manumission of his enslaved people, is Thompson, *"The Only Unavoidable Subject of Regret,"* especially 293–314.
47. [George Washington], "Last Will and Testament," in *PGW,* 1022–45 (1022, 1023 qtd).
48. See Wolf, *Race and Liberty in the New Nation,* 116–17.
49. Ibid., 125.
50. Jefferson to Madison, August 23, 1799, in *PTJ,* 31:172–74 (174 qtd).
51. Jefferson to John Wise, February 12, 1798, in ibid., 30:98–99 (98 qtd).
52. Jefferson to Gerry, January 26, 1799, in ibid., 30:645–50 (646–47, 648 qtd).
53. Ibid., 649.
54. Susan Dunn provides an excellent account of the New York City contest in *Jefferson's Second Revolution,* 175–81.
55. Quoted by Wood, *Empire of Liberty,* 282.
56. Quoted by Larson, *A Magnificent Catastrophe,* 126.
57. Quoted in Cox, *Champion of Southern Federalism,* 76.
58. Reprinted, with a long and insightful introduction, in *PAH,* 25:169–234.
59. Larson, *Magnificent Catastrophe,* 136, 140.
60. Boles, *Jefferson,* 308.
61. See Smith, *John Marshall,* 263–64.
62. In the Sixth Congress, in session from 1799 to 1801, the Federalists controlled both the Senate (22 to 10) and the House (60 to 46). See "Appendix," in Greenstein, *Inventing the Job of President,* 108. But despite their majority of total votes, the Federalists controlled only six state delegations, the Republicans eight, and two delegations (Maryland and Vermont) were tied.
63. A series of letters indicate Jefferson's concern: see Jefferson to Thomas Mann Randolph, December 12, 1800, in *PTJ,* 32:300; Jefferson to Burr, December 15, 1800, in ibid., 306–7; Burr to Jefferson, December 23, 1800, in ibid., 342–43; Jefferson to Hugh Henry Brackenridge, December 18, 1800, in ibid., 318; Jefferson to Madison, December 19, 1800, in ibid., 321–23; Jefferson to Madison, December 20, 1800, in ibid., 330; Jefferson to Madison, December 26, 1800, in ibid., 358.
64. See *PAH,* 25:185; Dunn, *Jefferson's Second Revolution,* 202–4; Chernow, *Alexander Hamilton,* 633–36.
65. Dunn, *Jefferson's Second Revolution,* 195.
66. Jefferson to Monroe, February 15, 1801, in *PTJ,* 32:594. See also Ammon, *James Monroe,* 192–93, for Virginia making preparations for such an exigency.

67. The best brief account of the dilemma the nation faced is Lewis Jr., "'What Is to Become of Our Government?,'" 329.

10 A Political Turning Point

1. My account of the balloting in the House is a composite portrait drawn from a number of secondary accounts, but see especially Sharp, *American Politics in the Early Republic,* 265–73; Dunn, *Jefferson's Second Revolution,* 208–13; Larson, *A Magnificent Catastrophe,* 262–70.
2. Quoted in Sharp, *American Politics in the Early Republic,* 272.
3. See Jefferson, comments on April 15, 1806, recorded in [Jefferson], *The Complete Anas of Jefferson,* 237–41.
4. Bayard is quoted in Borden, *Federalism of James A. Bayard,* 90. Borden supplies the most extensive coverage of this event in his chapter 7 (73–95).
5. "First Inaugural Address," in *TJW,* 492–96 (492–93 qtd).
6. Ibid., 493. Although in this edition "Republicans" and "Federalists" are capitalized, in Jefferson's original text they were lowercased because he was not referring to the parties as such.
7. Ibid., 494–95.
8. See Chervinsky, *The Cabinet.*
9. "Circular to the Heads of Departments," November 6, 1801, in *PTJ,* 35:576–78. See also Cunningham, *Process of Government;* White, *The Jeffersonians,* 8–9, 72–78; and Greenstein, *Inventing the Job of President,* 40–41.
10. The best account of Jefferson's residency in the White House is Conroy, *Jefferson's White House.*
11. Boles, *Jefferson,* 332–35; 371–73.
12. "First Annual Message to Congress," December 8, 1801, in *PTJ,* 36:58–65 (63 qtd).
13. See Greenstein, "Presidential Difference in the Early Republic," 373–90.
14. For congressional numbers, see Greenstein, *Inventing the Job of President,* 108, 111.
15. Malone, *Jefferson and His Time,* 4:113.
16. Ibid., 130–34; Richard Ellis, *The Jeffersonian Crisis,* 45–51, 65–68.
17. For this whole issue, see Smith, *John Marshall,* 309–26.
18. Rakove, *Revolutionaries,* 377.
19. See Hobson, *The Great Chief Justice,* 4–5. For Marshall at the ratification convention, see *DHRC,* 10:1431.
20. Newmyer, *John Marshall and the Heroic Age,* 157–75, 324; Hobson, *The Great Chief Justice,* 47–71 (48 qtd). Newmyer, relentlessly hostile to Jefferson, argues that he and Marshall were already inveterate enemies. For more on Marshall, see chapter 14 of this work.
21. Pasley, "1800 as a Revolution in Political Culture," 120–52, especially 146–47.
22. Jefferson to George Clinton, May 16, 1801, in *PTJ,* 33:127–28 (127 qtd).
23. William Branch Giles to Jefferson, March 16, 1801, in ibid., 310–12 (311 qtd).
24. Cunningham, *Process of Government,* 171–82; Appendix I of *PTJ,* 33:663–79.

25. See Sadosky, "How the Jeffersonians Learned to Love the State," 154–55.
26. Quoted in White, *The Jeffersonians,* 13.
27. Hamilton to Morris, February 29, 1802, in *PAH,* 25:544.
28. Ohio had become a state in 1803, so there were seventeen states in the 1804 election year.
29. See Scofield, "The Fatigues of His Table," 449–69.
30. Young, *The Washington Community,* 167–70.
31. Jefferson to David R. Williams, January 31, 1806, quoted in Cullen, "Jefferson's White House Dinner Guests," 25–43 (29 qtd). Jefferson's predecessors had not so entertained.
32. See Boles, *Jefferson,* 186–87.
33. Lambert, *Barbary Wars,* 118.
34. Ibid., 93.
35. Jefferson to Madison, August 28, 1801, in *PTJ,* 35:162–63 (163 qtd).
36. See "Notes on a Cabinet Meeting," May 15, 1801, in ibid., 34:114–15; for Dale's orders, see ibid., 115n.
37. Lambert, *Barbary Wars,* 132.
38. Quoted in Sofka, "The Jeffersonian Idea of National Security," 519–44 (539 qtd).
39. Lambert, *Barbary Wars,* 150–54. The attack on Derne later gave rise to the phrase "To the shores of Tripoli" in the official Marine hymn, composer and date unknown.
40. I have drawn on three major books for my discussion of the Louisiana Purchase, DeConde, *This Affair of Louisiana;* Lewis, *The Louisiana Purchase;* and Kukla, *A Wilderness So Immense.* See also Boles, *Jefferson,* 350–56, 363–71; and Kaplan, *Jefferson and France,* 98–99.
41. Jefferson to Robert R. Livingston, April 18, 1802, in *PTJ,* 37:263–66 (265 qtd).
42. Jefferson to Thomas Mann Randolph, January 17, 1803, in ibid., 39:341.
43. Robert R. Livingston to James Madison, September 1, 1802, in the *PJMSSS,* 3:536–37 (536 qtd).
44. Quoted in DeConde, *This Affair of Louisiana,* 151.
45. Monroe to Madison, July 11, 1804, quoted in Ammon, *James Monroe,* 220.
46. Robert R. Livingston to Madison, April 11, 1803, in *PJMSSS,* 4:500–502 (500 qtd); Livingston to Madison, April 14, 1803, in ibid., 511–15.
47. Livingston to Jefferson, April 14, 1803, in *PTJ,* 40:198–200 (199 qtd). Jefferson would receive this letter on June 13.
48. Livingston to Jefferson, May 2, 1803, in ibid., 301–3 (302 qtd).
49. Cited in Kukla, *A Wilderness So Immense,* 280.
50. Barbé-Marbois, *The History of Louisiana,* 310–11.
51. Livingston to Madison, June 25, 1803, in *PJMSSS,* 5:119–21 (120 qtd).
52. "Resolution for Introduction of Constitutional Amendment," [August 1803?], in *PTJ,* 41:305.
53. Quoted in Jackson, *Thomas Jefferson and the Rocky Mountains,* 95.
54. Jefferson to Martha Jefferson Randolph, May 28, 1801, in *PTJ,* 34:200–201 (200 qtd).
55. Jefferson, "To the Senate and the House of Representatives," January 18, 1803, in *PTJ,* 39:350–53 (352–53 qtd).

56. Ibid., 354n.
57. The most convenient source for the letter is Jefferson to Lewis, June 20, 1803, in *TJW,* 1126–32 (1127 qtd).
58. Ibid., 1128.
59. Ibid., 1130.
60. An extensive literature exists on the expedition. A widely read popular account is Ambrose's *Undaunted Courage,* but there are books on every single aspect of their journey. Their journals, cited in the next note, make for fascinating reading.
61. Meriwether Lewis, journal entry for July 4, 1805, in Moulton, *The Definitive Journals of Lewis and Clark,* 4:362.
62. Jefferson to Lewis, October 20, 1806, quoted in Boles, *Jefferson,* 399.
63. See note 60, above.
64. For the biographical sketch, see Thomas Jefferson to Paul Allen, August 18, 1813, in *PTJRS,* 6:418–24. In part, Jefferson said of Lewis, "of courage undaunted, possessing a firmness & perseverance of purpose which nothing but impossibilities could divert from it's direction . . . I could have no hesitation in confiding the enterprise to him" (421).

11 Jefferson, Madison, and John Bull

1. See Albert Gallatin to Jefferson, January 31, 1803, in *PTJ,* 39:422 and 422–25n; and Jefferson, "To the House of Representatives," February 3, 1803, in ibid., 443.
2. See Turner, "The Impeaching of John Pickering," 485–507; and Ellis, *The Jeffersonian Crisis,* 71–72.
3. Jefferson to Joseph H. Nicholson, May 13, 1803, in *PTJ,* 40:371–72 (372 qtd).
4. Smith, *John Marshall,* 336–37.
5. See Ellis, *The Jeffersonian Crisis,* 81–90; and Haw et al., *Stormy Patriot,* 209–41.
6. Ellis, *The Jeffersonian Crisis,* 96–107.
7. "Second Annual Message," in Jefferson, *The Complete Jefferson,* 394–98 (398 qtd).
8. "Fourth Annual Message," November 8, 1804, in ibid., 406–10 (410 qtd).
9. "Sixth Annual Message," December 2, 1806, in ibid., 421–26 (425–26 qtd).
10. Jefferson to Benjamin Austin, January 9, 1816, in *PTJRS,* 9:333–36 (335, 336 qtd).
11. See Boles, *Jefferson,* 385–86.
12. Jefferson to Samuel Kercheval, July 12, 1816, in *PTJRS,* 10:222–28 (226, 227 qtd).
13. Jefferson to John Breckinridge, August 12, 1803, in *PTJ,* 41:184–86 (186 qtd).
14. The literature on the Burr-Hamilton duel is immense; see particularly the modern accounts in Chernow, *Alexander Hamilton,* 680–709; Stewart, *American Emperor,* 26–43; and Freeman, "Dueling as Politics," 289–318.
15. Two centuries later, there still is no consensus about what Burr had in mind. Abernethy, *The Burr Conspiracy* is thorough and very critical; Isenberg's *Fallen Founder,* is highly favorable. I find Stewart, *American Emperor,* convincing; he argues that Burr was guilty of conspiring against the interests of the United States.
16. What appears here is an abridgment of the longer account in Boles, *Jefferson,* 398–405.

17. Quoted in ibid., 401–2.
18. See "Sixth Annual Message," in Jefferson, *The Complete Jefferson,* 421–26, especially 422.
19. "Special Message," January 22, 1807, in ibid., 427–31 (427 qtd).
20. Quoted in Newmyer, *The Treason Trial of Aaron Burr,* 63.
21. Quoted in Malone, *Jefferson and His Time,* 5:339.
22. First Inaugural Address, in *TJW,* 492–96 (493 qtd).
23. For background, see Perkins, *Prologue to War.*
24. For the size of the British navy and number of crewmembers and impressments, see Stagg, *The War of 1812,* 28.
25. Madison to Jefferson, September 14, 1805, in *PJMSSS,* 10:230.
26. Jefferson to Pierre Samuel Du Pont de Nemours, July 14, 1807, as quoted in Boles, *Jefferson,* 413.
27. "Seventh Annual Message," October 27, 1807, in Jefferson, *The Complete Jefferson,* 434–39 (434 qtd).
28. "Special Message on Commercial Depredations," December 18, 1807, in Jefferson, *Works of Thomas Jefferson,* 10:530–31. For background on the embargo, see Spivak, *Jefferson's English Crisis;* and Malone, *Jefferson and His Time,* 5:393–657.
29. Quoted in Cheney, *James Madison,* 343.
30. See Allgor, *A Perfect Union,* 126–38.
31. See Frankel, "The 1807–1809 Embargo Against Great Britain," 291–308. He concludes that the embargo "failed through a lack of the political will and perseverance to use it, rather than through a lack of economic power" (291–92).
32. Jefferson to Monroe, January 28, 1809, in Jefferson, *Works of Jefferson,* 11:93–96 (96 qtd).
33. Jefferson to Thomas Mann Randolph Jr., July 14, 1793, in *PTJ,* 26:503–4 (504 qtd). For background on the Haitian Revolution there is a large literature, but see Dubois, *Avengers of the New World* and James, *The Black Jacobins.*
34. See Scherr, *Rightful Liberty.*
35. Monroe to Jefferson, September 15, 1800, in *PTJ,* 32:143–45 (143 qtd). For Gabriel's revolt in general, see Sidbury, *Ploughshares into Swords;* and Egerton, *Gabriel's Rebellion.*
36. Jefferson to Monroe, September 20, 1800, in *PTJ,* 32:160.
37. "Sixth Annual Message," December 2, 1806, in Jefferson, *The Complete Jefferson,* 421–26 (424 qtd).
38. 9th Congress, Records of the United States Senate, Record Group 46, National Archives.
39. For Dolley Madison's role, see Allgor, *A Perfect Union,* xx; and Stewart, *Madison's Gift,* 282–90.
40. Sir William Congreve had perfected the weapon based on rockets the Kingdom of Mysore had employed against the British East India Company in the 1790s.
41. Ketcham, *James Madison,* 496–500; Feldman, *Three Lives of James Madison,* 512–13.
42. The best account of this tempest within the administration is Feldman, *Three Lives of James Madison,* 522–31; see also Perkins, *Prologue to War,* 266–70.

43. Feldman, *Three Lives of James Madison,* 517–21; Cheney, *James Madison,* 367–68. Madison justified the move in a letter to Jefferson on October 19, 1810, in *PTJRS,* 3:177–78.
44. See Perkins, *Prologue to War,* 372–73; Hickey, *The War of 1812,* 24.
45. See Risjord, *Jefferson's America, 1760–1815,* 274–81; Hickey, *War of 1812,* 24; Wood, *Empire of Liberty,* 675–76; Perkins, *Prologue to War,* 283–84; and Feldman, *Three Lives of James Madison,* 533–35.
46. Newspapers quoted in Hickey, *War of 1812,* 25–26.
47. Monroe to John Tyler, June 13, 1812, in Monroe, *The Papers of James Monroe,* 6:197–200.
48. This was the conclusion of his private secretary, Edward Coles. See *PJMPS,* 4:xxv.
49. "Annual Message to Congress," November 5, 1811, in ibid., 1–5 (2 qtd).
50. Ibid., 3.
51. Ibid., 5.
52. Madison to Jefferson, February 7, 1812, in ibid., 168–69 (168 qtd); Jefferson to Madison, February 19, 1812, in ibid., 195–96 (195 qtd).
53. Madison to Jefferson, March 6, 1812, in ibid., 228.
54. This so-called Henry Affair is discussed in Perkins, *Prologue to War,* 369–72; Ammon, *James Monroe,* 303–4; and Feldman, *Three Lives of James Madison,* 537–39.
55. "To Congress," March 9, 1812, in *PJMPS,* 4:235.
56. "To Congress," April 1, 1812, in ibid., 279.
57. "To Congress." June 1, 1812, in ibid., 432–38 (432–33 qtd).
58. Ibid., 433.
59. Ibid.
60. Ibid., 434.
61. Ibid., 436.
62. Ibid., 437.

12 Mr. Madison's War

1. "Presidential Proclamation," [June 19, 1812], in *PJMPS,* 4:489–90. For the congressional votes, see Stagg, *The War of 1812,* 46–47.
2. A good general account of the war is Hickey, *The War of 1812,* 81–84.
3. Ibid., 131–33.
4. Beschloss, *Presidents of War,* 70.
5. For the success of the privateers, see Wood, *Empire of Liberty,* 682.
6. Hickey, *War of 1812,* 283–84; Stagg, *War of 1812,* 80, 96; Feldman, *Three Lives of James Madison,* 561, 564, 572.
7. See Wallace, *The Long, Bitter Trail;* and Holland, *Andrew Jackson and the Creek War.*
8. Hickey, *War of 1812,* 167–73.
9. Taylor, *The Internal Enemy,* 3, 271, 442.
10. For Winder's appointment, see Lord, *The Dawn's Early Light,* 22–23. This is a reprinting of a classic account first published in 1972 by W. W. Norton.
11. Quoted by Feldman, *Three Lives of James Madison,* 581.

12. Ibid., 582.
13. Allgor, *A Perfect Union,* 311–13.
14. The most vivid account of the stunning defeat is in Lord, *Dawn's Early Light,* 123–43.
15. Allgor, *A Perfect Union,* 314.
16. See Graves, "Why the White House Was Burned," 1095–127 (especially 1099–101).
17. Every history of the War of 1812 recounts the burning of Washington, but the most vivid account is Lord, *Dawn's Early Light,* 145–87.
18. Stewart, *Madison's Gift,* 391n20.
19. "Presidential Proclamation," [September 1, 1814], in ibid., 166–68 (167–68 qtd).
20. Vogel, *Through the Perilous Fight,* 371–72; and Pitch, *The Burning of Washington,* 222–25.
21. There is an extensive literature on the Battle of Baltimore. Again, Lord, *Dawn's Early Light,* 227–300, is colorfully written. But Vogel, *Through the Perilous Fight,* is now the definitive treatment of the entire Chesapeake campaign.
22. See Filby and Howard, *Star-Spangled Books,* especially "Some Facts About a Legend," 41–62.
23. See Buel, *America on the Brink,* is the best account of New England attitudes toward the war.
24. On the New England sense of moral superiority, see Banner, "A Shadow of Secession," 24–30.
25. For the Hartford Convention, see Banner, *To the Hartford Convention;* Hickey, *War of 1812,* 255–80; Wood, *Empire of Liberty,* 692–94; and especially Buel, *America on the Brink.*
26. Madison to Wilson Cary Nicholas, November 25, 1814, quoted in Ketcham, *James Madison,* 593.
27. Feldman, *Three Lives of James Madison,* 599.
28. Smith, *John Marshall,* 409–10.
29. "Presidential Proclamation," November 16, 1814, in *PJMPS,* 8:386–87.
30. In addition to Buel, *America on the Brink,* for the Hartford Convention, see Banner, *To the Hartford Convention.*
31. There is an immense and distinguished body of scholarship on the negotiations at Ghent and even more so at Vienna. Convenient summaries are Hickey, *War of 1812,* 281–99; Stagg, *War of 1812,* 143–47; and Cooper, *Lost Founding Father,* 112–23. The definitive treatment is now Bickham, *The Weight of Vengeance,* though still valuable is Perkins, *Castlereagh and Adams.*
32. Quoted in Cooper, *Lost Founding Father,* 116.
33. Remini, *The Battle of New Orleans,* 16–17.
34. My description of the entire New Orleans campaign is drawn from Remini, *The Battle of New Orleans;* Hickey, *Glorious Victory;* and Drez, *The War of 1812.*
35. Quoted in Hickey, *War of 1812,* 212.
36. The classic account of how Jackson's fame spread and captured the imagination of much of the nation is Ward, *Andrew Jackson.*
37. Monroe to Madison, February 3, 1815, in *PJMPS,* 8:554.

38. Feldman, *Three Lives of James Madison,* 604–5.
39. "Presidential Pardon," February 6, 1815, in *PJMPS,* 8:557–58 (557 qtd).
40. "To Congress," February 18, 1815, in *PJMPS,* 8:599–601 (599, 600 qtd). Although Tchaikovsky's "1812 Overture" is often played today at Fourth of July celebrations, it has nothing to do with US history. It was written to celebrate the Russian victory over France's invading army in 1812.
41. Ibid., 600.
42. Here I am following the interpretation of Feldman, *Three Lives of James Madison,* 608.
43. "To Congress," in *PJMPS,* 8:599–601 (601 qtd).
44. Ibid.
45. "To Congress," February 23, 1815, in ibid., 9:23.
46. "Presidential Proclamation," March 4, 1815, in ibid., 56–57 (56 qtd).
47. For the naval action against the Barbary nations, see Lambert, *The Barbary Wars,* 189–99.
48. Jefferson to Samuel H. Smith, September 21, 1814, in *PTJRS,* 7:681–83 (682–83 qtd).
49. See Jefferson to James Madison, September 24, 1814, in ibid., 691–93; *PJMPS,* 8:248n4. The Federalists in Congress voted 51–4 against the purchase. For an example of strident Federalist opposition to the purchase, see Jedediah Morse Sr. to Madison, November 23, 1814, in ibid., 398–99.
50. "To the Prince Regent of Great Britain," March 4, 1815, from James Madison and James Monroe, in *PJMPS,* 9:52; "From George III," July 31, 1815, in ibid., 499–500 (499 qtd).
51. See Baker, *Building America,* 168–84.
52. See "Annual Message to Congress," December 5, 1815, in PJMPS, 10:66–72.
53. Ibid., 66, 67, 68, 71, 72. He would go on to submit a bill to the House in February 1816 for a national university, but it went down to a resounding defeat in April.
54. "Eighth Annual Message," December 3, 1816, available via UVa Miller Center, https://millercenter.org/the-presidency/presidential-speeches/december-3-1816-eighth-annual-message.
55. Ibid.
56. Ibid.
57. "To the House of Representatives of the United States," March 3, 1817, in Madison, *The Mind of the Founder,* 391–94.
58. Adams to Jefferson, February 2, 1817, in Adams, *The Adams-Jefferson Letters,* 506–8 (508 qtd).

13 A Maturing Nation

1. Long seen as a heroic part of American history, the steady march westward of white settlers and their dispossession of Native peoples' land is now often portrayed as a tragic and shameful example of colonial and racist imperialism. See, for example, such recent works as Saler, *The Settlers' Empire;* Seeley, *Race, Removal, and the Right to Remain;* and Witgen, *Seeing Red.*

2. “Inaugural Address,” March 4, 1817, in *WJM,* 6:6–14 (6, 7, 10, 11, 12, 13–14 qtd).
3. James Monroe to Andrew Jackson, December 14, 1816, in ibid., 5:342.
4. For Jackson’s letter and Monroe’s response, see Cunningham, *Presidency of James Monroe,* 19–20.
5. My account of Monroe’s travels is based on the descriptions in ibid., 31–40; Unger, *The Last Founding Father,* 268–76; and Ammon, *James Monroe,* 373–77.
6. [Boston] *Columbian Centinel,* July 19, 1817.
7. Monroe to Jefferson, July 27, 1817, in *PTJRS,* 11:568–69 (568 qtd).
8. Monroe to George Hay, August 5, 1817, quoted in Unger, *The Last Founding Father,* 274.
9. Ammon, *James Monroe,* 349–50; Herring, *From Colony to Superpower,* 149; and Howe, *What Hath God Wrought,* 96.
10. See Howe, *What Hath God Wrought,* 96; and Ammon, *James Monroe,* 516–17.
11. For brief background on the situation in Florida, see Herring, *From Colony to Superpower,* 145–48; Cunningham, *Presidency of James Monroe,* 55–69; Ammon, *James Monroe,* 412–25. For a detailed account, see the definitive study by Watson, *Jackson’s Sword,* a tour de force of research.
12. For full accounts of Adams’s role, see Bemis, *John Quincy Adams* and Weeks, *John Quincy Adams;* but for a succinct summary, see Cooper, *The Lost Founding Father,* 159–68.
13. Both quotations in Cooper, *Lost Founding Father,* 167–68.
14. “Inaugural Address,” *WJM,* 6:7.
15. “First Annual Message,” in Israel, *The State of the Union Messages,* 1:148–56 (148 qtd).
16. Browning, *The Panic of 1819,* 3, 62, 64.
17. For a recent summary of these developments, see Browning, *Panic of 1819,* 49–74. Foundational studies on these topics include Taylor, *The Transportation Revolution;* and Sellers, *The Market Revolution.*
18. Browning, *Panic of 1819,* 93.
19. “Second Annual Message,” November 16, 1818, in Israel, *State of the Union Messages,* 1:156–65 (156, 164 qtd).
20. Browning, *The Panic of 1819,* 162.
21. Wilson Cary Nicholas to Jefferson, April 19, 1818, in *PTJRS,* 12:649; Jefferson to Madison, February 17, 1826, in *RL,* 3:1964–67 (1966 qtd).
22. “Third Annual Message,” December 7, 1819, in Israel, *State of the Union Messages,* 1:165–74 (165, 172 qtd).
23. For the itinerary of the trip, see Cunningham, *Presidency of James Monroe,* 71–75.
24. Quoted in ibid., 89.
25. Quoted in Forbes, *The Missouri Compromise,* 40.
26. Congressmen John W. Taylor of New York quoted in Cunningham, *Presidency of James Monroe,* 89.
27. Dangerfield, *The Era of Good Feelings,* 2–4.
28. Jefferson to Adams, December 10, 1819, in Adams, *The Adams-Jefferson Letters,* 548–49.

29. The scholarship on Monroe and slavery is extremely limited, but see Preston, "James Monroe and the Practicalities of Emancipation and Colonization," 129–45.
30. Clay to Adam Beatty, January 22, 1820, quoted in Peterson, *The Great Triumvirate,* 60.
31. Monroe to Jefferson, February 7, 1820, in *WJM,* 6:113–15 (114 qtd).
32. Clay to John J. Crittenden, January 29, 1820, as quoted in Cunningham, *Presidency of James Monroe,* 98.
33. The active role of Monroe in finding a working solution is emphasized by Forbes, *The Missouri Compromise,* as well as by Cunningham, *Presidency of James Monroe,* both building on Harry Ammon's pioneering biography of the fifth president. A more recent account, which I do not find convincing, dismisses Monroe's moderation and unionism and sees him as a protector of the interests of the planter class. See Hammond, "President, Planter, Politician: James Monroe," 843–67.
34. Monroe to Madison, November 16, 1820, in *WJM,* 6:159–61 (160 qtd).
35. For the final resolution, see Cunningham, *Presidency of James Monroe,* 109; and Peterson, *The Great Triumvirate,* 62–66
36. The best treatment of Monroe's leadership style is Ammon, "Executive Leadership in the Monroe Administration," 111–31.
37. See the brief discussion in Perkins, *History of the Monroe Doctrine,* 25–26.
38. Quoted in ibid., 31.
39. Canning to Rush, August 20, 1823, in *WJM,* 6:365–66 (365 qtd).
40. Monroe to Jefferson, October 17, 1823, in ibid., 323–26 (325–26 qtd).
41. Jefferson to Madison, October 24, 1823, in *TJW,* 1481–83.
42. Madison to Monroe, October 30, 1823, in *WJM,* 6:394–95 (394 qtd).
43. Madison to Jefferson, November 1, 1823, in ibid., 395–96.
44. Adams quoted in Cunningham, *Presidency of James Monroe,* 154.
45. For the cabinet discussions and the working out of all the details, see Perkins, *History of the Monroe Doctrine,* 39–64; Cunningham, *Presidency of James Monroe,* 154–60; Herring, *From Colony to Superpower,* 154–62; Cooper, *Lost Founding Father,* 183–87; and especially Ammon, *James Monroe,* 476–92.
46. "Seventh Annual Message," in *State of the Union Messages,* 202–14 (204 qtd).
47. Ibid., 212–13.
48. Perkins, *History of the Monroe Doctrine,* 62.

14 Institution Builders

1. Monroe to Madison, May 10, 1822, in *WJM,* 6:284–91 (286 qtd).
2. Levasseur, *Lafayette in America,* 1:174–75.
3. Ibid., 175.
4. See Unger, *The Last Founding Father,* 328, 115–16; and Cheney, *The Virginia Dynasty,* 152–53.
5. A succinct discussion of the election may be found in Peterson, *The Great Triumvirate,* 123–31.
6. "Eighth Annual Message," in Israel, *The State of Union Messages,* 1:214–30 (229 qtd).

7. Levasseur, *Lafayette in America,* 2:268.
8. See Marshall quotation in Smith, *John Marshall,* 583.
9. The best modern biography of Marshall is Smith, *John Marshall.* The best one-volume analysis of his most influential decisions is Newmyer, *John Marshall and the Heroic Age;* but Hobson, *The Great Chief Justice,* is also indispensable.
10. Hobson, *Great Chief Justice,* 29, 33–34.
11. For Kentucky landholdings specifically, see Smith, *John Marshall,* 75n; and, for more details, *PJMar,* 1:100–104 and 2:140–49; Newmyer, *John Marshall and the Heroic Age,* 9–10, 16–17. For Marshall's frequent purchases of enslaved people, see Finkelman, *Supreme Injustice,* 37–40.
12. Smith, *John Marshall,* 282.
13. See Newmyer, *John Marshall and the Heroic Age,* 157, 398, 403; Smith, *John Marshall,* 402–3.
14. For the percentages of opinions, see Newmyer, *John Marshall,* 459.
15. Newmyer, *John Marshall and the Heroic Age,* 424; Finkelman, *Supreme Injustice,* 27–28; Thomas, *A Question of Freedom,* 183, 184–85.
16. For the whole issue, see Magrath, *Yazoo.*
17. For succinct analyses of the case, see Hobson, *The Great Chief Justice,* 82–88; Newmyer, *John Marshall and the Heroic Age,* 388–94, 222–35.
18. Newmyer, *John Marshall and the Heroic Age,* 235.
19. Kelly, Harbison, and Belz, *The American Constitution,* 185.
20. Quoted in Smith, *John Marshall,* 435. Emphasis in the original.
21. "*Opinion in* Dartmouth College v. Woodward," in *JMW,* 391–411 (391 qtd).
22. Ibid. 394, 402, 401.
23. Ibid., 399.
24. See Hobson, *The Great Chief Justice,* 94–95, and Newmyer, *John Marshall and the Heroic Age,* 246–53.
25. Quoted in Hobson, *The Great Chief Justice,* 100.
26. "*Opinion in* McCulloch v. Maryland," in *JMW,* 412–36 (414 qtd).
27. Ibid., 415–16, 419.
28. Ibid., 426.
29. Ibid., 431.
30. Ibid., 432, 433.
31. Ibid., 436.
32. Ibid., 436.
33. Smith, *John Marshall,* 446–81, has a good account of this legal back-and-forth.
34. "*Opinion in* Cohens v. Virginia," in *JMW,* 528–64 (529, 531, 533, 537 qtd).
35. Ibid., 553.
36. Hobson, *The Great Chief Justice,* xii.
37. On the reaction to the decision, see Smith, *John Marshall,* 463–69; Newmyer, *John Marshall and the Heroic Age,* 374–75; and *RL,* 3:1848–52.
38. "*Opinion in* Gibbons v. Ogden," in *JMW,* 607–32 (608, 609 qtd).
39. Ibid., 610.

40. Ibid., 613.
41. Ibid., 631.
42. See Ragosta, Onuf, and O'Shaughnessy, *The Founding of Thomas Jefferson's University.*
43. Jefferson to Littleton Waller Tazewell, January 5, 1805, in *TJW,* 1149–53 (1152 qtd).
44. Jefferson to Messrs. Hugh L. White and Others, May 6, 1810, in ibid., 1222–23.
45. Wagoner, *Jefferson and Education,* 75–80.
46. Jefferson to Peter Carr, September 7, 1814, in *PTJRS,* 7:636–41.
47. O'Shaughnessy, *The Illimitable Freedom of the Human Mind,* 60–61. This is by far the best, most fair-minded account of Jefferson as university builder.
48. See "Report of the Commissioners for the University of Virginia," August 4, 1818, in *TJW,* 457–73.
49. Ibid., 459–61.
50. Jefferson to William Roscoe, December 27, 1820, quoted in Boles, *Jefferson,* 497.
51. O'Shaughnessy, *Illimitable Freedom,* 58–59, 107–9.
52. See McInnis and Nelson, *Educated in Tyranny.*
53. O'Shaughnessy, *Illimitable Freedom,* 176–78.
54. "Speech on Lafayette," in Jefferson, *The Complete Jefferson,* 447–48 (448 qtd).
55. O'Shaughnessy, *Illimitable Freedom,* 11–12, and chapter 9 generally.
56. Taylor, *Thomas Jefferson's Education,* emphasizes the way the university failed to meet Jefferson's aspirations for it.
57. *AIA Journal* 65 (July 1976): 91. For the World Heritage designation, see www.worldheritagesite.org, accessed October 2, 2015. They were so designated in 1987.

15 Legacy Deferred and the End of a Dynasty

1. Quoted in Boles, *Jefferson,* 28. My entire discussion of Jefferson's antislavery is drawn from this book, especially chapter 19, "Living with Paradox," 460–77.
2. The best analysis of *Notes* is Rogers, "Jefferson's Changing Audiences," 171–208.
3. Over the years Jefferson freed several enslaved persons, all part of the Hemings clan, like James Hemings, and at his death he freed five more, including two of Sally's children still living at Monticello. He petitioned the Virginia House of Delegates to exempt them from having to leave Virginia. He asked his daughter Martha to allow Sally to live as free, in a house he provided for her. But he did not free the great bulk of his enslaved people.
4. There is an immense body of scholarship on these developments; see, for example, Rothman, *Slave Country;* Johnson, *River of Dark Dreams;* and Baptist, *The Half Has Never Been Told.*
5. Gordon-Reed, *The Hemingses of Monticello.* See her nuanced treatment of Hemings's experience in France. See also Boles, *Jefferson,* 150–54.
6. Quoted in Ketcham, *James Madison,* 625.
7. Madison to Jefferson, February 24, 1826, *Founders Online,* National Archives, https://founders.archives.gov/documents/Madison/04-03-02-0714.
8. See Wulf, *Founding Gardeners,* 197–202.

9. Guasco, *Confronting Slavery.*
10. For a general history of the movement, see Burin, *Slavery and the Peculiar Solution;* but also see Tomek, *Colonization and Its Discontents.*
11. For his later years, see Ammon, *James Monroe,* 566–72.
12. We know he owned various plantations replete with enslaved laborers because of his gifts by will to his sons. See Finkelman, *Supreme Injustice,* 37–48.
13. As such he was quite typical of a Federalist politician in Virginia, who according to Broussard, *The Southern Federalists,* was "a town-dwelling lawyer or commercial man" (199).
14. The best general treatment of Marshall and slavery is Newmyer, *John Marshall and the Heroic Age,* 414–34.
15. Quoted in Peterson, *The Jefferson Image,* 7.
16. The population numbers are drawn from Jordan, *Political Leadership in Jefferson's Virginia,* 6, 28.
17. This is the theme of an important article by Sutton, "Nostalgia, Pessimism, and Malaise," 41–55.
18. Garnett and Wirt cited in ibid., 42–43.
19. See Jordan, *Political Leadership in Jefferson's Virginia,* 207–24.
20. William Henry Harrison was a resident of Ohio when named to head the Whig ticket in 1836, and Woodrow Wilson ran and won after having served as the governor of New Jersey. John Tyler did not lead the ticket; he became president only after Harrison died in office.
21. Ellen Randolph Coolidge to Thomas Jefferson, August 1, 1825, in Jefferson, *Family Letters of Thomas Jefferson,* 454–57 (454–55 qtd).
22. Jefferson to Ellen Randolph Coolidge, August 27, 1825, in ibid., 457–59 (457 qtd).
23. Sutton, *Revolution to Secession,* 75.
24. The publication history of the letters is outlined in *PTJRS,* 10:220–21n.
25. Jefferson to "Henry Tompkinson" [Samuel Kercheval], July 12, 1816, in ibid., 222–28. Tompkinson was a pseudonym used on occasion by Kercheval.
26. *Proceedings and Debates of the Virginia State Convention,* 476.
27. Ibid., 17.
28. Ibid., 76.
29. Ibid., 116.
30. Ibid., 154.
31. Ibid., 158.
32. Ibid., 160.
33. Ibid., 102.
34. Ibid., 313, 321.
35. The new constitution is included in ibid., 896–902.
36. Ibid., 789, 492.
37. For the session, see Dunn, *Dominion of Memories,* 49–55.
38. See Freehling, *Drift toward Dissolution,* 129–30ff.
39. Quoted in *Proceedings and Debates,* 54.

40. Most conveniently found today in Faust, *The Ideology of Slavery,* 23–77. This is the version published in the *American Quarterly Review,* and my quotations will be from the essay as published in Faust.
41. "Abolition of Negro Slavery," 27, 28.
42. Ibid., 61.
43. Ibid., 63–72.
44. Ibid., 77

BIBLIOGRAPHY

Abernethy, Thomas Perkins. *The Burr Conspiracy.* New York: Oxford University Press, 1954.

Adams, John. *The Adams-Jefferson Letters: The Complete Correspondence between Thomas Jefferson and Abigail and John Adams.* Edited by Lester J. Cappon. Chapel Hill: University of North Carolina Press, 1987.

Adams, John Quincy. *The Jubilee of the Constitution: A Discourse Delivered at the Request of the New York Historical Society, in the City of New York, on Tuesday, the 30th of April, 1839: being the Fiftieth Anniversary of the Inauguration of George Washington as President of the United Sates, on Thursday, the 30th of April, 1789.* New York: Samuel Colman, 1839.

Allgor, Catherine. *A Perfect Union: Dolley Madison and the Creation of the American Nation.* New York: Henry Holt and Company, 2006.

Ambrose, Stephen E. *Undaunted Courage: Meriwether Lewis, Thomas Jefferson, and the Opening of the American West.* New York: Simon & Schuster, 1996.

Ammon, Harry. "Executive Leadership in the Monroe Administration." In *America: The Middle Period: Essays in Honor of Bernard Mayo,* edited by John B. Boles, 111–31. Charlottesville: University Press of Virginia, 1973.

———. *The Genet Mission.* New York: W. W. Norton, 1973.

———. *James Monroe: The Quest for National Identity.* New York: McGraw Hill, 1971.

Appleby, Joyce. *Capitalism and a New Social Order: The Republican Vision of the 1790s.* New York: New York University Press, 1984.

Baker, Jean H. *Building America: The Life of Benjamin Henry Latrobe.* New York: Oxford University Press, 2020.

Banner, James M., Jr. "A Shadow of Secession: The Hartford Convention, 1814." *History Today* 38 (September 1988): 24–30.

———. *To the Hartford Convention: The Federalists and the Origins of Party Politics in Massachusetts, 1789–1815.* New York: Alfred A. Knopf, 1970.

Baptist, Edward E. *The Half Has Never Been Told: Slavery and the Making of American Capitalism.* New York: Basic Books, 2014.

Barbé-Marbois, François. *The History of Louisiana, Particularly the Cession of That Colony to the United States of America.* Philadelphia: Carey & Lea, 1830.

Beeman, Richard R. *Patrick Henry: A Biography.* New York: McGraw, Hill, 1974.

———. *Plain, Honest Men: The Making of the American Constitution.* New York: Random House, 2009.

Bemis, Samuel Flagg. *John Quincy Adams and the Foundations of American Foreign Policy.* New York: Alfred A. Knopf, 1949.

———. *Pinckney's Treaty: America's Advantage from Europe's Distress.* New Haven: Yale University Press, 1960.

Beschloss, Michael. *Presidents of War.* New York: Crown, 2018.

Bickham, Troy. *The Weight of Vengeance: The United States, the British Empire, and the War of 1812.* New York: Oxford University Press, 2012.

Billings, Warren M., John E. Selby, and Thad W. Tate. *Colonial Virginia: A History.* White Plains, NY: KTO Press, 1986.

Bird, Wendell. "Reassessing Responses to the Virginia and Kentucky Resolutions: New Evidence from the Tennessee and Georgia Resolutions and from Other States." *Journal of the Early Republic* 35, no. 4 (Winter 2015): 519–51.

Boles, John B. *Jefferson: Architect of American Liberty.* New York: Basic Books, 2017.

Borden, Morton. *The Federalism of James A. Bayard.* New York: Columbia University Press, 1955.

Bordewich, Fergus M. *The First Congress: How James Madison, George Washington, and a Group of Extraordinary Men Invented the Government.* New York: Simon & Schuster, 2016.

Boswell, James. *The Life of Samuel Johnson.* 3 vols. New York: The Heritage Press, 1963.

Bowen, Catherine Drinker. *Miracle at Philadelphia: The Story of the Constitutional Convention, May to September 1787.* Boston: Atlantic Monthly Press, 1966.

Bowling, Kenneth R. *Creating the Federal City, 1774–1800: Potomac Fever.* Washington, DC: American Institute of Architects Press, 1988.

Breen, Timothy H. *Tobacco Culture: The Mentality of the Great Tidewater Planters on the Eve of Revolution.* Princeton: Princeton University Press, 1985.

Broadwater, Jeff. *George Mason: Forgotten Founder.* Chapel Hill: University of North Carolina Press, 2006.

———. *Jefferson, Madison, and the Making of the Constitution.* Chapel Hill: University of North Carolina Press, 2019.

Broussard, James H. *The Southern Federalists, 1800–1816.* Baton Rouge: Louisiana State University Press, 1978.

Browning, Andrew H. *The Panic of 1819: The First Great Depression.* Columbia: University of Missouri Press, 2019.

Buel, Richard, Jr. *America on the Brink: How the Political Struggle over the War of 1812 Almost Destroyed the Young Republic.* New York: Palgrave Macmillan, 2005.

Burin, Eric. *Slavery and the Peculiar Solution: A History of the American Colonization Society.* Gainesville: University Press of Florida, 2005.

Burstein, Andrew, and Nancy Isenberg. *Madison and Jefferson.* New York: Random House, 2010.

Cheney, Lynne. *James Madison: A Life Reconsidered.* New York: Penguin Books, 2014.

———. *The Virginia Dynasty: Four Presidents and the Creation of the American Nation.* New York: Viking, 2020.

Chernow, Ron. *Alexander Hamilton.* New York: Penguin Books, 2004.

———. *Washington: A Life.* New York: Penguin Books, 2010.

Chervinsky, Lindsay M. *The Cabinet: George Washington and the Creation of an American Institution.* Cambridge: Harvard University Press, 2020.

Coleman, Aaron. "'A Second Bounaparty?' A Reexamination of Alexander Hamilton during the Franco-American Crisis, 1796–1801." *Journal of the Early Republic* 28, no. 2 (Summer 2008): 183–214.

Combs, Jerald A. *The Jay Treaty: Political Background of the Founding Fathers.* Berkeley: University of California Press, 1970.

Conroy, James B. *Jefferson's White House: Monticello on the Potomac.* Lanham, MD: Rowman & Littlefield, 2019.

Cooke, Jacob E., ed. *The Federalist.* Middleton, CT: Wesleyan University Press, 1961.

Cooper, William J. *The Lost Founding Father: John Quincy Adams and the Transformation of American Politics.* New York: Liveright Publishing Corporation, 2017.

Cox, Joseph W. *Champion of Southern Federalism: Robert Goodloe Harper of South Carolina.* Port Washington, NY: Kennikat Press, 1972.

Cullen, Charles T. "Jefferson's White House Dinner Guests." *White House History* 17 (Winter 2006), 25–43.

Cunningham, Noble E., Jr. *The Jeffersonian Republicans: The Formation of Party Organization, 1789–1801.* Chapel Hill: University of North Carolina Press, 1957.

———. *The Presidency of James Monroe.* Lawrence: University Press of Kansas, 1996.

———. *The Process of Government under Jefferson.* Princeton: Princeton University Press, 1978.

Curran, Andrew S. *The Anatomy of Blackness: Science & Slavery in an Age of Enlightenment.* Baltimore: Johns Hopkins University Press, 2011.

Dangerfield, George. *The Era of Good Feelings.* New York: Harcourt, Brace and Company, 1952.

DeConde, Alexander. *This Affair of Louisiana.* New York: Scribner, 1976.

———. "Washington's Farewell, the French Alliance, and the Election of 1796." *Mississippi Valley Historical Review* 43, no. 4 (March 1957): 641–58.

Drez, Ronald J. *The War of 1812: Conflict and Deception; The British Attempt to Seize New Orleans and Nullify the Louisiana Purchase.* Baton Rouge: Louisiana State University Press, 2014.

Dubois, Laurent. *Avengers of the New World: The Story of the Haitian Revolution.* Cambridge: Harvard University Press, 2004.

Dulany, Daniel. *Considerations on the Propriety of Imposing Taxes in the British Colonies for the Purpose of Raising a Revenue.* Annapolis: Printed and sold by Jonas Green, 1765.

Dunbar, Erica Armstrong. *Never Caught: The Washingtons' Relentless Pursuit of Their Runaway Slave, Ona Judge.* New York: Simon & Schuster, 2017.

Dunn, Susan. *Dominion of Memories: Jefferson, Madison, and the Decline of Virginia.* New York: Basic Books, 2007.

———. *Jefferson's Second Revolution: The Election Crisis of 1800 and the Triumph of Republicanism.* Boston: Houghton Mifflin Company, 2004.

Egerton, Douglas R. *Gabriel's Rebellion: The Virginia Slave Conspiracies of 1800 and 1802.* Chapel Hill: University of North Carolina Press, 1993.

Elkins, Stanley, and Eric McKitrick. *The Age of Federalism.* New York: Oxford University Press, 1993.

Ellis, Joseph J. *American Sphinx: The Character of Thomas Jefferson.* New York: Alfred A. Knopf, 1997.

———. *His Excellency: George Washington.* New York: Alfred A. Knopf, 2004.

———. *The Quartet: Orchestrating the Second American Revolution, 1783–1789.* New York: Alfred A. Knopf, 2015.

Ellis, Richard E. *The Jeffersonian Crisis: Courts and Politics in the Young Republic.* New York: Oxford University Press, 1971.

Farrand, Max, ed. *Records of the Federal Convention of 1787.* 3 vols. New Haven: Yale University Press, 1911.

Faust, Drew Gilpin, ed. *The Ideology of Slavery: Proslavery Thought in the Antebellum South, 1830–1860.* Baton Rouge: Louisiana State University Press, 1981.

Feldman, Noah. *The Three Lives of James Madison: Genius, Partisan, President.* New York: Random House, 2017.

Filby, P. W., and Edgar G. Howard. *Star-Spangled Books* . . . Baltimore: Maryland Historical Society, 1972.

Finkelman, Paul. *Supreme Injustice: Slavery in the Nation's Highest Court.* Cambridge: Harvard University Press, 2018.

Forbes, Robert Pierce. *The Missouri Compromise and Its Aftermath: Slavery and the Meaning of America.* Chapel Hill: University of North Carolina Press, 2007.

Frankel, Jeffrey A. "The 1807–1809 Embargo against Great Britain." *Journal of Economic History* 42, no. 2 (June 1982): 291–308.

Freehling, Alison Goodyear. *Drift toward Dissolution: The Virginia Slavery Debate of 1831–1832.* Baton Rouge: Louisiana State University Press, 1982.

Freeman, Joanne B. "Dueling as Politics: Reinterpreting the Burr-Hamilton Duel." *William and Mary Quarterly* 54, no. 2 (April 1996): 289–318.

Gaustad, Edwin S. *Sworn on the Altar of God: A Religious Biography of Thomas Jefferson.* Grand Rapids, MI: William B. Eerdman's Publishing Company, 1996.

Glover, Lorri. *The Fate of the Revolution: Virginia Debates the Constitution.* Baltimore: Johns Hopkins University Press, 2016.

———. *Founders as Fathers: The Private Lives and Politics of the American Revolutionaries.* New Haven: Yale University Press, 2014.

Gordon-Reed, Annette. *The Hemingses of Monticello: An American Family.* New York: W. W. Norton, 2008.

Gordon-Reed, Annette, and Peter S. Onuf, *"Most Blessed of the Patriarchs": Thomas Jefferson and the Empire of the Imagination.* New York: Liveright Publishing Company, 2016.

Graves, Donald E. "Why the White House Was Burned: An Investigation into the British Destruction of the Public Buildings at Washington in August 1814." *Journal of Military History* 76, no. 4 (October 2012): 1095–1127.

Greenstein, Fred I. *Inventing the Job of President: Leadership Style from George Washington to Andrew Jackson.* Princeton: Princeton University Press, 2009.

———. "Presidential Difference in the Early Republic: The Highly Disparate Leadership Styles of Washington, Adams, and Jefferson." *Presidential Studies Quarterly* 36, no. 3 (September 2006): 373–90.

Guasco, Suzanne Cooper. *Confronting Slavery: Edward Coles and the Rise of Antislavery Politics in Nineteenth-Century America.* DeKalb: Northern Illinois University Press, 2013.

Gutzman, K. R. Constantine. "The Virginia and Kentucky Resolutions Reconsidered: 'An Appeal to the *Real Laws* of Our Country.'" *Journal of Southern History* 66, no. 3 (August 2000): 473–96.

Halperin, Terri Diane. *The Alien and Sedition Acts of 1798: Testing the Constitution.* Baltimore: Johns Hopkins University Press, 2016.

Hamilton, Alexander. *The Papers of Alexander Hamilton.* Edited by Harold C. Syrett and Jacob E. Cooke. 27 vols. New York: Columbia University Press, 1961–1987.

Hammond, John Craig. "President, Planter, Politician: James Monroe, the Missouri Crisis, and the Politics of Slavery." *Journal of American History* 105, no. 4 (March 2019): 843–67.

Haw, James, Francis Beirne, Rosamond Beirne, and R. Samuel Jett. *Stormy Patriot: The Life of Samuel Chase.* Baltimore: Maryland Historical Society, 1980.

Hayes, Kevin J. *The Mind of a Patriot: Patrick Henry and the World of Ideas.* Charlottesville: University Press of Virginia, 2008.

Henriques, Peter R. *Realistic Visionary: A Portrait of George Washington.* Charlottesville: University of Virginia Press, 2006.

Herring, George C. *From Colony to Superpower: U.S. Foreign Relations since 1776.* New York: Oxford University Press, 2008.

Hickey, Donald R. *Glorious Victory: Andrew Jackson and the Battle of New Orleans.* Baltimore: Johns Hopkins University Press, 2015.

———. *The War of 1812: A Forgotten Conflict.* Urbana: University of Illinois Press, 1989.

Hobson, Charles F. *The Great Chief Justice: John Marshall and the Rule of Law.* Lawrence: University Press of Kansas, 1996.

Hofstadter, Richard. *The Idea of a Party System: The Rise of Legitimate Opposition in the United States, 1780–1840.* Berkeley: University of California Press, 1969.

Holland, James W. *Andrew Jackson and the Creek War: Victory at the Horseshoe.* Tuscaloosa: University of Alabama Press, 1968.

Holton, Woody. *Forced Founders: Indians, Debtors, Slaves, and the Making of the American Revolution in Virginia.* Chapel Hill: University of North Carolina Press, 1999.

Howe, Daniel Walker. *What Hath God Wrought: The Transformation of America, 1815–1848.* New York: Oxford University Press, 2007.

Hunter, Thomas Rogers. "The First Gerrymander? Patrick Henry, James Madison, James Monroe, and Virginia's 1788 Congressional Districting." *Early American Studies* 9, no. 3 (Fall 2011): 781–820.

Isenberg, Nancy. *Fallen Founder: The Life of Aaron Burr.* New York: Penguin Books, 2007.

Israel, Fred L., ed. *The State of the Union Messages of the Presidents, 1790–1966.* 3 vols. New York: Chelsea House, Robert Hector, Publishers, 1966.

Jackson, Donald. *Thomas Jefferson and the Rocky Mountains: Exploring the West from Monticello.* Norman: University of Oklahoma Press, 1993.

James, Cyril Lionel Robert. *The Black Jacobins: Toussaint Louverture and the San Domingo Revolution.* New York: Vintage Press, 1989.

Jefferson, Thomas. *The Complete Anas of Jefferson.* Edited by Franklin B. Sawvel. New York: The Round Table Press, 1903.

———. *The Complete Jefferson, Containing His Major Writings, Published and Unpublished, Except His Letters.* Edited by Saul Padover. New York: Duell, Sloan & Pearce, Inc., 1943.

———. *The Family Letters of Thomas Jefferson.* Edited by Edwin Morris Betts and James Adam Bear Jr. Charlottesville: University Press of Virginia, 1966.

———. *Notes on the State of Virginia.* Edited and with an introduction by William Peden. Chapel Hill: University of North Carolina Press, 1955.

———. *The Papers of Thomas Jefferson.* Edited by Julian P. Boyd, L. H. Butterfield, Charles T. Cullen, and John Catanzariti. 44 vols. to date. Princeton: Princeton University Press, 1950–.

———. *The Papers of Thomas Jefferson, Retirement Series.* Edited by J. Jefferson Looney. 17 vols. to date. Princeton: Princeton University Press, 2004–.

———. *The Republic of Letters: The Correspondence between Thomas Jefferson and James Madison, 1776–1826.* Edited by James Morton Smith. 3 vols. New York: W. W. Norton, 1995.

———. *Thomas Jefferson and the National Capital: Containing Notes and Correspondence . . .* Edited by Saul K. Padover. Washington, DC: Government Printing Office, 1946.

———. *Thomas Jefferson: Writings.* Edited by Merrill D. Peterson. New York: Library of America, 1984.

———. *The Works of Thomas Jefferson.* Compiled and edited by Paul Leicester Ford. 12 vols. New York and London: G. P. Putnam and Sons, 1904–1905.

———. *The Writings of Thomas Jefferson.* Edited by Paul Leicester Ford. 10 vols. New York: G. P. Putnam and Sons, 1892–1899.

Johnson, Walter. *River of Dark Dreams: Slavery and Empire in the Cotton Kingdom.* Cambridge: Harvard University Press, 2013.

Jordan, Daniel P. *Political Leadership in Jefferson's Virginia.* Charlottesville: University Press of Virginia, 1983.

"Journal of a French Traveler in the Colonies, 1765." *American Historical Review* 26, no. 4 (July 1921): 726–47.

Kaminski, John P., and Gaspare J. Saladino, eds. *Documentary History of the Ratification of the Constitution.* 14 vols. Madison: State Historical Society of Wisconsin, 1988.

Kaplan, Lawrence S. *Jefferson and France: An Essay on Politics and Political Ideas.* New Haven: Yale University Press, 1967.

Kelly, Alfred H., Winfred A. Harbison, and Herman Belz. *The American Constitution: Its Origins and Development.* 6th ed. New York: W. W. Norton, 1983.

Ketcham, Ralph. *James Madison: A Biography.* Charlottesville: University Press of Virginia, 1990.

Kidd, Thomas S. *Patrick Henry: First Among Patriots.* New York: Basic Books, 2011.

———. *Thomas Jefferson: A Biography of Spirit and Flesh.* New Haven: Yale University Press, 2022.

Klarman, Michael J. *The Framers' Coup: The Making of the United States Constitution.* New York: Oxford University Press, 2016.

Koch, Adrienne. *Jefferson and Madison: The Great Collaboration.* New York: Oxford University Press, 1964.

Koch, Adrienne, and Harry Ammon, "The Virginia and Kentucky Resolutions: An Episode in Jefferson's and Madison's Defense of Civil Liberties." *William and Mary Quarterly* 5, no. 2 (April 1948): 145–76.

Kolchin, Peter. *American Slavery, 1619–1877.* Rev. ed. New York: Hill and Wang, 2003.

Kraut, Julia Rose. *Threat of Dissent: A History of Ideological Exclusion and Deportation in the United States.* Cambridge: Harvard University Press, 2020.

Kukla, Jon. *A Wilderness So Immense: The Louisiana Purchase and the Destiny of America.* New York: Alfred A. Knopf, 2003.

———. *Patrick Henry: Champion of Liberty.* New York: Simon & Schuster, 2017.

Lambert, Frank. *The Barbary Wars: American Independence in the Atlantic World.* New York: Hill and Wang, 2005.

Larson, Edward J. *A Magnificent Catastrophe: The Tumultuous Election of 1800, America's First Presidential Campaign.* New York: The Free Press, 2007.

Lee, Henry. "Funeral Oration on the Death of General Washington. Delivered at the Request of Congress, Dec. 26, 1799." In *Eulogies and Orations on the Life and Death of General George Washington, First President of the United States of America, 9–18.* Boston: Manning & Loring, 1800.

Leibiger, Stuart. *Founding Friendship: George Washington, James Madison, and the Creation of the American Republic.* Charlottesville: University Press of Virginia, 1999.

———. "Thomas Jefferson and the Missouri Crisis: An Alternative Interpretation." *Journal of the Early Republic* 17, no. 1 (Spring 1997): 121–30.

Levasseur, Auguste. *Lafayette in America in 1824 and 1825, or, Journal of a Voyage to the United States.* Translated by John D. Goodman. 2 vols. Philadelphia: Carey and Lea, 1829.

Lewis, James E., Jr. *The Louisiana Purchase: Jefferson's Noble Bargain?* Chapel Hill: University of North Carolina Press, 2003.

———. "'What Is to Become of Our Government?' The Revolutionary Potential of the Election of 1800." In *The Revolution of 1800: Democracy, Race, and the New Republic,* edited by James Horn, Jan Ellen Lewis, and Peter S. Onuf, 3–29. Charlottesville: University of Virginia Press, 2002.

Lord, Walter. *The Dawn's Early Light.* Baltimore: Johns Hopkins University Press, 2012.

Lyon, E. Wilson. "The Franco-American Convention of 1800." *Journal of Modern History* 12, no. 3 (September 1940): 305–33.

Maclay, William. *The Diary of William Maclay and Other Notes on Senate Debates.* Edited by Kenneth R. Bowling and Helen E. Veit. Baltimore: Johns Hopkins University Press, 1988.

Madison, James. *The Mind of the Founder: Sources of the Political Thought of James Madison.* Edited by Marvin Meyers. Indianapolis: Bobbs-Merrill Company, 1973.

———. *Notes of Debates in the Federal Convention of 1787, Reported by James Madison.* Paper ed. Athens, OH: Ohio University Press, 1985.

———. *The Papers of James Madison.* Edited by William T. Hutchinson, William M. E. Rachal, and Robert Allen Rutland. 18 vols. Chicago: University of Chicago Press, 1962–2000.

———. *The Papers of James Madison, Presidential Series.* Edited by Robert A. Rutland et al. 10 vols. Charlottesville: University of Virginia Press, 1984–2019.

———. *The Papers of James Madison, Secretary of State Series.* Edited by David B. Mattern et al. 10 vols. to date. Charlottesville: University Press of Virginia, 1986–.

Magrath, C. Peter. *Yazoo: Law and Politics in the New Republic.* Providence: Brown University Press, 1966.

Maier, Pauline. *Ratification: The People Debate the Constitution, 1787–1788.* New York: Simon & Schuster Paperbacks, 2011.

Malone, Dumas. *Jefferson and His Time.* 6 vols. Boston: Little, Brown & Company, 1948–1981.

Marshall, John. *John Marshall: Writings.* Edited by Charles F. Hobson. New York: Library of America, 2010.

———. *The Papers of John Marshall.* Edited by Herbert A. Johnson et al. 12 vols. Chapel Hill: University of North Carolina Press, 1974–2006.

Mason, George. *The Papers of George Mason, 1725–1792.* Edited by Robert A. Rutland. 3 vols. Chapel Hill: University of North Carolina Press, 1970.

Mayo, Bernard. *Myths and Men: Patrick Henry, George Washington, and Thomas Jefferson.* Athens: University of Georgia Press, 1959.

McCoy, Drew R. *The Elusive Republic: Political Economy in Jeffersonian America.* Chapel Hill: University of North Carolina Press, 1980.

McCullough, David. *John Adams.* New York: Simon & Schuster, 2001.

McInnis, Maurie D., and Louis P. Nelson, eds. *Educated in Tyranny: Slavery at Thomas Jefferson's University.* Charlottesville: University of Virginia Press, 2019.

Meacham, Jon. *Thomas Jefferson: The Art of Power.* New York: Random House, 2012.

Meade, Robert Douthat. *Patrick Henry: Patriot in the Making.* Philadelphia and New York: J. B. Lippincott Company, 1957.

———. *Patrick Henry: Practical Revolutionary.* Philadelphia and New York: J. B. Lippincott Company, 1969.

Mearns, David C. *The Story up to Now: The Library of Congress, 1800–1946.* Washington, DC: Government Printing Office, 1947.

Monroe, James. *The Papers of James Monroe.* Edited by Daniel Preston. 6 vols. Westport, CT: Greenwood Press, 2003–2017.

———. *The Writings of James Monroe.* Edited by Stanislaus Murray Hamilton. 7 vols. New York: G. P. Putnam's Sons, 1898–1903.

Morgan, Edmund S. *American Slavery, American Freedom: The Ordeal of Colonial Virginia.* New York: W. W. Norton, 1975.

Morris, Richard B., ed. *Encyclopedia of American History.* 3d ed. New York: Harper & Row, Publishers, 1965.

Moulton, Gary E., ed. *The Definitive Journals of Lewis and Clark.* 13 vols. Lincoln: University of Nebraska Press, 1987–2001.

Newman, Richard S. "Prelude to the Gag Rule: Southern Reaction to Antislavery Petitions in the First Federal Congress." *Journal of the Early Republic* 16, no. 4 (Winter 1996): 571–99.

Newman, Simon P. "Paine, Jefferson, and Revolutionary Radicalism in Early National America." In *Paine and Jefferson in the Age of Revolutions,* edited by Simon P. Newman and Peter S. Onuf, 71–94. Charlottesville: University of Virginia Press, 2013.

Newmyer, R. Kent. *John Marshall and the Heroic Age of the Supreme Court.* Baton Rouge: Louisiana State University Press, 2007.

———. *The Treason Trial of Aaron Burr: Law, Politics, and the Character Wars of the New Nation.* Cambridge: Cambridge University Press, 2012.

"Notes of Major William Pierce on the Federal Constitution of 1787." *American Historical Review* 3, no. 2 (January 1898): 310–34.

Oakes, James. *The Crooked Path to Abolition: Abraham Lincoln and the Antislavery Constitution.* New York: W. W. Norton, 2021.

O'Shaughnessy, Andrew J. *The Illimitable Freedom of the Human Mind: Thomas Jefferson's Idea of a University.* Charlottesville: University of Virginia Press, 2021.

Otis, James. *The Rights of the British Colonists Asserted and Proved.* Boston: Edes and Gill, 1764.

Pasley, Jeffrey L. *The First Presidential Contest: 1796 and the Founding of American Democracy.* Lawrence: University Press of Kansas, 2013.

———. *"The Tyranny of the Printers": Newspaper Politics in the Early American Republic.* Charlottesville: University Press of Virginia, 2001.

———. "1800 as a Revolution in Political Culture." In *The Revolution of 1800: Democracy, Race, and the New Republic,* edited by James Horn, Jan Ellen Lewis, and Peter S. Onuf, 120–52. Charlottesville: University of Virginia Press, 2002.

Perkins, Bradford. *Castlereagh and Adams: England and the United States, 1812–1823.* Berkeley: University of California Press, 1964.

———. *Prologue to War: England and the United States, 1805–1812.* Berkeley: University of California Press, 1961.

Perkins, Dexter. *A History of the Monroe Doctrine.* Boston: Little, Brown and Company, 1963.

Peterson, Merrill D. *The Great Triumvirate: Webster, Clay, and Calhoun.* New York: Oxford University Press, 1987.

———. *The Jefferson Image in the American Mind.* New York: Oxford University Press, 1960.

———. *Thomas Jefferson and the New Nation: A Biography.* New York: Oxford University Press, 1970.

Pitch, Anthony S. *The Burning of Washington: The British Invasion of 1814.* Annapolis: Naval Institute Press, 1998.

Preston, Daniel. "James Monroe and the Practicalities of Emancipation and Colonization." In *New Directions in the Study of African American Recolonization,* edited by Beverly C. Tomek and Matthew J. Hetrick, 129–45. Gainesville: University Press of Florida, 2017.

Proceedings and Debates of the Virginia State Convention, of 1829–30. To Which are Subjoined the New Constitution of Virginia, and Votes of the People. Richmond: Ritchie & Cook, 1830.

Ragosta, John A. *Patrick Henry: Proclaiming a Revolution.* New York: Routledge, 2017.

Ragosta, John A., Peter S. Onuf, and Andrew J. O'Shaughnessy, eds. *The Founding of Thomas Jefferson's University.* Charlottesville: University of Virginia Press, 2019.

Rakove, Jack. *Beyond Belief, Beyond Conscience: The Radical Significance of the Free Exercise of Religion.* New York: Oxford University Press, 2020.

———. *Revolutionaries: A New History of the Invention of America.* Boston: Houghton Mifflin, 2010.

Remini, Robert V. *The Battle of New Orleans.* New York: Viking, 1999.

Reps, John W. *Washington on View: The Nation's Capital Since 1790.* Chapel Hill: University of North Carolina Press, 1991.

Risjord, Norman. *Chesapeake Politics, 1781–1800.* New York: Columbia University Press, 1978.

———. *Jefferson's America, 1760–1815.* Madison, WI: Madison House Publishers, 1991.

Rogers, Cara J. "Jefferson's Changing Audiences: A Reevaluation of *Notes on the State of Virginia.*" *Journal of Southern History* 87, no. 2 (May 2021): 171–208.

Rohrs, Richard C. "The Federalist Party and the Convention of 1800." *Diplomatic History* 12, no. 3 (Summer 1988): 237–60.

Romano, Renee C., and Claire Bond Potter, eds. *Historians on Hamilton: How a Blockbuster Musical Is Restaging America's Past.* New Brunswick: Rutgers University Press, 2018.

Ross, Marc Howard. *Slavery in the North: Forgetting History and Recovering Memory.* Philadelphia: University of Pennsylvania Press, 2018.

Rothman, Adam. *Slave Country: American Expansion and the Origins of the Deep South.* Cambridge: Harvard University Press, 2005.

Rush, Benjamin. *Letters of Benjamin Rush.* Edited by L. H. Butterfield. 2 vols. Princeton: Princeton University Press, 1951.

Rutland, Robert Allen. *The Ordeal of the Constitution: The Antifederalists and the Ratification Struggle of 1787–1788.* Norman: University of Oklahoma Press, 1966.

Sadosky, Leonard J. "How the Jeffersonians Learned to Love the State: Consumption, Finance, and Empire in the Madison Administration." In *Jeffersonians in Power: The*

Rhetoric of Opposition Meets the Realities of Governing, edited by Joanne B. Freeman and Johann N. Neem, 148–77. Charlottesville: University of Virginia Press, 2019.

Saler, Bethel. *The Settlers' Empire: Colonialism and State Formation in America's Old Northwest.* Philadelphia: University of Pennsylvania Press, 2014.

Scherr, Arthur. "Alexander Hamilton and Slavery: A Closer Look at the Founder." *The Historian* 83, no. 2 (July 2021): 130–70.

———. *Rightful Liberty: Slavery, Morality, and Thomas Jefferson's World.* Macon, GA: Mercer University Press, 2021.

Schiff, Stacy. *A Great Improvisation: Franklin, France, and the Birth of America.* New York: Henry, Holt and Company, 2005.

Scofield, Merry Ellen. "The Fatigues of His Table: The Politics of Presidential Dining during the Jefferson Administration." *Journal of the Early Republic* 26, no. 3 (Fall 2006): 449–69.

Seeley, Samantha. *Race, Removal, and the Right to Remain: Migration and the Making of the United States.* Chapel Hill: University of North Carolina Press, 2021.

Selby, John E. *The Revolution in Virginia, 1775–1783.* 2nd ed. Charlottesville: For Colonial Williamsburg by the University Press of Virginia, 1988.

Sellers, Charles G. *The Market Revolution: Jacksonian America, 1815–1846.* New York: Oxford University Press, 1991.

Sharp, James Roger. *American Politics in the Early Republic: The New Nation in Crisis.* New Haven: Yale University Press, 1993.

Sidbury, James. *Ploughshares into Swords: Race, Rebellion, and Identity in Gabriel's Virginia, 1730–1810.* Cambridge: Cambridge University Press, 1997.

Slaughter, Thomas P. *The Whiskey Rebellion: Frontier Epilogue to the American Revolution.* New York: Oxford University Press, 1986.

Smith, James Morton. *Freedom's Fetters: The Alien and Sedition Laws and American Civil Liberties.* Ithaca: Cornell University Press, 1966.

Smith, Jean Edward. *John Marshall: Definer of a Nation.* New York: Henry Holt & Co., 1996.

Smith, Page. *John Adams.* 2 vols. Garden City, NY: Doubleday & Company, 1962.

Sofka, James R. "The Jeffersonian Idea of National Security: Commerce, the Atlantic Balance of Power, and the Barbary War, 1786–1805." *Diplomatic History* 21, no. 4 (October 1997), 519–44.

Spivak, Burton. *Jefferson's English Crisis: Commerce, Embargo, and the Republican Revolution.* Charlottesville: University Press of Virginia, 1979.

Stagg, J. C. A. *The War of 1812: Conflict for a Continent.* Cambridge: Cambridge University Press, 2012.

Steele, Brian. *Thomas Jefferson and American Nationhood.* Cambridge: Cambridge University Press, 2012.

Stewart, David O. *American Emperor: Aaron Burr's Challenge to Jefferson's America.* New York: Simon & Schuster, 2011.

———. *Madison's Gift: Five Partnerships That Built America.* New York: Simon & Schuster, 2016.

Sutton, Robert P. "Nostalgia, Pessimism, and Malaise: The Doomed Aristocrat in Late-Jeffersonian Virginia." *Virginia Magazine of History and Biography* 76, no. 1 (January 1968): 41–55.

———. *Revolution to Secession: Constitution Making in the Old Dominion.* Charlottesville: University Press of Virginia, 1989.

Taylor, Alan. *The Internal Enemy: Slavery and War in Virginia, 1772–1832.* New York: W. W. Norton, 2013.

———. *Thomas Jefferson's Education.* New York: W. W. Norton, 2019.

Taylor, George Rogers. *The Transportation Revolution, 1815–1860.* New York: Holt, Rinehart and Winston, 1951.

Thomas, William G., III. *A Question of Freedom: The Families Who Challenged Slavery from the Nation's Founding to the Civil War.* New Haven: Yale University Press, 2020.

Thompson, Mary V. *"The Only Unavoidable Subject of Regret": George Washington, Slavery, and the Enslaved Community at Mount Vernon.* Charlottesville: University of Virginia Press, 2019.

Ticknor, George. *Life, Letters, and Journals of George Ticknor.* Edited by George S. Hillard. 2 vols. Boston: J. R. Osgood & Co, 1876.

Tomek, Beverly C. *Colonization and Its Discontents: Emancipation, Emigration, and Antislavery in Antebellum Pennsylvania.* New York: New York University Press, 2011.

Turner, Lynn W. "The Impeaching of John Pickering." *American Historical Review* 54, no. 3 (April 1949): 485–507.

Unger, Harlow Giles. *The Last Founding Father: James Monroe and a Nation's Call to Greatness.* Philadelphia: Da Capo Press, 2009.

Van Cleve, George William. *We Have Not a Government: The Articles of Confederation and the Road to the Constitution.* Chicago: University of Chicago Press, 2017.

Vogel, Steve. *Through the Perilous Fight: Six Weeks That Saved the Nation.* New York: Random House, 2013.

Wagoner, Jennings L. *Jefferson and Education.* Charlottesville: Thomas Jefferson Foundation, 2004.

Waldstreicher, David. *Slavery's Constitution: From Revolution to Ratification.* New York: Hill and Wang, 2009.

Wallace, Anthony. *The Long, Bitter Trail: Andrew Jackson and the Indians.* New York: Hill and Wang, 1993.

Ward, John William. *Andrew Jackson: Symbol for an Age.* New York: Oxford University Press, 1955.

Washington, George. *George Washington: Papers.* Edited by John H. Rhodehamel. New York: Library of America, 1997.

———. *The Papers of George Washington, Colonial Series.* Edited by W. W. Abbot, Dorothy Twohig, and Philander D. Chase. 10 vols. Charlottesville: University Press of Virginia, 1983–1995.

———. *The Papers of George Washington, Confederation Series.* Edited by W. W. Abbot and Dorothy Twohig. 6 vols. Charlottesville: University Press of Virginia, 1992–1997.

———. *The Papers of George Washington, Presidential Series.* Edited by Dorothy Twohig, W. W. Abbot, and Philander D. Chase. 20 vols. Charlottesville: University of Virginia Press, 1987–2019.

———. *The Writings of George Washington from the Original Manuscript Sources.* Edited by John C. Fitzpatrick. 37 vols. Washington, DC: Government Printing Office, 1931–1944.

Watson, Samuel J. *Jackson's Sword: The Army Officer Corps on the American Frontier, 1810–1821.* Lawrence: University Press of Kansas, 2012.

Weeks, William Earl. *John Quincy Adams and American Global Empire.* Lexington: University Press of Kentucky, 1992.

Whitaker, Arthur Preston. *The Spanish-American Frontier, 1783–1795: The Westward Movement and the Spanish Retreat in the Mississippi Valley.* Boston: Houghton Mifflin, 1927.

White, Leonard D. *The Jeffersonians: A Study in Administrative History, 1801–1829.* New York: Macmillan, 1951.

Wilentz, Sean. *No Property in Man: Slavery and Antislavery at the Nation's Founding.* Cambridge: Harvard University Press, 2018.

Witgen, Michael John. *Seeing Red: Indigenous Land, American Expansion, and the Political Economy of Plunder in North America.* Chapel Hill: University of North Carolina Press, 2022.

Wolf, Eva Sheppard. *Race and Liberty in the New Nation: Emancipation in Virginia from the Revolution to Nat Turner's Rebellion.* Baton Rouge: Louisiana State University Press, 2006.

Wood, Gordon S. *Empire of Liberty: A History of the Early Republic, 1789–1815.* New York: Oxford University Press, 2009.

———. "Rhetoric and Reality in the American Revolution." *William and Mary Quarterly* 23, no. 1 (January 1966): 3–32.

Wulf, Andrea. *Founding Gardeners: The Revolutionary Generation, Nature, and the Shaping of the American Nation.* New York: Vintage Books, 2011.

Young, James Sterling. *The Washington Community, 1800–1818.* New York: Columbia University Press, 1966.

INDEX